Praise for
Cicero and *Augustus* by Anthony Everitt

"Gripping . . . Everitt combines a classical education with practical expertise. . . . He writes fluidly."   —*The New York Times*

"Everitt is an attentive biographer who continuously rehearses and refines his account of the motives of his subject."   —*Financial Times*

"Excellent . . . Cicero comes across much as he must have lived: reflective."   —*The Wall Street Journal*

"Everitt is a skillful, deft, articulate, and often humorous expositor."   —*Seattle Times/Post-Intelligencer*

"As an explicator, [Everitt] is admirably informative and free from breathlessness. He has a sophisticated conception of character, too, including a willingness—so crucial in biographers—to embrace contradictions."   —*Independent on Sunday*

"A strong sense of drama sustains [*Augustus,* which thrills] the intellect as well as [stirs] the imagination." —*The New York Times Book Review*

"[Everitt makes Cicero]—brilliant, vain, principled, opportunistic and courageous—come to life after two millennia." —*The Washington Post*

"Anthony Everitt . . . is a brilliant guide to the intricacies of Roman politics." —Dublin Sunday *Independent*

"Wonderful . . . [*Cicero*] is biography at its best—excellent research, an approachable writing style, a knack for making an ancient ancestor relevant to today's world without overreaching." —*Denver Post*

"[*Augustus* is] fascinating and brisk to read. . . . All the stuff of adventure is here, from court intrigue to roving armies to shipwreck." —*The Washington Post Book World*

"Riveting . . . a clear-eyed biography . . . Cicero's times . . . offer vivid lessons about the viciousness that can pervade elected government." —*Chicago Tribune*

"Lively and dramatic . . . By the book's end, [Everitt's] managed to put enough flesh on Cicero's old bones that you care when the agents of his implacable enemy, Mark Antony, kill him." —*Los Angeles Times*

"Everitt's writing is elegant and worldly. . . . His cultural insights are particularly refreshing." —*The Guardian* (London)

"[*Augustus*] captures the color of the city and an era in a biography of Rome's first bona fide emperor. . . . Everitt's writing is so crisp and so lively he brings both Rome and Augustus to life in this magnificent work, a must-read for anyone interested in classical times."

—*Booklist* (starred review)

"Everitt makes Augustus's rapid rise through Roman society comprehensible to contemporary readers, deftly shifting through the major phases of his life. . . . This familiar story is fresh again in this lively retelling."

—*Publishers Weekly*

HADRIAN AND
THE TRIUMPH OF ROME

HADRIAN
AND THE TRIUMPH OF ROME

• • •

ANTHONY EVERITT

RANDOM HOUSE TRADE PAPERBACKS • NEW YORK

2010 Random House Trade Paperback Edition

Published in the United States by Random House Trade Paperbacks,
an imprint of The Random House Publishing Group,
a division of Random House, Inc., New York.

RANDOM HOUSE TRADE PAPERBACKS and colophon are trademarks
of Random House, Inc.

Originally published in hardcover in the United States by Random
House, an imprint of The Random House Publishing Group,
a division of Random House, Inc., in 2009.

Maps © 2009 by David Lindroth

Everitt, Anthony.
Hadrian and the triumph of Rome / Anthony Everitt.
p.   cm.
ISBN 978-0-8129-7814-8
eBook ISBN 978-1-58836-896-6
1. Hadrian, Emperor of Rome, 76–138.   2. Emperors—Rome—
Biography.   3. Rome—History—Hadrian, 117–138.   I. Title.
DG295.E84 2009
937'.07092—dc22   [B]   2009005683

Printed in the United States of America

www.atrandom.com

2 4 6 8 9 7 5 3 1

Book design by Simon M. Sullivan

For the shade of
TOR DE AROZARENA

PREFACE

. . .

Hadrian lived through tempestuous and thrilling times. He ruled the Roman empire in the second century A.D. and has a good claim to have been the most successful of Rome's leaders. An experienced soldier and a brilliant administrator, he presided over the empire at its height.

He had two very good ideas, which helped to ensure that the empire had a long and successful future. First of all, he saw that Rome could not go on expanding. The empire, which stretched from Spain to Turkey, from the Black Sea to the Maghreb, was unmanageable enough as it was and he ruled out any more wars of conquest. As a demonstration for the literal-minded, he built walls along all the frontiers, except where natural boundaries already existed in the shape of rivers and mountains. On this side was civilization and the *pax Romana;* on the other lay the untamed territory of barbarism, of everything that was not-Rome. In Germany the wall was a wooden palisade, long since gone, but in northern Britain, for want of trees, it was built of stone and remains today one of the most evocative symbols of Roman dominion.

Hadrian's second idea stemmed from his love of Greece. The eastern half of the empire spoke Greek and boasted a culture that went back to Homer. Rome in the west was the superpower of the Mediterranean basin and commanded irresistible armies. Hadrian took steps to transform the empire into a joint project, where the cultural and the military, art and power, could meet on equal terms. He brought Greeks into government and through massive building projects developed Athens into the empire's spiritual capital.

In these two ways Hadrian ushered in, as Edward Gibbon wrote, perhaps a little fulsomely, in his *History of the Decline and Fall of the Roman Empire,* "the fair prospect of universal peace." He and his successors, Antoninus Pius and Marcus Aurelius, both of whom he appointed and who continued his policies, "persisted in the design of maintaining the dignity of the empire without attempting to enlarge its limits. By every honourable expedient, they invited the friendship of the barbarians; and endeavoured to convince mankind that the Roman power, raised above the temptation of conquest, was actuated only by the love of order and justice."

This is my third Roman biography and completes a triptych. *Cicero* traces the fall of the old flawed Republic, and *Augustus* the establishment of rule by one man. Here now is the story of an emperor who brought a period of disorder and military aggression to a prosperous conclusion, and showed how monarchy could be compatible with good governance. Some of the personalities of the previous books, although long dead, put in cameo appearances, especially Augustus, whom Hadrian greatly admired and emulated.

I attempt not only the portrait of a man, but of an age, during which an unstable system of power, proceeding by fits and starts, managed to regain its balance. While the fall of the Roman Republic is a well-trodden pasture, for many readers the epoch from the end of Nero to the reign of Hadrian is terra incognita; they may find its bloodstained twists and turns all the more exciting for the personalities and the plot being novel.

Hadrian was by no means the first Roman to be extravagantly philhellene. For centuries most members of the ruling elite had been bilingual in Latin and Greek. That poetical narcissist the emperor Nero had had much the same unifying idea as Hadrian, but been incompetent to carry it out.

In Hadrian's childhood, two unforgettable events took place: the Colosseum, that vast humanities slaughterhouse, opened its doors to the public, and the destruction of Pompeii seemed to prefigure how the world would end.

In his late teens Hadrian witnessed the emperor Domitian's murderous culling of the ruling class. Civil strife was narrowly avoided after the emperor's assassination, and in due course Hadrian's cousin and onetime guardian, Trajan, a popular general, took up the reins of power. From Trajan, the young man learned the art of soldiery in two terrifying campaigns against a fierce barbarian kingdom on the far side of the Danube. The reliefs that wind their way up Trajan's Column in Rome follow these tumultuous events. Like carved newsreels, they speak across time with the immediacy of a CNN report.

Then followed triumph and, in equal measure, disaster. In a campaign that has a sharp contemporary resonance, Trajan invaded the Parthian empire (roughly what is now Iraq). Victory was swift, for the Parthians offered little or no resistance. But then insurgencies broke out across the eastern empire. Sick at heart and in body, the emperor handed over command to his former ward, and soon afterward died on the journey back to Rome.

The legions acclaimed Hadrian as the new emperor. It had been a long, arduous, and perilous apprenticeship. But now, at the age of forty, the new master of the known world was eager to make history, and was determined that no one should stop him. An indefatigable traveler, Hadrian spent as much time as possible on the road, inspecting everything and reforming everything. The frontiers were secured, the army trained, the laws codified, infrastructure improved, the economy fostered.

There was a terrible exception to this record of benevolent success. Hadrian's politics had a dark side. The one people that refused to be reconciled to the imperial system was the Jews. A great revolt against Rome broke out. The outcome was a catastrophe for the rebels; according to one estimate, many thousands of Jews were killed, and many others driven from the land. In an attempt to annihilate this thorny and unyielding race from memory, Hadrian renamed Jerusalem and replaced Judaea with a newly minted word, Palestine. All Jews were forbidden from entering their own capital city. It took two thousand years before they were able to return and resume their independence.

Hadrian is the most enigmatic of ancient Romans.

Why is so little said of him? Why have his achievements been so sparsely celebrated? Although he has attracted scholarly attention, the last full-dress biography in English for the general reader appeared as long ago as the 1920s. One explanation of this silence lies in the man's prickly personality. A fine administrator, Hadrian was brave, intelligent, and, on the main political issues of the day, astute. But he was also irritable and excessively pleased with himself: like many talented amateurs, he took malicious fun in contradicting experts. Hadrian sometimes turned on his friends and threw them over without regret. That great classical historian of the nineteenth century Theodore Mommsen found him "repellent" and "venemous."

There was an even more damaging threat to Hadrian's posthumous reputation. Hadrian had a doomed love affair with a beautiful Bithynian boy, Antinous, who drowned mysteriously in the Nile. Victorian and early-twentieth-century commentators shied away from the embarrassing topic of same-sex relationships. One of them argued, hopefully, that Antinous was the emperor's illegitimate son. Bastardy was bad enough, to be sure, but almost respectable when compared with the love that dared not speak its name.

The most serious problem has been the ancient literary sources, of which a mere handful survive, mangled and mutilated. We know of Hadrian's autobiography and many other histories of his age, but only by name. The books themselves were consumed in the bonfire of the vanities over which the Church presided during the Dark Ages.

So writing a life of Hadrian promised to be a thankless task. Would there even be enough material to bulk out a book? Heaving a sigh of relief, the historian made way for the historical novelist. Not long after the Second World War, the French writer Marguerite Yourcenar published her *Memoirs of Hadrian* to loud applause; the book takes the form of a letter addressed by the dying emperor to the young Marcus Aurelius, his successor-but-one on the imperial throne. Poetic and melancholy, it colored in the gaps in our knowledge and offered a speaking likeness of a world-weary autocrat and connoisseur of life. It is no exaggeration to say that for a while Mme. Yourcenar supplanted the academics. Her Hadrian was received as a true image of the real thing.

Since then more than fifty years have passed. The *Memoirs* are a masterpiece, but (just as a fake antique, completely convincing when it first appears on the market, loses its authenticity with the passage of time) they now reveal as much about mid-twentieth-century French literary attitudes as they do of second-century Rome. Yourcenar's Hadrian is a romantic rationalist with a taste for the exotic, a classical André Gide.

Scholarship has moved forward as well. Wherever Hadrian traveled in his endless journeying across the empire, he commissioned theaters, temples, aqueducts, arches. Inscriptions record the emperor's decisions, speeches, and official correspondence, sometimes in great detail. They amount to a second autobiography, this time penned in marble. Archaeologists have deciphered a mass of new material, adding many insights to the literary record.

Important incidents in Hadrian's career, we must suppose, have entirely vanished beneath the historical horizon or have survived as barely understood vestiges (for example, the British uprising at the beginning of his reign). However, just about enough is known to tell a life and describe the times. And what a remarkable life it was, and what extraordinary times! We have very little information about Hadrian's childhood and youth, but we are well informed about the public events of the day, so it is at least possible to give an account of what he witnessed or heard about when he was a boy. I also offer a sketch of how the empire worked and trace the origins of the political world that Hadrian would be entering once he had grown up.

It turns out that the poisonous pervert of past imaginings was, in fact, a fascinating figure—full of contradictions, certainly, infuriating and charming, ruthless and well-wishing, hardworking and playful, a man of action and an aesthete, occasionally cruel, but, all in all, a richly endowed, rounded human being. Himself a poet and painter and an enthusiast for everything Hellenic, he was a *good* Nero.

Now for some practicalities. It is difficult to be precise about the value of money in ancient Rome. The basic unit of account was the sesterce, a small silver coin, four of which made a denarius, also of silver. Goods and services had different relative values when compared to similar ones of today. As a rule of thumb a sesterce could be exchanged for between two and four dollars. But it is more sensible to consider a range of specific instances of income and expenditure. In the first century B.C. the fortune of Rome's richest man (reputedly), Marcus Licinius Crassus, has been reported as 200 million sesterces. One of Hadrian's averagely wealthy contemporaries, Gaius Plinius Caecilius Secundus, known as Pliny the Younger, was worth about 20 million sesterces. A legionary soldier's annual pay was 1,200 sesterces. A Roman citizen could live decently on an annual income of 20,000 sesterces; this modest affluence would presuppose capital worth 400,000 sesterces (the minimum qualification for membership of the *eques,* or business class). Graffiti at Pompeii show that a *modius* of wheat (rather more than fourteen pounds) in the mid–first century A.D. cost three sesterces and a loaf of bread weighing just over one pound less than an *as,* or one quarter of a sesterce. A measure of wine, a plate, or a lamp could each be purchased for an *as,* which was also the price of admission to the public baths. The minimum wage—whether in cash, or in cash plus keep—will seldom have fallen below four sesterces a day.

As a rule I refer to people and places by their Latin names, while making a few exceptions of those best known by Anglicized versions (thus, Rome not Roma, Pliny not Plinius). I sometimes employ the term *barbarian,* which the Greeks and Romans applied to peoples who lived outside the empire: this is for convenience, although I recognize that its negative connotations do an injustice to some sophisticated and successful societies. As in my previous books I adopt our contemporary method of dating, which pivots around the supposed year of Jesus Christ's birth, rather than the Roman chronology, which counted time from the traditional foundation of the city of Rome in 753 B.C. Years A.D. are usually mentioned by number alone.

Roman personal names had a complex significance. First came the *praenomen,* which would be used in everyday conversation. This was chosen from a limited number of names in common use, such as Gaius, Marcus, Lucius, Publius, and Sextus. An eldest son was usually given the same *praenomen* as his father. The clan name, or *nomen gentilicium,* followed. The *cognomen* (or *cognomina,* for it was possible to have more than one) may originally have indicated a personal characteristic—for example, Agricola (farmer) and Tacitus (silent). It often signified the family within the clan or a branch within a family or the name of another family into which someone had married. So with Hadrian his *praenomen* was

Publius; to his *nomen* Aelius were added two *cognomina*—Hadrianus, referring to his town of origin in Italy, Hadria, and Afer, a Latin word for "African," which may denote a family branch that had had some connection with the Roman province of Africa, or is possibly an acknowledgment that Carthaginian blood ran through his veins (as it very probably did). Victorious generals might be awarded a *cognomen;* so the emperor Trajan's conquest of the Dacian kingdom was marked by the title Dacicus.

Women were generally known by the feminine form of their *nomen,* although this rule had been relaxed by Hadrian's day; thus, his sister was not called Aelia, but was known by her mother's names, Domitia Paulina.

Most people these days encounter ancient Rome through sword-and-sandals epics in the cinema or television miniseries. These can be entertaining, but often leave us unsatisfied. This is because they dump inappropriate contemporary viewpoints onto classical attitudes. For example, we today regard the arena as an inexplicable display of mass sadism. But, although spectators certainly took a cruel pleasure in what they saw, one purpose of gladiatorial combat was to witness courage and to be strengthened or inspired by it. Rome was a military society and physical bravery—*virtus*—was at a premium.

This book will have succeeded if it introduces the reader not only to the man Hadrian, but also to his world. This means making the unfamiliar familiar; for without a sense (however tentative and provisional) of what it was like to be alive in those distant days, the reader will make little sense of the events that follow in these pages and the people who acted them out.

CONTENTS

. . .

CHRONOLOGY

. . .

B.C.

753	Romulus founds Rome (legendary)
509	Monarchy overthrown; Roman Republic founded
264–241	First war with Carthage
239–169	Ennius, epic poet
234–149	Cato the Censor
218–201	Second war with Carthage
185–129	Scipio Aemilianus
160–91	Caecilius Metellus Numidicus
146	Carthage destroyed
62	Pompey the Great returns from the east
49	Julius Caesar launches civil war
44	Julius Caesar assassinated
31	Octavian wins battle of Actium; end of civil wars
27	Octavian, now Augustus, establishes the imperial system

A.D.

14	Augustus dies; succeeded by Tiberius
37	Tiberius dies; succeeded by Gaius (Caligula)
41	Gaius assassinated; succeeded by Claudius
c. 46	Birth of Publius Aelius Hadrianus (Hadrian's father)
53 *September 18*	Birth of Marcus Ulpius Traianus (Trajan)
54	Claudius poisoned; succeeded by Nero
c. 60	Marcus Ulpius Traianus *pater* proconsul of Baetica
66	Jewish revolt
c. 67	Marcus Ulpius Traianus *pater legatus legio* X Fretensis in Syria; under Vespasian's command for the Jewish war
68 *June 9*	Nero commits suicide
69	"Year of the Four Emperors"

early July	Eastern legions declare for Vespasian
70 *June*	Vespasian enters Rome
September 8	Titus captures Jerusalem
	Defeat of Batavian revolt
71 *spring*	Titus returns from the east
June	Jewish Triumph
71–75	Banishment from Rome of *astrologi* and *philosophi*
72	Annexation of Commagene
	Armenia Minor added to Cappadocia
73 or 74	Fall of Masada
74	Grant of Latin rights to Spain
c. 75	Trajan *tribunus laticlavius* with legion in Syria
	Birth of Domitia Paulina, Hadrian's sister
75	Banishment of Helvidius Priscus
76 *January 24*	**Birth of Publius Aelius Hadrianus Afer (Hadrian)**
c. 77–84	Agricola governor of Britain
c. 77	Trajan transferred as *tribunus laticlavius* with legion in Germany
c. 78	Trajan marries Pompeia Plotina
78	Death of Gaius Saloninus Matidius Patruinus, the husband of Trajan's sister Marciana; she goes to live with Trajan and Plotina
79 *June 24*	Death of Vespasian
	Accession of Titus
August 24	Eruption of Vesuvius; destruction of Pompeii and Herculaneum
	Fire at Rome
80	Dedication of Colosseum
	Destruction of temple of Capitoline Jupiter by fire
	Dedication of Arch of Titus
81 *September 13*	Death of Titus
	Accession of Domitian
82 *December 7*	Dedication of restored temple of Jupiter on the Capitol
83	Domitian's triumph over the Chatti
83–84	Increase of legionary pay
85	Domitian *censor perpetuus*
85 or 86	Hadrian's father dies; Trajan and P. Acilius Attianus are appointed guardians

85–88   Dacian war

86   Inauguration of Capitoline games

Trajan praetor

c. 87   Trajan *legatus legionis* VII Geminae

89   Rebellion of L. Antonius Saturninus

90 *January*   Trajan takes the VII Geminae to Moguntiacum against
Saturninus

90   Edict against *astrologi* and *philosophi*

Hadrian comes of age, and visits his Spanish estates

91   Trajan *consul ordinarius*

93   Pliny praetor

Trials of Baebius Massa, Herennius Senecio, Helvidius
Priscus, Arnulenus Rusticus

93–120   Vindolanda tablets written

94   Hadrian enters public life: *decemvir stlitibus iudicandis, sevir
turmae equitum Romanorum,* and *praefectus urbi feriarum
Latinarum*

95   Philosophers expelled from Italy

Flavius Clemens put to death

Hadrian *trib. militum legionis* II Adiutrix Pia Fidelis in
Pannonia

96 *September 18*   Domitian assassinated

Accession of Nerva

Trajan defeats the Suebi

October 25   Adoption of Trajan

Hadrian *trib. militum legionis* V Macedonica in Lower Moesia

98   Trajan *consul* (2) *ordinarius* with Nerva

99 *January 28*   Death of Nerva

February   Hadrian brings news of Nerva's death to Trajan at Colonia
Agrippinensis

Accession of Trajan

spring   Trajan inspects Danube frontier

Hadrian *trib. militum legionis* XXII Primigeniae Piae Fidelis in
Upper Germania

Tacitus, *Agricola* and *Germania*

99 *autumn*   Trajan enters Rome

100   Trajan *consul* (3) *ordinarius*

Alimenta schemes initiated

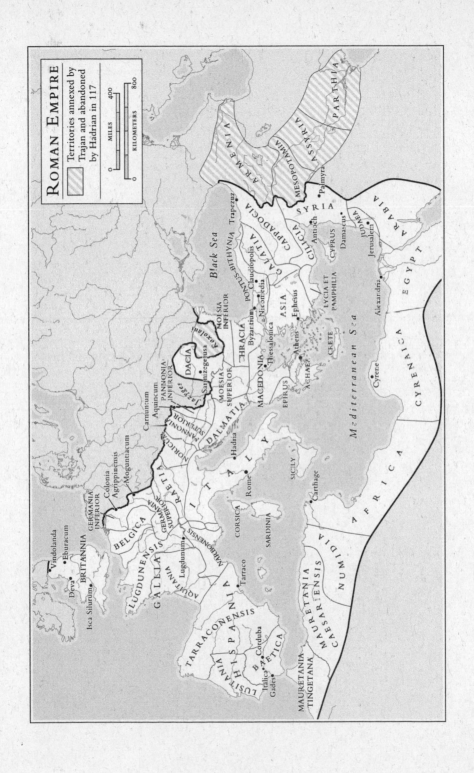

ROMAN EMPIRE

Territories annexed by
Trajan and abandoned
by Hadrian in 117

MILES
0   400
KILOMETERS
0   800

PARTHIA

ARMENIA

ASSYRIA

MESOPOTAMIA

Palmyra

SYRIA

Black Sea

CAPPADOCIA

CILICIA

Antioch

Damascus

ARABIA

Trapezus

PONTUS-BITHYNIA

GALATIA

CYPRUS

JUDAEA

Jerusalem

Claudiopolis

Nicomedia

Byzantium

LYCIA ET
PAMPHILIA

Ephesus

Alexandria

EGYPT

MOESIA
INFERIOR

ASIA

CRETE

Mediterranean Sea

Kossolum

THRACIA

Thessalonica

Athens

Cyrene

CYRENAICA

DACIA

Sarmizegetusa

MOESIA
SUPERIOR

MACEDONIA

EPIRUS

ACHAEA

Aquincum

PANNONIA
INFERIOR

DALMATIA

Carnuntum

PANNONIA
SUPERIOR

NORICUM

Hadria

SICILY

Carthage

AFRICA

Colonia
Agrippinensis

Moguntiacum

RAETIA

GERMANIA
INFERIOR

GERMANIA
SUPERIOR

ITALY

Rome

SARDINIA

NUMIDIA

BELGICA

SEQUANENSIS

CORSICA

Vindolanda

Eburacum

Deva

Isca Silurum

BRITANNIA

LUGDUNENSIS

GALLIA

AQUITANIA

Lugdunum

NARBONENSIS

Tarraco

MAURETANIA
CAESARIENSIS

Italica

Corduba

BAETICA

Gades

TARRACONENSIS

HISPANIA

LUSITANIA

MAURETANIA
TINGETANA

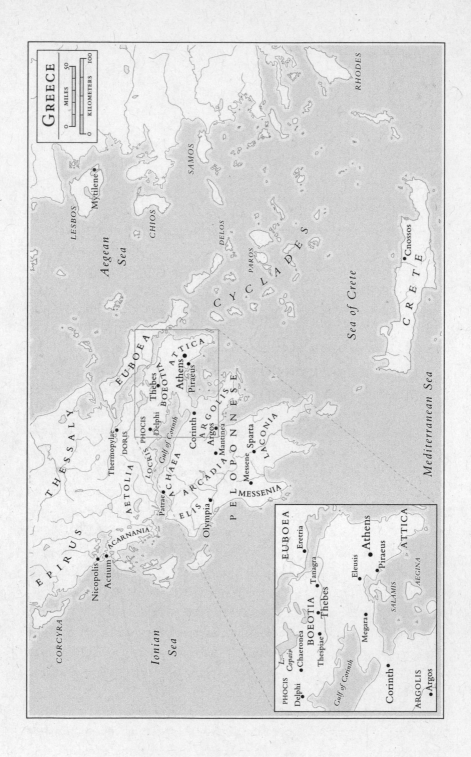

INTRODUCTION

. . .

This is the loveliest of places—and also among the most mysterious.

After walking half a mile uphill into countryside, you will arrive at a great but ruined wall, some thirty feet high. A wide opening gives onto a long pool beyond which lies a calm vista of hills and valleys. Cypresses abound, together with holm oaks, beeches, hornbeams, and ancient olive trees. Maritime pines spread their lofty canopies like bursts of frozen green fireworks.

The twenty-first century dissolves into the second, for everywhere among the trees stand Roman ruins—broken colonnades, collapsed apses, steps up to higher terraces, steps down to underground tunnels, stretches of water and broken fountains, the surviving columns of a circular temple, a grassed-over open-air theater.

Here is what remains of one of the wonders of European architecture, the villa of the emperor Hadrian near Tivoli, less than twenty miles from Rome. It was an inspiration to Renaissance architects seeking to learn the secrets of the ancient world, and as well as stealing its ideas they stripped the walls of their marble facings and the floors of their mosaics. Every statue they could find they removed for their brand-new palazzi. At least 250 have been identified, and there were certainly many more around every corner in the villa's heyday.

Among the portraits of emperors and images of gods, forty or more memorial statues of the emperor's doomed lover, a young Bithynian called Antinous, looked down from niches and plinths, an inescapable, ubiquitous presence.

The word *villa* is a misnomer. This was no single building, but a township or a campus: more than thirty-five structures of one kind or another have been counted over an area of at least three hundred acres.

It is a mark of its scale that, after being looted for centuries as if it were a city captured by drunken soldiery, so much remains.

The emperor did not commission a rural retreat for a tired autocrat; he had in mind a working and ceremonial center of government, hence the extraordinary number of banqueting rooms and reception halls. But, if we leave aside its practical uses, the most curious feature of the complex is that it was a representation in miniature of the Roman world as Hadrian saw it—or, more precisely, those parts of it that held most meaning for him. It was his metaphor in brick and stone for the empire itself.

Greece took pride of place. Here was a version of the Painted Porch of Athens, famous for its wall paintings and its association with the Stoic philosophers; and over there the Academy, the olive grove where the great Plato taught. The real Vale of Tempe is in Thessaly, land of sorceries and enchantment: it was here that Apollo, god of the sun, came after slaying a dark chthonic power, the Python, a serpent that guarded the center of the earth at Delphi, and replaced it with his famous oracle. This luxuriant gorge was evoked at the northern end of the villa.

Elsewhere, in a dip of the grounds a long rectangle of water was flanked by colonnades and statues, and was reportedly inspired by the Canopus, a canal and popular tourist trap outside Alexandria. At one end of the pool was a monumental half-domed open-air dining room, backed by a cooling display of fountains and falling water. In the pool lurked a marble crocodile, and marble images of Egyptian gods looked down benevolently on the emperor's summer-evening parties.

"And in order not to omit anything, Hadrian even made a Hades," writes an ancient historian, referring to the underworld where the dead eked out a gloomy half life. We do not know where this was located. One of the villa's most remarkable features is that beneath the grand edifices where the emperor and his guests took their leisure or held their assemblies was a subterranean network of tunnels, storerooms, and windowless sleeping areas where servants and slaves lived and labored—out of sight, out of hearing, and out of mind—to provide all the necessary services for those upstairs in the light. But these utilitarian spaces were unlikely to have been the Hades that Hadrian had in mind.

Another possibility suggests itself. Toward the far end of the imperial estate rises a high upland, with few buildings on it, where Hadrian and his companions could ride and hunt. However, below rough fields one of the villa's most astonishing features is to be found—four uniform passages, half a mile long in all and wide enough for a chariot to clatter along, join to form a rough rectangle or trapezium. A huge amount of labor went into their creation: 26,000 cubic yards of rocks had to be cut out and removed. Vents in the ceiling let in light and air at intervals. These long, dim corridors look and feel much as they did in Hadrian's time. The atmosphere in them is chilly even on hot days.

They present an enigma, for they can be entered only from one end, the northern side of the rectangle. So what were they for? Perhaps here we find an allusion to the afterlife, a disorienting space for religious rituals where the living were able to reencounter the shades of great ancestors, and even lost lovers.

Equally enigmatic was the man who brought this wonderland into being. His villa raises more questions than answers about the strange personality of one of Rome's greatest rulers, and to understand him fully we must visit the scenes of his life.

HADRIAN AND
THE TRIUMPH OF ROME

I

INVADERS FROM THE WEST

. . .

This is a tale of two families and an orphaned boy.

The Aelii and the Ulpii had the usual share of irritations and friendships, marriages and estrangements, and their influence on the child lasted for his entire life. He was called Publius Aelius Hadrianus Afer, and he was born on the ninth day before the Kalends of February in the year when the consuls were the emperor Vespasian and his son Titus— that is to say, January 24, A.D. 76. Hadrian (for this is the English version of his name) first saw the light of day in Rome, but his hometown was far away, on the extreme edge of the Roman empire.

Andalusia, in southern Spain, is well sited, for it is the bridge between Europe and Africa and its coastline joins the Mediterranean Sea to the Atlantic Ocean. For many centuries it has been among the poorest regions of Europe. Farm laborers there are still among the worst paid in the Continent.

Barren lands and snowcapped mountains alternate with fertile fields watered by the Guadalquivir River, which rolls down the wide valley it wore away from rock through prehistoric millennia and pours itself into the main. A few miles upstream of the fine city of Seville is the undistinguished little settlement of Santiponce. Here, way below tarmac, apartment buildings, and roadside cafes, below the feet of its more than seven thousand inhabitants, lie hidden from view the unexcavated remains of Roman Italica. The population then was about the same as that of today, and the Aelii were among the leading families of this provincial backwater. This was little Hadrian's *patria,* his place of origin.

On an eminence overlooking Santiponce, the splendid ruins of New

Italica, added on to the original town by the adult Hadrian much later in his life, bake in the sun. Wide avenues, lined with the footings of vanished shady colonnades, crisscross a vast scrubby field, once an opulent and busy urban center but now populated only by a few dusty, undecided butterflies. Along a main street are the foundations of a public baths complex and the mosaic floor, displaying the signs of the zodiac, of a rich man's villa. Through tall trees, the visitor glimpses one of the empire's largest amphitheaters, all of it still in place except for some fallen upper arches.

Today's Andalusia is beginning to recover its long-vanished prosperity, thanks to a revived democracy and membership in the European Union. From a viewing platform over which a nude statue of the emperor Trajan presides, new, snaking motorways look as if they are tying a knot around the ancient monuments; and nearby yet another Italica, this time "Nueva," is rising from the ground. Blinding white high-rises and empty streets await their first occupants.

Two thousand years ago the region was among the wealthiest of the Roman empire. The Latin name for the Guadalquivir was the Baetis, and the province was called Baetica after it. The great geographer Strabo, writing in the first quarter of the first century A.D., had little time for most of Spain, which he found rugged, inhospitable, and an "exceedingly miserable place to live." But Baetica was a different story.

> Turdetania [another name for Baetica, after its aboriginal inhabitants] is marvelously blessed by nature; and while it produces all things, and in large quantities, these blessings are doubled by the facilities for exporting goods, [including] large quantities of grain and wine, and also olive oil, not only in large quantities, but also of the best quality.

Olive oil sold exceptionally well. A staple of the ancient world, it was part of everyone's diet as well as being used for indoor lighting, cosmetics, soap equivalents, and medicine. Demand from a large city such as Rome was huge (perhaps as many as 5 million gallons a year were consumed), and Baetican landowners sold as much as they could produce.

Evidence for this is provided by the largest rubbish dump of the classical world, Monte Testaccio in Rome—an artificial hill 165 feet high and 1,100 yards wide composed entirely of broken-up amphorae, or earthenware storage jars, perhaps 45 million in all. They were often stamped with their contents and exporters' names; most of those from Baetica contained oil, and it has been estimated that 130,000 of them, having contained not less than 2 million gallons, were deposited on the hill every year. Among the largest oil producers of southern Spain were the Aelii.

An Aelius first came to Italica when it was founded during Rome's second long war with the merchant city-state of Carthage; strategically located on the coast of what is now Tunisia, in northern Africa, Carthage had dominated trade in the western Mediterranean for centuries.

For a long time the struggle went very badly. Hannibal, the Carthaginian general and one of history's great commanders, spent more than ten years marching up and down Italy, winning battle after battle. At the time southern Spain was a Carthaginian colony, and the twenty-four-year-old Publius Cornelius Scipio led an expeditionary force there. After a masterly campaign, the young commander provoked a battle a few miles from Italica. Despite being outnumbered, he won a complete victory, interrupted only by a downpour. The battered and drenched Carthaginians tried to escape, but Scipio followed after and butchered them. Only six thousand men survived from a force of more than fifty thousand.

Scipio went on to invade Carthage itself, where he routed Hannibal on his home ground. The war was over, and the triumphant general was honored with a title to add to his ordinary names—Africanus.

A large number of sick and wounded legionaries were left behind in Spain and were settled in the new town of Italica, named after Italy. This was not, or not just, a case of convenient abandonment of veterans who had become a liability; once recovered, they would make themselves useful by keeping an eye on the locals, introducing them to the Roman way of life, and, in case of unrest, using military force.

Our Aelius, whose hometown was Hadria, about ten miles from the sea on Italy's eastern coast, was among the human detritus of the war. How happy he was to be deposited permanently in a foreign land far from home cannot be determined. However, his children and his children's children settled into the agreeable task of making money and rising in the world.

For about 150 years we have no news of the Aelii. Baetica prospered and, attracted by economic opportunity, immigrants from Italy poured in. Then in 49 B.C. civil war broke out in Rome. This was a struggle to the death between a charming, unscrupulous, and farsighted politician and general, Gaius Julius Caesar, and the aristocratic establishment that ran the Roman Republic. Most of the leading personalities in Italica had the ill judgment or the ill luck to choose the losing side. More than ten thousand men with an Italian background joined up to serve in the Republican army. Roman legions twice fought each other on Spanish soil and twice Caesar won; the second of these campaigns won him the war, too.

At about this time Hadrian's great-great-great-grandfather, a certain Aelius Marullinus, was the first member of the family to become a senator. He was more astute than his compatriots, for the promotion can only have been at the victorious Caesar's behest, a reward for loyalty.

Hadrian's father—like him, named Publius Aelius Hadrianus Afer—was born a century later and married a woman from Gades, Domitia Paulina. Gades had been founded and colonized by Phoenicians from Tyre and Sidon on the Palestinian coast, just as Carthage had been. Some passing member of the great Roman clan of the Domitii must have conferred Roman citizenship on an ancestor, but Paulina's origins were most likely to have been Punic (a Roman term for Carthaginian). The couple had two children, Hadrian and an elder daughter.

Aelius Hadrianus was among the growing number of wealthy Baeticans who decided to pursue political ambitions in Rome. Little has come down to us about his career, but he was evidently intelligent and able. He served in the senior post of praetor, probably in the year of his son's birth. The authorities must have thought well of him, for he was probably only about twenty-nine or thirty years old, the minimum qualifying age for the praetorship. As praetor he either acted as a judge in Rome or received a commission to command a legion. This may have been followed by a provincial governorship (possibly in Baetica itself).

The Aelii were friendly with the Ulpii, another of Italica's leading clans. The historian Dio Cassius, writing in the third century A.D., claimed dismissively that the Ulpii were of Spanish origin; they did not even have Italian or Greek blood from southern Italy in their veins, let alone Roman. But they, too, were probably among the town's first settlers and originated from Tuder (today's Todi), a hill town in northern Umbria, in those days celebrated for its martial valor.

Hadrian's paternal grandfather married an Ulpia. This was an excellent match, for her brother was Marcus Ulpius Traianus (the *cognomen* doubtless derived from a marriage with one of the Traii, a Baetican clan with an interest in the mass production of amphorae). Traianus had once been governor of Baetica, and at the time of Hadrian's birth was serving as governor of Syria, one of Rome's most senior provincial posts. He had with him on his staff his talented and affable son—in the Roman way, also Marcus Ulpius Traianus, whom we know as Trajan.

The Ulpii were rich and grand, and Traianus was not the first member of his family to enter the Senate, the necessary but not sufficient qualification for which was a fortune of at least 1 million sesterces. Access to the Senate lay in the emperor's hands, and conferred membership of the senatorial class, or *ordo senatorius,* on a man's male offspring. It has been estimated that there were only at most four hundred active senatorial families throughout the empire, so a place such as Italica that boasted several was fortunate indeed.

The Aelii and Ulpii boasted no aristocratic Roman forebears in them. They were "new men," the condescending phrase that the great and ancient families who had governed Rome for centuries applied to unknown politicians from outside their magic circle. They had exploited the economic opportunities that fertile Baetica offered, and were now determined to make their mark in Rome itself.

The baby Hadrian was in great peril. This was because the most life-threatening period of anyone's life in the ancient world was that from birth to seven or eight years of age. Medical science was in its infancy, and while some doctors were pragmatists who encouraged healthy lifestyles and prescribed treatments that had been seen to work, others regarded medicine as a branch of philosophy or of magic, and allowed theory, often of the most bizarre kind, to replace observation.

Having managed to survive his arrival in the world, Hadrian was not yet accepted as being completely alive. Like other Roman newborn boys, he received his *praenomen,* or personal name, only on the ninth day after his birth, the delay reflecting the fact that many infants perished in the first week or so of life. The most common fatal diseases were gastric disorders—diarrhea and dysentery. The latter remained a threat throughout early childhood.

One of the consequences of the high rate of infant mortality was that upper-class parents took care not to become too attached to their children until they were reasonably confident that they would live. Mothers tended to avoid breast-feeding (despite the fact that this accelerated their liability to conception), and Paulina was no exception.

So a wet nurse had to be found. It was essential to recruit the right type of woman. According to a leading gynecological textbook of the period, the *Gynaecologia* of Soranus, she "should be not younger than twenty and not older than forty years, who has already given birth twice or thrice, who is healthy, in good condition, of large frame of a good color. Her breasts should be of medium size, lax, soft, and unwrinkled." In addition, she should be "self-controlled"—that is, she should abstain from sexual intercourse and alcohol.

Paulina appointed a woman called Germana to this essential task, and we may suppose that she fulfilled the job specification. Her name suggests that she was a slave who originated in northeastern Europe. She was evidently a success, for she was later given her freedom and, in the event, reached a considerable age, outliving her charge.

Little else is known for certain of Hadrian's infancy. His father, being a senator, was obliged by law to live in or near Rome, unless on a foreign posting. No doubt the family had a town house, and also a place in the country within striking distance of the capital. A colony of well-to-do Spaniards built or occupied villas at Tibur (today's Tivoli), and the Aelii will surely have been among them. This fashionable resort about eighteen miles east of Rome was built on the lower slopes of the Sabine Hills, at the end of a valley through which the river Anio (today's Aniene) passes. The town stands at the point where the valley narrows to a gorge.

The river rushes past with spectacular cascades and makes a loop around the town, and eventually joins the Tiber. Tibur was noted for an abundance of water and its cool, refreshing climate. Wealthy Romans escaped there from the suffocating summer heat of the capital, and sometimes lived in or near the town all year round. Their villas were often of great splendor. The fashionable author Statius wrote a eulogy of one palatial residence, a *villa Tiburtina,* in its wooded park by the banks of the rushing Anio. Hadrian must have visited it and marveled.

> Should I express wonder at gilded beams,
> or Moorish citrus wood for all the doorposts,
> or shining marble shot with colored veins,
> or water piped to flow through all the bedrooms?

The poet went on to describe every appurtenance of luxury, the mosaics, the works of art in ivory and gold, the gemstones, the statuary.

Hadrian probably spent much of his childhood in this enchanted spot, for which he harbored a lifelong affection.

For his first eight years Hadrian was left in the charge of his mother. Then, in 84 or thereabouts, Hadrian became the direct responsibility of his father and his formal schooling began. It is uncertain whether he was educated by a home tutor or sent to school. The leading educationist of the day, Marcus Fabius Quintilianus (in English, Quintilian), was worried that the typical family no longer offered reliable role models. Children were corrupted by kindness and were excessively spoiled ("they grow up lying around in litters"); he recommended the "broad daylight of a respectable school" in preference to the solitariness and obscurity of a private education. The Aelii may well have taken his advice.

Elementary school classes were usually held in a rented shop with an open frontage, like a porch, in a main square. The day started at dawn or earlier and ended in the afternoon with a visit to the baths. Teaching methods were both brutal and boring, testing memory rather than intelligence. Hadrian and his fellow pupils learned the names of letters before their shapes. They sang them forward and backward from *a* to *x* (there were no *y* or *z* in the Latin alphabet) and *x* to *a*. They then memorized groups of two or three letters and finally graduated to syllables and words. The basics of practical mathematics were also taught, to enable a Roman to act confidently in the daily to-and-fro of buying and selling, and of managing his money.

The schoolmaster, or *ludi magister,* guided Hadrian's hand over his tablet when learning to write. Later he gave his students sentences to copy with their styluses on waxed tablets or with a reed pen and ink on papyrus or cardboard-thin wooden sheets. They had an abacus for counting and recited their multiplication tables in chorus.

In 85 or 86, when Hadrian was about ten years old, an event took place that transformed his world. His father died unexpectedly at the age of forty. A promising career near the summit of imperial politics was cut short. The cause of death has not been recorded, but he was most likely to have succumbed to one of the numerous epidemics in the ancient world, which struck impartially at rich and poor alike.

Domitia Paulina was in a difficult, but not altogether unusual situation. Women married young, sometimes as early as thirteen years old, soon or immediately after the onset of puberty, whereas their husbands would typically be much older, in their mid- or late twenties as a rule. Despite the high rate of mortality when giving birth, women were more likely to see their children into adulthood than were their spouses; it is estimated that only one third of twenty-five-year-olds had a living father, while nearly half still had a mother.

Hadrian's mother or her family advisers considered what was best for the boy. He was heir to a fortune, and it was agreed that masculine guidance was required to keep a watchful eye over him as he grew up and to ensure that the family estate in Baetica was well managed. So two guardians were appointed, both of whom were townsmen of Italica. One was an *eques* (or "knight," a member of the business or country gentry class, one rank below that of the political, or senatorial, elite), Publius Acilius Attianus.

The second was a glamorous and impressive figure—one of the Ulpii, and the son of Hadrian's maternal great-uncle. He was Trajan, whom we first met in his youth when he served in the army under his father. Now thirty-two, he was proving to be an able soldier. A great admirer of Alexander the Great, he was ambitious for military glory. Tall and well made, "with a noble appearance," he had a beak of a nose and a wide mouth. He had recently been praetor and had his eye on the crowning glory of a consulship, the public office that was the apex of a Roman's political career (unless he dangerously aspired to the purple).

Trajan followed outdoor pursuits and was a keen huntsman. He seems to have been something of a mountaineer, an unusual hobby in his day, who enjoyed "setting foot on rocky crags, with none to give a helping hand or show the way." He was a heavy drinker, and liked having sex with young men. He was on affectionate terms with his wife, Pompeia Plotina (in full, Pompeia Plotina Claudia Phoebe Piso), whom he married in 78. The union seems to have been a *mariage blanc,* and there were no children.

The quality that contemporaries noted and most respected in Trajan was his fair-mindedness. He had a reputation for never allowing his private pleasures to impinge on his public duties, a little-observed quality in the governing elite.

At the time, the guardianship of a ten-year-old Spanish boy was of little interest except to those directly affected; but, as it turned out, this was the moment when the fortunes of the Aelii and the Ulpii tied themselves together in an inextricable knot, with imponderable consequences for the future of Rome.

II

A DANGEROUS WORLD

. . .

Hadrian's two guardians were busy men and cannot have had much time to supervise their ward's progress closely; but they shared Domitia Paulina's ambitions for her son. Hadrian was sent to a secondary school when he was about twelve years old. It was one of the best, or at least best known, in Rome, for its *grammaticus,* a Latin word meaning both secondary-school teacher and grammarian, was the celebrated Quintus Terentius Scaurus. Author of a manual on grammar and books on spelling and the correct use of prepositions, he was a master of scholarly ratiocination at its driest.

Grammatical cruxes were popular talking points among educated Romans, and evidently went down well with the bright young student from Baetica; or so we infer, for the adult Hadrian made himself out to be something of an expert on linguistics. He was the author of *Sermones,* or "Conversations," two volumes on grammatical topics (sadly, lost), and once engaged in scholarly debate with his former teacher. He challenged Scaurus, still alive and working, on his interpretation of the word *obiter*—"by the way" or "in passing"; he cited many learned authorities, including a letter Augustus wrote to Tiberius in which the emperor criticized his stepson for avoiding the word. Of course, Hadrian added bumptiously, the emperor was only an amateur.

Here we have the unmistakable tones of the precocious and competitive teenager who insists on outdoing the expert, and who will never altogether grow up. It was the authentic Hadrian.

Going to school—or, more exactly, to the *grammaticus*'s house—was to enter the dangerous world of grown-ups. Well-to-do parents understood this and appointed a *paedogogus,* a trusted slave who supervised children at home and accompanied them to the classroom. He was all the more necessary as his charges approached puberty and attracted the attentions of men in the street. Boys were more at risk than girls, if only because the latter went out in public less often and were usually educated at home. Unsavory encounters were common, and a handsome bribe could transform the home tutor into a go-between. And it did not take more than a gift or two to persuade an inquisitive child to a fumble.

It was to ward off this kind of threat that the poet Horace's father refused to delegate accompanying his son to school.

> . . . he preserved my chastity
> (which is fundamental in forming a good character), saving me
> Not only from nasty behavior but from nasty imputations.

Unfortunately the trouble was not over once a pupil had walked through a *grammaticus*'s door. If a contemporary of Hadrian, the great poet and satirist Decimus Junius Juvenalis (his full name is uncertain; we know him as Juvenal), is to be believed, the classroom was the scene of much furtive sexual experimentation. Observing that the teacher was expected to act *in loco parentis,* he wrote that fathers

> require that he take the father's role in the scrum,
> ensuring that they don't play dirty games
> and don't take turns with one another.
> It is no light thing to keep watch on all those boys
> with their hands and eyes quivering till they come.

Covert sexual abuse was commonly accompanied by overt physical abuse. Masters routinely flogged idle or rebellious or just lively students. A mural at Pompeii reveals a typical scene: the schoolmaster stands sternly on the left, students are seated quietly at their desks, and a boy carries the almost fully stripped culprit on his shoulders. Another grabs his legs. A classroom assistant raises a cat-o'-nine-tails, ready to strike. So central was the experience of corporal punishment to the learning process that an expression for being too old for school was *manum sub-ducere ferulae*—"to withdraw the hand from the cane."

The curriculum Hadrian settled down to study was narrow. The notion of a liberal education that catered to mind and body was little valued. Mathematics and science were not on the syllabus, nor music and the arts, with the sole exception of literature. Gymnastics and athletics were left to the holidays.

There were, in essence, only two related subjects of study—literature and oratory—and two languages to be learned, Latin and Greek. Hadrian was introduced to the classics of both tongues, foremost of which were the two epics of Homer, the *Iliad* and the *Odyssey,* composed by one or more oral poets in the eighth and seventh centuries B.C. In Latin he studied masterpieces from the more recent past—the speeches of Marcus Tullius Cicero, "that genius, the only possession of Rome to rival her empire"; Horace; and Publius Vergilius Maro, or Virgil, author of the great national epic, the *Aeneid,* which celebrated Rome's eternal empire, *imperium sine fine.*

Scaurus and his assistants were not directly concerned with literary criticism, although they did expound the "moral" of every passage. Texts were examined in great detail and their meaning explained, their meter and syntax analyzed, as well as the tonal and rhythmic aspects of the spoken word. Hadrian and his fellow students were taught to read aloud with intelligence and feeling. They broke down, or parsed, sentences into their constituent elements—subject, verb, object, and so forth—and scanned verse through a tough system of question-and-answer.

This could be dreary work, and the classes in oratory were much more fun. For centuries, the art of public speaking had been an essential skill for any upper-class Roman interested in a career as a politician and as an advocate in the courts. To get on in the world it was essential to be able to address large gatherings with confidence and to persuade listeners of the rightness of one's point of view. Even under the empire, when election to office had largely been replaced by imperial designation, oratory was a highly valued art.

Scaurus introduced Hadrian's class to the foundations of rhetoric. Boys learned to retell legends and stories from Rome's past in their own words. They took epigrams from the poets and developed them into arguments. A more complex task was to compose speeches around imaginary themes. These were either *controversiae,* exercises based on cases in a court of law, or *suasoriae,* the giving of advice at a public meeting.

Pupils spoke on one side of a case or the other. The issue debated, of course, had less to do with the law than with resolving a moral dilemma. This was no accident, for the study of oratory was an essential part of a boy's ethical molding. As Marcus Porcius Cato, called the Censor, a paradigm of Republican citizenship, observed in the second century B.C.: "An orator, son Marcus, is a *good* man good at speaking."

Whatever might have been the case in his day, theory was not now borne out by practice. As an induction to virtue, oratory left much to be desired. The subjects for debate were too remote from the challenges of ordinary life to be relevant, and encouraged the use of specious and hairsplitting arguments. The unscrupulous would knowingly strive to make the worse cause seem the better. Oratory's disjunction from the real world was reflected in the fact that it had become a highbrow entertainment. Speeches were honed to perfection and authors then read them aloud in lecture theaters. Audiences would applaud a particularly fine effect. The art of persuasion had dwindled into a work of art.

We are not told whether Hadrian liked going to school. Contemporary observers were highly critical, but we know of at least one man who looked back on his education as the "happiest days of my life." Hadrian may not have gone that far, but he had a lively, inquiring mind and his studies certainly won his attention.

Quite suddenly he became infatuated with all things Greek. Soon after the death of his father, he immersed himself in Greek studies so enthusiastically that he was nicknamed Graeculus, "little Greek boy." There is the slightest hint in the *Historia Augusta* that the two events were somehow linked; perhaps his philhellenism filled an emotional gap (especially if, as is possible, his father had taken him to Greece when on a foreign posting and introduced him in a simple way to the glories of its civilization). It is likely that his guardian's new wife, Plotina, encouraged him. She became very fond of Hadrian and was something of an intellectual and philhellene herself.

Caution is called for. The only thing unusual in Hadrian's passion was the length to which he took it. The Romans were a practical people who distrusted works of the imagination, unless they conferred an immediate and useful benefit. Law, architecture, engineering—these were disciplines they could understand, for they called for rigorous mental application but no flights of fancy.

However, they had little in the way of a homegrown intellectual or cultural tradition. Although they had been aware of the Greeks for all of their history, they were bowled over by what they found when they conquered the Greek world in the second century B.C. and incorporated it into their empire. The cities—Athens, Antioch, Ephesus, Alexandria (in every way Greek rather than Egyptian)—astounded with their beauty, elegance, and splendor. Greek philosophy and scientific inquiry, its poetry and drama, provoked a deep, if reluctant, admiration. Most well-educated Romans spoke Greek fluently; Latin poets copied the literary masterpieces of Athens and Italian architects modeled their buildings on its temples and pillared porches.

Horace famously wrote:

> When Greece was taken she took control of her rough invader,
>   and brought the arts to rustic Latium [the Italian region where
>   Rome can be found].

He added, with almost tangible disgust, that the "fetid smell" of primitive Italian verse forms gave way to clear and unpolluted air.

The Greece with which Hadrian was so fascinated was no longer simply that of the mainland, of the tiny city-states that drove off two Persian invasions, among whom the most powerful had been democratic Athens and militaristic Sparta, of Socrates and Plato, of Sophocles and Aristotle. Nor was it just the larger Greece of all the many colonies that the mainland city-states had scattered around the Mediterranean along the coastlines of the Black Sea, Asia Minor, and northern Africa, in Sicily and southern Italy.

In fact, "Greece" had grown further still to include the complete eastern half of the Roman empire. This was because four centuries earlier the Macedonian king, Alexander the Great, had overthrown the Persian empire, whose territory stretched from the Ionian Sea to the Indian Ocean. After his death, his generals divided his conquests into powerful independent kingdoms, and introduced Greek ideas, Greek and Macedonian colonists, and, above all, the Greek language to these vast oriental domains.

Any natives who wanted to get on were obliged to Hellenize themselves. As Peter Green remarks:

> Like Indians under the British Raj angling for the *entrée* to European club membership, they developed the taste for exercising naked, for worshipping strange gods, for patronizing the theatre; they courted municipal kudos by the lavish generosity of their benefactions.

Of course, the Greekness of many Asiatic provincials was only skin deep. Their Roman overlords thought them tricky, cowardly, greedy, and unreliable. They were venal confidence tricksters, and what could sometimes be a true talent for high-flying rhetoric was in the case of most Asiatics no more than a tiresome gift of the gab.

To many traditionally minded Romans, there was something still more threatening about the Greeks—their approach to religion. Official Roman religion was not intended to be emotionally satisfying; it entailed a web of complicated rituals in the home and in the public square, designed to preserve the *pax deorum,* the grace and favor of the gods. Eastern cults, by contrast, offered mysticism and their ceremonies induced out-of-body, ecstatic experiences. Initiates were often sworn to secrecy. The state, whether under the Republic or the empire, distrusted excessive excitement and was always on its guard against the *coniuratio,* the society bound together by a common oath and invisible except to its members. Cults were often expelled from Rome, but they were so popular that they kept creeping back.

This spiritual exoticism appealed to Hadrian's deepest levels of feeling far more than did Rome's traditional nit-picking *superstitio,* and would go on doing so for all his life. And so did two other oriental imports—magic and astrology. Magic had long been illegal, but became increasingly popular under the empire. It was employed for many purposes—healing illnesses beyond the reach of conventional medicine; hurting, even killing, one's enemies; stimulating erotic love; ensuring the victory or defeat of a charioteer at the races.

This last was the purpose of a curse tablet in lead found by archaeologists, which still conveys a strong stench of hatred two millennia later. It demands of a powerful spirit, or *daimon,*

> from this day, from this moment that you torture the horses of the Greens and Whites [chariot teams]. Kill them! The charioteers Glarus and Felix and Primulus and Romanus, kill them! Crash them! Leave no breath in them!

Spell books were published and "magical papyri" have been unearthed from the bone-dry sands of Egypt that reveal the lengths to which people were willing to go to unleash the powers of darkness.

One of magic's key principles was *sympatheia,* or "fellow feeling." This allowed the part to be taken for the whole, *pars pro toto*—hence the removal from barbershops of hair or nail clippings, which gave the spellbinder power over their owner. Alternatively, and more ambitiously, the principle of "like for like" explained the use of wax dolls which, when pierced with a needle, communicated pain, even death, to their human originals. Another version of *similia similibus* entailed human sacrifice, where one living person was killed either to save another or to preserve the state, or in an act of self-immolation volunteered his or her own life. But in these days such a tragic transaction was rare, and the Baetican teenager had no grounds for supposing that it would ever apply to him, or anyone he might come to love.

Hadrian was also fascinated by astrology and other arcane means of foretelling things to come. Because it depended on complicated mathematical calculations, reading the stars was felt to be more of a science than spells and incantations and, despite its inherent implausibility, was bracketed with astronomy as a legitimate form of inquiry. It gave humankind a godlike knowledge compared to which even kingship was insignificant.

It was precisely because the authorities were convinced that astrologers genuinely opened a door into the future that they frowned on their art; casting an emperor's horoscope was high treason, for it might predict the time and manner of his death. None of this deterred Hadrian from making himself something of an expert, at least in his own eyes; he developed a habit of casting his horoscope every New Year's Day, writing down all the things he would be doing in the coming year.

Hadrian was never frightened by contradiction. His philhellenism was essentially antiquarian and archaic: what he admired was Greece's glorious past. At the same time, he looked back with nostalgia and respect to the heyday of the Roman Republic, long before the catastrophic first century b.c., when it broke down in a welter of bloodshed and the "free state" gave way to the rule of emperors. He did not much enjoy studying the classics of the age, Virgil and Cicero, finding their styles too polished and orotund.

He came to prefer the rougher, more muscular writing of Quintus Ennius, who flourished in the third and early second centuries and was a close friend of Scipio Africanus, Hannibal's nemesis. Ennius was the author of the *Annals,* an epic poem that told the story of Rome from the fall of Troy and the arrival of the Trojan prince Aeneas on the shores of prehistoric Italy to the present day. For many years the *Annals* was a set text at school, although the *Aeneid* came to supplant it.

Ennius stood for old values. He set out his philosophy in a line that, like the best writing in Latin, requires at least twice the number of English words if a translation is to do it full justice: *moribus antiquis res stat Romana virisque,* "the Roman state depends on the customs and morals of ancient times and on real men, who deserve the name."

Another of Hadrian's heroes was Marcus Porcius Cato, whom Ennius knew well personally. Cato wrote *Origines* (sadly, lost), which traced the rise of the Italian cities and told the story of Rome from the time of the kings—a parallel track in prose to Ennius' epic. He loathed the noblemen of his day, whom he regarded as corrupt, self-serving, and softened by luxury. In his account of the Punic Wars (the usual name for the wars with Carthage), Cato refused to praise any of them by name, singling out for bravery only a one-tusked Carthaginian elephant called the Syrian.

At first sight Hadrian's respect for these authors contradicts his enthusiasm for all things Hellenic. But appearances deceive. Ennius was of Greek descent and came from southern Italy, an area so dominated by Greek cities that it was named Magna Graecia, or Greater Greece. As well as the *Annals,* he wrote many plays in the classical Greek manner, often closely imitating works by the Athenian tragedian Euripides.

And although Cato made much of his down-to-earth Romanness, a close examination of his writings reveals a detailed knowledge of Greek literature from Homer onward. He published a textbook on public speaking, inspired by Greek rhetorical theory, and was clearly familiar with the best Greek texts.

So what are we to conclude? Cato and Ennius represented a bridge between the two cultures at their respective and distinctive bests. By Hadrian's time it was evident that Cato's gloomy prognostications were mistaken. Rome could safely enjoy Hellenic thought, imagination, and artistry without risking its predominance. However, the Greeks *had* failed militarily and politically. By contrast, soldiering, military élan, and true grit were fundamental to a Roman's idea of himself; in the social sphere, so too was the rule of custom and law; and, in the public square, the old Republican elite had shown a talent for finding practical solutions to problems and for reasonably clean administration.

As Hadrian matured from boy to man, he understood that Rome's future good fortune required a commitment to the *mos maiorum,* to the way generations of forefathers had done things—even if he remained a Graeculus in the center of his being.

On January 24, 90, Publius Aelius Hadrianus Afer celebrated his fifteenth birthday. Roman boys usually attained their majority in their mid-teens, and sometime in the months that followed, he officially came of age. The occasion, marking the onset of physical puberty rather than psychological maturity, was usually celebrated in a special ceremony on

March 17, the day of the Liberalia. This was a festival of the ancient Italian fertility deities Liber (identified with Bacchus, god of wine) and Libera, to whom images of female and male genitalia were dedicated in their temple in Rome.

Hadrian put aside forever his *toga praetexta,* a purple-edged toga that was a boy's uniform on formal occasions, and his *bulla,* a golden plate- or boss-shaped amulet that hung from the neck; he then robed himself in the all-white *toga virilis* that signified adulthood. He sacrificed at home to the household gods and, if he was at Rome, made his way, surrounded by relatives, friends, and family clients, to the Capitol, the citadel overlooking the Forum Romanum, where he visited the colossal temple of Jupiter Optimus Maximus, Best and Greatest; he paid his respects to the divinity that protected the civic community of which he had become a full member.

On quitting the status of a child, Hadrian, like other Roman boys, left school. However, his education was not yet over. Wellborn young men were expected to spend time in the capital "shadowing" a senior political personality (rather as an intern does today), and to follow advanced studies in the art of rhetoric. He also undertook military training.

In Hadrian's case, though, there was to be a variation on the general rule. Officially he was now head of the family, and this presented his kin with a serious problem. In the ordinary course of events an adolescent adult's father would be alive and well, and empowered to exercise authority over his inexperienced son, guiding him away from the temptations that beset wealthy young men. Somehow the Aelii had to find a way of keeping their juvenile paterfamilias on the rails.

Perhaps as a holding measure, Domitia Paulina and his guardians, Trajan and Attianus, decided that Hadrian should go to Baetica to inspect the family estates in his capacity as the new master. Although he had spent most of his childhood in or near Rome, Hadrian had visited Baetica once before; we are not sure exactly when, but if, as has been suggested, his father had been posted there at some point after his praetorship, he would have taken his family with him. Hadrian was now back on home ground in his own right.

It is hard to imagine Domitia Paulina allowing her inexperienced son to travel alone, and she presumably accompanied him. She will have introduced him to relatives on her side of the family in the port of Gades. He definitely met a paternal great-uncle; the encounter was more than the fulfillment of a polite obligation, for this Aelius Hadrianus was, fascinatingly, a master of astrology. He cast the boy's horoscope and predicted imperial power. Prophecies of this sort were perilous and must have been kept secret, only to be revealed many years later in Hadrian's autobiography.

The young master visited his lands a few miles upstream from Italica; these were mostly devoted to the production and export of olive oil, and storage amphorae have been found stamped *port. P.A.H.*—"from the warehouse of Publius Aelius Hadrianus." This does not mean that Hadrian's father had run the estate directly himself, nor would his son be expected to do so. A senator—or for that matter a senator's son—was not supposed to soil his hands too openly with "trade." He took an interest in the exploitation of his assets, but often set up in business his more able slaves or freedmen and invested in their commercial activities. Bailiffs managed his estates, supervising the labor force and negotiating with tenants.

Duty done, Hadrian went on to have a thoroughly good time. He learned something of military life; this did not entail joining the army but becoming a member of a local *collegium,* or association, of teenage boys of good family. *Iuvenes,* as they were called (literally, the word means "youths"), received some training, and were also expected to do good works: we know of a *collegium* in the province of Africa that dedicated a basilica (a large building used for trials and as a conference and shopping center) and some storehouses for public use.

We can safely assume that they also enjoyed hunting, to which Hadrian was introduced when he was in Baetica. He cannot have known much about the sport beforehand, although Trajan, who was a keen huntsman, may have mentioned the subject, for most upper-class Italians saw it more as an amusement for slaves and freedmen, or as a spectacle in the amphitheater, than as a pursuit for gentlemen.

Hadrian had no time for such reservations, and hunting immediately engaged his impassioned attention. The animal most commonly pursued in the ancient world was the hare, often hunted on foot with the assistance of scent hounds and driven into nets. However, by the time of the empire sight hounds were in use, which were fast enough to have a good chance of catching the animal, and nets could be dispensed with. Huntsmen rode on horseback if they wanted to keep up with the chase without having to run long distances.

A larger and more alarming enemy than the hare was the wild boar, and in the eastern provinces and northern Africa, intrepid enthusiasts hunted the lion, the leopard, the lynx, the cheetah, and the bear.

One of hunting's attractions for Hadrian was that, even if it was not yet fashionable in Rome, it was popular with Greeks, for whom it was not just a pastime but an exercise in bravery and a religious act. It promoted good health, improved sight and hearing, delayed old age, and, in particular, trained men for war. Xenophon, an Athenian who studied under Socrates in the fifth century B.C., wrote a classic text on the subject, which was still widely read. The Olympian deities themselves enjoyed hunting, according to him, and liked to watch the sport. Pious huntsmen opened proceedings with a prayer to Apollo and his sister, Artemis (goddess of the chase, equivalent to the Roman Diana), to grant them a good bag, and closed them with a short thanksgiving.

So Hadrian was able to cite respectable justification for his new craze. He needed to, for his family was showing signs of anxiety about him. Hunting was not merely time-consuming but expensive. When a friend once complained about his son's extravagant expenditure on hounds and horses, Pliny counseled calm. "Surely everyone is liable to make mistakes," he remarked, "and everyone has his own foibles."

But, despite his own enjoyment of the chase, Trajan did not take such a relaxed view. His ward was getting above himself and had attracted criticism in Italica. His Hellenic posturing may also have irritated the thoroughly "Roman" Trajan; it is telling that years later he used Hadrian's old nickname when he referred dismissively to some Hellenic provincials as "these Graeculi." The boy needed to be taken in hand, so Trajan, then a legionary commander in northern Spain, ordered him back to Rome. From now on he treated his ward as his son, *pro filio*—a gesture that had as much to do with control as with affection.

Hadrian's interlude of independence was over. He would never again be in a position to kick over the traces. This may well have rankled, but not for long. Trajan was close to the seat of power, serving as consul in 91, and was well regarded by the emperor. The sixteen-year-old Hadrian found himself at the fulcrum of great events. It was an exciting time to be in Rome.

III

YOUNG HOPEFUL GENTLEMAN

. . .

Back from Spain, Hadrian was ready to complete his education by studying public speaking under the guidance of a *rhetor,* or specialist in oratory. By contrast with schoolteachers, *rhetors* were well paid and were often hired to give speeches on public occasions; some of them were celebrities and, as on today's lecture circuit, could command high fees.

There were plenty of these oratorical experts in Rome, and the leader in a competitive field was the educational expert Quintilian. Another Spanish import, he came from what is today Navarre. He founded a very popular school of oratory in Rome, for which he received an unprecedented state grant of 100,000 sesterces a year. The authorities saw the school as a means of creating a responsible, hardworking, and well-trained ruling class, for, in Cato's footsteps, Quintilian's aim was to educate the complete man rather than simply to impart a skill. He wrote:

> The man who can really play his part as a citizen . . . the man who can guide a state by his counsel, give it a firm basis by his legislation, and purge its vices by his decisions as a judge—that man is assuredly no one else than the orator.

As consul, Trajan was an influential figure at court and would have wanted to place the boy with Quintilian. Unfortunately, about the year 90, when in his late forties or fifties, the great man retired, partially or wholly, from teaching, in order to devote himself to writing. For some years afterward, though, he was tutor to the emperor's two grandchildren and it is perfectly possible that the consul was able to persuade Quintilian to take on another private student.

In an ancient version of the Grand Tour, many Romans in late adolescence spent some months or more topping up their oratorical training in mainland Greece or the eastern provinces. After a period studying in Rome, whether under Quintilian or some other *rhetor,* Hadrian may have been one of them. In that case he could have spent time in Athens. There is no direct evidence that he did so, but it is a happy speculation that the lover of Greek civilization seized the first available opportunity (as an adult at least) to linger in Plato's Academy; to join the audience in the grand open-air theater where the tragedies of Aeschylus, Sophocles, and Euripides had received their premieres; and to climb up to the Parthenon to pray before the colossal statue in ivory and gold that, more than five centuries previously, the sculptor Phidias had made of the city's tutelary goddess, Athene Parthenos, the Maiden.

As a member of a family heavily involved in imperial politics and military affairs, Hadrian was well placed to view and learn about the world around him. As the son of a senator he was destined, as of right, to become a senator himself. He was entitled to attend meetings of the Senate as an observer. More important, by attaching himself to a leading politician and orator he gained a practical insight into the process of government. Who was chosen has not been recorded, but one likely candidate is Lucius Licinius Sura, another Spaniard (this time from the northeastern port of Tarraco, today's Tarragona). As he was one of Trajan's closest friends, Hadrian would already have been known to him.

By chance an ancient horoscope of Sura survives, which casts an unfriendly light on his personality. Whatever the sophisticated mathematical computations the astrologer devoted to his task, the document reflected Sura's public image; reading the heavens is an art that hands back to the inquirer what he already knows.

The (person) who has the stars in this way (at his nativity) will be very distinguished, of very distinguished (ancestors), a person of authority and punisher of many, and very wealthy . . . but unjust and not brought to justice . . . very distinguished . . . And he was indifferent to female intercourse and sordid toward males . . . The moon (in Gemini) waxing in the trigonal configuration with Saturn (in Libra) and Jupiter (in Aquarius) also effected a happy and very wealthy (theme) and a person who provided many dedications and gifts for his fatherland.

It is interesting to note here that Sura, like Trajan, is reported to have slept with men, and this may indicate the existence of a well-placed cabal of intimates who shared their sexual preferences. Sura was an able military commander, as well as a noted man of letters. According to his friend Martial, he cultivated an old-fashioned Latin—"your antiquated vocabulary evoked our grave forefathers." He may have influenced Hadrian's literary taste, whether encouraging him to read the older Latin authors, or at least approving his admiration of them.

Through practical study and observation, Hadrian came to understand how the empire worked. Its inhabitants formed a colossal pyramid of mutual aid. A powerful Roman was a *patronus,* or protector, of many hundreds or even thousands of "clients," not just in Rome or Italy but across the Mediterranean.

A patron looked after his clients' interests. He would help them by giving them food, money, even land, or by standing up for them if they got into trouble with the law. In return, clients were expected to support their patron in any way they could—voting as he wished at elections and doing all kinds of useful service. In Rome, clients would pay their respects at their patron's house every morning and walk with him to the Forum.

Clientship was not legally binding, but its rules were almost always obeyed. A patron's client list lasted from generation to generation and was handed down from father to son. If someone freed one of his slaves, the *libertus* would automatically become a client of his former owner. Hadrian inherited his father's extensive client list and, when he visited Baetica, he would have made sure to assert his patronage of many citizens of Italica and beyond.

A man could have more than one patron, and a patron could, in turn, be a client. This benevolent reciprocity cut across social class and linked

Romans to people in the provinces. The greatest patron of all was the emperor, and the clientship system enabled him to exact loyalty and co-operation. It was a reliable and trustworthy network of communication in an age when travel was slow, administrative regulation uneven, and legal redress difficult. International trade and banking were advanced and political stability fostered.

Most men and women were very poor, and knew and saw little outside their immediate world. They tilled the fields either as smallholders or as laborers, often slaves, on someone else's land. Many produced little more than was needed for subsistence. Medium-size farms were more profitable and their owners often paid bailiffs to run them. Life was hard and often brutal. On one Italian farm the laborers recognized their good fortune when they paid for the gravestone of their farm manager, a slave himself, because he "gave orders respectfully."

Life for ordinary people in towns and cities was no great improvement. Many were jobless or only partly employed. Emperors went to a great deal of trouble to ensure the supply of grain for Rome from Egypt and Sicily and prices were carefully controlled. Some citizens received a grain dole and from time to time there were free distributions of other goods and money. Those who had jobs, whether slaves or freemen, mostly worked in the service industries or in manufacturing workshops. Tombstones from the early empire convey the manifold variety of the men and women Hadrian encountered as they strolled along the Roman street or snatched a bite to eat in one of the numerous fast-food bistros.

Those endowed with intelligence and luck were secretaries, personal maids, or barbers to the wealthy and the well-to-do. A bold and lucky few aspired to the social and political heights: one of these was Tiberius Claudius Zosimus, a freedman, who was manager of food-tasters for the nervous emperor Domitian. Others, unsuited to the exotic perils of the court, ran their own small businesses: a merchant of salted fish and Moorish wine commemorated himself in his own lifetime alongside his freedmen and freedwomen. Lucius Caelius was a tanner and leather-maker who lived to the ripe age (for the period) of sixty-one. There are fewer inscriptions to women, who tended to be wet-nurses, seam-stresses, midwives, and the like. But memorials to sword-makers, locksmiths, dealers in cloaks and skins, timber and marble merchants, potters, teachers of literature, interpreters for barbarian tribes, ship's pilots, goldsmiths, and bankers evoke the teeming labor landscape of a preindustrial society.

Freedmen owned and operated banks throughout the empire, but credit was fully secured, short-term, and usually took the form of bridging loans. Letters of credit enabled travelers to obtain cash when they needed it. When it came to large sums of money, the rich arranged loans among themselves. Seneca defined a praiseworthy man as one who "has a lovely family, a beautiful house, plenty of land under cultivation, and plenty of money out on loan."

The growing web of arrow-straight roads was primarily designed for military movements and the imperial courier service, but they were also open to traders. Nevertheless, transport by land was painfully slow and so expensive that a journey of any length would either eliminate profit margins or substantially raise prices for bulk goods. Sea travel was much cheaper, but dangerous and out of the question during the winter.

The operations of government were a technical matter that concerned few of the estimated 60 million or so men and women who lived under Roman rule. However, Hadrian, as he approached a career in public administration, needed to grasp the political realities of Rome toward the end of the first century A.D. And the lessons of the past informed an understanding of the present.

During the first six centuries since its legendary foundation in 753 B.C., Rome had devised and implemented an eccentric but surprisingly successful constitution— largely, the outcome of a long struggle between ordinary citizens (the *plebs*) and the nobility. Ostensibly a democracy, assemblies of adult male citizens passed laws and elected officials who doubled as civilian administrators and generals. In theory any citizen could stand for office, but in practice only candidates from a handful of old, aristocratic families had a chance of election (except for the occasional "new man"). Although senior officials held unlimited power, or *imperium,* their terms of office usually lasted for only one year and the Senate, once an advisory committee consisting of past and present elected officeholders, acquired overriding authority with the passage of time.

Rome was originally a monarchy, but after the kings had been expelled and a Republic established, the Romans were determined that no one man should ever again be allowed to control the state. So two consuls replaced a single head of government. Beneath the consuls, officials of different levels of seniority ranging from quaestors, who looked after treasury business at home or abroad, to praetors came in groups of various sizes. At each level, one officeholder could veto any decision taken by a colleague. In addition, ten "Tribunes of the People" were charged with the protection of citizens' interests as against those of the state: they could veto *any* officeholder's decisions. A tribune's person was sacrosanct; he could convene the Senate and lay bills before the people's assemblies for approval.

Every four or five years two censors were elected from among former consuls, with a duty to supervise public morals. They checked the list of Roman citizens and reviewed the membership of the Senate, expelling any who were guilty of reprehensible conduct.

For anything to get done, this complicated system of checks and balances required all those involved to cooperate. By the end of the first century B.C. the strain of running a large empire with such an incommodious constitution began to tell, and politics grew confrontational and violent. Soldiers of the victorious legions needed smallholdings so that they could earn a living as farmers when their terms of service came to an end. A mean-spirited Senate was reluctant to free up land for the veterans, and a succession of ambitious generals compelled it to do so by the use or threat of force.

These able and ruthless men made a laughingstock of the Republic, and the last of them, Julius Caesar, precipitated a series of civil wars that lasted from 49 to 31 B.C., leaving his great-nephew and adoptive son, Gaius Octavius, as the master of Rome.

Everyone was grateful to Augustus, or Revered One, the title the Senate gave him in recognition of his preeminence, for bringing peace after two decades of civil strife, but gratitude in politics is an emotion that quickly evaporates. He realized that the idea of the old, competitive commonwealth still meant a great deal to the political class. He needed to find a way of retaining power while at the same time "restoring the Republic." Otherwise, he ran the risk of sharing his adoptive father's fate: in the most famous assassination in history, Caesar had been struck down by fellow senators in the course of an official Senate meeting.

Augustus rose to the challenge. First, the forms of the old Republic were reinstated and nobles contended for all the offices of state, including the consulship, as they had always done. Augustus presented himself tactfully as *princeps,* or "leading citizen," merely the first among equals.

Second, Augustus was awarded a megaprovince, comprising the existing provinces of Spain, Gaul, and Syria. It was no accident that these were where most of Rome's legions were based, for in this way Augustus made sure he held an effective monopoly of military force. He appointed legates, or deputies, to run his provinces *in absentia.* As in the past the Senate appointed propraetors and proconsuls (that is, men who had served as praetors and consuls) to govern the empire's remaining provinces. Augustus reserved to himself an overriding authority—*imperium maius*—which allowed him to give orders to the provincial governors should that ever be necessary.

Finally, Augustus was granted *tribunicia potestas*—that is, all the powers of a tribune without the inconvenience of having to hold the office. As with tribunes, his person was sacrosanct and to offer him physical violence would be to break a grave taboo.

This system of government was a great success and, although some traditionalists still hankered after the "real" Republic and acted as an informal opposition, it won the cooperation of most of the ruling class. Augustus' constitutional arrangements were durable and, with some refinements, were still in place a hundred years later when the young Hadrian was becoming politically aware.

There was one major difference. The Augustan constitution depended, in the last analysis, on the threat, albeit hidden, of force. The pretense that the emperor was a senator like the rest, but just happened to be rather more powerful, was gradually abandoned. The autocracy was recognized for what it was. All that the ruling class requested was that their master did not rub their noses in their humiliation. Some emperors obliged, others did not.

A growing number of non-Italians—drawn from wealthy local elites—were invited to participate in power. The Aelii and the Ulpii were by no means the only provincial families to enjoy senatorial careers.

Men who were elected to public office in the latter days of the Republic had usually been Italians, but Julius Caesar in the 40s B.C. experimented with widening the recruiting pool. Claudius, who reigned between A.D. 41 and 54 and was the first emperor to have been born outside Italy, approved a standing policy that the Senate should include "all the flower of the colonies and municipalities everywhere."

In practice the early emperors did comparatively little to bring this about, but in the second half of the century the position changed markedly and a number of provincials attained high positions. In 56 the first Greek was appointed to the sensitive post of prefect of Egypt: this was Tiberius Claudius Balbillus, a noted court astrologer, who wrote a book about his journeys around the country he governed. By Hadrian's birth the complexion of the Senate was looking more representative of the empire as a whole. It has been estimated that perhaps 17 percent of its six hundred members came from outside Italy. Men from the thoroughly Romanized provinces of southern Gaul and southern Spain were recruited, among them (of course) Hadrian's father. Most of these were ultimately of Italian origin, but for the first time two Greek senators were elected.

Just below the senatorial class were the *equites,* literally "horsemen." In Rome's early days, these had been wealthy citizens who served in the army as cavalry, but now the term embraced businessmen and country gentry. The minimum entry qualification to the *ordo* was capital or property worth 400,000 sesterces (less than half the 1 million sesterces required of senators). Companies of *equites* collected taxes on behalf of the state, although cities in the provinces were beginning to take over this task from them. The loss was compensated by gains at court. From the time of Augustus emperors had appointed former slaves to run the burgeoning imperial bureaucracy. These men did not have a political constituency on which they could call and so had no choice but to be totally loyal to their employer. Perhaps for this reason, but also because they made large fortunes that they tended to spend on conspicuous display, imperial *libertini* became dangerously unpopular. Eventually, emperors replaced them with *equites;* they, too, carried little or no political weight, but, unlike freedmen, had the signal advantage of being accepted and respected members of the Roman commonwealth.

Meanwhile civic leaders throughout the empire were rewarded for their willingness to take part in public life with the grant of Roman citizenship. The Romans had a long tradition that can be traced back to the distant times when they were conquering their neighbors, local tribes in central Italy. They recruited their victims, inviting the vanquished to join the winning side. Rome awarded some of them full citizenship with privileges and others the lesser Latin Rights.

Once the lands encircling the Mediterranean basin were in Roman hands, the same principle was applied. More and more men from the provinces with not a single Italian gene became citizens. This made the empire a shared enterprise in the success of which those who might otherwise have opposed an occupying power had a common interest. The custom was that a man took on the *nomen* of the distinguished Roman who had granted him citizenship. Thus a Corinthian who was the son of Laco and the grandson of Eurycles added Gaius Julius to his Greek names, implying enfranchisement by Julius Caesar or Augustus; Gaius Julius Severus was a proud "descendant of kings and tetrarchs" in the Middle East and went on to become a senior Roman official and governor of Achaea (mainland Greece). Nothing is more expressive of someone's personal identity than how he or she is called, and the fact that throughout the empire everyone of any importance had a Latin name was a vivid assertion of Rome's unifying authority.

The long era of peace, the *pax Romana,* that Augustus had introduced after his victory over Antony and Cleopatra showed no sign of coming to an end a century later. We should not allow this to mislead us. The Romans were fundamentally belligerent. Since the Republic's earliest days they had been more or less continuously at war. As has been seen, their politicians also acted as military leaders. To be Roman was to place a high value on individual valor and state violence.

In theory the Senate condemned aggressive war, but it was usually not too difficult to devise a sufficiently plausible casus belli. And once they were in the field the legions obeyed few conventions. The remote Britannia offers a textbook example of imperial ruthlessness. The island was invaded and annexed in A.D. 43, but at the outset only England and parts of Wales fell under Roman control. Over the following decades, further campaigns led to the reduction of most of the island except for the far north. Although a patriot, Publius Cornelius Tacitus, an older contemporary of Hadrian and one of Rome's greatest historians, could see an enemy's point of view. In his biography of his father-in-law, Gnaeus Julius Agricola, who campaigned in Britannia, he puts a passionate speech into the mouth of a Caledonian leader, Calgacus—so passionate that it must have reflected the historian's real if not openly acknowledged feelings. It is an indictment of empire builders that rings true even today:

Robbers of the world, [the Romans] have exhausted the land by their indiscriminate devastation, and now they ransack the sea . . . They are unique in being as violently tempted to attack the poor as the wealthy. Robbery, butchery, rapine, the liars call empire. They make a desolation and they call it peace [in Tacitus's unforgettable Latin, *ubi solitudinem faciunt, pacem appellant*].

IV

CRISIS OF EMPIRE

. . .

The modern age opened for Hadrian a few years before his birth, with the emperor Nero and the catastrophe that engulfed him in A.D. 68. A revolt by provincial generals led to his suicide at the early age of thirty-two, and with that the dynasty founded by his great-great-grandfather Augustus came to an end. For most Romans Nero became a type of the bad emperor: he had murdered his mother, decimated the Senate, and been (mistakenly) accused of burning down his capital city. He displayed an unhealthy, an *un-Roman* obsession with poetry and the arts. Where was the austere *virtus* of his ancestors to be found?

Among philhellenes, though, Nero was celebrated as a martyr and his memory stayed evergreen for many years. His biographer, Gaius Suetonius Tranquillus, noted, "There were people who would lay spring and summer flowers on his grave for a long time, and had statues made of him, wearing his fringed toga, which they put up on the Speaker's Platform in the Forum." A well-known observer of the contemporary scene remarked: "Even now everyone wishes [Nero] to be alive, and most people think he really is." Indeed, pretenders emerged in the Greek east to cause brief trouble from time to time.

There was a straightforward explanation for this abiding popularity. Nero, who assumed the purple when he was only seventeen, had been as much of a Graeculus as Hadrian a generation later. As a boy he developed an interest in the arts, dashing off verses with facility; unusually, music was part of his childhood curriculum. The adult Nero aspired to be a great poet, musician, and performer. His aesthetic and sporting interests were essentially Hellenic: he drove a chariot at Olympia, the home of the Olympic Games, and he founded a Greek-style festival, the Neronia, in which musicians, orators, poets, and gymnasts competed for prizes. He visited Greece, where he took part in musical, literary, and dramatic contests.

Nero once remarked: "The Greeks alone are worthy of my efforts; they really listen to music." His enthusiasm was not entirely artistic, but had a political dimension. During his first of two Hellenic tours (probably in 67) he made the astonishing decision to liberate the province of Achaea—namely, mainland Greece up to Macedonia in the north.

The emperor announced his decision in a clumsy and pretentious speech (we have its text because it was taken down verbatim and carved onto a marble stele). "Other leaders," he said, "have liberated cities, only Nero a province." Greek opinion was delighted, and one of his critics, praising with a faint damn, remarked that the decree earned Nero reincarnation as a singing frog rather than as a viper. However, the boasted liberation did not last, for a later emperor soon rescinded it.

We do not know Hadrian's opinion of Nero, but, when he came to learn the history of his times, he must have been sympathetic to this attempt to rehabilitate the culture of Greece and to place the descendants of Pericles and Plato on something approaching level terms with their Roman masters. When many years later he found an opportunity to advance the same cause, he did not hesitate to seize it.

Two other significant events that took place in the years before Hadrian's birth molded his world and had serious consequences both for him and his contemporaries. The first of these was a military crisis toward the end of Nero's reign, which offered Hadrian food for thought as he looked back more than half a century later, with all the advantages of hindsight.

In A.D. 66 Judaea rose in revolt against Rome.

The Jews had long been the most awkward and annoyingly rebarbative of the conquered peoples, and the imperial authorities had never been certain how best to handle them, veering unpredictably between toleration and repression, ruling Judaea sometimes indirectly through a client king such as Herod the Great and sometimes directly as a province. Of an empire of about 60 million souls, a census conducted in A.D. 48 recorded some 6,944,000 Jews, not counting the many thousands still in Babylonian exile and living under Parthian rule. Perhaps 2.5 million lived in or around Judaea. Many had settled elsewhere in the empire, in Rome and especially in the eastern provinces; in an exodus in reverse, a million Jews lived in Egypt, and were a majority in two of the five districts of the city of Alexandria, second only to the imperial capital in economic importance and a learned center of Greek culture. At about 10 percent of the total subject population, they were numerous enough to create difficulties.

Although many Jews of the diaspora were willing to Hellenize themselves like everyone else in the eastern half of the empire, serious obstacles stood in the way of integration. Believing as they did in one invisible God, Jews abjured the multitude of overlapping divinities in whom both their Roman masters and their Greek-speaking neighbors confided their trust. However, respectful of their religious scruples, the emperor intermittently forgave them the duty of sacrificing to his well-being, allowed them freedom of worship, and exempted them from military service. They had the right to send an annual tax to Jerusalem for the upkeep of the Temple, splendidly rebuilt by Herod the Great, and to coin money without the emperor's head on it, or any other image.

Toleration was not accompanied by tolerance. For most citizens of the empire monotheism was a kind of atheism. While grudgingly admiring their obduracy, both Roman and Greek despised and distrusted Jews. Tacitus exemplifies the general opinion, in which falsehood and fact, unexamined prejudice and sharp perception jostle. He knew about Moses and the escape from Egypt, noting drily that they proceeded to "seize a country [Canaan], expelling the former inhabitants," an early case of ethnic cleansing.

Critics usually failed to specify what was wrong with the Jews. Tacitus remarks that they abstained from pork, buried rather than burned their dead, and avoided sex with non-Jews. The worst he could come up with was the (entirely fictional, so far as we know) erection in a shrine of the statue of a donkey, which "had enabled them to put an end to their wandering."

There were, in fact, two real, underlying difficulties— one of which marked a collision with Roman imperialism and the other with Greek cultural values. Jews' sense of themselves as the chosen people and the exclusiveness of their religious beliefs and practices led, among true believers, to an antagonistic nationalism, which prevented or at least hindered them from joining the Roman imperial enterprise.

One of the abiding symbols of being a Greek was the gymnasium and the wrestling ground, or *palaestra*. Here men and boys stripped naked (the Greek word for naked was *gumnos*, whence *gymnasium*) and exercised themselves. They ran, jumped, and leaped, boxed or wrestled, as well as taking part in two-person tugs-of-war or, less energetically, playing ball games in a special building or covered court. While nudity was completely acceptable to Greeks, it was taboo to reveal the tip, or glans, of the penis, and for this reason they found circumcision to be repugnant.

Gymnastics presented the Hellenizing Jew with a particular challenge. Since the beginning of their story, the Israelites stressed the importance of circumcision as a visible sign of the historic covenant with their sole and fiercely jealous God. According to the historian Josephus, Hellenizing Jews as long ago as the second century B.C. "hid the circumcision of their genitals, that even when they were naked they might appear to be Greeks. Accordingly, they left off all the customs that belonged to their own country, and imitated the practices of the other nations."

"Hiding" circumcision may have been essential, but it was painfully difficult. A Jew whose foreskin had been cut off in the first days of life had somehow to re-create it. This could be done by surgery. What was left of the prepuce was cut round with a scalpel; then the skin of the penis was pulled down as far as its base and then stretched back to cover the glans. The probability of inflammation and infection was high, and there was a nonsurgical alternative, albeit an equally unappealing procedure: weights could be attached to the skin of the penis to extend it over the glans.

True believers remained fiercely opposed to any reform or compromise. It was said: "Cursed be the man that rears a pig and cursed be those who instruct their sons in Greek wisdom." Paul Johnson sums up the position:

The great Jewish revolts against Roman rule should be seen not just as risings by a colonised people, inspired by religious nationalism, but as a racial and cultural conflict between Jews and Greeks. The xenophobia and anti-Hellenism which was such a characteristic of Jewish literature . . . was fully reciprocated.

No record exists of Hadrian's attitude to Judaism, but we can be certain that, as a fully committed Hellenist, he felt nothing but scorn for this unruly community, the only one in the empire whose ideologues openly resented Roman rule and resisted the universal appeal of the Hellenic idea.

Jerusalem was a marvelous sight. It was larger than today's Old Jerusalem, with a population perhaps of 100,000. From a distance travelers were known to mistake the city for a snowcapped mountain peak, for it perched on two hilltops above which towered the Temple to the one true God with its walls of gleaming white marble. Gold and silver decorations flashed in the sunlight and on a bright day forced onlookers to avert their gaze.

Built on an eminence extended by massive vaults, the Temple occupied a rectangular courtyard, thirty-five acres in area and a mile in circumference, and was lined with long, double-pillared colonnades in the Greek manner. In the center stood a tall building with turreted walls, which only Jews were allowed to enter. Here was a courtyard for women from which a flight of steps led through an arch into an area reserved for men, where they could witness sacrifices on a great altar. Beyond rose the Temple itself, a magnificent keeplike structure, one hundred feet high. Its façade was pierced by a great entranceway. Golden doors were shielded by a veil made from Babylonian tapestry of linen embroidered in blue, scarlet, and purple.

Inside was the Holy Place. This large room contained three fine works of art—a seven-branched lampstand, a table, and an altar for burning incense. The seven lamps represented the planets; twelve loaves on the table the circle of the zodiac and of the year; thirteen fragrant spices for the altar signified that all things were of God and for God. A small, lightless inner recess, measuring fifteen feet square, was screened in the same way as the outer entrance by a veil. According to Josephus,

> In this stood nothing at all. Unapproachable, inviolable, invisible to all, this was called the Holy of Holy.

The original Temple had been destroyed in the sixth century B.C. when the Jews were exiled to Babylon, but was rebuilt on their return. Augustus appointed to the throne of Judaea a Hellenizing client king, Herod the Great, who commissioned a wholesale reconstruction on a much enlarged scale. This was one of the great construction projects of antiquity, and only now in the 60s A.D. was the new Temple finally approaching completion.

Judaea was an unhappy place at this time. The economy was weak and there were tensions between rich and poor. Political opinion was sharply divided and religious sects were at one another's throats—among them the Sadducees, who monopolized the Temple management; the Pharisees, who were willing to render unto Caesar what was Caesar's; and the ascetic Essenes, who believed that the end of the world was at hand and that Israel would be rescued from tyranny by a militant savior, or messiah.

The province was small, and Rome sent out only the incompetent or (at best) the third-rate as junior governors, or *procuratores*. A dispute about the civic status of the town of Caesarea led to disturbances. Heavy-handed measures in an attempt to restore order only made the situation worse. In May or June the young captain of the Temple (a post junior only to that of the high priest) persuaded the authorities to halt the then regular sacrifices for the emperor's well-being. Gang warfare between opposing factions broke out. Leaders of those wanting to avoid war with Rome were killed. The rebels seized city and Temple and a small Roman garrison was massacred.

When the governor of the neighboring province of Syria heard the news of the revolt, he decided on a show of strength and marched down to Jerusalem with a sizable army. But after some indecisive skirmishing he saw that he did not have the resources to take the high-walled, well-defended city, and withdrew. The rebels harried his columns and a retreat became something approaching a rout.

For the first time since the Babylonian captivity, Judaea was a free state.

In Rome, Nero was nervous. The Jewish revolt had to be put down firmly, but whom should he appoint to accomplish this? He was fearful of his generals and provincial governors: the larger the number of legions they commanded and the greater the luster of their victories, the more he suspected them of designs on the throne.

Nero found just the man he needed to recapture Judaea in Titus Flavius Vespasianus, or Vespasian. He had a number of useful qualifications. Most important of all, at fifty-eight he was approaching the end of a successful but not brilliant career. His family background was reassuringly humble and he would pose no political threat if victorious.

By June 67 Vespasian was in Ptolemais (today's Acre or Akko) at the head of three legions. One of them was commanded by his son Titus, a dashing and handsome twenty-eight-year-old. Another was led by Marcus Ulpius Traianus, the father of the man who was to become Hadrian's guardian in twenty years' time. Young Trajan was around fourteen at the time, and probably accompanied his father on the campaign.

Vespasian proceeded south without undue speed toward Jerusalem, methodically capturing and securing every town and strongpoint in his way. A military incident from this time throws light on why the Spanish clan of the Ulpii were doing so well in the slippery world of Roman politics. Traianus was dispatched with a thousand horse and two thousand foot to reduce the large fortified village of Japha. This was not only in a naturally strong position, but was protected by a recently erected double ring of walls.

Luckily for Traianus, some of the inhabitants came out to offer battle, and the Romans charged and routed them. The rebels fled back into the first enclosure, closely pursued by Traianus' legionaries, who followed them inside. In order to prevent a further break-in, the defenders in the inner enclosure closed the gates, but had to shut out not only the

Romans but also their own people. A swarming, desperate crowd banged on the gates and begged the sentinels by name to let them back in. Cooped up and huddled together, they were butchered to the last man. Josephus reports that, abandoned by their friends, they did not even have the heart to resist.

Traianus saw that Japha would soon fall, but instead of proceeding to an easy victory, he paused. He sent a message to Vespasian asking him to send his son to complete the siege. Titus arrived with reinforcements, and the place was captured in short order. Little wonder that father and son valued the services of a man who combined military expertise with the tact of a courtier.

The course of the campaign in Judaea was halted by the second great event that shaped Hadrian's age. It was an upheaval that shook every part of the empire. A new civil war broke out, imperiling the stability of the entire grand enterprise.

Nero's worst fears were eventually realized in 68. When some provincial governors rose against him, it was not merely he that was destroyed, but the dynasty too. If he had put up a fight, he might have won the day, but, too soon fearing the worst, he brought on the worst. Anathematized by the Senate and abandoned by all but a few followers, he fled. Suicide was his best option, but, although his pursuers were almost in sight, he could not bear to kill himself. He kept saying, "What an artist the world is losing!" Someone had to help Nero drive a dagger into his throat.

The four emperors after Augustus had all been his familial descendants and so, in a sense, had an entitlement to the purple. Now, with the fall of the *domus Caesarum,* there was no obvious candidate for the succession, simply claimants with soldiers to back them. The next eighteen months saw three men successively seize the purple—only to lose it and their lives. Roman legions fought each other in murderous battles. In Judaea, Vespasian watched the situation develop, and eventually decided to bid for the purple himself. Troops loyal to him captured Rome, and the latest imperial incumbent was put to death.

No one stood forward to challenge Vespasian, the fourth and final pretender, and, to universal relief, peace returned. The Roman world had had a bad shock. However, it would be wrong to exaggerate. The storm was mercifully brief; peasant farmers in the Apennines, boatmen on the Nile, and fishermen in Attica were not greatly disturbed. Life went on. But much treasure had been wasted and many lives lost; the capital of the empire had been ablaze and blood let in its holy places.

With the elimination of the imperial system's founding family, it was evident that some means had to be devised not only of ensuring a reliable succession from one emperor to another, but also of identifying a competent man for the job. Rome had had enough of unbalanced despots. When the next crisis came, when in due course another dynasty crashed, Hadrian would be a young man. He and his contemporaries were to look to the decision makers of the day to avoid the errors of the past.

Meanwhile, there was the Jewish revolt to crush. Before Vespasian set sail for Rome in 70 to establish the Flavian regime, he handed over command of four legions to Titus, to which were added auxiliaries and contingents contributed by client kings—all in all between thirty thousand and forty thousand men. He also appointed a *consilium,* or advisory committee, of tried-and-tested generals and politicians, probably including Traianus, who was relieved of his day-to-day duties as a legionary commander. This was wise, for Titus was dashing and brave, but sometimes careless.

Four years had passed since the insurgency had begun and an independent state had proudly come into being. The Jewish authorities struck their own fine silver coins and bronze small change, some of which have been unearthed by archaeologists: one of these, a silver shekel, bears the image of three pomegranates and the words *Jerusalem the holy,* and the obverse shows a chalice and the inscription *Shekel of Israel Year Two*. Other signs of a stable state include the minutiae of public administration, such as the continuation of the law courts and municipal arrangements for pauper burials.

However, the fighting among radicals continued and opposing factions controlled different parts of Jerusalem. With the return of the Romans they joined in mutually distrustful alliance and, whatever their disagreements, resisted their besiegers with ferocity and ingenuity. When Titus rode out to reconnoiter the city's defenses, he strayed a little too close to the walls and was nearly captured by a sudden sortie of enemy fighters.

He returned to his camp, shaken and now fully seized by the daunting challenge that awaited him. At first sight, Jerusalem appeared impregnable. The walls of the old city (what were called the Upper Town and the Lower Town) stood on the top of sheer cliffs and on the east side overlooked a valley: the Temple itself rose up like a citadel and was defended by a huge four-turreted fort, built by Herod the Great and named the Antonia in honor of his friend Mark Antony.

The weakest part of the city's defenses was the third wall, around suburbs, and this was where Titus planned the first attack. Battering rams, protected by an artillery barrage from stone-throwing *ballistae* designed to clear defenders from the walls, took two weeks to create a breach. The rebels rallied and counterattacked, but gradually the Romans overturned every obstacle placed in their way.

At last Titus faced the culminating test—how to take the Antonia. The rebels tunneled out from the fort beneath Titus' siege towers, set alight the pit props and other combustible material, and withdrew. The towers collapsed in a blaze of flames.

A quite unexpected occurrence followed. The Antonia itself suddenly collapsed, destabilized by the tunneling. For all the rebels' efforts, the Romans slowly advanced, fighting every inch of the way through the Temple, both sides setting parts of it alight. Finally, a legionary flung a piece of burning timber through a gold-plated window into the central Temple complex. Its sacred contents were looted, and then the Holy Place and the innermost recess, the empty Holy of Holy, burned to the ground.

Titus razed what was left of the Temple and gave his soldiers leave to burn and sack the city. Tacitus estimated the Jewish body count at 600,000, which seems high; but clearly casualties were very numerous. Titus took the veil from the entrance to the Holy of Holy and hung it in his palace.

To underline the fact that the Temple no longer existed and would not be rebuilt, the tax levied on Jews everywhere for its upkeep was replaced by a poll tax payable to a new *fiscus Judaicus,* or Jewish Treasury, in Rome.

Awards and honors were distributed. Traianus's services as a legionary commander and later on the general's *consilium* had been exemplary, for about the time of, or shortly after, the fall of Jerusalem he was made a patrician. This was a glittering prize indeed for a provincial from Spain: patricians were Rome's oldest nobility—descended, legend had it, from the original members of the Senate as first established in the time of the kings. Promotion to patrician status indicated very high favor with the emperor.

Resistance in Judaea did not come to an immediate end. Zealots held out in the desert fortress of Masada for some time, eventually committing mass suicide after a long Roman siege. That tragic detail aside, the war was over.

Each of the contestants offered his account of events. In Rome, a commemorative arch was erected at the top of the Via Sacra, or Sacred Way, the street that led into the Forum—where it still stands. The dedicatory inscription reads: "Following the directions and plans and under the auspices of his father, [Titus] tamed the race of the Jews and destroyed the city of Jerusalem, a thing either sought in vain by all commanders, kings, and races before him or never even attempted."

Among the empire's Jewish community, the extent of the catastrophe was very hard to understand. As the Babylonian Talmud put it:

Why was the First Temple destroyed? Because of three transgressions: because of idol worship, sexual immorality, and wanton bloodshed. But the Second Temple, [whose generation] studied Torah, observed the commandments, and engaged in charitable works, why was it destroyed? Because of baseless hatred—which demonstrated that baseless hatred is as weighty as three transgressions: idol worship, sexual immorality, and wanton bloodshed.

The Jews had obeyed the Lord, but, like Job, still been punished. The explanation, mysterious except to the divine mind, was that the enmity of others was potent enough to outplay virtue.

V

A NEW DYNASTY

. . .

Vespasian inherited his family's reputation for stinginess, but this probably signified no more than financial realism. He liked to present himself as a common man, and enjoyed a dirty joke. When he decided to introduce a new tax on public latrines (these were profitable enterprises, because urine was much in demand by laundries for bleaching clothes whiter than white), his son Titus demurred. The emperor is reported to have responded that a coin did not smell (*pecunia non olet*).

The Flavians reintroduced competence into government. According to Tacitus, Vespasian was the first man to improve after becoming emperor. Rebellions in Germany and Britain, overhangs from the Year of the Four Emperors, were efficiently quelled. Increased taxes and the manipulation of the supply of certain commodities removed a large deficit at the treasury, the consequence of Neronian extravagance and the luxury of civil war.

The emperor and his sons, Titus Flavius Vespasianus and Titus Flavius Domitianus (known as Domitian), who succeeded him on the throne, did all they could to signal a break with the empire's original first family, and more particularly with Nero.

Vespasian reestablished a working relationship with the ruling class, which provided trustworthy and responsible personnel to govern the provinces and command the armies. Without its backing, even if this was only tacit, experience had shown that an emperor would be unable to manage the empire. However, one dangerous continuity with the discredited past remained obstinately in place—the existence in the Senate of an opposition party, or at least a faction of critics.

• • •

Imagine a perfect human being, virtuous and wise. If he sees his child in danger of drowning, it is natural for him to do all he can to rescue it. But if, despite his best efforts, he fails, he will accept what has happened without feeling distress or pity. In this way happiness cannot be compromised.

For most of us, this scenario is both disagreeable and implausible, but it epitomizes in a single *exemplum* the essence of Stoicism, a philosophical tradition that Rome's elite had long made its own. It was founded by Zeno of Citium, who lectured at the end of the fourth century B.C. in the Painted Porch in Athens, the ποικίλη στοά (Poikile Stoa), whence the name of his doctrines. The stoa was a roofed colonnade on the northern side of the Agora, or marketplace, where paintings on wooden panels of great events in Athenian history were on display. It was a convenient spot where a teacher and his students could hold their classes.

For the Stoic the universe consisted of matter inspirited by a divine breath. This creative fire (or warm air) was called the Word (the Greek term is λόγος, or *logos,* which we know from the Christian Gospel of Saint John, perhaps written about this time, when Hadrian was a young man). The *logos* fashioned the universe into a rational and purposive whole, of which an individual human soul formed a small part.

To lead a good life and attain happiness a man or woman had to live in harmony with this principle of energy and order. The ordinary aspirations of human life—health, wealth, friendship, family—have a real value, but they are subordinate to the imperatives of the *logos,* which can do no wrong. What seems like misfortunes cannot be so in the eyes of the cosmos and must be accepted with a cheerful heart. Ergo the inhuman imperturbability of the bereaved father. The universe has its reasons, of which reason knows nothing.

The living embodiment of Stoicism was the philosopher Epictetus. He was born in about A.D. 55, a slave of one of Nero's freedmen, Epaphroditus, who helped his patron Nero to kill himself, and had been lame from childhood. At a certain point he was probably handed on to a new owner, for his name is the Greek for "acquired." It is not known when or how he won his freedom; perhaps Epaphroditus let him go in the confused and violent aftermath of the fall of the Julio-Claudian dynasty.

One of Epictetus' catchphrases was 'ανέχον καί 'απέχου—"bear and forbear," or more precisely, "endure and renounce." In one of his lectures, he spoke of an appropriately calm approach to being executed.

> This is what it means . . . to have made desire and aversion free from every hindrance and proofed them against chance. I must die. If immediately, then I die. But if a little later, I will have some lunch, for it's lunchtime, and then I will die at the appointed time. How shall I face my end? As becomes a man who is giving back what belongs to someone else.

Epictetus held philosophy classes in Rome. Like Socrates, he wrote no books, and his thought survives thanks to verbatim notes of what he said, taken down by one of his students. He lived in the greatest simplicity and was modest about himself and his achievements. Children were only half-complete human beings, he felt, but their straightforwardness in play impressed him, and he loved to get down on his hands and knees and speak baby talk with them.

Ever since Augustus replaced the noisy, competitive, semidemocratic Republic with an efficient autocracy toward the end of the previous century, a minority of senators had kept their distance from the government and criticized successive administrations. It was never altogether clear to the emperor of the day whether or not they were a loyal opposition. Some of them cherished a long-term ambition to restore the Republic, but most intelligent observers of the political scene recognized that the past could not be recalled. What they sought was temperate rule by an intelligent and experienced emperor.

These dissidents have been named the Stoic opposition because their chief tactics—a refusal to cooperate with an unworthy government and a willingness to endure uncomplainingly the punishment of the state—could be justified in philosophical terms. They knew they were going to lose, but nonetheless proceeded on their dangerous course with stoicism—as well as with Stoicism.

Families that shared common political views intermarried over the years and one generation picked up where the previous one left off. Women played a key role and on occasion were braver and more decisive than their husbands. One of these was Arria, wife of Aulus Caecina Paetus, who supported an abortive revolt against the emperor Claudius in A.D. 42 by the governor of Illyricum, a province on the far side of the Adriatic Sea (roughly today's Albania and Croatia).

The emperor let it be known that he expected Paetus to commit suicide (a civilized alternative to execution for the wellborn or well-connected). However, when the last moment came, Paetus succumbed to nerves and it looked as if he would not behave in the expected high Roman fashion. Arria took his sword from him and stabbed herself with it. She said: "Paetus, it doesn't *hurt*," and handed back the weapon. The couple were soon both dead, and the words *Paete, non dolet* became a catchphrase for selfless courage.

Although Vespasian and the Flavians promised better government, the Stoic opposition remained unreconciled. An able but obstinate senator, Helvidius Priscus, opposed measures aimed at pleasing Vespasian. Helvidius insisted on addressing the emperor by his original preimperial name and delivered speeches attacking Vespasian personally and the office he held.

Epictetus recalls a memorable exchange. Vespasian asked Helvidius to stay away from a meeting of the Senate. Helvidius replied:

"It is in your power not to allow me to be a member of the Senate, but so long as I am I must attend its meetings."

"Very well then, but when you attend, hold your tongue."

"Don't ask for my opinion and I *will* hold my tongue."

"But I am obliged to ask your opinion [as a senior senator]."

"Then I am obliged to reply and give you my opinion."

"But if you speak, I will have you executed."

"All right, then, but when did I ever claim that I was immortal? You play your part, and I will play mine."

This may or may not be a verbatim account, but it epitomizes the strengths and weaknesses of the Stoic opposition—brave but to little effect, content to condemn but not to overthrow. But in one sense they posed the imperial idea a real and irresoluble threat. Although they suffered persecution from time to time, they remained an integral part of the political elite whether through friendship, family ties, or a dour underpinning philosophy of life. They could not be liquidated without risking the alienation of those on whose cooperation emperors depended.

An abiding problem with Rome's system of imperial government was the succession. In constitutional theory the emperor was merely the senior official in a republic, and so the future could not be spelled out. However, Vespasian believed reasonably enough that with two capable sons his own bloodline would be sufficient to ensure governmental continuity.

The calculation bore fruit, at first. In 79 the emperor was struck down by a bowel complaint. His sense of humor did not betray him, even when he realized that he was not to recover. In the confident expectation that, as was customary, the Senate would vote to deify him posthumously, he remarked: "Dear me, I seem to be becoming a god!" He continued with his official duties and received embassies. His doctors complained, but he replied, "An emperor ought to die on his feet." There is another version of this story. According to this, he made the remark when he was overtaken by a sudden and painful attack of diarrhea, and nearly fainted. He struggled to his feet and expired in the arms of those around him.

Hadrian was only an infant at the time, but as an adult he spread the word that Vespasian had in fact been poisoned at a banquet by his good-looking and able son Titus. This is an improbable claim. Such evidence as there is suggests that Titus loved and was loyal to his father; at any rate, in his brief reign he maintained Vespasian's policies.

On August 24, two months almost to the day after Vespasian's death, Mount Vesuvius in Campania erupted and buried the towns of Herculaneum and Pompeii beneath ash.

The event made a profound impression and talk of it may have been among Hadrian's early memories. Dust was reported to have spread to Africa, Syria, and Egypt. At Rome it filled the air overhead and darkened the sun for several days. According to Dio Cassius, "people did not know and could not imagine what had happened, but, like those close at hand, believed that the whole world was being turned upside down, that the sun was disappearing into the earth and that the earth was being lifted to the sky." Pliny the Younger was in Campania at the time, and was convinced that "the whole world was dying with me and I with it."

It soon became clear that this was not the case, but the terror that the end of the world was at hand fed the millenarian anxieties of the age. It was a fearful reminder that humankind was at the mercy of uncontrollable forces, which reason alone could not vanquish.

In 81, shortly after the endless *munera* with which he had marked the opening of a new amphitheater, the Colosseum, and some splendid public baths, Titus sickened unexpectedly with a fever and died. Domitian succeeded Titus without challenge. According to the literary sources, he was of a solitary and suspicious disposition. As a child, his father and brother had spent much of their time at Nero's court and during his teens had been largely absent on public business in the east. He seems to have been often left to his own devices and grew up unsupported by the day-to-day affection and supervision of his closest relatives.

Domitian was ill at ease socially and was sometimes reported to feign madness. He enjoyed the solitude of his vast villa outside Rome in the Alban Hills. According to Suetonius,

> At the beginning of his reign he used to spend hours in seclusion every day, doing nothing but catch flies and stab them with a keenly sharpened stylus. Consequently, when someone once asked whether anyone was in there with [him], Vibius Crispus made the witty reply: "Not even a *fly*."

Thirty years old when he assumed power, Domitian proved to be a competent administrator, and he performed his judicial duties conscientiously. He has had a bad press, for he alienated the Senate, and the literary sources reflect its antipathy. So what was said against him needs to be treated with caution. However, the antipathy itself is telling, for the inability of an emperor to manage the political class represents a serious failure.

Like Nero, Domitian had no obvious qualifications for the job he held; his refractory nature did not inspire confidence and, although he had held public office during his father's reign, he had not been allowed the opportunity to gain military experience.

One senses that a fear of insufficiency lay behind his bossy and decidedly autocratic manner. He appreciated it when flatterers hailed him as *Dominus et deus noster,* "our lord and god." The imperial system, as invented by Augustus, depended on everyone accepting the necessary fiction that it was the old Roman Republic reborn and that the emperor was merely the first among equals. Domitian was too impatient to waste time on this, and offended senators by his lack of *civilitas,* or polite affability.

Evidence survives of sensible measures taken by provincial governors, usually following precedents set by previous emperors. Where Domitian himself intervened, the most notable characteristic was not any special concern for justice or efficiency, but a censorious tone of voice.

His moralizing approach to governance found its most intense expression in a revival of the Julian Laws, with the aim of "shaking the thunderbolt of purity." The emperor sought to implement legislation dating from Augustus' day that encouraged marriage and protected the family, and the old Scantinian law that penalized male-to-male sexual activity.

As *censor perpetuus,* or censor for life, Domitian gave himself oversight of public morals. He took his responsibilities with the utmost seriousness. He twice acted against Vestal Virgins, whom he charged with *incestum,* illicit sexual intercourse. The six Vestals were the only priestesses in the Roman religious system, and their main task was to watch over Rome's eternal flame, or symbolic hearth. If it was allowed to go out, the well-being and prosperity of the city was put at risk.

Recruited when a little girl from the nobility, a Vestal served for thirty years and was under the care of the *pontifex maximus,* chief priest.

She could expect a life of luxury and high prestige. But she had to be careful. If a Vestal was found to have slept with a man a terrible fate awaited her—to be buried alive. Early in the reign three Vestals, half the complement, were found guilty of *incestum,* but Domitian was in a forgiving mood and allowed them to choose their own form of death.

Some years later the senior Vestal, Cornelia, who had already been acquitted of the same charge, was again arraigned. Domitian tried her and, although she protested her innocence vigorously, convicted her. In his capacity as *pontifex maximus* he accompanied her to a stretch of rising ground just inside the city walls called the Campus Sceleratus, the "field polluted by crime." Here a small underground chamber had been prepared, containing a couch, a lamp, and a table with food on it.

Cornelia's dress caught as she descended a ladder into the tiny vault, and Domitian, who was standing beside her, politely offered her his hand. She drew back in disgust and pushed his arm away. She took care to lower herself onto the couch without offense to her modesty. The ladder was pulled up and the access hole filled with earth. Cornelia was left alone to meet her death, whether through eventual asphyxiation or, perhaps, a more immediate suicide with poison or knife.

The affair left a bad impression. A former praetor was persuaded to make a tardy confession of having slept with the Vestal, but many doubted her guilt.

Domitian was unfazed by the contrast with his own private life. According to Dio, "he was not only physically lazy and emotionally timorous, but also extremely promiscuous and indulged in rough sex both with women and boys." Apparently he liked to call copulation by the Greek word for "bed-wrestling."

Domitian spent much of his time outside Rome on campaign, no doubt to the Senate's relief. Like all the Flavians, he recognized that military success would help to stabilize the regime. He defeated the Chatti, a Germanic tribe beyond the middle Rhine, and permanently occupied the Taunus region, in this way strengthening the frontier by eliminating an awkward re-entrant. He enclosed this new acquisition with a *limes,* a line of blockhouses and forts, that showed exactly where the imperial boundary was as well as demonstrating Rome's firm intention to maintain and defend it.

Domitian made more of his immediate victory than was warranted, and it was some years before the territory was fully pacified. However, he bought popularity with the troops by raising their wages by one third—the first time there had been an increase since the days of Augustus—as well as offering them three costly *congiaria,* or one-off bonuses. This was the kind of emperor the rank and file appreciated.

If the Rhine frontier was more or less settled, the same could not be said for the Danube. North of the river lay the Transylvanian basin, surrounded by the rugged Carpathian Mountains. Here was the home of the Dacians, a rich and powerful people who had originated in northwestern Asia Minor. They controlled substantial mineral reserves, especially of gold and silver, which they traded with their Celtic and Germanic neighbors and the Greek cities on the coast of the Black Sea.

In the early part of the first century B.C., a certain Burebista transformed the disparate and decentralized Dacians into a unified kingdom for the first time and established alliances with adjoining tribes. A great power began to emerge that in time might challenge Rome. Julius Caesar saw the danger and was planning an expedition against Burebista before his assassination, in 44 B.C. Luckily for Rome, the king died in the same year and the threat receded.

A century or so later, however, a new, energetic, and talented ruler came to the fore, Decebalus, "shrewd in his understanding of warfare, and shrewd too in the waging of war." His ambition was to reestablish the Dacian empire. He judged that Rome would not countenance the reappearance of an expansionist power on its frontier, and decided on a preemptive strike. In A.D. 84 a horde crossed the Danube and invaded the province of Moesia (parts of modern Serbia, Bulgaria, and Romania), killing the governor.

Domitian took immediate action. He made his way to Moesia to mastermind a military response. However, he did not lead the legions himself, staying in a town well behind the front line. Instead, he gave command of the army to Cornelius Fuscus, who had helped Vespasian to the throne and was praetorian prefect. He is listed among flattering *amici Caesaris* in a satire by Juvenal as an incompetent warmonger,

dreaming of battle while lolling in marble villas,
His guts a predestined feast for Dacia's vultures.

The poet was not the prophet he seemed, for he wrote long after the campaign had ended in a second bad defeat and Fuscus' death.

The emperor now faced a serious crisis. The ruling class expected the emperor to pursue a policy of imperial expansion and was liable to lose confidence in him were territory to be abandoned, legions destroyed, or a compromise peace agreed with the enemy. To deal with Decebalus the emperor assembled a new force, perhaps six legions strong, by withdrawing troops from elsewhere in the empire. A legion was ordered to the Danube from Britannia, as a result of which a successful campaign to extend the territory under Roman control had to be put into reverse. A new fortress at Inchtutil in Scotland was abandoned.

This time the Romans scored a decisive victory. Decebalus feared that they would proceed to his capital, Sarmizegetusa. Short of men, he anticipated the trick played on Macbeth at Dunsinane. Trees were cut down and dressed in military uniforms to give an impression that his forces were more numerous than in fact they were.

In the event, the maneuver proved to be unnecessary. Domitian's attention—and his legions—was diverted to the neighboring province of Pannonia, where dangerous revolts among Germanic tribes needed urgent attention. To avoid fighting a war on two fronts, the emperor agreed to terms with the Dacians. Decebalus was awarded a substantial annual subsidy of about 8 million sesterces. In a further dangerous concession, the emperor agreed to provide military engineers and artillery to help Decebalus fortify his realm against attack.

The emperor staged victory celebrations back in Rome. Informed opinion was derisive and word spread that exhibits displayed as campaign spoils really came from the imperial furniture store. Perilous laughter circulated around the best dinner tables.

With the indestructible optimism of veteran social climbers, the Ulpii did not allow themselves to be dismayed by the emperor's eccentricities. They remained loyal supporters of the dynasty. Just as Traianus had been close to Vespasian, so his able son Trajan was promoted by Titus and Domitian. Trajan spent much of his youth in the army as a military tribune *laticlavius:* every legion was allocated six tribunes, general staff officers who reported to the legionary commander, or *legatus.* The senior tribune was called *laticlavius,* or "broad-banded." This was a reference to the red stripe senators wore on their togas, and the *laticlavius* was usually a young man of senatorial rank at the outset of his political career.

Trajan had the physical strength and height for effective soldiering. He spent time in the east and on the German frontier and gained the respect and affection of the legionaries under his command. He became praetor in 86 and was a colleague of Hadrian's father. In the following year, at the age of thirty-one, he received his first legionary command. He was appointed the *legatus* of the VII Gemina. Founded less than twenty years previously, the legion was recruited in Spain, almost certainly from the Romanized citizenry of Baetica in the south. It was based at Legio, on a plateau beneath the mountains of Asturia and Cantabria; this is today's León, where the outline of the army camp can still be detected. This northwest region of Spain had been the last part of the peninsula to have been conquered by Rome, as recently as the first century B.C., and the hardy and aggressive mountaineers needed watching. But Trajan's main task was to protect the export of gold from this mineral-rich region.

It was not the most demanding of jobs, managing a backwater, but the appointment was a useful step up the military ladder. Then fate provided an unexpected opportunity that propelled Trajan to the center of events, and into the emperor's highest favor.

News arrived that the governor of Upper Germania, Lucius Antonius Saturninus, had raised the standard of revolt on January 1, 89. When the news of this insurrection reached Trajan, he did not hesitate to spearhead a counterattack. On the emperor's orders, he immediately led his legion on the long march across Gaul to Upper Germania to face down and fight the rebels.

The emperor himself left Rome on January 12, for the same destination. In fact, neither man was required. Saturninus had expected help from a Germanic tribe that failed to turn up, and a colleague, the governor of Lower Germania, was able to outflank and defeat him. The revolt was at an end by January 25—almost before it began.

Domitian was a conspiracy theorist, and once remarked: "Rulers find themselves in an extremely invidious position, for when they discover a conspiracy no one believes them, unless they are killed." He was determined that there had been one on this occasion, and held an inquiry, although so far as we can judge, Saturninus acted on his own.

In 91 Trajan received the culminating reward for his services. He was appointed consul *ordinarius*— a high accolade that the Flavians seldom conferred outside the imperial family: the two *ordinarii* entered office at the beginning of the year, which was named after them, and were a cut above the *suffecti*, or substitute consuls, who took their places after a few weeks or months.

Our impoverished literary sources do not specify Trajan's activities for the next few years after his consulship, but it is possible to make an informed guess. There were eleven imperial provinces, whose governors were directly chosen by the emperor (the others lying in the care of the Senate), and a former consul could expect appointment to one of them. Trajan, having been the junior of the two *ordinarii,* was likely to have found the German provinces open to him. A couple of years or so later he probably moved on to one of the militarily much more challenging Danube provinces, perhaps Pannonia, where Rome was engaged in a difficult conflict with a powerful Germanic tribe, the Suebi.

Hadrian had spent his entire life under Flavian rule, and by his late teens he would have absorbed the history of his times. His guardian was a rising man and this placed him close to the center of power, although too young to have arrived at mature judgments. Indeed, mature judgments came at some risk to life and limb for anyone within range of a suspicious and nervous ruler. Nevertheless, two conclusions were evident to an intelligent bystander, however inexperienced.

First, for it to run sweetly the imperial system depended on its chief executive and its senior management being on reasonably good terms.

For how long could an atmosphere of distrust last without the eventual need for a painful adjustment? Second, it was a brave emperor who abandoned, whether from choice or necessity, the traditional policy of military aggression. In Augustus' day, Virgil, the poet laureate of Roman power, had sung of an *imperium sine fine*. A century later he still pointed the way to an empire without end and without frontiers.

VI

ON THE TOWN

· · ·

In A.D. 93 Hadrian was nineteen years old; it was time for a public career.

Senators' sons with ambition, such as Hadrian, joined the *vigintivirate,* a college of twenty men who were allocated a variety of duties, some laborious and tiresome and others ceremonial. The most interesting job was usually restricted to those of patrician background; this was appointment as one of the three controllers of the mint, or *tresviri monetales* (only a nonpatrician, or plebeian, who commanded the most powerful political patronage could hope to capture one of these posts). The *tresviri* administered the production and design of the coinage—an important task, for coins were an effective and universal means of publishing state propaganda. We can infer that they worked closely with government officials.

At the other extreme, two boards were responsible for street maintenance in Rome and supervision of basic police duties (arrests, executions, and the collection of fines), and were to be avoided if at all possible.

Hadrian, being a plebeian, failed to win a post in the mint, but at least he was able to avoid the fatigue duty of civic administration. In 94 he served on the fourth and last of the *vigintivirate* committees, as *decemvir stlitibus iudicandis,* member of the Board of Ten for Civil Judgments. This demanded less onerous work than might at first appear. The *decemviri* chaired sessions of the Centumviral Court, which handled such noncriminal matters as disputed wills. The court enrolled 180 jurors, as a rule divided into up to four individual panels, each determining a different suit. Cases were heard in the Basilica Julia, a large conference hall in the Forum, Rome's main square—once, before Augustus and the establishment of one-man rule, the arena of political debate and power, but now merely a legal and shopping center.

Large crowds gathered to witness legal encounters. They had no interest in the youthful presiding judges, whose task was little more than to preside. The advocates were the real attraction. Their speeches created great excitement and were popular cultural events, rather as sermons used to be in seventeenth-century England. A well-informed commentator argued that he knew oratory was not dead when he noticed that a "young patrician who had had his tunic torn off, as often happens in a crowd, stayed on in nothing but his toga to listen for seven hours."

As a *decemvir* Hadrian had attendants, or *viatores,* at his disposal and secretaries who recorded proceedings and, it may be surmised, were able to offer legal advice on those occasions when he had to make a decision.

Hadrian was also appointed a *sevir turmae equitum Romanorum,* commander of one of six squadrons of young Roman "knights." Unless a man was a member of a *turma,* he was excluded from holding significant public office. It was a high honor to be a *sevir.* Here we have the first evidence that Hadrian was being fast-tracked for future preferment, presumably because of official interest on the part of someone at the imperial court if not of the emperor himself. The discreet helping hand of Trajan can be suspected; as we have seen, at this time he may have been serving as governor of one of the two German provinces, Upper Germania and Lower Germania, but a letter to Rome would have been sufficient. Sura, too, could have put in a word.

In the same year an even more distinctive honor came the young man's way, probably at the behest of one of the consuls for 94, who was a friend of Trajan and had served under Trajan's father. He was appointed *praefectus urbi feriarum Latinarum,* city prefect for the Latin Festival. This great celebration, originally a sacred truce among the warring towns of Latium, took place on the Alban Mount, a hill overlooking the Alban lake about twenty miles southeast of Rome and not far from the emperor's great villa. All the leading officeholders and public figures of Rome processed out of the city to sacrifice an ox at the antique shrine of Jupiter Latiaris, which stood on top of the hill. Offerings of lamb, cheese, and milk were made, and long and joyful feasting followed.

In theory, the *praefectus* was left in charge of the deserted city, in place of the consuls. But his duties were purely symbolic, and the post was awarded to young men with prospects. Julius Caesar appointed his great-nephew, the teenage Augustus (in those early days, called Gaius Octavius), and the emperor Claudius the youthful Nero. Hadrian was not in that league, but he was being singled out as a boy of promise.

Life was not all duty and ritual. Rome offered many opportunities for amusement and excitement. Apart from hunting, no record survives of young Hadrian's leisure activities, but there was plenty for him to sample.

By the middle of the first century, Rome boasted more than ninety *feriae,* annual festivals or holidays. On these days no public business could be conducted and various forms of religious ceremony were conducted. However, no one in the Mediterranean world had yet picked up the Jewish notion of a seven-day week, and the concept of a Saturday or Sunday as a day of rest was unknown—let alone a weekend of leisure. Whether everyone laid down tools during the *feriae* and took time off may be doubted, but they were the only breaks in laborious routine.

Interspersed among and between the *feriae* were the games, or *ludi.* By the first century there were six sets of games at different times of the year over a total of fifty-seven days. Their purpose, at least in origin, was to reward the gods for Rome's prosperity and success. They included the spring games in honor of the eastern goddess, the Great Mother, which took the form of a drama festival, and the licentious *Ludi Florales,* running from late April to early May, which featured naked actresses and prostitutes and took place partly at night. The last day of the Floral Games would have pleased Hadrian, for deer and hare were hunted in Rome's premier racecourse, the Circus Maximus, whose grand marble stands, accommodating some 250,000 spectators, have long since gone and been replaced by today's long, scrubby stretch of grass and dirt.

The greatest celebrations took place in the autumn, the Roman Games, or *Ludi Romani,* and the Plebeian Games, the *Ludi Plebei.* Programs of events were dominated by theatrical performances that were not universally popular; discontented audiences would shout, "We want bears!" or "We want boxers."

Comedy and tragedy fell out of fashion under the emperors and were supplanted by the *pantomimus,* a dancer, usually male, who acted out all the parts in complex narratives. He was backed by flute and lute, sometimes even a full orchestra, and a singer or chorus. Plots were historical, mythological, or based on the masterpieces of Greek tragedy. A dancer's repertoire was extensive and might even include a dialogue by Plato. What would one not pay to witness a dance performance that gave a wordless account of the philosopher's theory of ideas?

Pantomimi had a reputation for sexual immorality, and at the same time were sought after and patronized by the upper classes. The emperor Caligula included a *pantomimus* among his favorites, and Nero acted as one himself. In Hadrian's day there was an eccentric old noblewoman, Ummidia Quadratilla, who kept a troupe of *pantomimi* in her home; when she found herself at a loose end she used to watch them dance. Her priggish grandson Gaius Ummidius Quadratus lived with her; he disapproved and took care never to see them perform.

Pantomime should not be confused with the mime, which was a much coarser, more highly spiced kind of spectacle. It encompassed a wide range of performance styles: words, usually prose but sometimes verse, mingled with music and acrobatic displays. The titles of the shows suggest an affinity with today's tabloid newspapers—"Millionaire on the Run," "The Locked-Out Lover," "From Rags to Riches."

Sometimes condemned criminals joined the cast and were compelled to suffer, in character, real-life punishment. Apuleius, in his picaresque novel *Metamorphoses,* written in the second century A.D., described a typical provincial company as it planned a very singular display. As a climax of the entertainment, a murderess was to "marry" and have sex with a donkey. The donkey selected for the purpose was, in fact, the author's hero Lucius, a young man transformed by a malevolent witch.

Lucius was led to the local theater and left to graze outside the entrance while warm-up acts were presented. Then a new stage set appeared, a bed shining with Indian tortoiseshell, piled high with a feathered mattress and covered with a flowery silk coverlet. At this point, Lucius the donkey took fright. He realized that the woman was to be fastened to him in some way, and once copulation had taken place (or was supposed to have done so) wild animals would be brought on to kill her. Lucius suspected that in the process he would lose his life as well, and seizing an unguarded moment galloped away.

Apuleius' story is fiction, and the intended atrocity did not take place. However, it is known that a similar spectacle actually occurred in Rome, this time involving a bull: it replayed the legend of Pasiphaë, wife of King Minos of Crete, who fell in love with a bull and after copulation gave birth to the monstrous Minotaur, half bull and half man. Martial remarked approvingly on the event.

A minority of days during the games was given over to a sport that was hugely popular among all social classes—namely, chariot racing. Drivers and chariots belonged to four teams, or factions—red, white, green, and blue. In Rome these were substantial organizations that employed buyers, trainers, doctors, vets, grooms, and stablemen and were controlled by a team manager, or *dominus*. The factions attracted fierce, sometimes violent, loyalty among their fans.

There were two main racecourses in Rome, the Circus Maximus beneath the Palatine Hill and the smaller Circus Flaminius in the Campus Martius (the Field of Mars, a large area originally used for military training to the north of the city, but now largely covered with public buildings). Chariots were usually drawn by four horses, but on occasion up to ten; novices drove two-horse chariots. They waited in twelve starting boxes, charged down a long straight, maneuvered sharply and dangerously around a cluster of three turning posts, galloped back, turned again, and so on for seven laps. Races at the Circus Maximus, whose track was almost a quarter of a mile long, lasted about fifteen minutes.

Charioteers were hugely popular. Many of them began their careers as slaves, but bought their freedom with their prize money. They could earn giddyingly large sums: one of the most successful was a Spaniard from Lusitania, one Appuleius Diocles, who styled himself as the "most eminent of charioteers" and drove teams of chariot horses for twenty-four years. During this time he ran in more than four thousand races and came first nearly fifteen hundred times. He won a staggering total of

35,863,120 sesterces, although presumably some of this was payable to his faction management, and he earned himself a place among the superrich of ancient Rome.

Of course, few charioteers were as successful as Diocles. The twenty-two-year-old Eutyches was obviously not much good at his job. He died young, and the epitaph on his gravestone admits, touchingly, that

> In this grave rest the bones of an inexperienced charioteer . . .
> I was brave enough to drive the four-horsed chariots,
> But never won promotion from the two-horse teams . . .
> Please, traveller, lay some flowers on my grave.
> —Perhaps you were a fan of mine while I lived.

Chariot racing was reserved for professionals, and young men from the upper classes were excluded from entering and driving their own chariots. The more raffish emperors might encourage an exception. Nero, predictably, allowed men and women of both the equestrian and senatorial orders to take part in the games whether as stage performers or as gladiators and charioteers. In Dio Cassius' day, audiences were able to sit and watch members of Rome's great families "standing down there below them [in the arena or onstage] and doing things some of which they formerly would not even watch when performed by others."

This kind of permissiveness was not on offer under the Flavian emperors. In any event, Hadrian's days as a tearaway were over and, even if he watched the thrills of the circus with a certain envy, his attention was now focused on climbing the lower rungs of the political ladder. While he enjoyed his distractions, from now onward he never let himself be distracted from the main business of ambition.

In A.D. 94 Hadrian was able to enjoy one of Domitian's most extravagant innovations—the Capitoline Games, founded eight years previously to mark the rebuilding of the great temple of Jupiter Optimus Maximus on the Capitol and staged every four years. They were founded on the Greek model and were evidence that the Hellenizing ideas of Nero were not dead. They attracted the disapproval of old-fashioned Roman moralists, who were shocked that the city's most sacred precinct and its divine custodian should be sullied by non-Roman rites. Not so Hadrian. Whatever else he made of the Flavian regime, these games will have pleased a young man who was more Greek than the Greeks.

Everything was done on the grandest scale. Rather as with today's Olympic Games, vast sums of money were spent on specially designed buildings. The Stadium in the Campus Martius held seats for about fifteen thousand spectators (its arcades were soon given over to brothels) and was reserved for athletic contests. Not far away, the Odeum was erected for musical performances. For centuries these were among the city's most admired buildings (they have since completely disappeared).

The games featured chariot racing, gymnastics, and athletics (unusually, there was even a foot race for girls); also poetry, music, singing, and oratory. The emperor himself presided, wearing a purple toga in the Greek manner, with a golden crown on his head featuring images of Jupiter, his wife, Juno, and daughter, Minerva. This first year there were fifty-two contestants for the Greek poetry prize alone.

Competition was fierce and the games soon became very popular throughout the empire. They sent a powerful message of the high value that the government accorded to Hellenic culture. It was a message with which Hadrian heartily concurred, and to which he would return later in his life.

To modern eyes, the most disgraceful aspect of Roman culture was the gladiatorial display. Fights in the arena were called *munera* (literally, a *munus* meant a service, favor, or gift), and had nothing to do with the *ludi*. Slaves and criminals, complemented by a few volunteers, fought one another in costly spectacles.

The origins of this bloodthirsty practice are uncertain, but what evidence we have suggests that it began with sacrificial combats at the funerals of great men. By the end of the Republic, a century before Hadrian's day, educated Romans such as Cicero found the whole business vulgar and boring, but acknowledged that watching men trying to kill one another was a training in physical courage.

Gladiatorial shows were so expensive that even emperors had to ration the number of days devoted to them in a year. In Rome, they were usually held in March and December, but also at other times when the emperor chose to celebrate particular events. Thousands of gladiators might take part in imperial spectacles, although other promoters were restricted to no more than 120 pairs. Small teams of gladiators toured the provinces.

Fighters wore different types of armor; some were heavily armed, whereas others, such as the Thraeces, or Thracians, were provided with a light shield and sickle. The most distinctive gladiator was the *retiarius;* he simply wore a tunic and was equipped with a net, a trident, and a dagger.

An ingenious recent calculation allows us to estimate a total of four hundred gladiatorial venues across the empire. Perhaps on average two shows a year were staged at each of them, featuring teams of about thirty gladiators, who would each fight twice. This would have meant about twelve thousand fighters in total. Perhaps four thousand were killed annually, a death rate of one in six per show. Numbers were made up by recruitment, signifying an annual throughput of sixteen thousand men.

In the public eye, gladiators were extremely sexy; they were the ultimate in masculinity, and their charms were much enhanced by their mortality. Juvenal evokes an upper-class woman's fondness for "her Sergius," who had

> one dud arm that held promise
> of early retirement. Deformities marred his features—
> a helmet scar, a great wen on his nose, an unpleasant
> discharge from one constantly weeping eye. What of it?
> *He was a gladiator.* That makes anyone an Adonis.

The Romans liked animals, and especially liked to see them killed. With considerable difficulty, elephants, bears, crocodiles, ostriches, leopards, even polar bears and seals (another first for Nero) were caught, transported to Rome, and trained to do tricks or fight against each other. Elephants were particularly popular, being attributed with a humanlike intelligence: Pliny the Elder claims that one beast, beaten for failing to learn a trick, was discovered at night practicing what he had to do.

As well as gladiators, the program for a *munus* would usually include one or more of three spectacles—armed men fighting animals, animals driven to fight each other, and unarmed condemned criminals exposed to starved carnivores. The first of these was not unlike hunting in the open, and so may have interested a keen huntsman such as Hadrian. Martial, with his unerring eye for the unpleasant, describes the death of a pregnant wild sow; a *bestiarius* wounded her in the stomach and, as she expired, a piglet ran out of her into the arena.

The government devoted much attention to, and spent resources on, the *munera* and the *ludi*. The powers of the people to vote politicians into office had been steadily whittled away, but emperors knew that their authority lay in part with popular support in and around the capital. State provision of subsidized grain and free public entertainment helped to ensure the loyalty of the masses. Juvenal's sharp eyes saw this with poetic clarity. He noted that citizens no longer had a vote to sell, or even the wish to have one.

> Time was when their plebiscite elected
> generals, heads of state, commanders of legions; but now
> they've pulled in their horns. Only two things really concern them:
> bread and the games [*panem et circenses*].

It was not surprising, then, that the Flavians sought to secure their new dynasty by a massive building commission. Within a few years of assuming the purple in 69, Vespasian began construction of the Flavian Amphitheater, or the Colosseum as we know it, still Rome's most striking and unforgettable monument. Its seating capacity was around fifty thousand, so only a minority of the city's inhabitants could squeeze in at one particular time. Although tickets for all public entertainments were free, gaining entry to a major show at the Colosseum must have entailed some string pulling.

The seating was arranged hierarchically in steeply serried ranks and, when the amphitheater was full, was a representation in small of Roman society. In the front row of the lowest tier, spaces were reserved for members of the Senate and for state priestesses, the Vestal Virgins. Next came places for the *equites* and so on to high up in the top rows, where slaves and women were allowed to sit. For the emperor himself was reserved an imperial box, or *pulvinar* (originally a cushioned couch on which images of the gods were displayed).

In 80, the Colosseum was at last ready. By that time Vespasian was dead and Titus had succeeded him. The new emperor opened the building with a spectacular celebration. One hundred days were set aside for an extravagant series of combats and animal hunts. The program, if uninterrupted, would surely have been too much for the most diehard enthusiast for slaughter and must have been broken up into manageable groups of days over the year.

Hadrian was only five years old when the Flavian Amphitheater first opened its doors and would not have been taken to the more bloodthirsty events. But it was a great moment in the history of the dynasty, and, as an associate of the Ulpian clan, which was high in favor at court, he would surely have been taken to some ceremony or other over which the emperor presided, or perhaps to a comparatively "safe" spectacle, such as the horse racing. Later, as a young man he had ample opportunity to experience the complete gallery of horrors.

Another kind of horror awaited Hadrian on the public stage. Domitian's darkening mood as his reign proceeded had serious implications for anyone in the senatorial elite. People whom the young Spaniard knew, or certainly knew of, faced exile and execution, in large part through the law courts.

The Roman state had no public prosecution service or anything resembling a modern police force, so the legal system depended on a private citizen laying an accusation that some other person had committed an offense. He was called a *delator,* a denouncer. Often the matter concerned him directly, and he would either prosecute the case himself or commission an experienced advocate to do so on his behalf.

As already discussed, an upper-class Roman received years of training in oratory. Many launched their political careers as young men by initiating prosecutions in the public interest—for instance, against embezzling governors at the end of their terms. The most brilliant speakers, such as Marcus Tullius Cicero in the final years of the Republic, were in great demand, whether for the prosecution or the defense.

Gradually there grew up a class of advocate who made a regular, one might say "professional," practice of informing against and prosecuting people on serious or capital charges. They flourished, for emperors found them useful tools with which to eliminate their opponents. Denunciations were accepted from every socioeconomic class, even slaves, but the *delatores* who were also advocates and were capable of prosecuting as well as naming their victims usually came from leading circles. They made large fortunes from their trade: if they attached *maiestas*, or high treason, to the list of charges, one quarter of a convicted man's assets went to the prosecutor. Domitian relied on men like this to terrorize the senatorial elite, and especially members of the Stoic opposition, under cover of judicial propriety. Juries, made up of senators, were likely to convict when they sensed that the emperor approved or had even provoked the prosecution.

But being a *delator* was not without its dangers. If a case failed, then he was subject to the same penalties as the accused. What is more, he was likely to be pursued in the courts on other charges by his victim's vengeful relatives or friends. One such was Baebius Massa. He served as governor of Baetica (and may have been in office during Hadrian's visit to his estates there in 90), where he acted so corruptly that the locals brought charges against him. He was arraigned in Rome before his peers in the Senate, which commissioned two of its members—Herennius Senecio, a native of Baetica himself, and the younger Pliny—to lead the prosecution. This was a great state event and, as a senator's son, Hadrian had the right to attend; if we bear in mind the Baetican connection and his interests as a leading landowner, he very probably did.

The case seems to have been straightforward. Massa was convicted, and his assets were frozen while compensation for the Baeticans was assessed. The consuls objected and quietly unfroze them. But this contradicted a senatorial vote and, when he learned of this unusual move, Senecio, supported by Pliny, protested and the consuls swiftly revoked their decision.

At this juncture matters took a sinister turn when a furious Massa prosecuted his prosecutor for high treason. *Horror omnium,* wrote Pliny, to a friend, of the Senate's reaction. "Universal horror."

A routine corruption case had been suddenly transformed into an attack on the Stoic opposition, of which Senecio was a leading and well-known member. One may well detect here the hidden hand of Domitian. In the aftermath of the Saturninus revolt, he was uncertain of the extent and sincerity of political support for him in the Senate. To begin with, he sought to conciliate potential troublemakers, but Massa's outburst signaled the end of this uneasy entente. The ex-governor proceeded to prosecute Senecio, who had adopted a policy of dumb insolence toward the imperial government by refusing to compete for office after having won entry to the Senate as a quaestor. The implication was that the regime did not deserve his cooperation. Unsurprisingly, this was made much of during his trial, as was a political biography he had written of Helvidius Priscus, whom Vespasian had executed.

More trials followed, including that of Arulenus Rusticus, another author of incautious panegyrics of Stoic martyrs. Plutarch, the great Greek essayist and biographer, recounts that Rusticus was among the audience for a lecture he gave at Rome. "A soldier marched in and handed him a letter from the emperor. There was a silence. I stopped speaking so he could read the letter. But he did not, nor even open it, until I finished my lecture and the audience had left." Neither his sangfroid nor his recent consulship saved Rusticus. Another victim was also a former consul, Helvidius' son. Warned by his father's fate, he spent much of his time in quiet retirement, but he had the misfortune to have written a stage farce about Paris of Troy and his first lover, the wood nymph Oenone, whom he threw over for Helen. Domitian decided that the piece was a satire on his own divorce from his wife, Domitia, and thus a capital crime. From this distance it is hard to tell whether a paranoid ruler was imagining conspiracy where none existed or whether his irrational fears brought conspiracy about.

In any event, all these men were put to death, and some of their relatives sent into exile.

This chain of murderous events, with its Baetican associations, came a little too close for comfort to Rome's Spanish aristocracy, settled in its assembly of villas at Tibur. It felt as if the situation was foundering. Pliny, like many in the Senate a friend of the executed Stoics but no rebel and a trusty servant of empire, recalled these times: "I stood among the flames of thunderbolts dropping all round me, and there were certain clear indications to make me suppose that a like fate was awaiting me."

The Aelii and the Ulpii were protected from personal harm by Trajan's rise to favor, but Hadrian would have been upset by the emperor's decision in 95, following Senecio's death, to expel philosophers from Rome. "Philosopher" was code for teachers of Stoicism. Hadrian was much impressed by the Stoic outlook and at some point in his life became an admiring friend of Epictetus, although not necessarily at this early stage. As a student he may well have attended some of his lectures in Rome, but now that Epictetus was banished the opportunity for any longer-term relationship was removed.

The philosopher took a dim view of the regime's approach to freedom of speech. He particularly resented its policy of entrapment. Speaking from experience (either of his friends or of himself), he said:

> In Rome reckless persons are entrapped by soldiers. A soldier in civilian dress sits down next to you and begins by speaking ill of Caesar, and then, as if you had received a pledge from him of trust—the fact that he began the reproaches—you also say what you're thinking. Then come the chains and the march to prison.

The expulsions did not come as much of a surprise. Philosophy was well enough respected, and even Domitian had no particular quarrel with Stoicism in itself, which (after all) accepted the principle of monarchy—always providing that the monarch was a philosopher-king. What the regime could not endure, though, was open criticism of the government and ostentatious withdrawal into private life by members of the senatorial class. These were the sins that had led to the recent purge, and now that the political practitioners of Stoicism had been disposed of, it was time to remove the theoreticians.

This was by no means the first occasion that foreign intellectuals had been cleared out of the city; indeed Domitian had ruled against them ten years previously. However, the Roman fondness for everything Hellenic meant that it did not take long for them to creep back, and some patrons at least took care to preserve their philosophical protégés from want.

Astrologers also felt the full brunt of the emperor's anger. Hadrian was by no means alone in consulting the heavens about the future. It was precisely because Domitian shared this belief that he profoundly disapproved of its practice. Anyone plotting against him could establish the date of his future death, and this could help them win adherents. He would also be able to compute the name of the next emperor—a serious threat, for the one man who was by definition sure to survive Domitian was his successor.

As we know, Hadrian had a fearful secret in his possession. The horoscope that his ancient great-uncle had cast years before promised him imperial power. This was a wonderful daydream for an ambitious boy, but potentially lethal if he told anyone about it. In these slippery times, he kept silent.

For a young man at the outset of a political career, the performance of the emperor gave pause for thought. A vicious circle was clearly in process. The more Domitian sensed he was losing the confidence of the ruling class, the more punitive he became; and the more punitive he became, the more he lost the confidence of the ruling class. Could a wiser ruler break out of the vortex? Was it possible to govern by consent? And, if the answers to these questions were yes, how could a transition be planned to a virtuous circle that would avoid yet another civil war, a return to the terrible Year of the Four Emperors?

VII

FALL OF THE FLAVIANS

. . .

Pannonia was as far away from the amenities of civilization as it was possible to reach within the boundaries of the empire. Now a part of Hungary, it was one of a chain of provinces running along the right bank of the wide and strong-flowing river Ister, our Danube, which rises in the Black Forest in Germany and empties itself into the Black Sea. The landscape was wooded and mountainous, with few towns. The vine and the olive did not grow there, and a local beer was brewed in place of wine. Pannonia was famous for a plant called the *saliunca,* which had a sweet smell and could be used to combat bad breath and "offensive exhalations of the armpits."

The territory was new to Rome, which had conquered and annexed it only a century previously. It was of no particular interest in itself, but tribal migrations in central Asia were pushing populations west and south toward the imperial frontier. Augustus saw a threat to Macedonia and Greece unless buffer provinces to their north were established, with the Danube as a defensible frontier.

The inhabitants of Pannonia were various Celtic tribes, with a reputation for being warlike and brave, but also cruel and treacherous. They were rumored to use human skulls as drinking cups. However, after the bloody defeat of a great rebellion in A.D. 9, they settled down to foreign rule and were beginning to adopt the Roman way of life, with new urban settlements springing up.

It is a sign of Roman self-confidence that the only fortresses they built lay along the Danube, and that there was no need to garrison the province itself. One such was Aquincum (today's Óbuda, or Old Buda, in Budapest), the headquarters of one of the province's four legions (at least), the II Adiutrix Pia Fidelis (the Second "Reserve" Legion Loyal and True). Originally a rectangular camp on the traditional military model, it lay on the riverside with a view of barbarian lands across the water, and was well on the way to becoming a substantial town with stone buildings replacing wooden structures and civilian dwellings spreading beyond the ramparts. The streets were paved and there was a small forum or public square, an aqueduct, and water conduits.

It was in this remote but flourishing outpost that the next phase of Hadrian's life opened. Having completed a stint with the *vigintivirate,* he was twenty years old and ready to move on to a new challenge. A spell of military service had once been more or less compulsory for wellborn young Romans, but it appears that this was no longer the case. Hadrian's personal wishes have not been recorded, but a lively and adventurous lad would surely have welcomed the thrill of travel to strange places and the scent of danger. In any case, his own inclinations weighed less than the opinion of his guardians. Whoever made the final decision, in 95 Hadrian accepted a commission as military tribune in the army and left Rome for Pannonia.

As I have suggested, Trajan was almost certainly governor of the province at this time, campaigning against the unruly Suebic Marcomanni, a Germanic tribe in central Europe on the far side of the Danube. In his early years of soldiering he had been a tribune himself, and had learned much about the art of warfare, which, according to Pliny, he was only too happy to communicate to the next generation.

> A distant look at a camp, a stroll through a short term of service was not enough for you; your time as tribune must qualify you for immediate command, with nothing left to learn when the moment came for passing on your knowledge.

So it was no surprise that Trajan found a tribuneship for his ward with the II Adiutrix.

In its upper reaches, the Roman military system was no more meritocratic than European armies up to the nineteenth century. At the II Adiutrix, as elsewhere, commissions were bought and sold, and political influence counted for more than experience. The legionary commander was a former praetor, or *legatus pro praetore,* and so possessed *imperium*. He was outmatched only by a former consul with proconsular rank—in practice, his immediate superior, Pannonia's governor.

Reporting to the *legatus* were six military tribunes. Hadrian was to be the most senior of them, the *tribunus laticlavius*. Hadrian was expected to serve for between one and three years. In theory he was the *legatus's* deputy, but in practice his duties were undefined. His primary task was to learn the business of soldiering. The other tribunes were *equites* (*tribuni angusticlavi,* or "narrow-banded"); they had already seen service and tended to be in their late twenties or early thirties. In essence, tribunes were equivalent to today's young staff officers.

The II Adiutrix, like other Roman legions, consisted of 5,120 soldiers, although like other Roman legions it may not have been up to full strength, and was subdivided into ten cohorts. A cohort was large enough to be a fairly powerful unit in itself on the battlefield, but small enough to maneuver flexibly to cope with awkward terrain or to respond to the enemy's tactics.

A legion was actually *run* by the centurions. These were usually men who had risen from the ranks on merit, although good connections could engineer appointment. They have no exact modern equivalent; if a *legatus* is similar to a colonel, who commands a regiment, then they resemble both a sergeant-major and, at the most senior levels, a major. There were six to a cohort, each of whom commanded centuries of eighty men, or five in the first cohort. A lead centurion was probably also in charge of each cohort (although our sources do not make this absolutely clear).

The fifty-nine centurions carried immense prestige, especially those in the first cohort. An ordinary private earned 1,400 sesterces a year, but even the most junior centurion received an estimated salary of 18,000 sesterces. The *primus pilus,* the master centurion and commander of the first cohort, who led the first file, or *pilus,* on the battlefield and was a valued adviser of the *legatus,* made as much as 72,000 sesterces annually. No wonder even affluent *equites* entered the army with an ambition to attain the status of centurion.

Life was tougher for the ordinary soldier. However, the army gave him security in the form of a reliable income in coin, a regular healthy diet, access to good medical treatment, and a sense of common purpose.

On the debit side he had to sign up for most of his adult life, a term of twenty-five years (extensions were permitted), and was not allowed to marry, although many acquired mistresses and children with the passage of time. He was usually recruited from *coloniae,* or veterans' settlements, in northern Italy, southern Gaul, and Spain. He was meant to be a Roman citizen, but when there was an urgent need for manpower he might be awarded citizenship on joining up.

Legionaries were highly skilled at multitasking. Some were *principales,* men with particular and highly responsible duties. Others were simply *immunes,* specialists who had no particular seniority. They might be clerks in the governor's *officium.* Alternatively, they worked in the camp hospital, were armorers and artillerymen, trumpet and horn blowers, bridge builders, construction workers, road makers, butchers, horse trainers, medical orderlies, and so forth. A cavalry contingent of 120 riders provided scouts and messengers.

Soldiers with a record for bravery were standard-bearers for cohorts and centuries, and to be a legion's *aquilifer,* the man who carried into battle its precious "eagle," a pole topped by an eagle emblem surrounded by a laurel wreath, was a high but perilous honor. Almost the most shameful thing that could happen to a legion was to lose its eagle to the enemy.

A soldier was a member of an army, of a legion, of a cohort, and of a century. But the most important institution in his life was the *contubernium,* a fellowship of eight men who shared the same living accommodation, tent or hut, and messed together. He wore a bronze or iron helmet, a scale, mail, or segmented metal cuirass, a rectangular semicylindrical shield (the *scutum*), a heavy javelin (the *pilum*), a short thrusting sword (the *gladius*), and in all probability a dagger. In addition, when on the march he carried cooking and digging equipment, provisions for at least a fortnight, and three or four stakes for use when forming the palisade of a temporary, or "marching," camp. In total, he carried a load weighing at least sixty-five pounds. No wonder legionaries were affectionately called (after one of Rome's greatest generals) "Marius' mules."

Hadrian found Aquincum to be a busy place. In addition to the II Adiutrix, a similar number of auxiliary troops were billeted there: recruited from provincials, auxiliaries did not need to be Roman citizens and played a supporting role for the legions. If many of these soldiers had a partner and offspring, not to mention a slave or two, it is reasonable to suppose a community of fifteen thousand military personnel and family members. In addition, traders and suppliers of various commodities and services, all kinds of camp followers, will have been drawn from both sides of the Danube to do business with the Romans. All in all, Aquincum played host to as many as twenty thousand souls.

As the legate's deputy, the young *laticlavius* commanded spacious and ornate accommodation. He had his own house with many rooms, and imported freedmen and slaves from his household in Rome to look after him. If he so wished he could live in grand style and pay little attention to his flock, the *gregales*. However, we can take it that Hadrian did not follow this course. Later in life he was well known for his unpretentious, informal manner, and was able to converse easily with every class and type of person; he won a reputation for being "an ostentatious lover of the common people." Following Trajan's example, he developed an uncanny memory for names, not least among ordinary legionaries and long-serving veterans, and made a point of sharing the soldiers' simple diet. It was at Aquincum that he laid the first building blocks of this reputation.

Only 120 miles upstream the governor, Trajan (I assume), ruled from the provincial capital, Carnuntum, keeping an eye on his ward and having him visit for the conduct of army business. We hear no more complaints of excessive hunting—despite the fact that Pannonia was famous for its hunting dogs, robust enough to pursue and fight with boars and bison.

A scintilla of evidence suggests that Hadrian was making friends with at least one of the legion's centurions. A soldier's gravestone from Aquincum notes that his centurion bore the rare name of M. Turbo; he has been identified as Quintus Marcius Turbo, who years later himself became legate of the II Adiutrix and governor of Pannonia (probably Lower), ending up as prefect of the Praetorian Guard. It was a remarkable career from lowly beginnings, and Turbo became one of Hadrian's close friends and advisers. It was at Aquincum that the two men must have first met.

Hadrian's tour of duty came to an end in the summer of 96. He had been a year in Pannonia and learned a good deal. Most military tribunes were only too happy to leave at the earliest opportunity for Italy and all the amenities of city life and country retreats. Exceptionally, though, Hadrian accepted a second posting as *laticlavius* with one of the legions of Lower Moesia, the V Macedonica. He may have been copying his guardian's example, for (as we have seen) Trajan had spent a number of years as a military tribune and valued the in-depth professional expertise he had acquired.

Hadrian was based at Oescus, another fortress along the Danube, at its confluence with the river Oescus (near today's Pleven, in Bulgaria). The province was long and narrow and led to the coast of the Black Sea: hence Moesia's alternative name of *ripa Thracia,* the Thracian Shore. Here at the port of Tomis a century before, the fluent and fashionable poet Ovid had dragged out long years of exile for having offended the pitiless Augustus, dying miserable and alone.

But the real point about the Lower and Upper Moesias was that they acted as a cordon sanitaire between the dangerously aggressive kingdom of Dacia and Rome's Mediterranean lands—Dalmatia, Thrace, and, above all, the cradle of classical culture, Greece. When Hadrian stood on the rampart at Oescus and surveyed the forests and mountains beyond the wide river, he knew that sooner or later a Roman army would be obliged to cross to the other bank and march into terra incognita. The victims of Decebalus had to be avenged.

Toward the end of September extraordinary news arrived from Rome. Domitian was dead, killed by members of his own household. The deed was done behind closed doors in the palace and no bulletin was gazetted. Different versions percolated around the Roman world, but Hadrian and his army colleagues were able to establish the broad shape of what had occurred.

In the last year or so, the emperor's behavior had become increasingly erratic. Anxious about his future, he consulted his own and other people's horoscopes and tried to work out the exact hour of his death. Despite the fact that he had occupied the throne for fifteen years, he still feared, or sensed, that he had not been accepted as ruler. He now un-wisely began to persecute people within his circle. The most eminent of these victims was Titus Flavius Clemens, Vespasian's nephew and the emperor's first cousin. High in favor, Clemens served as consul *ordinarius* in 95 and was married to Domitian's niece Flavia Domitilla.

Clemens stayed in office as consul until May 1. Then, soon afterward and without warning, he and his wife faced grave accusations. Accord-ing to Dio Cassius, "the charge brought against them both was that of atheism, a charge on which many others who drifted into Jewish ways were condemned." "Jewish ways" could mean that Clemens and the rest were flirting with Judaism; Domitian would have been seriously of-fended that a member of the imperial family was interesting himself in the religion of a people against whom the Flavians had waged a pitiless war and expelled from their native land. The term could equally mean Christian, for many Romans were unclear about the distinction be-tween Christianity and Judaism. There has been a long tradition that Clemens and Domitilla were, in fact, Christian converts.

Whatever the nature of his spiritual life, Clemens left a poor impres-sion on his contemporaries, who saw him as a "man of the most con-temptible laziness." He was executed, and Domitilla banished to Pandataria, a small island off the coast of Campania with a large impe-rial palace (today's Ventotene), much favored by emperors who wished to hide away an inconvenient relative.

What struck the people around Domitian—the *amici,* the Flavian "party" in the Senate, the freedmen and the relatives—was the lack of substantive evidence against Clemens, who (they felt) had been liqui-dated "on the slightest of suspicions." If even members of his inner cir-cle could fall victim to the emperor's paranoid whims, *who* was safe?

Some of them began the potentially fatal business of planning an as-sassination. Two leading conspirators were Stephanus, Flavia Domi-tilla's procurator, or business manager, and Parthenius, the emperor's *cubicularius,* master of the bedchamber or valet de chambre, with routine access to the imperial presence.

They knew better than to act alone. They did not support an opposi-tion party (and certainly not the Stoic opposition); rather, they wanted to act on behalf of the Flavian establishment of senators and administrators by removing an increasingly unreliable ruler who was imperiling their personal security and the stability of the imperial system. Discreet contact was made with key personalities in the regime.

Of these by far the most important were the two prefects of the Praetorian Guard, Titus Petronius Secundus and Norbanus (this is his only appearance in history and his full name is unknown). The Praetorian Guard was a force of ten thousand highly trained and well-paid troops based in and around Rome. They were the imperial bodyguard, and were also powerful enough to deal with civil dissent. One cohort at a time stood guard in the imperial residence on the Palatine, carrying weapons but in civilian dress.

Gradually the Praetorian Guard came to expect a role in the transition from one emperor to another, especially when no generally accepted heir had been determined in advance. In A.D. 41 when the emperor Caligula was assassinated, the guards found his uncle Claudius hiding behind a curtain in the palace, carried him triumphantly to their camp outside the city boundary, and acclaimed him as Caligula's successor. The cowed Senate acquiesced in their decision. This proved to be a sinister precedent, and from then onward the Praetorian Guard was only too willing to dictate its wishes when occasion arose. As we have seen, Domitian was popular with the military and the Praetorian Guard was unlikely to approve of his removal, so it was important for it to be neutralized. The two prefects agreed to pacify their men.

A successor had to be identified who would command general support. No more suitable Flavians existed, so the field was open. Doubtless there were ambitious provincial governors in the far corners of the empire who would wish to be considered for the top job, but conspiracies are meant to be secret and widespread discussion was out of the question. So a stopgap candidate was required, one who would not create a dynasty and would last only long enough for a permanent solution to be negotiated. The plotters believed they had found just the man.

He was Marcus Cocceius Nerva, and he was conveniently old, childless, and sick. He was a handsome man, but with a large nose. His health was poor; he had a habit of vomiting up his food and was a heavy drinker of wine. Born in 35 into a family of legal experts, he was descended from Republican nobility and related to the founding house of the imperial system, the Julio-Claudians. He was a poet whose slim volumes of verse had a certain reputation. Martial observed: "Whoever is familiar with the poet Nero's verses knows that Nerva is the Tibullus [one of Rome's finest lyric poets] of our time." Nero was acknowledged to be the worst poet of the age, so the compliment was distinctly double-edged.

Nerva had thrived under Nero, but executed a neat switch of loyalty and became one of the Flavians' stalwart supporters. He liked a quiet life and knew how to get on in the world without irritating people. A discreet and able balancer of conflicting interests, he was twice consul *ordinarius,* alongside Vespasian and then Domitian—tokens of high esteem. Nerva was an intimate of the Flavians in another sense, for he is reported to have seduced Domitian, who had been a pretty young man. The affair would appear to have advanced rather than damaged his prospects.

All the pieces on the board were now in place, and it was time to act. Parthenius removed the blade of a dagger that the emperor kept under his pillow. Stephanus, who pretended an injury and had been wearing a bandage on his arm for some days, now secreted a knife inside it.

Domitian spent the morning of September 26 judging in the law courts, and then retired to his bedroom, where he prepared to take a bath. Stephanus, claiming to have uncovered a plot, asked for an immediate audience and entered the room. A boy was also present, preparing an offering for the Lares, or household gods, statuettes in a small shrine. The freedman said, "Your great enemy, Clemens, is not dead as you suppose, but I know where he is and that he is arming himself against you." He handed over a confirmatory document and while the emperor was reading it struck at him in the groin. Domitian shouted to the boy to get him his dagger and call the servants; but there was only a hilt and the doors were barred.

The emperor put up a fight, pulling Stephanus to the floor and struggling with him. He alternately tried to grab the dagger and pushed his lacerated fingers into his assailant's eyes in an attempt to gouge them out. Parthenius or one of his men rushed in to lend Stephanus a hand. At last the emperor was dead, with seven wounds on his body. Some other servants entered who knew nothing of the plot, and promptly killed Stephanus before there was a chance for explanation.

Waiting on tenterhooks, presumably in another room of the palace, was the emperor-to-be. At first a rumor came in that Domitian was still alive. Nerva went pale and could hardly stand up, but Parthenius told him that he had nothing to fear.

For Hadrian the news of the fall of the ruling dynasty called for careful interpretation. Signposts pointed in different directions. The Aelii and the Ulpii had done well out of Vespasian, Titus, and Domitian. After his long march from Spain to Germany in response to Saturninus' ill-judged revolt, Trajan was one of the regime's most high-profile supporters—and at times like these a high profile could be unhelpful. The fact that the assassination of Domitian was a coup by the Flavian faction did not mean that the future would be as safe and prosperous as the past.

Senators in Rome might congratulate themselves on the overthrow of a despot, but the next year or so promised uncertainty. By definition, the caretaker emperor was ill placed to deliver firm government and stability, and the competition would soon open to identify the leader who would follow him. If past history was anything to go by, provincial governors at the head of their legions would soon be carefully eyeing one another and weighing their chances. How long before civil war broke out again?

From his vantage point in a faraway fortress on the Danube, Hadrian was able to see that opinion in Rome was much too sanguine. Domitian had been well liked by the rank and file, and most legionaries and probably many centurions were furious about his removal. Some units of the Danubian army, perhaps in Lower Moesia, were mutinous. But without support from the general staff, without a commander to lead them, there was little they, or the Praetorian Guard in Rome, could do. For the moment the skies were calm, but a storm threatened.

VIII

THE EMPEROR'S SON

. . .

The affable and cultivated Nerva got off to a surprisingly good start, working in partnership with the Senate and promoting reconciliation. He moved fast and with sure judgment.

The first step was to sweep away the evidence of his predecessor's reign. The Senate withheld the compliment of deification, which they had conferred on his father and brother, and endorsed a condemnation of his memory—*damnatio memoriae*. Now that the tyrant was dead, this was the worst punishment they could inflict. His body was disposed of with the minimum of ceremony, buried by his nurse in the temple of the Flavian clan. Innumerable statues and arches, symbols of Domitian's personality cult, were removed. To refill a depleted treasury, imperial possessions, from estates to clothes, were sold off.

Rome did not possess the bureaucracy to establish a police state, but Domitian had gone as far in that direction as possible through the use of denunciation and what were in effect show trials, with death or banishment the almost invariable outcomes. Now all those facing trial for treason, or *maiestas,* were immediately released, and all the exiles recalled. For the future, *maiestas* charges were outlawed, as was the accusation of "adopting the Jewish mode of life": in other words, Flavius Clemens was rehabilitated. The emperor swore never himself to put a senator to death.

These negative, if necessary, measures underpinned a positive vision that carried signs of forethought. Nerva used the coinage as a universal means of conveying his message. An aureus, a gold coin worth one hundred sesterces, showed the head of the new emperor on one side and on the other the personification of Liberty holding a *pileus* and a ruler's scepter: a *pileus* was a felt cap shaped like half an egg that was given to a slave on his enfranchisement. A legend read "Public Liberty."

Other coins marked achievements, either real or wished for, that indicated fault lines about which the regime was worried. One of them celebrated the provision of grain for the capital city, underlining Nerva's anxiety to keep the plebs on his side. They had welcomed Domitian's departure but needed practical reassurance that the new emperor could feed them. Another numismatic image reflected hope rather than experience—beneath a pair of clasped hands a slogan read "Harmony of the armies." It was still unclear whether or not the military *would* accept Domitian's demise.

This in no way signified a return to the old days of the Republic. Even the most idealistic "noble Roman" could see that a rowdy six-hundred-strong committee, the Senate, was a defective mechanism of government. Nerva's clever trick was to transform the Flavian despotism into something approaching a constitutional monarchy. The emperor kept his all-trumping *imperium,* but framed it within the rule of law and institutional convention. The days of the *dominus et deus* were over and the old term devised by Augustus—*princeps* or leading citizen, first among equals—regained its common use. Tacitus, ferocious critic of imperial misrule, offered words of warm praise:

> Assuredly we have been given a signal proof of our submissiveness; and even as former generations witnessed the utmost excesses of liberty, so we have the extremes of slavery . . . Now at last heart is coming back to us. From the first, from the outset of this happy age, Nerva has united things long incompatible—autocracy and liberty.

In the opening weeks of the new reign, vengeful prosecutions had been brought against run-of-the-mill *delatores.* One of the consuls remarked that it was a bad thing to have an emperor under whom no one was allowed to do anything, but worse to have one under whom *anyone* was allowed to do anything. Nerva agreed, and ordered that cases of this kind should cease.

Despite the embargo, Pliny the Younger found it unjust that no senator had yet been charged. "Once Domitian was dead," he confessed, "I decided on reflection that this was a truly splendid opportunity for attacking the guilty, avenging the injured, and making oneself known."

His colleagues in the Senate did not agree. "Let us survivors stay alive," one of them said. Too many of their number had compromised themselves under Domitian, and they were determined that bygones should be bygones.

Nerva appointed many onetime supporters of the Flavian dynasty to high office, and had no intention whatsoever to revisit the "bloodstained servility" of the recent past. A discreet forgetfulness veiled it from view. An exchange at a small dinner party summed up the situation well. Nerva was lying next to one of Domitian's closest supporters, a noted *delator.* The conversation turned to another even more celebrated *delator,* the blind Lucius Valerius Catullus Messalinus, a man "whose loss of sight increased his cruel disposition." An *amicus,* he was a member of Domitian's *consilium.*

"I wonder what would have happened to him if he were alive today," Nerva remarked.

"He would be dining with us," said another guest drily, a member of the Stoic opposition who had recently returned from exile.

Nerva was able to bring together sworn enemies not only in a dining room, but also into a harmonious administration. His policy of reconciliation was generally popular. The emperor remarked with satisfaction: "I have done nothing that would prevent my laying down the imperial office and returning to private life in safety."

The elite may have been content, but the Praetorian Guard had sharp memories. They had been reluctantly persuaded to accept the change of regime, but Domitian's removal still rankled. In the autumn of 97 their simmering anger brimmed over.

Nerva ill-advisedly, as it turned out, appointed a new prefect of the guard, a certain Casperius Aelianus, who had held the same post late in the previous reign, to serve alongside the compliant Petronius Secundus, who had calmed the Praetorian Guard in the immediate aftermath of the assassination. Casperius sided with his soldiers and gave them the leadership they had lacked twelve months before. The Guard took over the palace, arresting the emperor and keeping him in custody. They demanded that Nerva hand over his predecessor's murderers, especially Petronius and the freedman Parthenius, who was still in the imperial employ.

Although sick with fear, the emperor strongly resisted, baring his throat and challenging his captors to kill him. As the men were found and led out to execution, Nerva vomited and suffered an attack of diarrhea, but he went on protesting. It would be better for him to die, he said, than to befoul his *imperium* by colluding in the deaths of those who had given it to him. He was ignored. Petronius was dispatched with a merciful single blow, but Parthenius had his genitals torn off and stuffed into his mouth before being strangled.

Nerva was then forced to address an assembly of the people and offer public thanks to the Praetorian Guard "since they had killed the basest and most wicked of all human beings." Casperius was paid off, but the damage had been done. The emperor's humiliation was complete and his authority fatally undermined.

Nerva's position was untenable, but what was to be done? Things would only be made worse if he were to abdicate or be deposed. No successor had been named and the outcome would very probably be civil strife. Yet again everyone's mind went fearfully back to the catastrophe of 69. The solution was, in fact, obvious. The emperor had to find an acceptable heir. Bearing in mind his age and state of health, and the fact that he now moved with commendable speed and decisiveness, we can assume that Nerva had already been laying his plans.

As soon as the emperor was ready he staged a compelling piece of political theater. A laureled dispatch arrived in Rome from Pannonia, announcing a victory—presumably by Trajan over Germanic tribes. The emperor walked up the winding path from the Forum to the temple of Jupiter Best and Greatest on the Capitol and laid the laurels on the altar. When he came out of the temple he announced in a loud voice: "May good fortune attend the Senate and People of Rome and myself. I hereby adopt Marcus Ulpius Traianus."

In theory, adoption was a private matter that brought no necessary political consequence. But the signal was clear, and a complaisant Senate awarded Trajan the *cognomen* of Caesar. He was also hailed as Germanicus, for his recent victory over the Suebi. In addition, the emperor endowed him with the two key mechanisms of imperial power: the first was the *proconsulare imperium maius,* which allowed him to give instructions to proconsuls, or provincial governors, and the second was the *tribunicia potestas,* the authority of a tribune of the people to propose laws, convene the Senate, and veto its decisions.

Nerva sent his adopted son, now styled Marcus Ulpius Nerva Traianus Caesar, a diamond ring with a message in which he quoted a line from Homer's *Iliad.* "May the Danaans by your arrows requite my tears." So prayed the soothsayer Calchas, when he called on the archer god Apollo to avenge his humiliations at the hands of the Greek army outside Troy. The emperor was hinting that he expected his adopted son to take measures against his Praetorian tormentors.

In the meantime, he moved Trajan from his posting in Pannonia to Germany, where he assumed overall command of the two provinces: it is not altogether clear why, but an unrecorded emergency had supervened. It may have been some unfinished business of Domitian—perhaps a recrudescence of trouble among the Germanic tribes on the far side of the Rhine, or some challenge to the new *limes,* the chain of forts that demarcated the limit of empire.

There was general surprise at the adoption, and general approval. Pliny noted: "All disturbances died at once." Although the promotion appeared to come out of the blue, Trajan was a rational choice. The son of a distinguished father, he was a second-generation patrician. He had made a name for himself as an able soldier, popular with both the men and their commanders.

According to Pliny, Trajan was reluctant to accept his appointment as Nerva's colleague in empire. "You had to be pressed. Even then you could only be persuaded because you saw your country in peril [from the Praetorian Guard] and the whole state tottering to a fall."

There is evidence that Trajan had been informally discussed as *capax imperii,* worthy of rule, for some time. Tacitus states that his father-in-law, Gnaeus Julius Agricola, a general who was responsible for much of the conquest of Britannia, "foretold" the principate of Trajan "in our hearing both as something to be prayed for and something that would happen." The point here is that Agricola had died as long ago as 93, at the height of Domitian's terror. Gossip of this kind was dangerous then not only to the speaker but to the person he was speaking about. Trajan was lucky that it did not reach the emperor's ears.

A remark by Pliny, that not to have adopted Trajan would have indicated the "wanton tyranny of power," suggests that Nerva's hands were tied in advance. And a late source claims that the dexterous and unscrupulous Licinius Sura had engineered a coup d'état: in other words, the adoption had been a seizure, not a gift. So perhaps Trajan was not as retiring as he seemed.

It is impossible to be sure exactly what happened, but here is a plausible scenario that takes account of what we are told and of the changeless imperatives of political action. During the last terrifying years of the previous reign Trajan's name began to be whispered in opposition circles as a potential *princeps*. As a distinguished soldier he could be counted on to adopt a more aggressive military posture than Domitian, which would please the general staff. Domestically, he held moderate views and would be likely to cooperate with rather than browbeat the Senate. If he showed no uncomely enthusiasm for the throne, that was a reassuring bonus.

The conspirators nominated Nerva to the purple rather than Trajan because the latter was physically too distant from the center of events, and the imperial system could not tolerate a vacuum, even for a few days, without risking civil war. The Praetorian Guard needed to be confronted with an immediate fait accompli if they were to tolerate Domitian's violent removal from the stage. Trajan, marooned in his province, on security grounds surely could not have been informed of the plot to kill Domitian. He would have to wait until the next time for a chance of winning the purple. And to make sure that the next time actually arrived, Licinius Sura was on hand as his confidential "agent" in Rome (in fact, it is not known where he was at this period, but if he was looking after Trajan's interests, as suggested, he could hardly have done so effectively unless he was in the capital).

Leaving aside his uncertain political health, Nerva knew that he was in poor shape physically, and must already have been thinking about the succession. Trajan had a number of influential friends in Rome or at court who would have spoken for him. At least five of the seven consuls *suffecti* for 97 had friendly or family connections with him, and some were fellow Spaniards. One of these was Titus Arrius Antoninus, a wealthy man of traditional morals: on Nerva's accession he had famously congratulated the Senate and people of Rome, but not the emperor himself, so heavy was the burden of rule.

When news of the adoption reached the youthful military tribune in Lower Moesia, he saw at once that his life had reached a turning point. As a student of astrology, Hadrian was aware of the magical power of numbers (another word for an astrologer was *mathematicus*). He knew that this, his twenty-first year, was the second of his life's climacterics, a time of great change in fortune, and alterations in body and spirit, which could bring with it danger of death. The first was held to occur in a person's seventh year, and later ones were multiples of seven, a number believed to be of especial virtue. They culminated in the grand climacteric at the age of sixty-three. To pass that undamaged was no mean achievement, as Augustus noted with relief—once he had reached sixty-four. (It is interesting to note that the shadow of these climacterics survives in the modern convention that children attain the age of reason at seven years, and that in many countries until recently twenty-one years used to mark the onset of adulthood.)

Hadrian's kinship to Rome's next emperor meant that he had suddenly become a very important young man. This was more evident when it was remembered that, despite the fact that Trajan had been married to Plotina for nearly twenty years, the union had produced no offspring. They liked and were loyal to each other, but Trajan found sexual pleasure elsewhere. Everyone could see that by this stage, children were most unlikely to be forthcoming. As guardian, Trajan had treated his ward as if he were his own son, and astute men in public life took that into careful account.

Hadrian was intrigued by his prospects, but wished to make assurance doubly sure. Remembering the long-ago prediction made by his great-uncle during his visit to Spain, it was probably now that he checked its veracity with a *mathematicus* in Lower Moesia. The same golden story was foretold. From this moment on, Hadrian understood himself to be a marked man.

The legions in Lower Moesia asked Hadrian to present their congratulations to the new Caesar. This was an appropriate commission for a military tribune, but it must also have fitted in well with his own wishes—the sooner he joined Trajan, the better he would be able to assess and promote his personal interests and join the new governmental team. A long and arduous journey ensued, riding upriver through the wild and mountainous provinces adjoining the Danube—Upper Moesia, Pannonia, Noricum, and Raetia (in today's terms, Hungary, Austria, and Switzerland). He reached the Rhine and Upper Germania (so-called because it was upstream of Lower Germania), through which he passed. Eventually, toward the end of November or early December, he arrived at Colonia Agrippinensis (today's Cologne), the capital of Lower Germania, which commanded the wide flow of the Rhine. This was where Trajan had elected to spend the winter of 97–98.

It soon emerged that, for whatever reason, Trajan did not want to keep Hadrian by his side, and he sent him away to the neighboring province of Upper Germania for an unprecedented third posting as a military tribune. He joined the legion XXII Primigenia (the "First Born" of a new breed of legions, formed by Caligula for his abortive invasion of Britain in 39) at Moguntiacum (today's Mainz). The fortress town stood on the shoulder of the dangerous re-entrant between the upper Rhine and the source of the Danube, where the Black Forest was a wedge pressing into eastern Gaul. Domitian's *limes* of forts crossed the eastern, broad end of the wedge to discourage Germanic incursions. The Primigenia was to be a reserve alongside another legion based at Argentoratē (today's Strasbourg), ready to repel any enemy forces that penetrated the *limes*. Hadrian was able to see for himself the new system of border defenses, and was impressed.

It is impossible to say whether Hadrian's third military tribuneship was in recognition of his growing military skills and gave him an opportunity to further perfect them, or a penalty for poor behavior. What is certain is that he made a bad impression on the province's governor, Lucius Julius Servilius Ursus Servianus. Born about 47, he was a leading member of Rome's Spanish set and was the husband of Hadrian's sister, Aelia Domitia Paulina. He may have been a widower (there is speculation that a first wife died during a putative epidemic of 90 that Dio attributed to a wave of poisoning). The couple are likely to have wed at about this time, when Servianus was in his early forties and Paulina about fifteen.

Presumably Servianus was on cordial terms with his wife, but he had little time for his brother-in-law. They got on uncomfortably at Moguntiacum and Servianus complained to Trajan about his ward. He revealed "what he was spending and the debts he had contracted." The news angered Trajan, as was intended, and reminded him of the boy's irresponsible goings-on in Baetica. Was he ever going to learn self-discipline?

It is not immediately obvious how easy it was to be extravagant in a frontier fortress. However, Hadrian was a dedicated huntsman and may have bought expensive dogs and horses; he could also have whiled away time by unlucky gambling. Not far away on the eastern side of the Rhine, the small military spa of Aquae Mattiacae offered the pleasures of relaxation: the water of the springs was high in calcium and piping hot, and was reputed to retain its temperature for three days. Baths are seldom far removed from the provision of sexual services, so here was another way of spending money.

Fortunately the standoff between proconsul and tribune did not last long. In early February a courier arrived at Moguntiacum with the news that Nerva had unexpectedly died. The emperor had lost his temper with a notorious *delator*. His voice rose in anger, he worked himself up into a sweat, and contracted a fever, which he could not shake off. He died on January 28. He was in his sixty-third year, having attained but not passed his grand climacteric.

For most of his life Nerva had subordinated principle to self-interest, but he had common sense and an intelligent understanding of what the imperial system needed if it was to last. He had the tolerance of a man without convictions—a useful quality after two decades of Domitian.

Hadrian seized the hour. If only he could be the first person to give Trajan the news eighty-odd miles downstream at Colonia Agrippinensis, he might be able to retrieve his approval. He set off quickly in a carriage, and made good progress until it broke down. This was no accident, apparently, for according to the *Historia Augusta* (which probably drew on Hadrian's lost autobiography), Servianus had found out about his plan and arranged for the carriage to be sabotaged. Nothing daunted, the military tribune walked on for a while until he could find some fresh horses, and made it to Cologne before Servianus' messenger. Just as Hadrian had hoped, the exploit delighted Trajan and their relations improved.

The years of apprenticeship were at an end. The fortunes of the young Aelian were chained indissolubly to those of the forty-four-year-old Ulpian. The Spanish immigrants had scaled the summit of power. Nothing could alter the fact that, for better or worse, Hadrian was the new emperor's closest male relative. He was not an adopted son or an heir, Trajan was firm about that, but he was now a high personage in the *res publica*.

IX

"OPTIMUS PRINCEPS"

. . .

Hadrian became a favorite of the new emperor, despite the fact that he fell victim to some mysterious intrigue against him led by the tutors of Trajan's youthful bedfellows: a gap in the text leaves it uncertain what the problem was. Presumably the people around the emperor did not relish the new arrival, who was well placed to establish a new power base.

Once again Hadrian experimented with fortune-telling. This time he used the *Virgilianae Sortes,* the Virgilian Lottery. In this game the player picks at random a quotation from Virgil's *Aeneid;* often enough it produces suggestive or predictive results. Hadrian's "lot" was taken from the poem's sixth book:

> Who is that in the distance, bearing the hallows, crowned with
> a wreath of olive? I recognize—gray hair and hoary chin—
> the Roman king who, called to high power from humble Curēs,
> a town in a poor area, shall found our system of law
> and thus refound our city.

Virgil's reference is to one of Rome's early kings, Numa Pompilius. A legendary figure, he succeeded the great Romulus. Pious and plain-living, he was a pacific ruler and the city's first legislator.

It is not easy to judge the historicity of this anecdote. However, it is consistent with Hadrian's recurrent dabbling in clairvoyance and his life-long fascination with the law, and may well derive from his lost autobiography. While the gist is clear, the quotation does not have an elegantly close relevance to Hadrian's circumstances, which tends to support its authenticity.

Hadrian's return to favor was not simply a consequence of the ride from Moguntiacum to Colonia Agrippinensis. He also benefited from some promotion: Licinius Sura took a personal interest in him (we do not know how personal) and persuaded the emperor to advance his prospects.

The emperor presided over a household of women, all of whom had known Hadrian since he was a little boy, certainly once he became Trajan's ward and probably before. He had a devoted friend in the empress, Plotina. He was also extremely fond of Salonina Matidia, the daughter of Trajan's much-loved sister Ulpia Marciana. Marciana had lived with Trajan and his wife after her husband died in 78; Matidia joined her after her own widowhood, a few years into the reign. This female household was mutually affectionate, and Trajan's well-being was its exclusive priority.

Plotina was probably in her mid-thirties at this time. She originated in Nemausus (modern Nîmes) in the province of Narbonensis (Languedoc and Provence). An interest in the ideas of Epicurus reflected her calm and constructive character. He argued that the gods were remote and ineffectual. Death marked the end of body and soul, and so a punitive afterlife was not to be feared. A happy, tranquil life could be achieved by kindness and friendship, and by moderation of appetite (although nothing was forbidden).

Matidia was about thirty, and her first marriage produced two daughters, one of whom was Vibia Sabina, now about thirteen years old and marriageable. Matidia remarried after her husband's death and had two more daughters by successive husbands. They both also died and from then onward Matidia remained single. She often traveled with her uncle and apparently gave him political and administrative advice.

The official statues of these women are marked by a heavy, idealizing passivity, although Marciana's likeness has a lively, inquisitive look. The conventions of coinage allowed more realistic images: Matidia appears on a silver denarius with a hawklike nose, pendulous cheeks, and a slightly recessive chin, and a sesterce reveals Plotina's sharp, birdlike profile and similarly full cheeks.

As well as assuring his own position at court, Hadrian was well placed to observe a transformation of the political world. The new emperor gave a master class in moderation combined with firmness, and Hadrian would long remember the lessons he learned in these months.

Trajan knew that ultimately his power rested with the army, but the fact that he was a distinguished soldier meant that he won the legions' loyalty without having to take any special measures apart from the usual bonus, or donative, that emperors gave at the outset of their reigns. By contrast, the Senate was weak, but, although he could act as he pleased, Trajan's policy was to conciliate it. His aim was to stabilize the political class. He reported that, before assuming power, he had a dream that conveniently illustrated his careful deference: according to Dio, "he thought that an old man in a purple-bordered toga and vesture and with a crown upon his head, as the Senate is represented in pictures, impressed a seal upon him with a finger ring, first on the left side of his neck and then on the right."

On his accession, Trajan immediately sent a letter to the Senate, written in his own hand. He promised, among other things, that "he would not kill or disenfranchise any good man; and he confirmed this by oaths not only at the time but also later." This restated Nerva's similar oath, and by "good man" he was guaranteeing that he would not persecute senators. It was an assertion of constitutional monarchy and the rule of law.

However, death *was* a fate in store for those who had humiliated the old emperor. Trajan felt strong enough to summon the Praetorian prefect Casperius Aelianus and his accomplices to attend him in Germania. Casperius duly turned up at Colonia Agrippinensis expecting a job with the new ruler, but to his surprise suffered execution instead. As requested, Nerva's tears had been requited. A new prefect was chosen. As the emperor's protector, he was the only person allowed to carry a weapon in his presence: at the ceremony of appointment, Trajan handed him his sword of office, famously saying, "If the public interest demands it, I have placed a weapon in the hands of my prefect for him to use against me."

Trajan went further: he was determined to break the Praetorian Guard's armlock over its employers once and for all. It was impractical to abolish it, as he might well have wished, but he created a counterweight by establishing a new cavalry force, the *equites singulares Augusti,* with a specific duty to protect the person of the emperor. Trajan re-cruited it from the Batavians, a Germanic tribe living on the near side of the Rhine and on a river island, encouraged by the Romans to specialize in warfare. Some believe that *Batavi* derives from the West Germanic *beter*—that is, better or superior men.

The emperor showed no eagerness to return to Rome in a hurry. He stayed for a time on the German frontier. Was he perhaps planning a campaign against the barbarians? Tacitus wrote at this time of the "ridicule that had greeted [Domitian's] sham triumph over Germania, when he had bought slaves to have their dress and hair made up to look like prisoners-of-war." He was not the only senior Roman who would welcome a real victory over the unruly tribes beyond the Rhine. How-ever, the emperor moved on to the Danube frontier, where he con-ducted a tour of inspection. Doubtless Hadrian accompanied him, for he had recent firsthand experience of conditions in Moesia. There were signs of a Dacian resurgence and the arrangement whereby Rome paid the Dacian king, Decebalus, a large and regular subsidy was intolerable.

It was too early in the reign to launch a major campaign, but not so to begin detailed planning and organization. A Greek traveler, the orator and historian Dio Chrysostom (Dio of the Golden Tongue), passed through the area at this time and reported major military preparations at a legionary base.

> One could see swords everywhere, and cuirasses, and spears, and there were so many horses, so many weapons, so many armed men . . . all about to contend for power against opponents who fought for free-dom and their native land.

Dio had spent time in Dacia and sympathized with its cause. Trajan dis-agreed and, for those who could read the signs, was actively meditating invasion. It was probably during this visit that he established forts on the far side of the Danube and cut a canal to circumvent some rapids. But, first, before he could commit himself to a war, pressing business called for attention at home.

•   •   •

At last, in September or October of 99, nearly two years after his accession, Trajan arrived in the empire's capital. On his journey from the frontier he behaved as if he were a private citizen. Ordinary carriages were requisitioned from the state posting system, no fuss was made about where Trajan lodged for the night, and everyone in his party ate the same rations. He walked on foot into the city. The effect was carefully judged, and well received.

The Senate en masse greeted him outside the city gates, and he met each member with an egalitarian kiss. After visiting the Capitol, where Nerva had announced his adoption, he made his way across the Forum Romanum to the twin imperial residences on the Palatine Hill, once a smart address for Rome's *gratin* but now expropriated as a center of government.

The first of these was the Domus Tiberiana, or House of Tiberius (Rome's second emperor and the building's first occupant), which overlooked, almost overshadowed, the Forum. Remodeled on a grand scale by Domitian after a fire, it was an unplanned labyrinth of accretions and annexes, loggias and peristyles, with hidden green spaces beside a sun terrace and a pavilion (now mostly covered by the Farnese Gardens). Here the imperial archives were stored.

Meanderingly splendid as the Domus Tiberiana was, it served merely as an entrance and appendix to an even more spectacular edifice, commissioned by Domitian and completed only a few years before his death. The public part of this palace, the Domus Flavia, or House of the Flavians, was dominated by a series of vast audience chambers. Columns were of polychrome marble, floors and walls were lined with marble veneer, and vaulted ceilings were painted with frescoes. A banqueting hall, spacious enough to accommodate the entire Senate, gave on to the gardens of a majestic courtyard surrounded by a covered colonnade. The adjoining Domus Augustana, or House of Augustus (not to be confused with Augustus' modest home on another part of the hill), contained the private apartments, the façade of which towered above the Circus Maximus, the racecourse.

Trajan and Plotina walked into this marmoreal embodiment of hubris "with the same modest demeanor as if it had been a private house." Before entering, the empress turned around to announce: "I enter here such a woman as I would wish to be when I leave." She fulfilled her promise, living quietly and attracting little or no criticism of her lifestyle.

Although there had been a brief bloodbath of *delatores* in the first days of his reign, Nerva had discouraged any further persecution. Trajan took a firmer line (although apparently leaving senior personalities in the Senate alone). In his inaugural games, he replaced the public execution of convicted criminals with an unprecedented spectacle. This was a parade of informers. An observer wrote:

> Nothing was so popular, nothing so fitting for our times as the opportunity we enjoyed of looking down at the *delatores* at our feet, their heads forced back and faces upturned to meet our gaze. We knew them and rejoiced.

The men were adjudged too ignoble for death by fighting in the arena or by execution. They were crowded onto ships and pushed out to sea, where it was assumed they would be wrecked and drown. Any survivors had already lost their homes and property, and, dead or alive, nobody expected to hear from them again. "Well, let them go!" was the happy verdict.

On September 1, 100, Pliny the Younger entered on a suffect consulship, and he gave a speech in the Senate, thanking the emperor for his appointment. It is probable enough that Hadrian was in the audience, but if he was he might well have dozed off, for the consul spoke at length and on a single, unvarying note of praise. Should he have missed the performance, the book was soon available. Pliny published the speech, although not before revising and massively enlarging it. In this version, the *Panegyricus* (as it is called) took a good six hours to deliver, enough to test the patience of the most pacific of emperors.

Pliny staged a public reading of the address. He took care not to issue formal invitations, but simply asked people to drop by if they had a moment. He had tolerant friends with a great deal of free time at their disposal, for he got a good house. After the event he proudly informed a correspondent:

> The weather was . . . particularly bad, but for all that they turned out for two days running—and when discretion would have put an end to the reading they insisted I continue for a third.

Pliny, a kindly man but inclined to self-love, admired the "critical sense of my audience."

For all its tedium, the *Panegyricus* marked a crucial turning point in the governance of the Roman empire. Pliny may have overdone the eulogy, but he was sincere. He was heralding nothing less than the end of the Stoic opposition, which now takes its leave of history. The achievement of Nerva and Trajan was to settle the quarrel between emperor and Senate, government and political class.

Pliny spoke for all when he said:

> Times are different and our speeches should show this . . . Nowhere should we flatter [Trajan] as a god or a divine spirit. We are talking of a fellow citizen, not a tyrant, one who is our father not our overlord. He is one of us.

It is a telling phrase, "one of us," which distills the Senate's longing for a citizen-emperor.

In the same year as Pliny's consulship Hadrian's career moved forward again. In early December, a couple of months after the *Panegyricus,* he was appointed one of twenty quaestors, and so ex officio entered the Senate. He was approaching his twenty-fifth birthday (which fell on January 24, 101), the minimum qualifying age for the post since Augustus had reduced it from thirty years. It was a rule that emperors often broke for members of their family, but in the case of his onetime ward Trajan did not offer any major promotion. However, Hadrian did have the honor to be one of two *candidati principis,* nominees of the emperor, in which capacity his main duty was to read in the Senate any written communications Trajan wished to make to it. In addition, he was made curator of the *acta Senatūs,* the record of senatorial debates.

His first attempt at standing in for Trajan was an embarrassment. According to the *Historia Augusta,* when he read out an address of the emperor's he "provoked a laugh by his somewhat provincial accent." Stung, he immediately gave attention to the study of Latin pronunciation until he became fully fluent. Presumably what was meant was that Hadrian spoke with a Spanish accent. However, he had spent very little of his life in Baetica, and some scholars argue that he picked up un-Italian speech patterns from the centurions and other ranks during his lengthy military postings. But these had lasted only four or five years in total, and it is more likely that he picked up a Spanish accent from his family and the colony of Baeticans in Rome and Tibur, among whom he passed his childhood. Also, as a Hellenophile, he may have devoted more time to speaking Greek than Latin.

Now that he was a senator, Hadrian probably acquired two additional distinctions at about this time, which conferred prestige and set him slightly apart from his contemporaries. Both of them brought him into direct contact with Roman religious observance at its most emotionally arid—and least appealing to a nature more inclined to the ecstatic and the spiritual.

Two vacancies among the *septemviri,* or Seven Men, needed to be filled. They were the college of *epulones,* or Banqueters, one of Rome's four great religious corporations. The senior college was that of the *pontifices,* or Pontiffs; headed by the emperor as *pontifex maximus,* it set the annual calendar of holy days, or holidays, and working days and kept the official state archive. Next came the *augures,* or Augurs, whose main job was to interpret the divine will by studying the flight of birds; and beneath them the *quindecemviri,* or Fifteen Men, who guarded the Sibylline Books, a collection of oracular sayings consulted in times of grave crisis.

The *epulones* were last in order of seniority, having been founded as recently as 196 B.C. They were responsible for arranging all the public banquets at the many festivals and games in the city. Catering to large numbers was no easy administrative matter, especially seeing that the work had an important political dimension. Feasts were an attractive addition to the free or heavily subsidized grain dole.

Hadrian's second religious function was as one of the twenty-one *sodales Augustales,* or Companions of Augustus. These were priests responsible for the worship of the god Augustus (similar priests attended to the cults of later emperors after their deaths if the Senate agreed to their deification). Fortunately, Hadrian and his colleagues were, in effect, trustees and were not expected to conduct time-consuming sacrifices and services themselves; these seem to have been left to priestly officiants, or *flamines*.

Progress was made in Hadrian's personal life as well. It was time for him to take a wife. This was a business decision, as few Romans married for love. Marriage—in the upper classes at least—was a property transaction. Wealthy clans entered into mutually profitable alliances with others, and deals, both economic and political, were sealed by an arranged union.

Hadrian, of course, had lost his father many years previously, and his guardians had exercised full *patria potestas,* or paternal authority, over him until he came of age. However, Roman law recognized that young adults, especially those with property, were inexperienced in the ways of the world and, to guard against fraud or extravagance, needed continued monitoring up to the age of twenty-five years. So Trajan and Attianus doubtless took on a looser role as *curatores.* Hadrian being only months away from full independence, they may have decided that he should be guided into a good marriage while they still had legal standing to influence the decision.

As it turned out, it was not so much the emperor but the women around him who played the key role, probably backed by Sura. Plotina did all she could to advance Hadrian's career. Some said she was in love with him, but if there is anything in the story a physical relationship is surely out of the question, he being more interested sexually in men than women and she having a reputation for virtue that none of the sources contradict. The empress argued that Trajan's closest male relative should marry into the Ulpian clan. The choice fell on Vibia Sabina, daughter of Hadrian's beloved Matidia. As usual with Hadrian, Trajan was of two minds, but allowed the project to go ahead, perhaps to preserve the domestic peace.

The couple probably first entered into an engagement. Written on tablets and signed by them both, this was legally binding unless both parties agreed to cancel. Hadrian bought Sabina some presents and gave her a ring, either of gold or of iron set in gold, which she wore on what is still the ring finger today. According to Aulus Gellius, this finger had a special property in that a delicate nerve ran from it directly to its owner's heart.

The wedding ceremony presumably took place in the imperial palace, where Matidia and Sabina lived, and was a simple statement in front of witnesses that the man and the woman intended to bind themselves to each other. An *auspex,* a personal family augur, examined the entrails of a sacrificed animal and ensured that the auspices were favorable. Bride and groom then exchanged vows: *Ubi tu Gaius, ego Gaia. Ubi tu Gaia, ego Gaius*. "Where you are Gaius, I am Gaia." "Where you are Gaia, I am Gaius."

In the evening, Hadrian seized Sabina, dressed in saffron with a flame-colored veil, in a pretence of kidnap. He then escorted her, surrounded by friends and family, back to his house. Flute players headed the procession, followed by torchbearers. People sang bawdy songs. Sabina was lifted over the threshold of her new home and guided to the marriage bed. Here Hadrian removed her cloak and began to undo the girdle of her tunic. At this point the wedding party withdrew.

From the bridegroom's perspective this was a good match, and both Ulpians and Aelians must have applauded a further bonding of their two families. As for Sabina, we do not know whether she was pleased, but we can be reasonably certain on one point. For many pubescent girls the bloodstained encounter of the wedding night and continuing sexual penetration by a fully grown man was painful and distasteful. Thanks to her husband's tastes Sabina did not have to endure much or any of this. That she did not become pregnant suggests that Hadrian left her alone. Another *mariage blanc* was in the making.

Sabina also benefited (or would when she grew older) from a form of marriage that became increasingly popular under the empire. In the old days, a wife would either fall under her husband's complete authority (*cum manu,* or "with his hand") or remain governed by her father's *potestas*—in other words, *sine manu,* without the husband's control. It was common now for women to be married *sine manu,* and although that meant they were theoretically accountable to their paterfamilias or an appointed guardian, in practice they could act independently and manage their own property. Augustus brought in a rule that mothers of three or more children did not need to have a *tutor,* and gradually the system of guardianship was discarded.

Little is known of Sabina's personality; inscriptions found throughout the empire show that she was a wealthy woman. She owned a mansion in Rome and records of numerous freedmen are evidence of a large household. When very young, she made a generous contribution of one hundred thousand sesterces to her local youth support, or *alimenta,* scheme (see pages 132–34).

Plotina was a fine example of how a woman could be happily chaste and become her husband's affectionate friend. Sabina did not follow her lead, and never warmed to Hadrian. Nor did he to her. The ancient authors do not tell us why, presumably because they did not know. But, apart from any other consideration, Hadrian's close relationship with Sabina's mother, Matidia, was surely a hard thing for a teenage girl to accept. From her perspective, there may have been three of them in the marriage, so, as a more recent princess remarked, "it was a bit crowded."

X

BEYOND THE DANUBE

. . .

King Decebalus in his aerie felt completely safe—above all, safe enough to challenge the Romans with every prospect of success. So much stood in his favor.

First of all there were the mountains, impenetrable to strangers. The heartland of the Dacian kingdom was the Transylvanian basin, inside the great semicircular sweep of the Carpathian Mountains north of the Danube. They vary from about four thousand to more than eight thousand feet in height, and were heavily forested. A rich habitat for brown bears, wolves, and lynxes, even today the range hosts more than a third of all Europe's plant species.

Second, the Dacians took care to defend themselves. Their craggy kingdom was guarded by half a dozen great fortresses, whose ramparts were constructed from the unique *murus Dacicus,* literally "Dacian wall." Heavy masonry facings covered a timber-reinforced rubble core. The wood made these defenses flexible, and they resisted battering rams. The Dacians also erected rectangular projecting towers, on the Greek model, which allowed archers and missile-throwing engines, the technology acquired courtesy of Domitian, to provide flanking fire.

The greatest of the fortresses was Sarmizegetusa, perched on a crag almost four thousand feet high (its extensive remains can be seen in the Orastie Mountains of Romania). It formed a quadrilateral made of huge stone blocks and was constructed on five terraces. Nearby stood two sanctuaries, one circular and the other rectangular, consisting of rows of wooden columns, symbolic groves from which hung offerings to the gods. Civilians lived outside the fortress walls: tens of additional terraces housed dwelling compounds, craftsmen's workshops, storehouses, warehouses, aqueducts, water tanks, and pipes. Roads were paved and there was a sewage system.

The Dacians had a civilization of which they could be proud. Their lands were rich in minerals, and they acquired great skill in metalworking. They traded with the Greek world, importing pottery, olive oil, and wine, and may have engaged in slave dealing. Compared with their neighbors they enjoyed a high standard of living as well as a rich spiritual life.

Militarily, the Dacians were less advanced. Unlike the Roman legions, they did not field a standing army, although there was a warrior class, the *comati,* or "long-haired ones." Instead, they depended on annual levies after the harvest had been gathered in, thus limiting the length of time a military force was able to stay in arms. The chieftains and warriors—Dacia's nobility—protected themselves with armor and helmets, and the rank and file wore ordinary clothes and were defended only by an oval shield. They marched into battle accompanied by the howl of boar-headed trumpets and following their standard, the *draco,* or "dragon," a multicolored windsock. Their principal weapon, the *falx,* was a fearsome curved machete, used for slashing rather than thrusting. As intended, a Dacian horde made a terrifying audiovisual spectacle.

On March 25, 101, a group of men wearing odd-looking hats gathered together on the Capitol in Rome. They were members of an ancient club, the *fratres arvales,* or Brothers of the Plowed Field, and their suitably agricultural headgear consisted of a white band holding in place a garland made from ears of corn. Founded by Rome's legendary second king, Numa Pompilius, they faded into obscurity during the later centuries of the Republic, but were reinvented by that most antiquarian of emperors, Augustus.

There were twelve Arvals, and at this time they were among the most distinguished personalities in Rome; they included former consuls, one of whom was in office when Domitian was assassinated and was probably involved in the conspiracy. All were seasoned players of the political game, exactly the kind of dinner guests favored by the late emperor Nerva.

The task of the Arvals was the worship of Dea Dia, an old rural fertility goddess, whom some thought to be the same as the Etruscan divinity Acca Larentia, Romulus' adoptive mother. They celebrated her in May at the festival of Ambarvalia.

The society also offered thanksgiving of a more contemporary and comprehensible kind. On this occasion only half a dozen brothers were in attendance. The emperor was an Arval ex officio, and sent his apologies. This was because today he was leaving Rome to lead an expedition against the Dacians, and the brothers wordily wished him the best of fortune.

> O Jupiter, Greatest and Best, we publicly beseech and entreat thee to cause in prosperity and felicity the safety, return, and victory of the emperor . . . and to bring him back and restore him in safety to the city of Rome at the earliest possible time.

It is highly probable that one of the first decisions of Trajan's reign was to deal with the threat posed by Decebalus. This was why he had visited the Danube provinces before returning to Rome for his inauguration. However, an attack on Dacia was high risk, and it is no wonder that an underlying impression of unease can be detected in the Arvals' good wishes; after all, previous campaigns had failed, with generals come to grief and legions mauled or (even) wiped out.

The new emperor had two good reasons for proceeding—one specific and the other general. First, Decebalus was an ambitious, able, and expansionist leader who threatened the stability of the imperial frontier; second, Trajan shared Augustus' perception that an aggressive foreign policy cemented consent for the autocracy at home.

That said, a careful and well-prepared approach would be essential to success. Trajan was an admirer of the ancient world's greatest conqueror, Alexander the Great. But although the Macedonian was justly famed for his bravery and bravura on the battlefield, Trajan understood the invisible key to his unbroken record of victory. Alexander was a master of logistics; he took great care of his supply lines and well understood the need to protect a victorious army's rear as it advanced into enemy territory.

The Danube was an essential line of communication for the movement of troops and supplies. However, in places rapids made it impassable; so one or more navigable canals were dug alongside stretches of the river, a characteristically ambitious *grand projet,* traces of which have been discovered.

Trajan built two great but temporary bridges resting on tethered boats, crossing the Danube at Lederata (near the present-day village of Kostolac, east of Belgrade) and Bononia (today's Vidin). These bridges gave the legions points of entry into the mountains of Dacia.

However, to ensure maximum security the emperor needed to provide a reliable connection between them. This was more easily said than done, for at the so-called Iron Gates of Orsova the Danube narrows to a gorge bounded by steep cliffs. At their feet on the southern, or Moesian, side the Romans cut a roadway-cum-towpath through sheer stone for a length of twelve miles. It was widened by cantilevered planks overhanging the water that were supported by wooden beams inserted into holes driven into the rock. This triumph of the legionary engineer can still be seen today.

Trajan was also justifiably proud of his achievement, as he made clear in a votive inscription of the year 100.

Imperator Caesar, son of the deified Nerva, Nerva Traianus Augustus Germanicus, pontifex maximus, holding the tribunician power for the fourth time, father of his country, consul for the third time, cut down mountains, erected the projecting arms, and constructed this road.

A year later another inscription boasted that "because of the danger of cataracts, [Trajan] drew off the stream and made the Danube's navigation safe."

All these preparations—not to mention the reorganization and strengthening of existing military bases north of the Danube, building accommodation for the invasion force, and increasing the capacity of ports during winter's inclement weather—took time, perhaps as much as two or three years. As the work drew to a conclusion, a large army was assembled in Moesia—nine of the empire's total of thirty legions. In addition, there was a roughly equal number of auxiliary troops, which included cavalry (which would face the fearsome Dacian *cataphracts,* or heavily armored horsemen), ten regiments of archers, and irregular forces such as the semibarbarian *symmacharii*—essential for warfare in rugged territory where set-piece battles were not feasible.

Soldiers were summoned from many parts of the empire—Spaniards, Britons, and a body of fierce Moorish riders commanded by the fiery Lusius Quietus, son of a tribal chieftain in Mauretania (roughly today's Morocco), who recruited his bareheaded cavalry from the free Berber tribes of northern Africa: they rode bareback and without reins, hurling light javelins at the enemy. A brilliant commander but a notorious rogue, he had been dismissed from the service for some unnamed conduct unbecoming, but was now forgiven for his prowess. In all, the units deployed in Moesia added up to the largest army a Roman general had ever commanded. On the assumption that many units stayed in the rear to secure the Danubian provinces and protect supply lines, more than fifty thousand men were available for front-line duty. Trajan was a cautious commander, who countered the risk of marching into unknown territory by the application of overwhelming force.

We can be sure that it was not only the Arvals who turned out to mark Trajan's departure. The Senate will have gathered to see him off, accompanied by his wife, Plotina, with crowds of ordinary citizens lining the streets. The imperial entourage included some of the best military talent of the day and most astute political minds—among them, the scion of an eastern royal house, C. Julius Quadratus Bassus from Pergamum, a splendid city in today's western Turkey, with its citadel modeled on the Acropolis of Athens; Hadrian's bugbear and brother-in-law, Servianus, now in his fifties; and the inevitable Licinius Sura.

The youngest *comes Augusti,* "companion of the Augustus," or official associate, was a twenty-five-year-old quaestor. Although obviously a competent junior officer who had useful firsthand knowledge of Moesia and the Roman frontier troops, Hadrian owed his elevated position to being a relative of the emperor. He was rising fast, but he knew he could fall faster. He had a good friend in Sura, but Servianus was a hostile critic and Trajan sometimes listened to one and sometimes the other. Hadrian was facing his first experience of war; all eyes were on him and he would have to work hard to win his spurs. What he had gained by birth, he would maintain only on merit.

Little has survived on paper about the course of the campaign, but the full story has been told in stone. It can still be "read" in Rome to this day. A visitor who walks down the wide, dusty viale dei Fori Imperiali from the Colosseum to the Vittore Emmanuele monument (looking more like a homage to Cecil B. DeMille than a true evocation of the classical world) will see on his right the ruins of the Forum, which Trajan commissioned later in his reign. The last, largest, and most magnificent of all the imperial fora, it dwarfed those of Julius Caesar, Augustus, Vespasian, and Nerva.

The emperor's architect was Apollodorus of Damascus, a designer and engineer of great virtuosity whose work exploited the revolutionary transition from traditional methods and materials to an architecture based on concrete, *opus caementicum,* a mixture of lime mortar, sand, water, and stones. Invented in the first century B.C., it was refined and developed and by the end of the following century had became the most popular building material. Thanks to concrete, the vault and the arch entered the Romans' architectural vocabulary, and buildings could rise as high as four or five stories.

The new forum stretched all the way from those of Caesar and Augustus northward to the Campus Martius. A large segment of the Quirinal Hill was removed to make room. A high arch, topped with a statue of Trajan in a war chariot, bounded the southern end of a vast rectangular piazza. This in turn led to a basilica, or conference and shopping center, and then a great temple, between which a tall freestanding column was erected, flanked by two libraries, one for Latin literature and the other for Greek.

Trajan's Column, the only component of this collection of massive edifices to remain intact, rises one hundred feet from the ground, as an inscription at its foot proudly claimed, to measure "how high a hill and place have been excavated for these great works." Inside the pedestal a small room was set aside to receive one day the ashes of emperor and empress in two golden urns (it is now empty); and a circular stairway ascends to the top of the column, where a gilt-bronze statue of Trajan once stood. He was displaced during the Renaissance by Saint Peter, who remains in occupation.

The exterior surface of the column takes the form of a stone ribbon about three feet wide and 670 feet long that winds its way up the column in twenty-three spirals. On this ribbon carved reliefs recount in realistic detail Trajan's struggle with the Dacians, rather in the manner of a modern cartoon strip. Its narrative is broadly trustworthy, although, just as ancient historians used to make up "appropriate" speeches for their protagonists, so the column's sculptor or sculptors sometimes inserted scenes that were typical of what could or should have happened rather than of what actually did. Hard to descry from the ground, the column could be readily admired and studied from windows in the libraries' upper floor or floors.

Winter was too much for classical armies and campaigns usually started in May, when there was enough fresh greenery to feed horses and pack animals, and the ground was firm underfoot. Fighting might be expected to start in June, or July after harvests had been brought in, and tailed out at the end of autumn.

So Trajan did not have to wait long after arriving in Moesia sometime in April 101 before launching the big push. The column picks up the tale. We see the flat riverbank across the wavy waters of the Danube and a series of blockhouses and watchtowers, the Roman *limes,* one and two stories respectively and surrounded by wooden palisades. In small ports on the Roman bank, stevedores are loading ships with supplies to be ferried across into Dacia. Bareheaded legionaries, their helmets hanging from their right shoulder and carrying their kit on the other, march in formation over the pontoon bridge, probably at Lederata.

On the second bridge a column of Praetorian standard-bearers is preceded by trumpeters and dismounted cavalry. At the head of the guard Trajan sets foot for the first time on Dacian territory. This emperor, it is clear, means to lead his men from the front.

The carvings pay close attention to engineering feats. Legionaries clear woodland and build camps, forts, bridges, and roads. Every advance into unknown territory is carefully secured to avert any danger of being outflanked by the enemy. Trajan is to be found everywhere, surveying terrain, confronting a Dacian prisoner, addressing respectfully attentive troops.

Decebalus avoids a full-scale encounter with the Romans and conducts a strategic withdrawal to his mountainous heartland and the royal citadel of Sarmizegetusa, but at Tapae, where years previously he had wiped out a Roman force, the king is either tempted or outmaneuvered into giving battle. This time he loses, and Trajan's auxiliaries, whom he placed in the front line, display before him the severed heads of fallen Dacians. However, the Romans suffer heavy casualties and the emperor gives some of his clothing to be torn into bandages. Decebalus cannot be prevented from retiring in good order.

In the absence of anything better to do, much territory is pillaged and many captives are taken. Among them we see a group of Dacian women, one of whom is richly dressed with a child in her arms—almost certainly the king's sister. The emperor is a gentleman and makes a point of treating them all generously (as Alexander did the womenfolk of the Persian king of kings). Autumn has arrived and the legions hole up in their winter quarters to await next year's spring. The fighting season draws to a close on a faintly equivocal note; Trajan has scored a victory, but failed to win the war.

In Italy the public was on tenterhooks. Everyone wanted news, and if they had a friend in the forces they wrote for the latest information. In a state of high anxiety, Pliny promised his friend Servianus, who was evidently a dilatory correspondent, that he would pay for a special courier to carry his reply if only he would put pen to paper (or stylus to waxed tablet).

I have had no letter from you for such a long time . . . Please end my anxiety—I can't bear it . . . I am well myself if "well" is the right word for living in such a state of worry and suspense, expecting and fearing to hear any moment that a dear friend has met with one of the accidents that can befall mankind.

Whether or not Servianus responded in writing is unknown, but Pliny did not have to wait long for an answer in person. While the emperor stayed behind on the front, Servianus and Sura returned to Rome, where their service to the state was rewarded with "ordinary" consulships. They were accompanied by Hadrian, still imperial quaestor until the end of the year; he carried with him Trajan's dispatches, a blow-by-blow account of the campaign, which he read out to the Senate.

Hadrian had had a good war, although what exactly he did has not come down to us. An inscription has been found in the theater of Dionysus in Athens that sets out his early career and notes that he was twice awarded military decorations. There were specific awards for different classes of officer, but as a *comes Augusti,* Hadrian held no particular command and, strictly speaking, did not qualify for any of them; so he must have won one or more of a range of decorations that honor particular acts of valor—the *corona civica,* for saving the life of a Roman citizen in battle; the *corona muralis,* for assault on a wall; the *corona vallaris,* for assault on a ditch or bastion; and the *corona obsidionalis,* for bravery during a siege. The Dacian campaign afforded plenty of opportunities for any of these risky specialties.

Also Hadrian at last managed to get "into a position of fairly close intimacy" with the emperor. He writes in his autobiography that he made sure to "fall in with Trajan's habits," in particular by getting drunk with him in the evenings. For this he received "opulent rewards." Evidently Hadrian had learned that essential aspect of the courtier's art—always to turn up, always to be on hand. Not only did this breed familiarity, but it reduced the monopolizing access to the presence that a carper such as Servianus needed to turn the emperor's mind against him.

As a small token of favor, Hadrian was permitted immediately to follow his quaestorship with appointment as *tribunus plebis,* tribune of the people, without the usual twelve months' interval between public appointments. In fact, there was an overlap of three weeks, for tribunes assumed office on December 10, while the term of all other "elected" officials ended on December 31.

While military tribunes were, as Hadrian knew only too well, junior officers in a legion, the ten tribunes of the people dated from the early days of the Republic when the patricians were locked in a political struggle with the plebs. They were not allowed to be patricians, for their task was to protect ordinary Romans from high-handed behavior by their betters.

At the height of their power in the first century B.C., they were able to bring the business of the state to a halt by the exercise of their veto over any decision taken by any other public officeholder, including the consuls. After the emperors assumed tribunician authority, the tribunes themselves dwindled in importance, although they continued to have the right to oppose decrees of the Senate and to act on behalf of injured individuals.

Hadrian and the Aelii had not been granted patrician status, as he might have expected if his kinship to the emperor was borne in mind. Trajan must have thought that this would be interpreted as a hint that his ward was well on course to being acknowledged as his heir. This was not his intention at all; he was still in his forties and the question of the succession could wait.

Once again Hadrian claims in his autobiography that he was given a sign that one day he would assume the purple. If we are to believe the *Historia Augusta,*

> he was given an omen that he would receive perpetual tribunician power [in other words, become emperor], in that he lost the heavy cloak, or *paenula,* which the Tribunes of the Plebs used to wear when it rained, but which emperors never wear.

There is some misunderstanding here, for it appears that everyone wore *paenulae* in bad weather, including emperors. But tribunes may well have worn some kind of uniform, to which Hadrian referred and which the author of the *Historia* confused with an ancient version of the raincoat.

• • •

On the Danube, Trajan was anxiously awaiting reinforcements. The fact that the governor of Britannia sent a small detachment from his personal bodyguard points to the emperor's urgent need: Tapae had evidently delivered more than just a bloody nose. The army was vastly expensive and emperors since Augustus had kept its complement to a minimum; the consequence was that they had no mobile reserve to call upon during an emergency. Trajan was diverting to Moesia every last soldier that could be safely spared from other frontiers.

The Romans could expect an even tougher and bloodier campaign in 102 than the year before, for they would be attacking Decebalus' precipitous heartland; not only were the mountains steeper, but desperation would fuel the Dacian resistance if and when the legions advanced. The plan was for Trajan to lead a frontal onslaught through the Iron Gates while, unobserved, Lusius Quietus and his Moors and a third force would launch pincer attacks from the rear.

It was hard going and much blood was shed, but the tactic worked. According to Dio Cassius, Trajan

> seized some fortified mountains and on them found the arms and captured artillery and siege engines as well as the legionary standard that had been captured in the time of Fuscus [Domitian's *amicus,* ambitious for military glory, who had lost the first battle of Tapae].

On the column we witness a large-scale engagement in which legionaries supported by artillery, archers, and slingmen drive through enemy ranks and storm a stronghold. An assault force forms a *testudo,* or tortoise, locking their shields above their heads to protect themselves from missiles hurled down from the ramparts.

Eventually the three divisions joined forces at the hot springs of Aquae (literally "Waters," today's Calan), only twenty miles from Decebalus' citadel at Sarmizegetusa. The game was up, and the king sent a high-ranking deputation of *pileati* to seek terms. These were granted, but, although they were punitive, Trajan meant to tame, not destroy,

Dacian power. The celebratory coins he issued referred to "Dacia Defeated," not "Captured" or "Annexed"—*victa,* not *capta* or *acquisita*.

In essence, the peace treaty between Rome and Dacia undid the humiliating settlement of Domitian, but went no further. Decebalus reluctantly

> agreed to surrender his weapons, artillery and artillery makers, to return Roman deserters, demolish his fortresses, withdraw from territory he had seized and furthermore to consider the same persons enemies and friends as the Romans did.

Large tracts of land north of the Danube were taken into the province of Moesia. Although he was allowed to stay on his throne, everything this able and aggressive king had achieved in his reign was now undone and Dacia returned to its former status as a minor kingdom, able to threaten nobody. Would he accept the war's verdict?

In Rome, in the intervals between the arrival of bulletins from the front, an almost certainly underemployed tribune of the people had no alternative but to enjoy the arts of peace. Hadrian would not have repined, for, as the *Historia Augusta* reports disapprovingly, he was "excessively keen on poetry and literature." He was skilled in painting and enjoyed music, too, both as a singer and as a player on the *cithara,* a kind of guitar.

Upper-class Romans were expected to practice the arts, write poetry, collect antiques, and generally lead a cultivated existence. Unlike Hadrian, however, a gentleman was not to be too keen, and would write verse as a relaxation rather than as a profession. The *cursus honorum,* or the "honors race," determined that the usual career was an alternation between brief periods in office in Rome or the provinces and interludes of unemployment.

Poetry readings were de rigueur in the best circles and Hadrian would have been among the audiences, even perhaps performing his own effusions. The experience could, on occasion, be trying, for amateur authors expected their acquaintances and their clients to put in an appearance. And not to show enthusiasm was bad form.

Some poets, such as Martial and Juvenal, were true professionals, but they were not members of the political elite and were obliged to make a living from their art. To win patrons and money, Martial wrote flattering epigrams and indecent squibs, but for the impoverished satirist Juvenal, whom Hadrian knew and helped, "rage powers my poetry"—*facit indignatio versum.*

As a rule, the noble dilettantes avoided deeply felt emotion, and explored or copied existing genres—elegies, pastorals, odes, and so forth. They agreed with the great Republican epic poet Titus Lucretius, who spoke of "the poverty of our native tongue"; to write elegantly in Greek was the highest attainment. Pliny praised the Greek epigrams and "iambic mimes" of the eminently respectable former consul Titus Arrius Antoninus (best known for commiserating with Nerva on his accession to the throne). "When you speak, the honey of Homer's Nestor seems to flow from your lips, while the bees fill your writings with sweetness culled from flowers . . . Athens herself, believe me, could not be so Attic."

Iambic mimes, or *mimiambi,* raise a ticklish question. They were a genre, invented in Syracuse and developed in Alexandria, that took the form of racy prose dialogues. Pliny explicitly compared Arrius with one of its most famous practitioners, Herondas, who flourished in the third century B.C. and wrote a celebrated dialogue, packed with double and single entendres, between two middle-class women about the virtues of a particular design of dildo.

At first glance it is more than a little odd for a man like Arrius to be mingling in this kind of company. However, there was a long-standing tradition that a writer's morals should not be inferred from his writings. In some cases this may have been a convenient "cover." Thus, Hadrian was on good terms with a poet of about the same age as he was, a certain Voconius Victor. On Voconius' death he wrote a neat, exculpatory epitaph for his friend: *lascivus versu, mente pudicus eras,* "Your lines were sexy, but your mind was pure."

Well, maybe. If, as is plausible, this Voconius is the same person as the Voconius Victor whom Martial teases on his impending marriage after an affair with a beautiful boy, it seems that, whatever might be claimed about his mind, his *body* was just as wanton as his verse.

In Rome, the empire's first indubitable victory over a foreign enemy since Claudius' invasion of Britannia half a century previously, as distinct from the blue-on-blue of civil war or the suppression of internal revolt, was received with delight.

Pliny's letter of congratulation would have been typical of many. He prayed that Trajan would bring about a further renewal of the "glory of the empire." Rome had returned with satisfaction to its age-old habits of aggression and territorial expansion.

Trajan returned to Rome in late 102, and was granted the title of Dacicus and held a Triumph. During the Republic this stupendous celebration had been open to any general who had scored a great victory, but it was now reserved to emperors, who were jealous of any military rival (not altogether groundlessly). The ceremony opened in the Campus Martius with speeches and the conferral of decorations for valor (perhaps this was when Hadrian received his awards). The Senate led the way into the city, followed by distinguished prisoners-of-war and floats carrying large pictures of heroic incidents in the campaign. Then came Trajan, who rode in a gilded four-horse chariot. Temporarily he was quasi-divine, with his face painted the same red as the statue of Jupiter Best and Greatest in the great temple on the Capitol; he wore an embroidered toga above a purple tunic interwoven with gold and decorated with designs of palm leaves. Behind him marched his troops in column of route. The men had immemorial license to sing scurrilous songs about their commander, and we may guess that on this occasion there was ribbing about the emperor's taste for wine and boys. The procession ended on the Capitol, where the god for a day sacrificed white bulls to the god of gods.

The emperor staged lavish gladiatorial combats and authorized the return of pantomime shows: banned by Domitian on the grounds of their obscenity, they had been reintroduced by the easygoing Nerva, and banned again by Trajan on his accession. But now Trajan changed his mind—according to gossip, because he had fallen in love with one of the artistes, Pylades.

In 103 Hadrian held no public office and we hear nothing of his activities. But in the following year, he was elected as praetor for 105, an important post only one tier below the consuls. For the first few weeks of the year he was technically ineligible to serve, for he ought to have been in his thirtieth year—which did not open until his twenty-ninth birthday on January 25.

There were eighteen praetors, and their main duties concerned the administration of justice, in both civil and criminal law. Hadrian seems to have been made urban praetor, not only the chief magistrate of the legal system but also the official responsible for staging the prestigious *Ludi Apollinares,* the Games of Apollo. These were instituted during the war against Hannibal and were held every July 6 in the Circus Maximus. No expense was spared, and Trajan gave Hadrian a large budget to make sure that the celebrations were as splendid as could be.

Every year the new holder of the office would issue an edict, a body of rules, priorities, and legal interpretations he intended to apply during his year of office. Often he adopted those of his predecessor, perhaps making his own additions to reflect the needs of the time. In some ways this was a convenient means of creating legislation; if a new rule was popular a praetor's successors would adopt it themselves, if not it would quietly be allowed to drop.

Hadrian was interested in law and would have enjoyed his praetorship. It is easy to imagine him presiding at court, attending to every procedural detail and unafraid to express his own self-taught legal views. However, he was not able to do so for long.

Trajan was not sure that Decebalus could be trusted, and he took sensible precautions against a return to war. Legionary fortresses north of the Danube provided an advance warning system, and Trajan's omniskilled architect Apollodorus built a permanent bridge east of the Iron Gates— twenty piers of hewn stone supported a timber roadway. It was a remarkable engineering feat for its day and made a profound impact on public opinion.

Over the next couple of years, the Dacian king began to make attempts to escape from the box into which the Romans had locked him.

He rearmed, and occupied land belonging to the Iazyges, a nomadic tribe that the Romans had settled in the province of Pannonia—without asking for Roman permission. He contacted other tribes to seek alliances, and once more welcomed Roman deserters. He even sought support from the powerful Parthian empire which lay beyond Rome's eastern frontier; as a personal token of goodwill, Decebalus sent the Parthian king a Greek slave, a certain Callidromus, once the property of one of Trajan's generals but captured in Moesia. Finally, he launched a preemptive strike and attacked Roman forces in southwestern Dacia, prophylactically occupied since 102.

The crisis, when it came, took Trajan by surprise, as evidenced by the fact that he left abruptly for the frontier in June 105—far too late in the year to initiate a full-scale campaign. New military appointments were posted, including a promotion to legionary commander, or *legatus*, for Hadrian. This meant he had to abandon his legal work in Rome and miss his costly *ludi*. In theory it was illegal for the urban praetor to leave the city for more than ten days at a time, but, as so often in Roman history, a rule gave way to an emergency.

Hadrian's new legion was the I Minervia (founded by Domitian, it was named after his favorite Olympian, Minerva, goddess of warriors and wisdom), a reward for his prowess in the first Dacian conflict and a sign of imperial confidence in his usefulness in the field. It had marched down from Upper Germania as a reinforcement, probably after the bloody conflict at Tapae, and was one of the fourteen legions now readying themselves for the next round of hostilities. Hadrian presumably first came across it when he was in Germania a few years previously.

The column shows the emperor's arrival in Moesia. Legions cross the Danube again, this time on Apollodorus' new stone bridge, and the slow and steady process of moving forward, fortification by fortification, is set in motion. The Dacians respond by unpredictable and dangerous guerrilla raids. In one scene Trajan rides at full gallop at the head of some auxiliary cavalry to beat off an attack on a powerful Roman camp. But, although the fighting was tough, the eventual outlook was bleak for Decebalus.

The king took an eccentric measure, suggestive of growing desperation. He had heard that Trajan did little to ensure his personal safety.

This was no doubt partly a tactic to maintain his posture as first citizen rather than despot, but it also reflected the emperor's genuine popularity with the rank and file. He made himself readily accessible and allowed any soldier who wished to attend his councils of war (not meetings of his *consilium* where confidential plans were discussed, but briefings for officers from all units). Decebalus persuaded some deserters to make their way back to the Roman army to see if there was a way of killing the emperor at such a gathering.

Many generations were to pass before the concept of suicide terrorism was invented, but it would appear that these would-be assassins were willing to strike at the very moment their target was surrounded by hundreds, possibly thousands of loyal armed soldiers. They could not have hoped to survive. In any event, the plot failed. One of the deserters was arrested "on suspicion"—perhaps he had been recognized by former colleagues or he had been caught making some kind of advance preparation. He was put to torture, and sang.

The incident may have had a happy ending, but it starkly exposed a political reality that the presence of a healthy, fairly young *princeps* usually masked. In the event of his death the emperor had no named successor. There was, of course, one male relative available for the purple, young but with potential; however, Trajan had gone out of the way on numerous occasions to avoid pointing to Hadrian as his heir. He had behaved perfectly appropriately to his former ward and encouraged his career; but one has a sense that he harbored some deep, unspoken distrust of him.

It may have been about this time that a telling exchange took place, if we are to trust the *Historia Augusta*. Rumor had it that Trajan, as a disciple of the great Alexander, wanted to follow his example and die without an heir. When the Macedonian king, lying in his death fever, was asked to whom he left his conquests, he was said to have replied ambiguously: "To the strongest." Although it distinctly appealed to Trajan, this was a pernicious precedent, for the consequence was internecine quarreling among Alexander's generals, and the breakup of his hard-won empire. Other gossip at Rome had it that, when the time came, the emperor intended to write to the Senate, asking them to choose a new *princeps* from a short list supplied by him.

The column makes it clear that the emperor saw action. Trajan could well fall in battle and was in no position to be vague about what was to happen then, if he wished to retain the army's confidence. After consulting his *amici,* he at last decided to reveal something of his intentions.

For whatever reason, he did not nominate his former ward and closest male relative, but seems to have let it be known that in the event of his death Lucius Neratius Priscus, who (it seems) was governor of Pannonia, should take his place. Apparently he told him to his face: "I commend the provinces to you if anything should happen to me." This was a curious form of words: Trajan may have used the emperor's direct control of the empire's most important provinces, where much of the army was based, as a shorthand for acceding to the throne. But perhaps he only meant the Danube provinces, and so was referring to the command of the Dacian war. One way or another, the sentence betrays a continuing reluctance to be absolutely clear.

Neratius Priscus was an interesting choice, for he was essentially a nonpolitical figure. By nominating him, Trajan knew that he was not giving momentum to a serious candidate for the purple. A very capable man, Neratius worked his way through the honors race, ending up as a suffect consul in 97 and then with his governorship. But his real passion was the law, to which he devoted himself for the rest of his life after his return home from the Danube. He became a well-known jurist, a legal adviser who offered opinions on points of law and on specific court cases to private parties as well as to elected officials and the emperor himself. His textbooks, notes, and responses were much cited by later experts.

We do not know whether the *legatus* of the I Minervia was disappointed that he had been overlooked. His clairvoyant interest in his imperial prospects is well enough attested, but at this stage they were not taken seriously by anyone else. Perhaps he was too busy to care. So far as we can tell he did not scheme against the emperor or seek to assemble a faction to support his claim; he remained loyal and got on with his career more or less as if he were just an ordinary member of the ruling class.

• • •

Decebalus, having failed to shortcut the war by an assassination, now tried another trick. He offered to negotiate without preconditions with a Roman commander north of the Danube, the former consul Cnaeus Pompeius Longinus, who had been successfully beating the Dacians back to their rocky heartland. Longinus incautiously made his way to the king's camp for the talks, where he and an accompanying escort of ten soldiers commanded by a centurion were immediately placed under house arrest and then interrogated in public about Trajan's plan of campaign. Longinus kept his counsel and said nothing.

Decebalus sent an ambassador to Trajan, asking for the restoration of all his lands north of the Danube and the payment of war reparations. A careful response was prepared, calculated to create the impression that Longinus was neither very highly nor very slightly valued. Trajan wanted to prevent his being put to death, or handed back on excessive terms. He succeeded, for the Dacian king could not make up his mind what to do next and temporized.

It was Longinus who bravely broke the stalemate. He made friends with one of Decebalus' Dacian freedmen and obtained some poison from him. He then promised the king that he would win Trajan over and in pursuit of this wrote the emperor a letter. He arranged for the freedman to deliver it in person and, in order to ensure the man's safety, he asked the emperor to treat him well.

Longinus hoped that Decebalus would not guess his true intentions and so not keep a very strict watch over him. That was how matters fell out, and one night after the freedman had left for the Roman headquarters Longinus took the poison and died. This was a fine example of self-sacrifice: for a leading Roman statesman or commander, suicide was recognized to be a courageous, even a noble, act in the event of *desperata salus,* of no hope of rescue or recovery.

The king refused to admit defeat and dispatched the captured centurion to Trajan, promising to send back Longinus' body and the escort in return for the freedman. The emperor refused, commenting that the freedman's safety was "more important for the dignity of the empire than the burial of Longinus." An honorable position to adopt, one might think, if one overlooks the fact that it left the escort out on a limb. The emperor evidently cared more for a dead general than ten other-rankers. History does not record their fate.

The reduction of Dacia now proceeded with little opposition from the enemy. The legions followed a direct route to Decebalus' capital via the Vulcan Pass, more than 5,300 feet high. The Dacians lost heart: the column shows members of the Dacian court pleading with their king to come to terms. Decebalus refused and retreated into the mountains with his family and bodyguard, to form a resistance movement. Meanwhile, Sarmizegetusa, for all its impregnable appearance, fell without a fight. It was looted and burned to the ground.

Some of the nobility decided to collaborate, and one of the king's companions revealed the secret location of Decebalus' treasure to Trajan. According to Dio Cassius,

> with the help of some captives Decebalus had diverted the course of the river [Sargetia], made an excavation in its bed, and into the cavity had thrown a large amount of silver and gold and other objects of great value that could stand a certain amount of moisture; then he had heaped stones over them and piled on earth, afterward bringing the river back into its course. He also had caused the same captives to deposit his robes and other articles of a like nature in caves, and after accomplishing this had made away with them to prevent them from disclosing anything.

Alaric, king of the Visigoths, borrowed the idea three hundred years later and was buried with his spoils beneath a river in southern Italy. But while his resting place has never been discovered, the Dacian treasure was dug up. It turned out to be of almost unbelievable value—about 500,000 pounds of gold and 1 million of silver.

And what of the king? Years afterward a proud cavalryman commissioned a gray marble inscription that recorded a long career of distinguished service in the army. A carved relief depicts the high moment of his life. We see him galloping on his horse and on the ground the prostrate trousered figure of Decebalus, a bearded man in a Dacian cap. The curved sword with which he has just cut his throat falls from his hand. The legend below reads that he captured the king, who killed himself moments before his arrest, and that he delivered his head to Trajan (it was later sent to Rome and was ceremonially thrown down the Scalae Gemoniae, a flight of steps that led up to the Capitol, where the bodies of executed criminals were exposed for a time).

The war was over. The victory was as complete as victory could be. Just as Titus in 70 had expelled the Jewish population from Judaea, so Trajan ethnically cleansed Dacia. Many thousands, perhaps hundreds of thousands, of Dacians were dispersed, some to appear as gladiators in the emperor's postwar celebrations and others to be sold into slavery. Colonists were imported to take their place and a new capital city was built in the name of the emperor's clan, Sarmizegetusa Ulpia. Dacia became Rome's first new province since Claudius had annexed Britannia in 43.

Once again, Hadrian had distinguished himself. Army life suited him and the I Minervia performed well. As so often, the detail of what he did is missing, but according to the *Historia Augusta,* "his many remarkable deeds won great renown."

Trajan began to blow hot again, after cold. He was so pleased with his former ward's successes that he presented him with a diamond he himself had received from Nerva. The intention seemed obvious, at least to Hadrian, who repolished his hopes of being acknowledged the emperor's official successor. People were reminded of the famous occasion when a seriously ill Augustus passed his signet ring, bearing the head of Alexander the Great, to his friend Marcus Agrippa to mark the transfer of authority. But the two events were not really comparable; a jewel was no official ring, and a healthy and triumphant Trajan was not transferring anything except a valuable gift. Whatever Hadrian liked to think, the diamond was a token of the emperor's esteem rather than the talisman of his power.

XI

THE WAITING GAME

. . .

Of more practical value than a jewel was the emperor's decision to promote Hadrian again, after only twelve months as commander of the I Minervia, to provincial governor—a clear demonstration of his usefulness in the field. As the campaign against Decebalus drew to its climax during the summer of 106, Trajan divided Pannonia into two jurisdictions, Upper and Lower. The latter was the smaller part, with only a single legion as garrison, and this he allocated to Hadrian. The wheel had come full circle, for the new province's capital was Aquincum, the fortress town on the Danube where the young military tribune had had his first real experience of army life ten years previously.

It was not the grandest of appointments and one of its consequences was that Hadrian probably missed the culminating excitements of total victory. But it was some compensation that the post was no sinecure. Lower Pannonia looked across the Danube to the Hungarian plain, home of the fierce, unmastered Sarmatian Iazyges. This tribe adjoined the western frontier of the Dacian kingdom; they were nervous of Decebalus' expansionist policy and unsurprisingly supported Trajan's invasion. According to the *Historia Augusta,* the new governor "held back the Sarmatians." We can take it that they had not chosen this unlikely juncture to turn on their victorious Roman friends, but were seizing the opportunity to grab or at least to raid defenseless Dacian territory. What they failed to grasp quickly enough was that Rome already regarded Dacia, no longer just *victa* but *capta,* or "taken," as its own property and did not welcome unfriendly incursions.

Dealing with the Sarmatians, probably by negotiation (for there is no report of fighting), by no means consumed all of Hadrian's energies and, for the first recorded occasion, his taste for intervention (or, his critics would argue, for interference or meddling) was given full rein. Archaeological evidence suggests that Hadrian had an impressive new governor's palace built: if so, this was his first opportunity to indulge in what was to become a lifelong passion for commissioning art and architecture and investing in what the French call *grands projets*. Ever the autodidact, Hadrian convinced himself that he had a talent for design that made him the equal of professional practitioners.

One of the more ingenious characteristics of the imperial system was a division of powers at the provincial level. A governor, a former praetor (as in Hadrian's case) or consul and a leading member of Rome's political elite, was responsible for the general administration of the province and the command of its garrison army. Alongside him, one or more procurators were charged with financial management and reported directly to Rome, not to the governor; their chief task was to collect taxes and other sources of revenue and to transmit this income to the *fiscus,* or exchequer, in Rome or to the emperor's privy purse (it can be presumed that these were sometimes in whole or in part paper transfers, with the actual cash being spent locally). By removing from him control over finance, this made it far more difficult for a discontented governor to mount an armed challenge to the emperor.

Although procurators enjoyed multiple opportunities for malfeasance, it was a brave governor who pried into their affairs. But, self-confident as ever, Hadrian did not hesitate to do so; no details have come down to us, but, according to the *Historia Augusta,* he "restrained the procurators, who were overstepping too freely the bounds of their power." One would like to know more, but what can be understood is that he took risks by acting *ultra vires*—and survived them. If he was wise, he would have cleared his plans with Trajan first, and there is evidence that the emperor would have strongly backed him.

The *Epitome de Caesaribus* claims that during Trajan's reign some procurators were disrupting the administration of the provinces by launching false accusations.

One was said to ask a wealthy man, "Why are you rich?"; another, "Where did you get it from?"; and a third, "Give me what you've got." The empress, Plotina, tackled her husband on the subject and reproached him for being so unconcerned to protect his good name. She returned to the subject so often that he came to detest unjust exactions. He used to call the *fiscus* the spleen because, as it grew, the rest of the body, its muscles and limbs, wasted away.

The incident is undated, but when we recall how close Hadrian was to the empress, it could be that it coincides with his governorship and that Plotina was preparing her husband's mind for the inevitable procuratorial complaints about Hadrian.

The governor was also the *legatus* of his legion, the II Adiutrix. He knew the men well, seeing that he had served with them as military tribune. One of the challenges facing commanders of troops on frontier duty was to find ways of keeping them at a high pitch of battle-readiness when they spent much of their time not doing anything very much apart from boring guard duty. This absorbed much of Hadrian's attention, and the *Historia Augusta* reports that he "maintained military discipline."

It is uncertain how long Hadrian stayed in his post at Aquincum, but he may still have been there when he reached the apex of a Roman's political career. In 108, two years or less after starting his governorship, he was awarded a consulship. According to the *Historia Augusta,* this was in recognition of his successful record in Lower Pannonia, evidence that his interventions had been met with approval. He was only thirty-two. The general rule, dating back to the days of the Republic, fixed the minimum age for holding the state's senior post at forty-two, but since the reign of Augustus this had been reduced to thirty-one for patricians and members of consular families.

Hadrian was neither, so the early appointment was a compliment. But, as ever, what Trajan gave with one hand he contradicted, or at least contraindicated, with the other. Instead of being one of the two *consules ordinarii,* who launched the year in January and gave their names to it (officially a year was referred to as "during the consulships of so-and-so and so-and-so"), Hadrian was simply a suffect or replacement consul, who probably took over in May.

* * *

Hadrian's great friend at court, Trajan's close adviser and companion Licinius Sura, was still putting in good words for him, to considerable effect according to the *Historia Augusta*.

Sura's years of power opened with the accession of Nerva, and from that point onward he was the empire's éminence grise. Dio Cassius claims that he acquired "great wealth and pride," as well as numerous enemies who schemed to undermine Trajan's confidence in his loyalty. They lost their labor.

> So great was the friendship and confidence he showed toward Trajan and Trajan toward him, that, although he was often slandered, Trajan never felt any suspicion or hatred toward him. On the contrary, when those who envied Sura became very insistent, the emperor went uninvited to his house to dinner, and having dismissed his whole bodyguard, he first called Sura's physician and caused him to anoint his eyes, and then his barber, whom he caused to shave his chin; and after doing all this, he next took a bath and had dinner. Then on the following day he said to his friends who were in the habit of constantly making disparaging remarks about Sura: "If Sura had wanted to kill me, he would have killed me yesterday."

The private man seems to have been more agreeable than the statesman. If we can draw conclusions from two letters Pliny wrote to him, he enjoyed being asked to address abstruse conundrums. One of these concerned a spring at Pliny's villa on the shore of Lake Comum (today's Como), which had the curious property of intermittently filling and emptying a pool in an artificial grotto. It can still be found at the sixteenth-century Villa Pliniana near Torno and has puzzled great minds down the ages, including such disparate figures as Leonardo da Vinci and the poet Shelley. In fact, water is siphoned off variably according to atmospheric pressure, but Sura's reply does not survive, so we cannot tell whether he proposed the correct solution.

During the year of Hadrian's consulship Sura let his protégé know that he was to be adopted by Trajan. This information was widely leaked and led to a new friendliness on the part of onetime critics and enemies, including members of the imperial *consilium*. "He was no longer despised and ignored by Trajan's *amici*."

This anecdote is hard to interpret. It very probably derives from Hadrian's autobiographical apologia, and so should be treated with caution. One indubitable fact undermines it: the emperor took no steps to implement his resolution. Did Sura or Hadrian simply make the story up? Unlikely; it would be risky to spread a false report at the time, which might well find its way to the emperor; if it was invented later, former members of the imperial entourage would have been able to deny knowledge of it.

Perhaps it is no coincidence that the reported incident took place not long before the death in about 110 of Sura, who may have been making one last attempt to reinforce Hadrian's position before quitting the stage. His passing brought a remarkable career to a close. As we have seen, he shared Trajan's sexual tastes. According to the *Epitome de Cae-saribus,* it was through Sura's "zeal that he had secured *imperium*." The strong implication was that he negotiated persuasively with Nerva, or (some speculate) threateningly, on behalf of his friend, then absent in Germania. Sura was appointed suffect consul in the crucial year of 98 when Trajan inherited the throne from Nerva; and, a rare honor, twice as consul *ordinarius* in 102 and 107. He served in Dacia and was appointed to lead an embassy to Decebalus—a move that came to nothing because of the king's fear for his own safety. Trajan's regard for Sura remained undiminished until the end and after. He awarded him a state funeral and erected a statue in his honor. He also named some splendid new baths on the Aventine Hill after his friend, built near or perhaps on the site of Sura's house; they remained in use for more than two hundred years.

An interval of peace followed the Dacian wars. After his governorship, Hadrian returned to Italy, and he did not hold further public office for some years. It is instructive that the emperor showed no interest in sharing the workload of empire with his now mature and experienced relative; Augustus had had Marcus Agrippa and Tiberius as nearly coequal partners, and Vespasian had worked very closely with his son Titus.

So far as we can tell, Hadrian betrayed no signs of disappointment or resentment. He remained loyal and patient. For a politically inexperienced aspirant to the purple, who had spent the last ten years—that is, most of his adult career—in the field rather than at Rome, he now enjoyed a front-row view of Trajan's performance as a civilian ruler. There were lessons to be learned.

The first of these concerned the limits of absolute power. Communications were slow; nobody could travel faster than a horse and journeying by ship was extremely dangerous in the winter months. Even an urgent correspondence took weeks to conduct and complete.

The state played a far more limited role than in today's world. Economic and social theory were little understood, and seldom translated into public policy. Military spending was by far the largest item in the imperial budget. However, the army, with its thirty legions, was hard put to guard the empire's borders along the Rhine and the Danube, in the sands of Mesopotamia and the Sahara, and in the rocky, contested landscape of northern Britannia. Rome could afford to defend its frontiers but, with a few notable exceptions such as Judaea, not to police heavily or "occupy" its domains as well.

Another factor restricting an emperor's freedom of action was the relatively small number of officials and bureaucrats that helped him administer the empire. In the days of the Republic a consul or other elected *magistratus* brought with him members of his household, usually slaves and freedmen, to help him manage his public business. Also, he depended on friends to advise him. Augustus adopted this model, if on a grander scale. He and his successors gathered around him able freedmen, usually Greek, to run an imperial secretariat. Among the most important were the *ab epistulis,* who handled the imperial correspondence, the *a rationibus,* in charge of the imperial finances, and the *a libellis,* who dealt with petitions.

These men accumulated great power and wealth. They were accountable only to the emperor; this meant they could operate out of the public view and, in the event of any scandal, were expendable. Unsurprisingly, they became so unpopular that emperors began to hire *equites,* men of standing from the business class, in their place.

The *princeps,* as the first among supposed equals, needed to maintain the confidence of the senatorial class, and to a growing extent the *equites.* With the support of the army and Rome's masses, he was in a position to act despotically if he so wished. But if he held all the cards, he needed others willing to play the game with him. As we have seen, the history of the previous century demonstrated only too clearly that if he did not at least go through the motions of working with the Senate he ran a number of unpleasant risks: at worst, assassination or revolt; at best, lack of cooperation.

For all these reasons it was extremely difficult for the center to impose policy on the periphery or to act without consultation, but this did not mean that the center was impotent. It was a reservoir of prestige, authority, money, and law, and Trajan demonstrated how an intelligent *princeps* could get his way with little difficulty.

To senators he behaved with unfailing affability; the contrast with Domitian could not have been plainer. He treated them as personal friends, visiting their houses if they were ill or were celebrating feast days. In turn, he was a lavish host, entertaining them at banquets "where there was no distinction of rank." Dio Cassius writes:

> He joined others in animal hunts and in banquets, as well as in their labors and plans and jests. Often he would take three others into his carriage, and he would enter the houses of citizens, sometimes even without a guard, and enjoy himself there.

It was claimed that he "took more pleasure in being loved than being honored," although this did not deter men like Pliny from lauding him in the most flattering terms. This easygoing social manner was very welcome, even if it was little more than intelligent public relations.

Despite all the difficulties, there was a mechanism by which Trajan was able to make his presence felt throughout the empire. Even if overarching policy interventions in provincial life were rare, Trajan was showered with petitions from all and sundry and requests for action of one kind or another. The imperial government interfered as little as possible in local politics and religion, expecting civic elites to maintain an orderly administration. Inevitably, though, disputes arose on almost every imaginable topic and Trajan was asked to adjudicate, just as his predecessors had been.

He was seldom governed by personal whim. The emperor stood at the apex of the legal system. Roman jurists wrote, "What the emperor decides has the same authority as the law of the people, because the people have made him their sovereign." Local jurisdictions retained their validity, but Roman law was applicable throughout the empire and had something of the force that international law has today. Local authorities and individual Roman citizens could appeal to the *princeps,* who acted as a kind of supreme court (Saint Paul was well within his rights about A.D. 60 when he said to Porcius Festus, procurator of Judaea, "*Appello Caesarem*"—"I appeal to the emperor").

Experienced jurists bore much of the heavy workload that the preparation of new laws, the promulgation of imperial edicts to clarify points of law, and the judging of particular cases entailed. Trajan was an active reformer; he ruled that defendants condemned in absentia should have the right to a retrial. Also, by banning anonymous accusations laid by *delatores* and the practice of torturing slaves in *maiestas* cases, he brought to an end the political show trials that rulers such as Domitian had used to quash suspected dissent.

Petitions did not only deal with legal matters; they also requested practical help with local building developments. As we have seen, Trajan spent vast sums of money on transforming urban spaces, not just in Rome but throughout the provinces. He made sure that his munificence was acknowledged with grateful inscriptions; even a remote bridge in Numidia proclaimed that it had been erected "with the labor of [Trajan's] soldiers and from his own money." So many buildings carried his name that he was nicknamed "the Wallflower."

The imperial archives are long gone, thrown away or destroyed among all the vicissitudes that beset Rome during its long decline and through the longer centuries of the Dark Ages. But we have the next best thing. Grateful provincials engraved their correspondence with the emperors and their replies on stone or bronze memorials, many of which the modern archaeologist has recovered from the ruined sites of lost cities. Reading these documents reveals a continuity of governance from *princeps* to *princeps,* with officials evidently looking up past decisions for precedents. Even the decisions of a "bad" emperor such as Domitian were consulted for guidance.

Every now and again something truly original emerges. In 1747 some plowmen in a field near Piacenza unearthed by chance the largest known inscribed bronze tablet of antiquity, measuring four feet six inches by nine feet six inches, the celebrated *tabula alimentaria.* Two others were discovered in southern Italy. The tablets give detailed information about an ambitious and extremely expensive child welfare scheme, funded by Trajan, as it applied to three communities—the modest township of Veleia in the north, which vanished long ago under a landslide, and places in Tuscany and near Beneventum in the south.

The emperor had a good track record with the young. He passed far-reaching laws to protect the rights of minors and abandoned infants. The exposure of newborn children was a feature of life in the classical world; sometimes they were rescued and brought up as foundlings. Trajan restored their rights as heirs of their birth parents. He also removed the absolute power fathers held over their sons, the *patria potestas,* in the event of maltreatment. The laws of guardianship (a subject of which he had personal experience as a *tutor*) were tightened and it was made more difficult for testators to leave their estates to single heirs at the expense of others with reasonable expectations of inheritance.

Probably founded by Nerva but developed by Trajan, the *alimenta* scheme, as revealed by the inscription, was an ingenious measure that apparently sought to meet two different objectives at once, one economic and the other social. The first step was to set a target number of beneficiaries in a given district and to identify needy children to fill the quota. Both freeborn boys and girls were eligible for financial support—sixteen sesterces a month for the former and twelve for the latter (and less for youngsters who were illegitimate). The treasury then made a capital sum available in the form of cheap 5 percent loans to local landowners on the security of their farms or estates. The interest on the loans was sufficient to cover the dole payable to the children. So far as we can tell, the loans were in perpetuity.

It has been estimated that the entire scheme throughout Italy cost the state annually 311 million sesterces, a very large sum equivalent to three quarters of the army's annual budget. But what exactly was it designed to achieve?

There is evidence that from the reign of Domitian Italy suffered from an agricultural crisis. Pliny, a substantial landowner, reports that his tenants were finding it hard to pay their rent and were falling into ever-larger arrears. "As a result, most of [them] have lost interest in reducing their debt because they have no hope of being able to pay off the whole."

The *alimenta* scheme must surely have transformed economic expectations. The subsidy for selected offspring of citizens (all the freeborn inhabitants of the peninsula held Roman citizenship as of right) would have removed the shadow of poverty from a young generation; Pliny, who ran a similar, much smaller scheme of his own on his estate, expected the boys to grow up into soldiers and the girls to marry and procreate—and so, too, we may surmise, did the emperor.

The cheap loans themselves were probably intended to enable investment in the land and in development projects. To judge from the bronze tablets, most of the mortgagees were of a middling sort and, although this is nowhere spelled out, must have been expected to invest the money in their farms or at least to make good any losses.

Did the inflow of so much cash to the Italian countryside have a beneficial impact? Nobody tells us in so many words, but the government was moved to boast, issuing a series of *alimenta* coins as well as one with the proud slogan *Italia restituta,* Italy renewed.

These policies for youth support and rural development have a familiar ring to them, but they were merely a pragmatic response to particular problems. Rome did not invent the welfare state. That said, here was the *optimus princeps* at his best—generous, well intentioned, and intelligent.

After Sura's death, Hadrian took over responsibility for writing the emperor's speeches; this meant that he was often in his presence and as a result relations between the two men warmed. One wonders if, from time to time, he also helped out with his correspondence. In that case, he would have observed that letters poured in unrelentingly from imperial officials in every corner of the empire, each of them posing a conundrum, often of only local significance and requiring detailed knowledge of the area, and asking for a decision.

By a great stroke of luck a bundle of letters between Trajan and a high official have evaded the worst that tidy-minded clerks, barbarian invaders, and Christian monks could do. For some years the province of Bithynia-Pontus on the southern littoral of the Black Sea had been in a state of endemic financial and administrative disarray, and in 110 the emperor commissioned the experienced Pliny as his special representative, *legatus Augusti,* with a mission to overhaul the political and financial governance of the province. We have sixty-one letters he wrote to Trajan, seeking guidance on a wide range of topics. Despite wide-ranging powers and an imperial letter of instruction, it is remarkable how many minor matters Pliny referred to the emperor. It was probably wise for officials on foreign postings to keep their employers fully informed of what they were doing to ward off misunderstandings or suspicion.

However, important questions *were* discussed, with the emperor regularly adopting a conservative approach. "My own view is that we should compromise," he remarked on one occasion, adding: "We should make no change in the situation resulting from past practice." The basic principle to which Trajan adhered was to interfere as little as possible in the lives and customs of provincials, as when he advised on an issue concerning local-authority senates in Bithynia: "I think then that the safest course, as always, is to keep to the law of each city."

However, the emperor's moderation did not stem from an inability to make up his mind; rather, it was a decisive cast of mind. An instructive exchange between him and his *legatus* is a case in point.

The Romans did not know what to make of the Christians, a new sect less than a century old. The travels of Saint Paul as recorded in the Acts of the Apostles and his letters reveal the existence of many Christian communities in the cities of the eastern empire, especially those that lay on major trade routes, and in the imperial capital itself. To begin with they were hardly noticed and their intentions were much misunderstood. They were accused of criminal depravity and, in a distorted allusion to the Eucharist, of cannibalism.

Nevertheless, conversions mounted and, if we can judge from those named in Paul's correspondence, believers were widely spread across social classes and in the city or nation of their origin. We have seen that a relative of Domitian was executed in the 90s, perhaps because he was a Christian convert, although at this stage in its evolution the religion did not usually appeal to ruling elites.

The apostle had tried to make his way to Bithynia-Pontus, but mysteriously failed to get there because of opposition from the "Spirit." However, a Christian community came into being and flourished, to the unease, years later, of the imperial *legatus,* Pliny. He knew that he was expected to act against the sect, but was uncertain of the nature of their offense. So he wrote to Rome for guidance. Was a Christian to be convicted simply of membership in the church? Or of the crimes allegedly associated with it? And what would be appropriate punishments? It appeared, Pliny found, that coreligionists sang hymns in honor of Christ "as if he were a god" and bound themselves by oath to abstain from theft, robbery, and adultery. At the eucharist, they took food of an "ordinary, harmless kind." No cannibalism there. What puzzled Pliny was the innocuousness of Christianity.

Typically, the emperor took a cautious line. It was impossible, he wrote, to lay down a general rule. If someone was proved to be a Christian, he should be punished (unhelpfully, Trajan failed to answer the question about penalties). But if he sacrificed to the Roman gods, he should be pardoned. He added:

> Pamphlets circulated anonymously must play no part in any accusation. They create the worst sort of precedent and are quite out of keeping with the spirit of our age.

Did Hadrian read this ruling? That cannot be determined, but it is perfectly possible. The matter was of some importance and Trajan is likely to have consulted, or at least informed, his close circle. Also, the bureaucrats in Rome must have recognized that the emperor's wishes had an empire-wide application and made sure the ruling was widely disseminated. In any event, we can safely assume that Hadrian consulted the imperial archives some years later, when he himself was obliged to take a view on Christianity.

XII

CALL OF THE EAST

. . .

For the wellborn Roman, educated as he had been to value Greek history and culture above his own, the first visit to Athens was a rite of passage. As Pliny put it to a young friend, he was going "to the pure and genuine Greece where civilization and literature, and agriculture too, are believed to have originated."

The voyager from Rome chose from two alternative itineraries. He rode down the Appian Way and a brand-new stretch of road commissioned by Trajan, took ship at Brundisium (today's Brindisi), then sailed across the Adriatic and down the coast of Greece into the Gulf of Corinth. There were no passenger ships as such, but places could be booked on merchant vessels: government officials or senior personalities in the imperial regime were in a position to commandeer a warship, fast although not comfortable. Landfall was made at Corinth's western harbor, and the traveler crossed over by land to its eastern counterpart. The adventurous alternative was to sail down the coast of Italy, turning east through the Strait of Messina and rounding the windswept peninsula of the Peloponnese.

Either way, journey's end was the port of Piraeus, with its three fine weatherproof harbors, which had once been the home of the eastern Mediterranean's most formidable fleet. As the traveler rode the few miles to the city, he could see on either side the ruins of the Long Walls, built to link Athens securely to its ships. Along the road stood the gravestones of past generations of Athenians.

Soon a spectacular distant view of the city presented itself against a horizon of high mountains. The sun caught the spear and helmet of a colossal statue of the goddess Athena that guarded the citadel, the crag of the Acropolis. Just to one side the columns of the Parthenon, shrine of the Maiden, shone whitely.

The famous words of Pindar were as apt as when minted six centuries previously.

> O glittering, violet-crowned, chanted in song,
> Bulwark of Hellas, renowned Athens,
> Citadel of the gods.

In 112 Hadrian made his way to Athens for an extended stay. This is his first recorded visit, although (as has been seen) it is possible that his father took him there when a young child. Also, he may have been in Athens a few years before, during the fallow period after his consulship. A man of some importance in the state, Hadrian doubtless journeyed in style with a considerable entourage; it was the done thing for elite wives to accompany husbands on their travels, so the little-loved Sabina was probably present.

Which of the two routes he took is uncertain. It is plausible that he chose the first, via Brundisium and Corinth. Although it entailed a good deal of walking or riding a mule or in a mule-drawn carriage and was slower and more tedious, it reduced the ever-present risk of shipwreck in a storm. En route, Hadrian was able to follow the example of many other Roman tourists and stop over at Nicopolis; this was the City of Victory, which Augustus founded near Actium after his victory at sea over Mark Antony and Cleopatra in 31 B.C.

The temptation was not so much Nicopolis itself, pleasant place though it was, as the fact that the philosopher Epictetus was living and lecturing there. We know that at some stage Hadrian became a friend and admirer and that he may have already met him in Rome. He would hardly have turned down the opportunity of an encounter.

At about this time an eager young man from Bithynia was studying under Epictetus, taking copious shorthand notes at his lectures. This was Lucius Flavius Arrianus Xenophon (Arrian in English), now in his mid-to late twenties. A capable and intelligent man, he had three heroes—the Greek author and adventurer Xenophon, whose name he took, most unusually, as a *cognomen;* Alexander the Great, about whom he wrote an influential biography; and Epictetus.

Deeply impressed by the philosopher's thought, Arrian was aware that, like Socrates, the sage never wrote anything down, and decided to publish his lecture notes so that an accurate memory of his philosophy survived. From these an unmistakable theme emerges—a scorn for authority and, more particularly, that of the emperors. Although Hadrian's name is not mentioned, a number of remarks in his lectures bear a certain aptness to the character of the imperial student.

At one point during a discussion in which Epictetus argues that everyone is a son of God, he remarks, "If the emperor adopts you, no one will be able to bear your conceit." Later he inquires, "Shall kinship with the emperor or any of those who wield great power in Rome be sufficient to enable men to live securely, proof against contempt and in fear of nothing whatsoever?" Whom, we muse, did Epictetus know among Trajan's very few politically important relatives, if not the man perhaps sitting in the lecture hall in front of him?

The philosopher pleaded for tolerance of those who chattered on about their war records in Dacia.

> Some men . . . have excessively sharp tongues and say: "I cannot dine at this fellow's house, when I have to put up with his telling every day how we fought in Moesia [Hadrian's province, one recalls]. 'I have told you, brother, how I climbed to the crest of the hill; well, now, I begin to be under siege again.' " But someone else says: "I would prefer to eat my dinner, and let him chatter on as he pleases."

Epictetus concludes with his advice to those who cannot bear it: "Never forget that the dining room door stands open."

It cannot be proved that the philosopher had Hadrian in mind when he made these good-humored jibes; but they do sketch a portrait of someone rather like him—bumptious, talkative, and a know-it-all.

What is more interesting is the fact that a man who had his eye on the throne should sit at the feet of a thinker who criticized the imperial system. Epictetus' view was that the "power" of power was much exaggerated. In a brief dialogue between an imperial official called Maximus and himself, Epictetus pricks the balloon of self-aggrandizement.

> MAXIMUS: I sit as a judge over Greeks.
> EPICTETUS: But do you know how to be a judge? And what has given you this knowledge?
> MAXIMUS: The emperor gave me my credentials . . .
> EPICTETUS: And there is another question—that is, how did you come to be a judge? Whose hand did you kiss? In front of whose bedroom door did you sleep so as to be the first to say good morning? To whom did you send presents? . . .
> MAXIMUS: Well, I can throw anyone I want into prison.
> EPICTETUS: Just as you can throw a stone away.
> MAXIMUS: And I can have anyone I want beaten to death with a club.
> EPICTETUS: As you can a donkey. That is not governing men.
> Govern us as rational beings by pointing out what is useful to us and we will follow you. Point out what is useless, and we will turn away from it.

Epictetus' final remarks suggest that for him the ideal wielder of power was very much like a philosopher whose task was to guide human beings down the path of reason.

We can take it that Hadrian was aware of Epictetus' political opinions. He may have attended a version of this lecture. Whether or not he agreed with everything he heard is immaterial; what matters is that Hadrian had an opportunity to meditate on the nature of government and to take seriously the concept of emperor as a philosopher-king.

After the short ride from Piraeus—or possibly walk, for he enjoyed exercise—Hadrian arrived at his destination. Once through the city gates, Hadrian found himself in a broad avenue, the Panathenaic Way; on either side were colonnades, with statues of famous men and women along their front, as the street passed through an industrial district, the Kerameikos, or Potters' Quarter, and led into the Agora, or marketplace.

Originally a triangular square planted with plane trees, the Agora once had been bisected by a racetrack for athletes. For the rest of the year it had been populated with traders' stalls. Here had been the beating heart of classical Athens. However, the Romans had arrived, with their passion for building. They constructed a new marketplace, the Roman Agora dedicated to Julius Caesar and Augustus, a large square courtyard surrounded by colonnades on all four sides, not dissimilar to a monastic cloister. And in the middle of the old Agora, Marcus Agrippa built a huge new multistory concert hall, which it completely dominated. It was a fine example of arrogance masked as generosity.

Hadrian was well aware that Athens had long lost its political importance, but it was a cultural center with a thriving intellectual life: a rough modern analogy would be Paris in the first half of the twentieth century. This was what appealed to him. Civic buildings also contained countless works of art. In the Propylaea, the grand (and still very beautiful) marble gateway up to the Acropolis, there was a picture galley. On every corner there were shrines, temples, statues, and altars. It was as if the city was a vast open-air museum celebrating the achievements of Greek civilization.

The rich and well connected did not expect to stay at the various inns and hostels that could be found in most cities. A local worthy—perhaps a friend or acquaintance—or government official would offer generous hospitality. The name of Hadrian's host at Athens has not survived, but we can make a guess. One possibility is Gaius Julius Antiochus Epiphanes Philopappus. He was one of a breed of rootless multimillionaires in whom Greek, oriental, and Roman cultural attitudes mingled.

His name contains his history: "Gaius Julius" signifies Roman citizenship, but he was of Asiatic origin, being the grandson of Antiochus IV, the last king of Commagene, a region of ancient Armenia just to the east of Cilicia. Although one of the wealthiest of Rome's tributary kings, Antiochus was not the most nimble of politicians. In 72 he wisely supported Vespasian when he made his bid for the purple and sent forces to help Titus during the siege of Jerusalem; but he was then found to be conspiring with Rome's great enemy in the east, the Parthians.

The new emperor had no time for slippery loyalties and promptly deposed him. Antiochus withdrew to Sparta, once a great power and

Athens' rival but now a quiet tourist backwater. Then, presumably after mending some bridges with the Flavian regime, he settled in Rome, where he lived with his two sons and was generally regarded with great respect.

His grandson was evidently fond of him, for his *cognomen* Philopappus means "lover of his grandfather." He spent most of his time in Athens, where he became an Athenian citizen and a member of the Besa *deme,* or district. A generous patron of the arts, he funded cultural and athletic events. Philopappus took care to keep his lines open to senior government officials; he became a Roman senator and was a suffect consul in 109.

This was a man who enjoyed living lavishly and prominently—as his other *cognomen,* Epiphanes, or "illustrious," indicates. He became a celebrity in the modern sense of the word, famous for nothing in particular except for conspicuous expenditure. The Athenians nicknamed him King Philopappus. Hadrian became a good friend of his and Sabina made much of his sister, a poet and bluestocking, Balbilla. The siblings will have been of special interest to him, for magic had been a family tradition: two of their ancestors were celebrated astrologers, the onetime prefect of Egypt Tiberius Claudius Balbillus and his father, Thrasyllus of Mendes, who survived holding the dangerous post of official astrologer to the emperor Tiberius.

There had been no emergency—political, military, or personal—forcing Hadrian to take to sea during the perilous winter months, so we may assume that he traveled in late spring—say, from May onward. He was well received, for almost immediately the Athenians offered him citizenship, which he accepted without demur, and, as with Philopappus, made him a member of the Besa *deme.* They then awarded him their highest honor, appointing him archon, or chief magistrate: only a handful of leading Romans had been so distinguished, among them Domitian, who, with typical tactlessness, appointed himself by imperial fiat and held the post in absentia. The official year ran from summer to summer and Hadrian took office immediately.

The new archon was soon hard at work, helping to ensure that the Panathenaic Games of 112 were a success. Philopappus was doubtless on hand to offer support (we know he was interested, for at some stage in his career he was appointed *agonothetes,* or games producer). The games were held every four years in the year preceding an Olympiad, in the height of the summer. Both body and mind were tested to the extreme.

As well as athletic contests, competitors in poetry competitions spoke or chanted excerpts from the works of Homer. Musical contests—solo lyre and flute performances and singing to one's own lyre or flute accompaniment—were held in one of the most curious of buildings. This was the Odeion, in the shadow of the Acropolis: a vast square structure with a roof supported by a forest of columns, it was a copy in stone and wood of the spectacular tent of the Persian king of kings, Xerxes, which he had had to abandon after his failed invasion of Greece in the early fifth century B.C.

Every year at the height of summer a great celebration, the Panathenaea, was staged in honor of the city's tutelary goddess, Pallas Athene. Priestesses, official seamstresses, and four specially selected little girls made a new tunic, or *peplos,* to clothe an archaic statue of Athena, housed in the little temple on the Acropolis, the Erechtheum. A great procession gathered at the Dipylon Gate, as depicted in the Elgin or Parthenon Marbles. Charioteers, horsemen, musicians, elders, resident aliens, three sheep and a bull for sacrifice, and girls carrying bowls and jugs for libations walked through the Agora and up to the Acropolis, where the *peplos* was handed over. The brilliantly painted marble frieze high up on the outside walls of the temple's sanctuary, or *cella,* showed the Olympian gods in benevolent attendance at the ceremony.

As archon, one of Hadrian's first duties on taking office was to select two deputies and some administrators to plan the following March's Great Dionysia. At this religious festival in honor of Dionysus, god of wine and ritual madness, patron of agriculture and theater, three days of drama were presented in the theater of Dionysus; built against the southern slopes of the Acropolis, this seated fifteen thousand to seventeen thousand spectators. Each day a playwright presented three tragedies, based on well-known legends, and a raucous farce, a so-called satyr play. Comedies and choric odes were also performed.

Originally all these were new works, but by Hadrian's day audiences preferred revivals of masterpieces by authors such as Aeschylus, Sophocles, and Euripides. Judges were elected by lot and awarded a prize of an ivy wreath to the producer of the best show, the *choregos*. Hadrian sat ex officio in the front row of the auditorium alongside the judges and other dignitaries.

If we may believe the *Epitome de Caesaribus,* he devoted every spare moment from his duties as archon to cultural pursuits (the author flatters, for Polycleitus and Euphranor were celebrated old masters).

He devoured the pursuits and customs of the Athenians, having mastered not merely rhetoric, but other disciplines too, the science of singing, of playing the harp, and of medicine: [he was] a musician, geometrician, painter, and a sculptor from bronze or marble who was next to Polycleitus and Euphranor [in artistry]. Indeed, like those things in a way, he, too, was refined, so that human affairs hardly ever seem to have experienced anything finer.

Now in his mid-thirties, Hadrian was in the prime of life. He was tall and very strongly built, but elegant in appearance, with carefully curled hair. According to Dio Cassius, he was "a pleasant man to meet and possessed a certain charm."

His features were reasonably good-looking, with a strong nose, high cheeks, and puckered eyebrows. He looked about him with an alert, even suspicious gaze. Flatterers said that his eyes were "languishing, bright, piercing and full of light," signs of a true Hellene and Ionian. One may suspect that this was exactly what Hadrian liked to hear (just as his revered Augustus prided himself on *his* clear, bright eyes). He had a way of compressing his mouth, with the lower lip projecting slightly forward. The overall impression he gave was of inquiry, decisiveness, and sharp, sometimes acid judgment. This was a self-confident man used to giving orders—but with few illusions that they would necessarily be carried out efficiently.

His face possessed one remarkable singularity. For centuries Romans of the ruling class had been clean-shaven (no painless task in the days before the invention of soap and tempered steel for razors)—that is, in civilian life, for they often let their beards grow when on military campaign, as the reliefs of Trajan's Column clearly show. The fashion had been set at the beginning of the second century B.C. by Scipio Africanus, the charismatic young general who defeated Hannibal. The lower classes did not bother to follow suit. Romans had a way then as today of kissing each other socially, and Martial writes disgustedly of the "bristly farmer with a kiss like a billy-goat's." In the twilight of the Republic gilded young men sported goatees to irritate their elders; Cicero called them *barbatuli* ("beardy boys"), but the tradition of beardlessness persisted into the empire.

Hadrian decided to follow his own taste and grow a beard. The *Historia Augusta* claims that he wanted to cover some natural blemishes, but, if true, that will not have been his only motive. Doubtless he listened to Epictetus, who had something to say on the subject. He posed a question to his students: "Can anything be more useless than hairs on the chin?" and immediately replied to himself in the negative. Facial hair, he claimed, was nature's sign for distinguishing men from women, and was more beautiful than a cock's comb or a lion's mane. "So we ought to preserve the signs which God has given. We ought not to throw them away. We ought not, so far as we can, confuse the sexes which have been distinguished in this way."

By implication Epictetus was advising a Roman, not a Greek. This was because Greek adult males usually wore short, trimmed beards as a matter of course, and these were an easy means of ethnic identification. The new archon of Athens did not wish to appear as a smooth-skinned imperialist in a toga and, although we do not know when he gave up shaving, it is very plausible that he did so now—as a gesture of solidarity with the city that had given him so warm a welcome and as a visible sign of his Greekness.

These months in Athens were a high point in Hadrian's life. He was a member of the Roman establishment and in no way did he resile from that; but, at least temporarily, he had become a leader of the culture he so greatly admired. He could imagine himself to be a true Hellene, an heir of Pericles and the great men of old.

After years of peace the thoughts of the *optimus princeps* were turning again to war. The enemy he had in mind was the Parthian empire. Onetime nomads from northeastern Iran, the Parthians defeated and expropriated the Seleucid empire, founded by Seleucus, one of Alexander the Great's Macedonian officers. At its height their realm stretched from today's Pakistan to the river Euphrates. Little is known in detail about them, for they left behind no written records, but they governed loosely, allowing a good degree of local autonomy to their vassal provinces. A coin issued by Chosroes, the present king, in about 110, hailed the ancestral founder of his dynasty as "Friend of the Greeks"; so it is evident that he had no wish to halt, reverse, or subvert the Hellenization of the Middle East.

The nobles were striking to look at. They always seemed to be on horseback, whether fighting or dining, traveling or relaxing. They wore long beards, used cosmetics, and elaborately styled their hair. Plutarch recalls how Roman soldiers were once thoroughly put out by the misleadingly effeminate appearance of an opposing Parthian commander with his "painted face and parted hair." He was as fierce a fighter as they had ever met.

Although militarily they could be most effective, the Parthians were greatly weakened by their eccentric constitutional arrangements. The king of kings was an absolute ruler and had to be a member of the Arsacid clan; however, he was elected by two councils. One represented the nobility—in effect, the Arsacids and their cadet branches, in other words all his relatives—and the second was drawn from the Magi, or "wise men," a priestly tribe responsible for religious and funerary arrangements. At any time, these committees could elect a new king. The succession was never undisputed and primogeniture often yielded to fratrigeniture, and a dispossessed elder son would contest his uncle's throne.

It was hard to see, even at the time, why Trajan was meditating an expedition against the Parthians. He had demonstrated his soldierly prowess against the Dacians, but in that case had been responding to a real military threat. In general, he presented himself as a man of peace.

Arrian, a friend of Hadrian as we have seen and a competent public official and historian, was absolutely certain that Trajan, while mindful of the dignity of the empire, did all he could to avoid war with Parthia.

Dio Cassius (albeit in a late summary) takes the opposite view: he is explicit that the emperor went to war on a pretext and that his true motive "was a desire to win glory."

In the light of the fragmentary state of the surviving evidence, it is impossible to decide definitively between the two opinions, but there are enough clues to suggest that Dio was right.

In 112 the emperor celebrated fifteen years of power. On January 1 he entered on his sixth consulship and formally dedicated his magnificent new forum and basilica. Coins were issued featuring the emperor's kindly wife, Plotina, and his much-loved sister, Marciana. For the first time each woman is named as Augusta, or "revered one." Sadly, Marciana died in August; her brother arranged for her deification and promoted Matidia to Augusta. Sabina was now the granddaughter of a Diva and the daughter of an Augusta.

Festive coin types in the same mintage celebrate Trajan's father, one-time holder of triumphal honors, *ornamenta triumphalia,* over the Parthians when he governed Syria, and deified by his son. Another shows Trajan himself with the curious legend "May fortune return him safely," *fort[una] red[ux].* This signified that the emperor was planning a *profectio,* an imperial expedition, of some kind; combined with a tribute to the last Roman to have beaten the Parthians, it could be interpeted by the Roman equivalent of Kremlinologists as a hint that battle was to recommence. Other coins of the period have a markedly martial flavor—with images of Mars, the god of war, of the emperor on horseback trampling on his fallen enemies, and of legionary eagles and standards.

The *Historia Augusta* remarks, but infuriatingly fails to date the event precisely, that Hadrian was appointed *legatus* to the emperor "at the time of the Parthian expedition." Dio reports that he "had been assigned to Syria for the Parthian war." This may mean that he traveled on from Athens sometime during 113 to Syria, the province that shares a frontier with the Parthian empire, and began to assemble an invasion army. In that case it would seem likely that he received the emperor's confidential instructions before setting off for Greece in early 112, and made preliminary preparations during his stay there.

So such particular evidence as there is suggests a long-planned intention only awaiting an opportunity. More generally, though, there was a traditional pattern in the relations between the two powers. The Parthians were usually too preoccupied with their internecine court politics to plot aggressive war; and their statesmen must have recognized that their system of governance would not readily permit them to manage a larger territory. However, from the perspective of a Roman general ambitious for glory (for example, Crassus, Julius Caesar, and Mark Antony), they were a tempting if often indigestible prey. It is reasonable to regard Trajan as the inheritor of this tradition.

The longed-for casus belli eventually presented itself in Armenia, a bone of contention for more than a century. Both parties saw the kingdom as falling within their legitimate sphere of interest. Long ago Augustus had negotiated a face-saving arrangement, confirmed by Nero: the Parthians nominated a Parthian prince to the throne of Armenia, but the Romans confirmed the choice and conducted a coronation in Rome. By and large this double-lock system had assured an uneasy but durable stalemate.

For some years, though, Parthia had been divided by two rival kings. During the second half of 113, the leading contender for the throne, Chosroes, self-confidently deposed the Armenian ruler, a nephew of his, and replaced him with the king's older brother, a certain Parthamasiris. Nothing particularly unusual here—except that Chosroes foolishly failed to consult Trajan. This certainly meant a loss of face for Rome, but no fundamental imperial interest was at risk. A rational response would have been to follow in Augustus' footsteps and send out a high official (say, Hadrian) to negotiate an acceptable settlement.

Trajan made it clear, though, that negotiation was the last thing on his mind. Public opinion was enthusiastically behind him and, amid cheering crowds, he set out from Rome for the east, accompanied (according to a late source) by a "large force of soldiers and senators." He probably chose for his departure the date of his adoption by Nerva, October 25. Chosroes panicked and sent an embassy, which met the emperor at Athens; it presented gifts and begged Trajan not to make war on him. Trying to make up for his earlier mistake, the king of kings asked that Armenia be given to Parthamasiris and requested that Rome send him the royal diadem as a token of endorsement. He had deposed his nephew, he claimed, for being "satisfactory neither to the Romans nor to the Parthians."

Trajan was unrelenting. He refused to accept the gifts and did not respond to Chosroes' requests, either orally or in writing. He merely stated, forbiddingly: "Friendship is decided by actions and not by words. When I have reached Syria, I will do everything that is proper."

So what were Trajan's true motives? What did he have in mind if not in word? We can only speculate, but one thing is certain—he was obedient to the long-established rhetoric of imperial expansion. As he was an admirer of Alexander the Great, an invasion of Parthia would be a happy echo for him of the Macedonian king's conquests. Now in his mid-fifties, this was Trajan's last chance to live a dream of youthful adventure.

Hadrian waited in Antioch (today's Antakya), then capital of Syria, for Trajan to take command of the legions he had assembled. Founded by Seleucus in the fourth century B.C., the city was squeezed in between the river Orontes (the modern Asi or Nehri) to the west and Mount Silpius to the east. It was laid out in imitation of the grid plan of Alexandria; two long colonnaded streets met in the center. With a population of about half a million, Antioch was the empire's third largest city after Rome and Alexandria.

About four miles away was Daphne, a large *paradeisos,* or walled park around a gorge with groves of laurel and cypress. There were formal gardens and cascades. A spring called the Castalian fount was believed to have prophetic properties; it was perhaps on this occasion that the superstitious Hadrian consulted it and was informed that he was to become emperor.

However, Daphne had a reputation less for religious observance than as a haunt for sexual promiscuity, as more generally did Antioch itself. This was the city that inspired the stereotype of the slippery, treacherous, and untrustworthy Asiatic—perhaps the closest Romans came to anything approaching contemporary racism. But it was also nicknamed the "Athens of the East" and its great wealth attracted artists, philosophers, poets, and orators from across the Mediterranean, and financed a luxurious and permissive lifestyle. Although he was busy, Antioch would have been an entertaining billet for a man like Hadrian, with an inquisitive mind and an openness to experience.

Toward the end of December he greeted the emperor when he disembarked at Antioch's port, Seleucia Pieria (near today's Samandağ). They made their way at once to the neighboring Mount Casius (Jebel Akra) for a religious ceremony at a temple of Zeus Casius. At nearly six thousand feet, this was the highest landmark in northern Syria, with views of Cyprus and the Taurus range in Cilicia.

The imperial pair presented an array of gifts for the god; more was promised if the Romans were victorious in the impending campaign. Hadrian composed a short poem in Greek (of course) elegiac couplets for the occasion.

> To Zeus Kasios has Trajan, son of Aeneas, dedicated this gift,
> the ruler of men to the ruler of the immortals:
> two artistically wrought cups and from a large ox
> the horn adorned with all-gleaming gold,
> chosen from his former spoils when, unyielding,
> he has wasted the Getae with his spear.
> But you, lord of the dark clouds, grant him the power
> gloriously to complete this Achaemenian conflict,
> so that your heart may be twice warmed by the sight
> of two spoils, those of the Getae and those of the Arsacids.

Aeneas was the prince who escaped the blazing ruins of Troy and settled in Italy, and whose descendants founded Rome; so Trajan is represented as the millennial inheritor of this great tradition. The Achaemenids (literally the name of the dynasty Alexander overthrew) and the Getae were poetic terms for the Parthians and the Dacians. Hadrian was associating past victories with an assured future one. But would the god smile on the enterprise?

XIII

MISSION ACCOMPLISHED

. . .

The emperor was in no hurry. He proceeded, by way of the pleasant gardens at Daphne, to Antioch, where he passed the winter of 113. His first destination was Armenia, the ostensible cause of the war, and he was obliged to wait until the winter snows had melted from the passes leading into that remote and high kingdom.

Trajan had promoted Hadrian to something like a modern chief of the general staff and so given him a key role in the management of the Parthian expedition. His ambivalent feelings had apparently firmed into wholehearted approval. Hadrian was for the moment the second man in the empire. However, despite the fact that he was well qualified for the purple, his position remained insecure. Despite his six decades, the emperor still showed no interest in securing the succession.

How are we to explain what looks like a dereliction of duty on the part of a levelheaded ruler? Perhaps Trajan obstinately refused to acknowledge the approach of old age, part of the same mind-set that encouraged him to emulate the ever-youthful Alexander. But just as powerful a factor may have been disagreements at court. Among the emperor's *comites* opinions were sharply divided. The *Historia Augusta* has a passage on the subject, typically condensed to the point of obscurity:

> At this same time [Hadrian] enjoyed . . . the friendship of Quintus Sosius Senecio, Marcus Aemilius Papus, and Aulus Platorius Nepos, both of the senatorial order, and also of Publius Acilius Attianus, his former guardian, of Livianus, and of Turbo, all of equestrian rank.

These men were the leaders of a meritocracy, for they had all reached the top through talent and endurance. Senecio held high command in

Dacia and had twice been consul; a cultivated man, he was a friend of Pliny, who gossiped to him about the difficulty of getting audiences for literary readings, and of Plutarch. Hadrian became a friend of his, probably as early as 101, at the beginning of his career. Papus and Platorius Nepos had Spanish connections and were members of the Baetican "mafia," with villas in and around Tibur. We have already met the now aging Attianus, when he and Trajan took responsibility for the child Hadrian when he was orphaned nearly three decades previously. He was now praetorian prefect and, as cocommander of the Guard, a guarantor of the stability of the regime. Titus Claudius Livianus had been one of his predecessors as prefect, and was perhaps of special interest to Hadrian as the owner of twin boys celebrated for their beauty.

Turbo we have also already met: he had been a centurion at Aquincum, where he probably first got to know the youthful Hadrian and join his circle, and rose swiftly from the ranks; he was now admiral of the fleet at Misenum (modern Miseno, at the northwestern end of the Bay of Naples). He was Hadrian's kind of soldier, hardworking and without airs and graces. Dio Cassius writes of him: "He displayed neither effeminacy nor haughtiness in anything he did, but lived like an ordinary person." (The fact that his character was the complete opposite of the not-long-dead Licinius Sura's illustrates the wide range of Hadrian's affections.)

On the debit side, the *Historia Augusta* pointed to Aulus Cornelius Palma and Lucius Publilius Celsus, "always his enemies." Palma was a younger friend of Trajan; trusted and trustworthy, he had twice been consul, and in 105 or 106 he had conquered the Nabataean Arabs, hardy nomads on the southern border of Syria who traded in frankincense and myrrh, and brought them within the empire. Celsus was consul for the second time in 113 and stood high in Trajan's favor. According to Dio, he and a colleague were awarded the signal distinction of public statues. In the shadows, other critics of Hadrian are to be suspected, among them his elderly brother-in-law, Servianus.

Grounds for the distrust of Hadrian are hard to determine. He was obviously competent and intelligent, and no reports have come down to us of serious disloyalty to Trajan. History shows that factions tend to gather around close relatives of a monarch and criticize official policy.

So one might speculate that Hadrian opposed the Parthian war, but if he did he surely held his tongue. Otherwise, as he played a large part in preparing the expedition and was working closely with the emperor, he would have been open to charges of subversion or hypocrisy.

There may have been objections to Hadrian's personality. A picture does emerge of a hardworking but cocksure man—a combination often irritating to colleagues. Not suffering fools gladly is insufferable to the fools.

Whatever the explanation, Trajan would have been rational to conclude that the eve of a major expedition was the wrong moment to alienate one side or the other by coming to a firm decision about his former ward. The question of the succession would have to wait.

In the spring Trajan marched with his army northward from Antioch to the town of Satala in Lesser Armenia, on the Roman bank of the river Euphrates. It was a long trudge—some 475 miles—across awkward terrain, and the Romans probably arrived toward the end of May. The advance precipitated a line of embassies from client kings and minor rulers, all wishing to make their peace with the emperor. One who stayed away was Abgarus, king of Osrhoene, a tiny kingdom on the far side of the Euphrates that he had purchased from the king of kings. "Afraid of Trajan and the Parthians alike," he sent gifts and kind words, but not himself.

At Satala the seven eastern legions, gathered by Hadrian, joined others dispatched from the Danube provinces (a risky step, one might have thought, to denude an unsettled region of its troops). Some of them were not at full strength, but Trajan now commanded the equivalent of eight full legions with the same number of auxiliaries—in other words, about eighty thousand men.

He also deployed his towering prestige. He marched into Armenia and then, before an arrow had been released or a spear cast, paused at a place called Elegeia. Here he staged a splendid ceremony—like the *durbars* of the British Raj—at which local satraps and princes came to meet him and offer their fealty. One of them presented Hadrian with a horse that had been trained to prostrate itself as if it were a subject in the presence of an eastern monarch. It knelt down on its forelegs and placed its head beneath the feet of anyone who stood by it.

The culminating event saw the arrival of the Parthian pretender, Parthamasiris. This should have been a significant propaganda coup, but it went badly, and mysteriously, wrong.

The emperor sat on a tribunal set up in the Roman camp and was forced to wait for his visitor. In a surprising breach of protocol, Parthamasiris turned up late, pleading as excuse the need to evade roaming supporters of his deposed rival, Exedares. He laid his diadem before Trajan, expecting to receive it back. The soldiers shouted in delight at this "victory." But the emperor refused to crown Parthamasiris, who protested loudly. Trajan replied that he would surrender Armenia to no one, and declared that it was now a Roman province. He gave Parthamasiris permission to leave.

This is a very odd incident. Parthamasiris had been in communication with Trajan and presumably agreed terms for the encounter in advance. He was to be recognized as king of Armenia provided that he accepted Rome's right of confirmation and coronation. Are we to suppose that events got out of hand by some mischance—or that Trajan had decided in advance to break the negotiated deal and trick Parthamasiris out of his throne? The accounts we have seem to imply confusion rather than conspiracy, except that it is unlikely that Trajan would announce out of the blue the annexation of Armenia. This was a strategic decision of some importance, and the humiliation of Parthamasiris was a striking means of dramatizing it. The Romans were well aware of the propaganda opportunity, as shown by several coin issues that depict the *rex Parthus* as a suppliant in front of Trajan.

But why let him leave the Roman camp? Surely the prince would be dangerous if set at large? Indeed. The Romans had thought of that. Parthamasiris and his entourage were given a cavalry escort to see them on their way, presumably to Parthia. Soon news arrived of the prince's death; apparently he had been cut down while trying to escape his guard—an explanation deployed by ruthless captors throughout the ages.

Over the centuries Rome placed great weight on honest and straightforward dealing; treaties were sacred. The episode damaged the good name of the *optimus princeps*. He must have known it would do so, and we can only assume that Parthamasiris could call on very powerful support in Armenia for it to be worth Rome's while to tolerate the moral cost of removing him.

Armenia was soon reduced. Various commanders, among them Lusius Quietus, the Moorish chieftain with his fierce horsemen, were dispatched to various parts of the kingdom to subdue resistance. The fighting seems to have gone on into the winter, for there are reports of soldiers making themselves snowshoes. But victory was complete, and previously hesitant local kings decided it was time to join the winning side.

Among them was Abgarus, who had the luck to have an extremely good-looking son, a certain Arbandes, who wore gold earrings and caught the emperor's roving eye. Thanks in part to the young man's intercession, his father's early reluctance to meet the emperor was pardoned. Dio Cassius remarks that the king "became Trajan's friend and entertained him at a banquet. During the meal he brought in his boy to perform some barbaric dance or other." History fails to record how the evening concluded.

It would have been difficult to retain control of Armenia without annexing a large slice of the Parthian empire to its south, Mesopotamia (today's Iraq), the fertile land between the rivers Euphrates and Tigris. That was to be the business of next year's campaign.

Entry into Parthian territory in 115 was an event of historic proportions, and Trajan led his troops in the field. Despite his age he made a point, as he always had done, of marching on foot with the rank and file, fording rivers with them and so forth. According to Dio, he paid special attention to training. "Sometimes he even made his scouts circulate false reports, so that the soldiers might at one and the same time practice military maneuvers and become fearless and ready for any dangers."

The campaign went well, and it appears that Mesopotamia was entrapped in a pincer movement with Lusius Quietus moving into eastern and Trajan into western Mesopotamia (taking care to march around the lovely Arbandes' Osrhoene).

The emperor returned to Antioch for the winter, and before the end of the year Trajan sent dispatches to Rome—a "laureled letter" betokening victory. He probably announced the creation of Armenia and Mesopotamia as two new Roman provinces. The Senate received the news on February 21 to loud acclaim. It awarded Trajan the title of *Parthicus,* despite the fact that much of the Parthian empire remained to conquer.

Meanwhile, the emperor had a narrow escape from death. Early one morning in January a severe earthquake occurred, with its epicenter near the city. The emperor's presence had attracted large numbers of soldiers, officials, visiting embassies, and tourists, so the loss of life was all the greater. Many people were trapped beneath collapsed buildings, "able neither to live any longer nor to find an immediate death." Two of the very few to be pulled out of the debris some days later were a mother and child; she had survived by feeding both herself and her baby with her own milk. One of the consuls for 115, Marcus Vergilianus Pedo, lost his life—and Trajan was lucky to have saved his by jumping out of a window.

The disaster did not materially impede the course of the war. With the beginning of spring the emperor "hurried" back into enemy territory. Settling the Armenian quarrel may have been the original war aim, but now he was determined, as one suspects he had been from the beginning, on the overthrow of the Parthian empire. He built a fleet of fifty river vessels on the Euphrates and marched alongside it down into the Parthian heartland. Meanwhile other forces followed the Tigris south; some of them passed through Gaugamela, where Alexander had scored the culminating victory over Darius III that had made him master of the Persian empire and its new, foreign king of kings. To Trajan's mind, history was ready to repeat itself.

By the summer he arrived at Seleucia, a city opposite the Parthians' winter capital, Ctesiphon, which stood on the far or eastern bank of the Tigris. At this point the two rivers flow within twenty miles of each other and the fleet was dragged overland from the Euphrates to the Tigris. The Romans entered Ctesiphon without encountering any resistance and found it empty.

It has been supposed that the Parthians had fled, but as the Romans arrived in the summer it was unsurprising that the place was deserted. Chosroes and his court were presumably to be found at their summer capital, Ecbatana, in the Zagros Mountains, where the air was cooler. However, the king had evidently decided against challenging the Romans in the field: according to Dio Cassius, civil strife had removed Parthia's capacity to the resist the invader.

For Trajan the moment was sweet. He now deserved the *cognomen* Parthicus, and new coins showed a military trophy (enemy shields and weapons fixed on a pole) with two captives and the legend *Parthia capta,* "Parthia taken." He busied himself with the details of administration—for example, raising the ferry charges across the Tigris and the Euphrates for camels and horses. He made arrangements to create a third new province, Assyria.

And then, a vacation, sailing down the Tigris with his river ships. According to Arrian,

four of them carried the royal flags and they led the way for the flagship furnished with long planks of wood. This ship was about the length of a trireme [about 130 feet], its width and depth those of a merchantman, like the largest Nikomedian or Egyptian vessel, and it gave the emperor satisfactory living quarters. It displayed stem-post ornaments [of gold] and on top of the sail the emperor's name was inscribed along with the rest of his imperial titles in gold letters.

Traveling downriver, the emperor continued the business of government, holding conferences on board the flagship. When navigating around an island in the Tigris delta, he was nearly sunk by a combination of storm and tide, but eventually reached the Persian Gulf at a place called Charax (today's Basra). He saw a ship sailing to India and said wistfully: "I would certainly have crossed over to the Indians, too, if I were still young." He counted Alexander, who reached the subcontinent, a lucky man.

The emperor built a statue of himself signaling the limit of his advance (it was still standing in 659) and lost no opportunity to send another laureled letter to Rome. Public opinion was astounded by the demolition of the Parthian empire and the stunned Senate voted him many honors, among them the privilege of holding triumphs over as many peoples as he pleased. The senators explained, helplessly:

> Because of the large number of peoples about whom you are constantly writing to us, we are unable in some cases to follow you intelligently, or even to use their names correctly.

If ever a mission had been accomplished, this was the occasion.

The Jews had never forgotten the destruction of Jerusalem at the hands of Titus. Scattered throughout the eastern Mediterranean, large settlements flourished alongside their Greek-speaking neighbors. Unhappily, they seldom got on with them well and there was regular intercommunal strife, for which both sides bore a fair share of the blame.

Many Jews remained bitterly opposed to their Roman oppressors and despised the pagan environment in which they lived. They especially disliked the *fiscus judaicus,* which Titus had imposed after the bloody end of the siege of Jerusalem in 70. Nerva had restricted its application to religious Jews, but it still rankled.

In 115 the Jews in Cyrene revolted and by the next year the insurrection had spread to Alexandria, where about 150,000 Jews lived, and to the island of Cyprus. The match that lit the fire is uncertain; it is not inconceivable that the Parthians incited the Jews to disrupt the Romans' supply chain to the legions in the east, but anti-Roman nationalism may be a sufficient explanation. Messianic fervor could also have played a part, for the Jewish leader in Libya, one Lukuas, was elected king by his coreligionists.

Dio Cassius paints a picture of unrelieved brutality. The Jews, he claimed,

> would eat the flesh of their victims, make belts for themselves of their entrails, anoint themselves with their blood and wear their skins for

clothing. Many they sawed in two, from the head downward; others they gave to wild beasts [in the arena] and still others they forced to fight as gladiators.

We do not need to give much credit to these anti-Semitic fantasies, but there is no doubt that ordinary people went in fear of their lives, in the countryside as well as in the towns, as papyri retrieved from desert sands testify. A glum rural correspondent noted: "The one hope and remaining expectation was the attack from our village against the unholy Jews—the opposite of which has now happened. For on the twentieth [?] we engaged them and were defeated, although many of them were killed." Another *strategos* apologized to the prefect of Egypt for being away from his post: "Not only because of my long absence do my affairs begin to be in complete disorder, but also, because of the unholy Jews' attack, just about everything I have in the villages of Hermopolis and in the metropolis needs repair from me."

That the Jews went on the rampage is beyond doubt; but their objective is mysterious. Could they seriously have hoped to drive the Roman occupiers out, or permanently suppress the indigenous populations among which they lived? We can only suppose that this was a spontaneous uprising. There was no strategic plan, simply a passionate thirst for revenge against an unjust world. In Cyrene many thousands of gentiles were massacred and temples destroyed. The death toll was also high in Cyprus, and the important town of Salamis razed. There was still a sizable Jewish community in Mesopotamia; Trajan suspected their loyalty and ordered his enforcer Lusius Quietus to "clean them out" of the province. Quietus achieved this by the straightforward means of a massacre.

Some legions were withdrawn from Mesopotamia under the able Quintus Marcius Turbo to confront the emergency and support the civilian power. The affected territories were pacified with some difficulty and the utmost ferocity. In Alexandria the Romans had to fight a pitched battle. The troubles were not over until 117. The impact on the Jewish diaspora was catastrophic. Jews were banished from Cyprus (a measure still in force a century later); they also appear to have vanished from the Egyptian and Cyrenian countrysides, and largely from Alexandria.

So far as Trajan was concerned, the Jewish rebellion was bad enough, but worse was to come. On his arrival at Babylon he learned that an insurgency had broken out in all the territories he had conquered. Legions were sent in every direction to meet the crisis. There were three theaters—Armenia, Mesopotamia, and Babylonia. The Armenians had found a replacement for Parthamasiris, another nephew of the king of kings, and although he lost his life in battle with the Romans, his son picked up the baton—to good effect. From a position of military strength, he asked the Roman commander for an armistice, and it was given. Subsequently, Trajan granted him a part of Armenia in return for a peace agreement. It is all too evident that the emperor had overextended himself and did not have the forces to retain his easy conquests.

Another general was defeated and killed in Mesopotamia, but (as well as killing Jews) Lusius Quietus recaptured a number of cities in the province, including the capital of Osrhoene (for Abgarus and his charming son had turned coat).

Finally, down in the south the thriving metropolis of Seleucia, on the Mesopotamian side of the Tigris, was sacked and the Romans, led in person by Trajan, won a great battle outside Ctesiphon. Nonetheless, the emperor could recognize reality. For the time being at least, he decided to cut his losses and pull back from the new provinces, spinning a humbling defeat into victory.

In 117, the Romans managed to find yet another member of the Arsacid clan, a certain Parthemaspates, and invited him to accept the Parthian throne. It took a bribe for him to accept this dangerous promotion. From a high platform erected on a plain not far from the Parthian winter capital, the emperor addressed a large assembly of Romans and Parthians and described "in grandiloquent language" all that he had achieved. The prince prostrated himself before Trajan, who placed the royal diadem on his head.

A coin of the day shows the emperor crowning Parthemaspates while a personification of Parthia kneels beside them. The legend reads proudly *rex Parthis datus,* "a king is given to the Parthians." A more honest assessment of the situation was given in a letter Trajan wrote to the Senate.

> So great and so boundless is this land and so immeasurable the distances that separate it from Rome that we do not have the reach to administer it, but let us present them with a king subject to the power of the Romans.

An attempt was made to rescue something from the debacle. If Rome was ever to project its power again beyond the Tigris, it was essential to recover the citadel of Hatra, which controlled a strategic road leading east to Babylon. Trajan placed himself in charge of the siege. It was a hard place to capture, for there were running springs inside its walls but little water in the surrounding desert.

The emperor was on his horse watching a failed cavalry attack and, although he had removed his imperial uniform, was recognized because of his "majestic gray head." An archer shot at him and killed a cavalryman in his escort. The weather was hot and wet, with rain, hail, and thunder. Whenever the soldiers ate, flies settled on their food and drink. Hatra refused to fall. Eventually Trajan lost heart and left. A little later he began to feel ill.

A bronze bust of the emperor, beautifully preserved, used to hang on a wall in the public baths in Ankyra (today's Ankara). It was made about this time by a fine and candid sculptor who, in place of the haughty, fleshy features of the usual official portraits, reveals a lined, worn face—the very image of disappointment. The adventure was over.

XIV

THE AFFAIR OF THE FOUR EX-CONSULS

. . .

From today's distant standpoint, Hadrian vanishes from sight during the Parthian war. He is not listed as an army commander, though presumably he accompanied Trajan on campaign and was responsible for some unglamorous but essential duty, such as the maintenance of almost impossibly long supply lines through inhospitable country. Dio Cassius records him at this time as being the emperor's companion, *comes Augusti,* "sharing his daily life"; but that is all we are told. Then, suddenly, he is back, center stage.

More bad news arrived at the depressed imperial headquarters. Serious disorder had broken out in the Danube provinces, from which substantial forces had been incautiously borrowed. The eastern expedition was threatening to loosen the bonds that held the empire together. Trajan appointed one of his best generals, Gaius Julius Quadratus Bassus, to restore order. An imperial administrator promoted on merit, he was a Galatian and related to one of those onetime royal families who (like Philopappus in Athens) had Romanized themselves when their kingdoms had been annexed and made provinces. He knew Dacia very well, for he had fought successfully in the Dacian wars.

At the time Bassus was governor of Syria. This was a frontline position in light of the insurgency and the more or less simultaneous Jewish revolt, and a competent successor was required. Trajan selected Hadrian. For the first time since the consulship, he was being given a proper job where he could display his talents for all to see.

This was not all. Hadrian was promised the consulship for 118. The story went the rounds that Plotina used her influence with the emperor to win him the appointment. According to the *Historia Augusta,* Hadrian was no novice himself in the dark art of palace politics. Well known for his promiscuity, he had no qualms in deploying his sexuality to secure advancement.

> Widespread rumor asserted that he had bribed Trajan's freedmen, had cultivated his boy favorites and had frequent sexual relations with them during the periods when he was an inner member of the court.

It looked very much as if the succession to Trajan, if he were to die now, was settled. Unsurprisingly, this stirred Hadrian's critics into action. Although we have no details, his enemies at court, Palma and Celsus, came under suspicion of planning a coup d'état and fell from grace. Hadrian's position was further strengthened.

The emperor's illness worsened. He was intending a fresh attack on Mesopotamia, but he was obliged to leave the front and withdraw to Antioch. Within the constraints of medical knowledge in the classical world, or (more accurately) ignorance, Dio Cassius gives a good description of Trajan's symptoms:

> The blood, which descends every year into the lower parts of the body, was in his case checked in its flow. He had also suffered a stroke, so that a portion of his body was paralyzed, and he was dropsical all over.

In modern terms, Trajan was suffering from peripheral edema, or water in tissues, and hemostasis in his legs, or halting of the blood flow. The cause of these symptoms, and of the stroke, appears to have been congestive heart failure, possibly caused by high blood pressure. He may have been genetically predisposed to the disease, but the stresses and strains of campaigning and his insistence on sharing the privations of his men must also have taken their toll. The prognosis was poor, as will have been apparent to anyone with access to the emperor.

Trajan was of a different opinion; he was sure, however unreasonably, that he had been poisoned. If so, could he guess by whom? If he considered the history of his assassinated predecessors, the only possible conclusion was that their deaths were inside jobs. The killers were family members, servants, or guards. Claudius, it was said, received poisoned mushrooms at the hands of his wife; and Domitian's wife had joined the conspiracy against her husband. So the fact of the emperor's suspicions may mean that he had begun to distrust his household, perhaps even the faithful Plotina.

The decision was taken for the emperor to return to Rome. If he were to die in Antioch, he would be the first emperor to do so outside Italy, and Trajan or his advisers may have sought to avoid this luckless eventuality. In any event, his condition deteriorated further, and after two or three days at sea the imperial party put in at the port of Selinus on the Cilician coast, once the haunt of pirates.

Trajan's life was approaching its end. It was said that he intended to send a list of likely candidates to the Senate and ask *them* to choose a new emperor. Perhaps an undated anecdote of Dio Cassius' took place in these days. Apparently Trajan at dinner asked his guests to name ten men who were capable of being sole ruler; after a moment's pause, he corrected himself. "I mean nine, for I have one name already—Servianus."

Whatever the truth of this, his sickness overcame him and he was no longer able to conduct public business. An attack of diarrhea, perhaps an infection caught on campaign, finally killed the emperor. Something had to be done. Plotina—aided and abetted by the city prefect, Attianus, and (we may suppose) the other Augusta, Matidia, made sure that an heir was produced before the death was announced. Dio writes:

> My father, Apronianus, who was governor of Cilicia, had ascertained accurately the whole story, and he used to relate the various incidents, in particular stating that the death of Trajan was concealed for several days in order that Hadrian's adoption might be announced first.
>
> This was shown also by Trajan's letters to the senate, for they were signed, not by him, but by Plotina, although she had not done this in any previous instance.

The empress went further, said the rumormongers. In a darkened bedroom, an impostor stood in for the lifeless Trajan and whispered commands in a tired voice for the adoption of Hadrian.

Whether or not Trajan himself agreed to the succession of Hadrian, it was essential that news of the decision be sent to Rome with all possible speed. For the sake of appearances, there should be as long a delay as possible before the emperor's demise was announced. Arrangements were made for the Rome mint to issue coinage celebrating the adoption, for dissemination throughout the empire. A gold piece showed Trajan Augustus wearing a laurel wreath on one side and Hadrian, also laureled, on the other, with the inscription *Hadriano Traiano Caesari,* or "Hadrian, son of Trajan Caesar." This was the first time the *cognomina* "Augustus" and "Caesar" were separated, with the former signifying the emperor and the latter the publicly announced heir and junior partner in government, as was to be the custom during the rest of the history of the empire.

On August 9 the beneficiary of this scheming, waiting impotently in Antioch, received his letter of adoption. If it is true that Trajan was already dead, he was surely told that as well. A few more days of patience were required. On the night of August 11 he experienced a portent. He climbed Mount Casius in order to see the sunrise (a very Hadrianic project, for most Romans were far too practical to waste energy on a fine view). A storm struck as Hadrian was preparing a sacrifice and lightning flashed down, striking both the victim and an attendant but leaving Hadrian unharmed and, it is reported, unfrightened. The event signified that he was serenely ready for his great promotion, and at last, on the following day, the official announcement of the end of the reign reached him. The little boy from Baetica, the Graeculus, had at last attained the purple. He had had to wait a long time. The new emperor was forty-one years old.

A sad, strange footnote to the intrigues at Selinus has been discovered in modern times. It is the gravestone of a certain Marcus Ulpius Phaedimus, which reads:

To [the memory of] Marcus Ulpius Phaedimus, imperial freedman, sommelier and head butler of the deified Trajan; chief *lictor* [official attendant of senior Roman officeholders] and secretary for grants and promotions. He lived for twenty-eight years and died at Selinus on August 12 in the consulships of Niger and Apronianus [117: this Apronianus was not connected with Dio]. His remains were removed [to Rome, where the gravestone was found] by permission of the College of Pontiffs after an atonement sacrifice [*piaculo*] had been made in the consulships of Catullinus and Aper [130].

Much can be deduced from this text, but the heart of a mystery remains. From our knowledge of Trajan's tastes, we can guess that Phaedimus, originally a slave, was an attractive young man. He was certainly an important one, for his duties gave him easy access to the emperor's person.

Two questions arise. Is it not a curious coincidence that Phaedimus died on the very day that Hadrian received the announcement of Trajan's death? And why did it take twelve years before his body was returned to Rome?

If the immediate cause of Trajan's demise (compounding his heart condition) was an infection contracted out east, then perhaps Phaedimus fell victim to it too, alongside his master. Conceivably (but certainly no more) he killed himself from grief. However, the delay in removing his remains is strange.

The only rational explanation is that some scandal attached to the dead man's name, for which a discreet silence, a forgetting, was the right response. So the trail leads to Attianus and Plotina. If there was truth in the rumor of subterfuges, a loyal Phaedimus may have known too much, seen too much to permit his survival. Liquidated to protect Plotina's credibility, the sooner he, and even his very existence, was forgotten, the better.

Hadrian needed to take swift, firm action, or other governors with armies under their command would themselves be tempted to bid for the purple. The memory of the Year of the Four Emperors was still green. He presented himself to his legions, who hailed him as emperor without demur. Hadrian was careful to be generous and gave the men—

and doubtless the rest of the army throughout the empire—a "double donative," or bonus.

The Senate needed delicate handling, for it treasured its constitutional right to approve the appointment of a new head of state. Hadrian drafted a polite, carefully worded letter in which he sought divine honors for Trajan. He apologized that he had not left the Senate the opportunity to decide on his accession. He explained: "The unseemly haste of the troops in acclaiming me emperor was due to the belief that the state could not be without an emperor."

The gesture seems to have been appreciated. He received the Senate's reply a few weeks later, in September. They had voted unanimously to deify the *optimus princeps* and added numerous other honors. So far as Hadrian was concerned, they offered him the high title of *pater patriae,* father of the people. He declined, taking Augustus' view that this was one honor that had to be *earned;* he would defer acceptance until he had some real achievements to his credit.

He was also awarded a Triumph—to mark Trajan's victories. He declined the offer, but because the pretense of success had to be preserved, Hadrian authorized one for the late *princeps*. Instead of the man himself, an effigy would, unusually, preside over the celebrations and ride in the triumphal chariot.

Coins were quickly issued to disseminate an image of benevolent continuity. One gold piece showed Trajan handing a globe to Hadrian, signifying the transfer of the rulership of the world. In another appears the image of the phoenix, the wonder bird of Egyptian legend. When it dies it burns itself on a pyre and from its ashes its successor arises, which then buries its parent's remains. The phoenix was an image of continual renewal—and Hadrian the new link in an eternal chain. A third coin from early in the reign reprises the phoenix theme, adding the more ambitious claim that the "Golden Age" had returned.

The dowager empress and Hadrian's mother-in-law, Matidia, received a due reward in the coinage; they share a splendidly preserved aureus (in the British Museum's collection) in which a bust of Plotina is partnered by one of Matidia. The message was clear: Trajan's women were going to remain key members of the imperial household.

Perhaps the most remarkable is a coin with two obverses—that is, one side carries a head of Trajan and the other of Hadrian, both laureled. What was unprecedented was the latter's short-cut beard. Those who met him from day to day were familiar with this artful innovation; as he well knew, in civilian dress it made him look like a Greek, and when wearing armor, like a down-to-earth soldier. Until his accession, emperors' faces, whether in statuary or on coins, had been clean-shaven. Now the fashion changed: men in every corner of the empire looked at their money and discarded their razors.

The elderly Attianus was fiercely protective of his onetime ward and wrote to him from Selinus warning of enemies who would do their best to ensure that the new reign was stillborn. In its abbreviating manner, the *Historia Augusta* provides a less-than-helpful précis:

> [He] advised him by letter in the first few days of his rule to put to death [Quintus] Baebius Macer, the prefect of the city, in case he opposed his elevation to power, also [Manius] Laberius Maximus, then in exile on an island under suspicion of designs on the throne, and likewise [Caius Calpurnius] Crassus Frugi [Licinianus].

Laberius carried substantial political weight. A senior figure, he made his name under Domitian and had distinguished himself in Trajan's Dacian wars. He was that increasingly rare thing in a multicultural court, an Italian, and more than that—a true Latin from Lanuvium, an ancient city near Rome in the Alban Hills. Nothing is known of his plotting, but he may have been implicated in the disgraces of Palma and Celsus. Also a banished man, Crassus labored under the dangerous disadvantage of an ancient aristocratic name. He appears to have been a serial conspirator, against Nerva as well as Trajan.

Emperors often removed favorites or relatives who had fallen from grace to one or other of the many tiny islands that lie off the Italian coast. Expelled from the Senate, these isolated and impotent captives seldom returned to public life. Why Attianus should have particularly feared this pair is unclear; as guard prefect in attendance on the emperor he would have seen secret reports on suspicious activity by dissidents, but perhaps he was being overcautious.

Baebius Macer was a different matter. He was *praefectus urbi,* prefect of the city of Rome; a combination of chief of police and mayor, the *praefectus* was responsible for law and order and had jurisdiction in criminal matters. He was of a scholarly disposition and a stickler for what he saw to be right. He was not only in a powerful position, but was likely to take a dim view of any constitutional irregularities as a new regime tried to establish its authority. Attianus had reason to fear a man without the moral flexibility for which the times called.

Hadrian disagreed. Whatever the guilt or innocence of those accused, this was not the moment for a ruler who had not yet established himself to put senior politicians to death. It was too soon to judge loyalties, and he turned down Attianus' request. To make his position clear publicly, he wrote again to the Senate. Among many high-minded sentiments,

he swore that he would do nothing against the public interest, nor would he put to death any senator, and he invoked destruction on himself if he should violate these promises in any way.

The prefect complied with the emperor's decision—or at least gave the appearance of doing so. Crassus unwisely left his island, so the official story went, and his keeper had him put to death. The emperor's writ did not yet run reliably.

Plotina and Matidia, accompanied by Attianus, boarded ship with Trajan's body and set sail to Antioch and the new emperor. Hadrian went out to meet them, probably at Seleucia, and viewed the remains. These were then cremated and the imperial party took ship for Rome. They carried the ashes with them and eventually they were laid to rest in the small burial chamber at the foot of Trajan's Column.

As autumn set in, embassies began arriving at Antioch bearing letters of congratulations from municipalities across the empire. Each needed a written answer, which would be taken home and proudly reproduced in stone in every main square. The *princeps* wrote, in formulaic mode, to the Youth Association of Pergamum:

> Noting from your letter, and through the ambassador Claudius Cyrus, the great joy you openly feel in our succession, I consider such sentiments to be indicative of good men. Farewell.

Celebrations were staged all over the Roman world, some of them elaborate. But in Antioch, merrymaking was the last thing on Hadrian's agenda. Fresh and insecure on the throne, he impulsively had the Castalian springs in the pleasure gardens of Daphne blocked up with a huge mass of stone; he did not want anyone else to receive the same message from the oracular waters that he had.

The empire was breaking up. Everywhere the enemies of Rome could not resist exploiting the tempting coincidence of an imperial military setback and an imperial death. The *Historia Augusta* summed up the situation:

> The nations that Trajan had conquered began to revolt; the Moors, too, were on the attack, and the Sarmatians were waging war, the Britons were running out of Roman control, Egypt was hard pressed by riots, and finally Libya and Palestine were showing the spirit of rebellion.

Within a few days of assuming power, the emperor took the two most important, and bitterly controversial, decisions of his entire reign. One of them was tactical and the other strategic. Neither was improvised, but must have been the product of hard thought.

Long imperial frontiers required a large standing army, and paying for this was extremely expensive, and new provinces meant new garrisons. The army was the state's largest single cost. There was also a limit to the available manpower that could be safely withdrawn from economically productive activity. The technology of warfare, the logistical difficulty of maintaining extended supply chains, and the slowness of long-range communications placed limits on the size of territory that a central government would find manageable. It is true that Rome ruled with a light touch and expected local elites to manage the day-to-day affairs of provincial towns and cities. However, government business seems to have grown inexorably.

In addition, it was not at all obvious that the benefits, the profits, that would accrue from new conquests would make the effort entailed worthwhile, at least in the medium term. Much of the land contiguous with the empire was ecologically marginal and, with the exception of the Parthian and Dacian empires, economically unrewarding—neither worth the trouble of annexing nor the expense of administering. What, one might ask, would be the point of taking over little-populated Scotland?

The historian Appian, who lived through the reigns of Trajan and Hadrian, made the point well.

> The Romans have aimed to preserve their empire by the exercise of prudence rather than extend their dominion indefinitely over poverty-stricken and profitless tribes of barbarians.

Emperors, needing to balance their books, settled for the minimum military establishment consistent with safety. They felt they could not afford a mobile reserve ready to meet crises as and when they occurred. (Such a reserve, when unemployed, would also present them with a potential threat to their own power.)

This parsimony had two main consequences. First, any military defeat would create a hole in the empire's defenses that would be difficult to plug—as Augustus had found when three legions were destroyed on the Rhine frontier in A.D. 9. Domitian had been forced to withdraw troops from Britannia to meet trouble in Dacia. Second, aggressive war, even when victorious, was just as dangerous to imperial stability. Trajan had raised additional legions during his Dacian campaigns (bringing the total establishment up to thirty); however, for his Parthian expedition, he still had to order legions from Pannonia to join him in the east, imperiling the Danube frontier. Once the expedition had been seen to fail, enemies of Rome on every side had seized the opportunity for rebellion. In fact, just to maintain the status quo was almost too much for the legions.

So military and financial reality argued against further enlargement of the empire. Intermittently, emperors recognized this. Augustus, who had been an out-and-out expansionist for most of his career, advised his successor, Tiberius, to stay within existing frontiers. Tacitus' *Annals,* a savage but authoritative study of the early empire, had recently appeared (perhaps published between 115 and 117, but possibly some years later). He reports that the aged Augustus produced a list of the empire's military resources very near the end of his life; the document was "all catalogued by Augustus in his own hand, with a final clause . . . advising the restriction of the empire within its present frontiers." Hadrian may well have seen a copy of, even read, the historian's masterpiece. In any event, he must have known of the policy. The first *princeps* being a man whom he greatly admired, he accepted his century-old advice without hesitation. Beneath the rhetoric of attack, Domitian, too, seems to have recognized the dangers of endless advance.

It was against this background that Hadrian issued orders to immediately abandon his predecessor's three new provinces—Armenia, Mesopotamia, and Assyria—and to regroup permanently behind Rome's traditional border, the Euphrates. Although this decision came as a great shock, it is evident that the dying Trajan, the aggressive warrior, had himself realized that a pull-back was inevitable. Hadrian deposed Trajan's puppet king, and as a polite compensation installed him in Osrhoene, from which Abgarus and son had been ejected. The emperor explained his decision by quoting from one of his favorite old Roman authors—Cato the Censor. In 167 B.C. Rome defeated the Macedonians with some difficulty and the Senate was considering what it should do about them. Cato pronounced: "Because it is impossible to keep them under our care, they will have to be left independent."

The emperor also meant to abandon Dacia, for the conquest of which many Roman lives had been sacrificed, but he was persuaded to reconsider. The original population had been killed or dispersed and their place taken by immigrants from the Roman empire. It would be unacceptable to hand them over to the untender mercies of their barbarian neighbors.

Hadrian went much further than pulling out of Parthia. So far as we know no formal announcement was made; it was unnecessary, and would have been incautious, to do so. However, a new long-term strategy can be inferred from his pacific behavior throughout the rest of the reign: Rome was to abjure military expansion of any kind in the future. Negotiation was to replace ultimatum. Trajan's eastern adventure had been the last straw, showing that while it was possible to project military power temporarily beyond the frontiers of the empire, it was difficult to preserve territorial gains.

The withdrawals are evidence of Hadrian's clear-sightedness and political courage, but they deeply angered many senior personalities. Opinion in Italy had fed on a diet of victories and as yet had no clear idea that Parthia had not, after all, been conquered. And even though Trajan's failure was common knowledge in leading circles, the ethos of aggression was too ingrained to accept that the days of *imperium sine fine* were over.

A contemporary observer summed up the conventional view. Publius Annius Florus was a poet and rhetorician from northern Africa and the author of a brief sketch for schoolboys of Roman history, largely drawn from Livy. In it he compares Rome to a human individual as it grows up, reaches maturity, and subsequently attains old age. So he identifies childhood with the rule of kings, the conquest of Italy with its youth, and manhood with the late Republic.

> From the time of Caesar Augustus down to our own age there has been a period of not much less than two hundred years, during which, owing to the inactivity of the emperors, the Roman people, as it were, grew old and lost its potency, save that under the rule of Trajan it again stirred its arms and, contrary to general expectation, again renewed its vigor—with youth, as it were, restored.

And now the next *princeps* was reverting to the unacceptable and passive norm, or so the elites angrily regarded his actions. As often happens, military adventures abroad lend stability and popularity to governments at home—provided that they bring victory. Lack of success in this regard helped seal the fate of Domitian. Would it do the same for Hadrian?

● ● ●

The emperor was too busy for hypothetical questions. The indispensable Marcius Turbo was bringing the Jewish revolt to a victorious conclusion in Egypt and Cyrene. But now the Greek community in Alexandria started rioting against the defeated Jews.

The emperor replaced Trajan's governor with a more competent and energetic figure, Quintus Rammius Martialis. It says much for his rapid decisiveness that Rammius was in his post on or before August 25, just over a fortnight since the news of Trajan's death had reached Antioch.

Hadrian himself probably paid a quick visit to Egypt. There was great economic distress in the country, and he rapidly produced generous and carefully thought-out measures that provided tax relief for tenant farmers. From now on assessments would be made on the actual agricultural yield rather than land value (the *tributum soli*). It was far more in character for him to investigate this situation directly, rather than rely at a distance on the recommendations of advisers.

It would have been too provocative to visit Alexandria, but he sent a Greek intellectual in his service who was known for his shrewdness and sharpness of wit, Valerius Eudaemon, as procurator, or financial director, for the city's local administration; his task was to be the emperor's eyes and ears.

Somewhere in Egypt—perhaps the border town of Pelusium or Heliopolis, at the southern head of the Nile delta—Hadrian presided over the trial, or at least some kind of official inquiry or hearing, of some hotheaded Alexandrian Greeks, led by a spokesman called Paul. A Jewish delegation was also present. From the reported proceedings it is possible to suppose the following savage sequence of events. After the failure of the Jewish revolt, many Jews were imprisoned and the triumphant Greeks put on a satirical stage show lampooning the rebel "king," Lukuas. Some of them sang songs criticizing the emperor for deciding to resettle Jewish survivors of the revolt in an area of the city from which they could easily launch new attacks on the native population.

The irritated governor (Rammius' predecessor) ordered the Greeks to produce their "*opera-bouffe* monarch." Unfortunately this "bringing forth" also brought many Greek rioters onto the streets. A Jewish witness asserted an unprovoked attack on a defeated community. "They dragged us out of prison and wounded us." Charges and countercharges followed. The Jews said of the Greeks: "Sire, they lie."

Hadrian was inclined to agree. He told the Greeks that the prefect was right to ban the carrying of weapons and that he disapproved of the satire on Lukuas. He advised the Jews to restrict their hatred to their actual persecutors and not to loathe all Alexandrian Greeks indiscriminately. This evenhanded treatment came as a pleasant surprise to the defeated insurgents.

At about the same time Hadrian dismissed the governor of Judaea. This was Trajan's mysterious and ferocious favorite, Lusius Quietus, who was also removed from command of his Moorish cavalry. According to the *Historia Augusta,* "he had fallen under suspicion of having designs on the throne," but this was an unlikely ambition for a tribal chieftain now an old man. More probably, he was feared as a potential "kingmaker" for a serious rival to Hadrian.

Lusius had been sent to Judaea to help suppress the Jewish revolt, for the Jewish community there had recovered, at least partially, from the destruction wrought by the Romans almost fifty years previously. He came to the task fresh from butchering the Jews in Mesopotamia, and his removal delighted the diaspora.

Hadrian was rewarded. In some anti-Roman oracular verses, originating among the Jews of Alexandria and widely read in the eastern Mediterranean, an emperor received a rare compliment.

> And after him shall rule
> Another man, with silver helmet decked;
> And unto him shall be the name of a sea;
> And he shall be a man the best of all
> And in all things discreet.

The name of the relevant sea is the Adriatic, so the reference is to Hadrian. Here at last, from the point of view of battered Jewry, the catastrophe of the revolt had given way, against every expectation, to a well-wishing ruler.

• • •

In early October the emperor left Antioch and proceeded urgently northward, with the troubled Danube provinces as his eventual destination. Meanwhile, Lusius Quietus' horsemen returned discontented to Mauretania, where they stirred up an anti-Roman revolt. The emperor immediately dispatched Turbo, fresh from his Egyptian success, to deal with the disturbance.

The worst possible news arrived. Quadratus Bassus was dead. We do not know if he fell in battle or was felled by natural causes but the depth of the loss was revealed by the arrangements for the long journey from Dacia to the dead man's home city, Pergamum. They matched what a prince of the blood might expect, with a military escort for the cortege and civic welcomes whenever it arrived at a town of any size and importance. The tomb was paid for at the public expense. In effect, Bassus received the Roman equivalent of a modern state funeral.

Fortunately, Quintus Pompeius Falco, a friend of Hadrian's, had been governor for at least two years of the huge Danubian province of Lower Moesia, originally a narrow strip south of the Danube and now also encompassing the kingdom of the Roxolani, Dacia's neighbor on the river's northern side. He was able to hold the line temporarily.

The emperor, chased by continuing congratulations, made his way to Thrace or perhaps Lower Moesia itself, and discussed with Falco what was to be done. He decided to appoint the reliable Gaius Avidius Nigrinus, who had been imperial legate in Achaea during Hadrian's stay in Athens in 112; the two men must have met then and had presumably got on well together.

Once again he came to the conclusion that it was pointless trying to hold on to territory that Rome could defend only at a vast expenditure of treasure and lives. So he instructed Falco and his legions to withdraw from the lands of the Roxolani in eastern Dacia (leaving only a narrow *cordon sanitaire* north of the river, named Lower Pannonia). The superstructure of Apollodorus' great bridge across the Danube was dismantled—probably only a temporary measure to foil a possible enemy attack. Under no circumstances could Hadrian's now controversial reputation survive a barbarian incursion into well-established provinces.

The demolition may have been a wise precaution, but it was also an unhappy metaphor for a perceived failure of nerve.

Hadrian reached an agreement with the king of the Roxolani, increasing Rome's ongoing subsidy (the price Trajan had been willing to pay for acquiescence in annexation), granting him Roman citizenship and, it is to be assumed, "most favored nation" status. He took the name Publius Aelius Rasparaganus, the "Aelius" showing respect for his patron. He may also have made Hadrian a valuable and soon to be much-loved gift. It was about now that the emperor's favorite horse, Borysthenes, was a colt. He was named after the river Borysthenes (today's Dnieper), which flowed through the land of the Alani, a tribe related to the Roxolani and their near neighbor. This could be the moment when horse and rider met for the first time.

As an official Friend of the Roman People, the king would rule a buffer state that kept the empire safe from unruly barbarians in the northern hinterland beyond the Roxolani—at a cost much lower than that of garrisoning a reluctant province.

A sensible-enough deal, one might think. But much of the Roman elite never forgave Hadrian for what they saw as pusillanimous behavior. Even half a century later, the rhetorician and friend of emperors Marcus Cornelius Fronto felt strongly enough about the issue to say acidly of Hadrian that he was "energetic enough in mobilizing his friends and eloquently addressing his army." He trained his legions "with amusing games in the camp rather than with swords and shields: [he was] a general the like of whom the army never afterward saw."

These sneers about a competent soldier were wide of the mark. Although designed to stress by contrast the supposed talents of a later emperor, they must have been credible to be worth making, and they illustrate the scorn that Hadrian's new strategy aroused.

It was against this gloomy backcloth that a strange and bloodstained sequence of events unfolded during 118. Attianus, the Praetorian Guard prefect, now back in Rome with the Augustas, laid before the Senate the details of a plot against the emperor and persuaded it to vote for the executions of the conspirators. These were four in number and of high seniority, for each of them was a former consul and had been close to Trajan.

Two of them, Celsus and Palma, were already in Hadrian's bad books: as already noted, they had fallen from grace in a court intrigue toward the end of the previous reign. Presumably they were living in retirement in Italy. Then there was the dismissed Lusius Quietus, traveling from his last posting in Judaea to an unknown destination—perhaps his homeland of Mauretania.

The fourth guilty man was the new governor of Dacia. Gaius Avidius Nigrinus was a senior politician and general, and a respected member of the Roman social scene. He appears in a very favorable light in Pliny's letters, as an intelligent public official dedicated to good governance. Once, when tribune of the people, he read out to the Senate

a well-phrased statement of great importance. In this he complained that legal counsel sold their services, faked lawsuits for money, settled them by collusion, and made a boast of the large regular incomes to be made by robbery of their fellow citizens.

He was that useful thing in politics, "a safe pair of hands," and Trajan had sent him to Greece on a delicate mission to resolve a three-hundred-year-old boundary dispute between Delphi and her neighbors.

Interestingly, Nigrinus had a distant family connection with the one-time Stoic opposition, for his uncle had been a friend of the Republican martyr Thrasea Paetus, one of Nero's most celebrated victims. Perhaps his hostility to Hadrian owed something to the political idealism that Nerva and Trajan's commitment to the rule of law and senatorial cooperation had largely made redundant.

But Nigrinus' motives may not have been so pure. His performance as governor of Dacia seems not to have satisfied the emperor, uncomfortably on the spot or at least close at hand. Hadrian brought his brief tenure to an end and replaced him with Turbo, who had taken little time in suppressing the Berber disturbances in Mauretania. He was given temporary command of both Dacia and Pannonia, with the obvious remit of reorganizing the frontier defenses after the withdrawals. This was a daring appointment, for Turbo was only an *eques,* and so strictly speaking ineligible for a post reserved for senators. But for Hadrian merit outweighed class.

So each member of the offending quartet had grounds for resentment; Palma's and Celsus' careers had been abruptly terminated in the recent past, and Nigrinus and Lusius Quietus had just lost their jobs. But if they all had motives for disaffection, it is not altogether certain that they acted on them. Some observers believed that they were set up. Dio Cassius, writing only a century later, remarked that they were victimized "in reality because they had great influence and enjoyed wealth and fame."

What was the actual offense of which they were accused? Two versions of the story have come down to us. According to the *Historia Augusta,* Nigrinus and the others planned an attempt on the emperor's life while he was conducting a sacrifice; but Dio claims that the occasion was a hunt. The contradiction is only an apparent one, for (as we have seen on page 23) hunts were preceded and followed by sacrifices to the gods—especially to Diana, goddess of the chase, and if the catch was good, to the goddess of victory. Hadrian was passionate about the sport, so we can be sure that he often went hunting with his *amici* as a relaxation from affairs of state and the crisis threatening the empire.

Two interlinked problems arise. First, the only alleged conspirator traveling with the emperor at the time was Nigrinus; the others were many miles away. Second, three of them were executed at their country houses in Italy—Palma at Tarracina (now Terracina), an ancient Latin town some thirty-odd miles southeast of Rome, Celsus at Baiae (today's Baia), a fashionable seaside resort for Rome's superrich in the bay of Naples, and Nigrinus at Faventia (modern Faenza) in the Po Valley in northern Italy, presumably his hometown. Lusius was put to death while on the move somewhere in the eastern provinces or northern Africa.

If we assume that there really was a plot to kill Hadrian, how can these data be reconciled with it? Why was Nigrinus not arrested at once in the wake of a failed attack, and why was he allowed to go home? Perhaps the attackers were hired men (legionaries or locals) and it was not immediately obvious who their employer was. But not only would it be hard to recruit people for such a risky mission and control them, but it would be unusual for a noble Roman, especially a distinguished public servant with a link to the brave Stoic opponents of the imperial system, to farm out the cutting off of a tyrant to anonymous others.

Here is a feasible scenario. A hunt was chosen for the attempt, for on no other occasion were armed men routinely allowed in an emperor's presence, apart from his guards. Nigrinus and some others of like mind in the party decided to strike down Hadrian with their hunting weapons at the ceremonies either at the beginning or the end of a hunt in Thrace or Moesia. Something held them back from making the attack—Nigrinus could have been ill or, most likely, Hadrian turned out to be too well guarded and the intended assassins too few in number for them to have a realistic chance of survival, even if they managed to destroy their victim. So nothing happened, and nothing was noticed.

The scheme came to light only a little later, when the dismissed Nigrinus had returned to Italy and private life. One or more plotters may have revealed it for irrecoverable reasons, or perhaps a servant in the know did so in the expectation of reward. More probably, their correspondence was intercepted, for, if they were to agree on their plans, the principals must have communicated with one another during the weeks following Hadrian's accession.

Such interception would have been no accident, for Trajan had accessed the public courier or postal service to keep himself informed about "state business"; Hadrian himself quietly put in place Rome's first organized secret service (before his time, emperors had indeed made use of informers and spies but in an ad hoc manner). To create a new bureau would have been politically controversial, so he added a confidential codicil to the job descriptions of the already-existing *frumentarii*. These were commissary agents in charge of organizing army supplies and were well placed to gather information about the activities of Roman officials in the provinces. Whether the new service was already in place so early in the reign is uncertain, but its establishment demonstrates Hadrian's abiding interest in uncovering the unspoken concerns of the senatorial elite. The exposure of the Nigrinus conspiracy thanks to secret surveillance could have been what prompted him to make use of the *frumentarii*.

A variant explanation for what happened may be found in the career of a German-born centurion, Marcus Calventius Viator. His name appears on two altars, one found in Dacia and the other in Gerasa (today's Jerash City in Jordan). In the first he appears as the training officer of Nigrinus' cavalry bodyguard. The second, ten years on, reveals a remarkable promotion; he is now in charge of the cavalry wing of Hadrian's own imperial bodyguard, the Germanic Batavi whom he inherited from Trajan. Someone close to a traitor could not usually count on a glittering future. Did the emperor take Calventius under his wing as a reward for informing on his commanding officer? It is a tempting speculation.

By a curious chance, the Arabian altar is dedicated to the goddess Diana. It was doubtless in her honor that a hunting party offered up its sacrifice on that dangerous distant day when an emperor was the quarry.

The executions were a political disaster. The fact that senators had been persuaded to vote for them was irrelevant. In their eyes, Hadrian had broken the spirit if not the letter of his guarantee of their personal security, foreshadowing a return to the days of Domitian. Although far away by the Danube, Hadrian immediately recognized the damage that had been done. Disaffection in the ruling class could bring about a return of the Stoic opposition and undo the political settlement, based on consent, that Nerva and Trajan had established.

At about this time the historian Tacitus was finishing the composition of his *Annals,* and a late passage expresses a melancholy exhaustion with his history of imperial victims during the time of the early emperors; he may also have been covertly alluding to the bloodstained opening of Hadrian's reign. "This slavish passivity, this torrent of wasted bloodshed far from active service, wearies, depresses, and paralyzes the mind."

Hadrian tried to extricate himself from blame. It was all Attianus' fault and what had been done had been done against his own will. Was the emperor protesting too much—or telling the plain truth? It is hard to tell. In a sense, whether or not the quartet did intend the emperor's death is immaterial. They were Hadrian's enemies and potentially dangerous. Perhaps what we have here is a prototype of the murder of Thomas Becket; rather as Henry II's knights made more than was meant of the king's exasperation with his archbishop, so the guard prefect may have guessed at a new emperor's fears, and acted. It is conceivable that he did so without informing his employer, in order to give him the deniability he would need when explaining himself to the Senate.

In any event, there was little Hadrian could do at the moment to retrieve the situation, but the sooner he could calm the provinces and return to Rome, the better.

XV

THE ROAD TO ROME

. . .

Hadrian stood on the bank of the Danube and reviewed his troops. To show how perfectly his Batavians, the imperial horse guard, were trained, he ordered them to swim across the river in full armor. This was something of a party trick, for they had a long tradition of crossing wide expanses of water en masse.

The Batavians had a deserved reputation for ferocity; Tacitus remarked of them: "They are made exclusively for war, like arms and weapons." There were about one thousand of them in the guard and, as intended, they made a daunting impression on the barbarian tribes to the north.

A tombstone found near the Danube celebrates in well-turned Latin verse the achievements of one of these guardsmen, a certain Soranus.

> I was once the most famous of men on the Pannonian shore . . .
> the one who could swim the wide waters of the deep
> Danube, with Hadrian as my judge, in full battle gear.

This was not the man's only skill. He was also an archer who could shoot one arrow in the air and hit it with another, splitting it in two—a feat of which Robin Hood would have been proud.

> No Roman or barbarian could ever defeat me . . .
> It remains to be seen whether anyone else will beat my record.

Who wrote these lines is unknown, but Hadrian was a frequent poet who liked to mark out his life in Greek or Latin meter. It is probable he was the admiring author.

Whatever his critics were saying, safe in their town houses in the capital or relaxing in their country villas, Hadrian understood and liked soldiers and enjoyed military life.

By June 118 the Danube frontier had been redrawn and hostile tribes—for example, the Iazyges on the Hungarian plain—pacified. Hadrian acquired the services of a Iazygian prisoner-of-war, a certain Mastor, who was a skilled huntsman "because of his strength and daring." With his steed, Borysthenes, and his groom both having been recruited from the wild regions north of the Danube, the emperor was equipped to enjoy the dangerous thrills of the chase as never before. His relationship with Mastor became close, and he kept him in his service for the rest of his life.

New governors, friendly to Hadrian, were appointed. Thus, Falco was tackling disturbances in the north of Britannia, and making progress. The Parthians were quiet as they reabsorbed the territory that Trajan had annexed. The brushfires of rebellion had been stamped out.

At last, in June the emperor was ready to leave for the long journey to Rome, confident that the military crisis following the failure of the Parthian expedition and Trajan's death was over. The task now was to pacify his civilian critics at home.

An emperor's entry into Rome on July 9, especially his first, tended to be a grand, noisy event. Hadrian had probably traveled overland from Pannonia to northern Italy, riding down the coast road to Ariminum and then over the Apennines on the via Flaminia.

As he approached the city, he met the consuls and other officeholders, with their guards of *lictors* carrying the axe and rods of *imperium,* who walked out beyond the walls to greet him. They were accompanied by all the senators, dressed in their whitest red-striped togas and leading representatives of the *equites.* Members of the emperor's *clientela,* or client list, were well represented—especially the young sons of senators and *equites* ambitious for public careers. The *praefectus urbi* was in attendance, together with other imperial officials.

The road became a long avenue as it crossed the built-over Campus Martius. He rode past the mausoleum of Augustus; this was now full, and at some point he would need to prepare a burial place for himself. A little farther down was the Ara Pacis, a masterpiece of Roman sculpture, albeit inspired by the reliefs on the Parthenon in Athens; its four walls showed the emperor Augustus and his family in the act of sacrificing to the gods. The altar was a celebration of the peace and prosperity that the empire had conferred on its inhabitants.

Next, a large open space to Hadrian's right gave onto the ruins of the temple to all the gods, the Pantheon, which Augustus' right-hand man, Marcus Vipsanius Agrippa, had erected ninety years previously. It had been burned down in 80. The emperor asked himself if it was not time to rebuild it.

The avenue was reaching its conclusion, passing through an old gate, the Porta Fontinalis. Here Rome's citadel, the Capitol, to the right and a colossal new structure, Trajan's forum and market, paid for from the loot of Dacia, created an architectural defile. The lesser forums of Julius Caesar and Augustus clustered nearby.

The emperor and his entourage entered the city's original central square, the Forum Romanum, and from there ascended the winding road to the summit of the Capitol, where stood the enormous temple of Jupiter Optimus Maximus. A sacrifice was offered in thanks for his safe return to Rome and to mark his assumption of the purple.

The ancient priestly association, the Arvals, met on the Capitol on the same day to mark the happy "arrival of Imperator Caesar Traianus Hadrianus Augustus"; in what must have been a lengthy and messy ceremony, they sacrificed an ox to Jupiter; a cow each to Minerva, the "Public Safety of the Roman People," "Victory," and Vesta, protectress of the city's undying flame; and a bull to Mars. The *princeps* was a new member of the priesthood ex officio, but as a rule he sent his apologies. On this occasion, Hadrian decided to put in an appearance. He was determined to please, and made himself available to everybody.

Hadrian's task was to relaunch his reign. The consuls convened the Senate, probably as early as the next day after his return. The mood on its benches must have been all the more gloomy for the fact that senators themselves had colluded in the deaths of the four ex-consuls. Many could recall the not-so-distant time when Domitian had insisted on their active cooperation when he struck down the final list of Stoic idealists.

The emperor was extremely sensitive to the comments that people were making about his behavior. For him the lesson of Domitian's end was that he had to avoid the vortex of violence and lost trust if he wanted to survive and thrive. Hadrian's reign had opened with violence, and it was essential that he break away from the potentially dire consequences and establish a reputation as a man of peace and legality.

He addressed the Senate as if he were making a speech for the defense at a trial, and declared on oath that he had not ordered the deaths of the four former consuls (later he repeated the denial in his autobiography). He also swore that he would never put a senator to death without the Senate's approval. In this he followed similar assurances given by Trajan and Nerva, and while these were welcome they did not mean very much, for history showed that the Senate routinely bowed to the wishes of an angry *princeps*. His listeners doubtless reserved judgment on the emperor's guilt, but will surely have attended to the passion with which he asserted his good intentions. Time would reveal whether these would translate convincingly into performance. (Somewhat cheekily, next year the emperor issued a coin boasting of his mercifulness: it showed Clemency, personified as a woman sacrificing at an altar.)

No one would begin to believe the emperor's assurance unless something was done about the man he was fingering as the real culprit—the elderly Attianus. The *Historia Augusta* has an odd tale that a murderous Hadrian wanted to do away with his former guardian because he was "unable to endure his power" and was deterred only by his existing notoriety as an executioner. There seems to have been a quarrel, and we can imagine the *princeps* losing his temper—but surely nothing more.

Praetorian prefects held their job for an indefinite period. Emperors fought shy of dismissing them out of hand for fear of trouble from the Guard. With some difficulty Attianus was persuaded to resign his post as prefect. Only an *eques,* he was given the signal honor of *ornamenta consularia*—these were the appurtenances of the consulship, without the post itself. He was not allowed to attend the Senate, but was entitled to sit with former consuls at public banquets and to wear a consul's richly embroidered *toga praetexta* on such occasions. Attianus was kicked upstairs.

Attianus' colleague as prefect was also an old man and sought permission to retire. It is a sign that the emperor was short of experienced and trustworthy talent that he refused to accept the resignation immediately. And who was to replace Attianus? The all-competent Turbo, who in little more than one year had ricocheted around the empire from Parthia, to Egypt, to Mauretania, to Pannonia and Dacia, was a wise choice and he now crowned his career with the top government job to which an *eques* could aspire.

Hadrian introduced a range of reforms designed to boost his popularity. The headline measure was breathtaking—nothing less than a cancellation of all unpaid debts owed by individual citizens to the public treasury (*fiscus* or *aerarium publicum*) and, according to Dio Cassius, to the privy purse (*fiscus privatus*). The period covered was the previous fifteen years.

The announcement was marked by a striking piece of street theater. In the great square of Trajan's forum all the relevant tax documents were assembled and publicly burned, to make it clear that this was a decision that could not be revoked. (Hadrian may have got the idea for the incineration from Augustus, for Suetonius records that in 36 B.C. he had "burned the records of old debts to the treasury, which were by far the most frequent source of blackmail.")

Public opinion was enthusiastic and a celebratory monument was erected on the site of the pyre. The inscription has survived, praising Hadrian,

> who remitted 900 million sesterces owed to the *fisci* and by this generosity was the first and only one of all the emperors to have freed from care not only his present citizens but those of later generations.

A carved relief shows the scene when Praetorian Guards entered the forum carrying wax tablets from the treasury archives. To spread the good news around the world a coin was issued showing a *lictor* setting fire to a pile of bonds in the presence of three taxpayers.

One of the most irritating burdens on local authorities in Italy and elsewhere was the cost of maintaining the government courier service, the *cursus publicus,* where it ran on main roads through their territories. They were obliged to pay for the horses, carriages, and privately owned hotels and hostels that those traveling on official business needed. The *fiscus* now took over financial responsibility for the service.

The "crown gold" was waived for Italy and reduced for the provinces; this was a contribution offered to a new emperor, in theory voluntary and in practice compulsory, to the cost of gold wreaths (in imitation of laurel) for grand imperial events such as triumphs.

A supplementary distribution of free and subsidized grain for citizens living in Rome was made, despite the fact that a generous donative of three aurei (that is, gold pieces worth seventy-five sesterces in total) had already been granted before the emperor's return.

The Italian countryside also benefited from the general largesse. The *alimenta* scheme had been close to Trajan's heart, and, as a gesture to the memory of his adoptive father, Hadrian increased its state funding.

It was essential to offer sweeteners that directly benefited the disaffected senatorial class. Existing rules set the minimum wealth a man had to possess if he wished to enter public life at the highest level at 1 million sesterces. Sometimes senators found themselves in financial difficulties; now Hadrian supplemented their income with an allowance, provided they could show that they were impoverished through no fault of their own.

Public office was expensive, for a consul or a praetor faced a number of necessary expenses (for example, the salaries of his *lictors*) and he was expected to demonstrate his *liberalitas* as a patron. The emperor made gifts of money to many needy officials—in effect, salaries.

Ever since the Proscriptions launched by the young Octavian (before his elevation to the title of Augustus) and Mark Antony in 43 B.C., rulers short of cash tended to execute opponents ostensibly for political or criminal offenses but in fact to confiscate their lands and wealth. Hadrian was determined to avoid that charge in the case of the four former consuls, so he passed a law assigning the property of condemned persons not to the privy purse but to the state *fiscus*. In this way he could demonstrate that the emperor was gaining no private advantage from their deaths.

Hadrian had implemented the first part of Juvenal's gloomy slogan "bread and circuses" by providing cash and grain. It was now time for blood to flow in the arena. To mark his forty-third birthday, January 24, 119, six successive days of gladiatorial games were held; many wild animals were slaughtered too, including one hundred lions and one hundred lionesses. Large numbers of little wooden balls were thrown into the audience: the names of various gifts were written on them—items of food, say, clothing, silver or gold articles, horses, cattle, and slaves—which could be claimed when presenting them later.

The package of reforms succeeded: it was well received and stabilized the new regime. Even if members of the elite were reserving judgment, there was no talk of outright opposition or even noncooperation. Despite a shaky start Hadrian had demonstrated his competence, both militarily and domestically. The empire was quiet and in the Senate no one now had any doubt who was in charge. From managing immediate challenges, the emperor could now take his time and plan a strategy for the longer term.

Hadrian was a man who knew his own mind and was impatient of inefficiency in others, but he also had a disarming talent for admiration. He learned much about the art of government from Trajan, but the true hero among his predecessors was Augustus.

We learn from the Arvals that when the emperor wrote to them in February 118 proposing a co-opted member of the association, "the waxed tablets, fastened with a seal showing the head of Augustus, were opened." For the image on Hadrian's signet ring to have been that of the first *princeps* was an elegantly simple way of acknowledging indebtedness to everyone throughout the empire who mattered. Later, he asked the Senate for permission to hang an ornamental shield, preferably of silver, in Augustus' honor in the Senate.

Ten years into his reign, Hadrian announced to the world that, speaking symbolically, he was a reincarnation of Augustus. He issued a high-value silver coin, a tetradrachm (worth twelve sesterces), with Augustus' head on one side, and on the other an image of himself holding corn ears, signifying prosperity, with the legend *Hadrianus Augustus Pater Patriae Renatus*—"Father of his People, Reborn."

When appointing the heads of his secretariat he chose an *eques,* the biographer Suetonius, to be his *ab epistulis,* the official secretary, who controlled the emperor's correspondence and as such was one of the most influential people at court. A bookish protégé and friend of Pliny, he had made a name for himself ten years or so previously for his *De Viribus Illustribus,* "On Famous Men," a copious collection of brief lives of literary celebrities—grammarians, rhetoricians, poets, and historians.

Suetonius was now working on what was to be his masterpiece, *De Vita Caesarum,* "The Lives of the Caesars." In the biography of Augustus, he writes of an unusual *cognomen* his subject was given as a boy, Thurinus—an allusion to the town of Thurii in southern Italy where his father's family had originated and where his father had won a battle.

> That he was surnamed Thurinus I may assert on very trustworthy evidence, since I once obtained a bronze statuette, representing him as a boy and inscribed with that name in letters of iron almost illegible from age. This I presented to the emperor [Hadrian], who cherishes it among the *Lares* [household gods] of his bedroom.

What was it that Hadrian valued so highly in his predecessor? Not least the conduct of his daily life. Augustus lived with conscious simplicity and so far as he could avoided open displays of his preeminence. A passage from Suetonius is almost echoed by another from the *Historia Augusta.* About Augustus the former observed:

> On the day of a meeting of the Senate he always greeted members in the House and in their seats, calling each man by name without a prompter; and when he left the House, he used to take leave of them in the same manner, while they remained seated. He exchanged social calls with many, and did not cease to attend all their anniversaries.

As for Hadrian, according to the *Historia Augusta,*

> he frequently attended the official functions of praetors and consuls, was present at friends' banquets, visited them twice or three times a day when they were sick, including some who were *equites* and freedmen, revived them with sympathetic words and supported them with advice, and always invited them to his own banquets. In short, he did everything in the style of a private citizen.

Both Augustus and Hadrian made a point of being *civiles principes,* polite autocrats.

It was not enough to placate the upper classes; it was also important to keep happy Rome's urban masses. Audiences at the games were infuriated if an emperor in his imperial box was inattentive and worked on his papers. Nor did they appreciate arrogant behavior on his part. Whenever Augustus was present, he took care to give his entire attention to the gladiatorial displays, animal hunts, and the rest of the bloodthirsty rigmarole. Hadrian followed suit.

He once nearly made a dangerous faux pas. The crowd was baying loudly for some favor or other, which he was unwilling to grant. He ordered the herald to call for silence. This had been Domitian's autocratic way, and the astute herald merely lifted his arm, without uttering a word. The shouting died down. The herald then announced: "That is what he wants." The emperor was not in the least put out, for he realized that by refusing to issue the tactless verbal order the herald had saved him from an odious comparison.

Augustus well understood that to hold power it was not necessary to *show* that one was holding power; in fact, it could be positively damaging to do so. While he was consolidating his authority in the 20s B.C. he held the consulship for eight years in a row. The post no longer commanded executive *imperium* as it had under the Republic, but it remained a great honor. For an emperor to treat it as if it were a permanent office was felt to be insulting, as well as being unnecessary. It also reduced by 50 percent the chance for a senatorial aspirant to become consul *ordinarius* and have "their year" named after him and his colleague. So from

23 B.C. the *princeps* more or less gave up the consulship, with only two more tenures during the rest of a long life.

By contrast, the Flavians were greedy; Vespasian held nine consulships in a ten-year reign, Titus eight, and Domitian a record-breaking seventeen. Trajan was more moderate, spreading six consulships across the reign. Hadrian followed Augustus' example to the letter—that is, once confirmed in place, he abstained. He was consul for the third and last time in 119.

An incoming emperor faced the challenge of making his power effective throughout such a wide domain. In this respect, there was one further characteristic of Augustus' dominance that must have attracted Hadrian's attention. The first *princeps* believed that communications were too slow and subordinates too unreliable for governing from Rome: in his view, he could run the empire only by being on the spot. For many years he spent his time on the move in the provinces, checking, settling, supervising, solving problems. And so did his dear friend and colleague in government, Agrippa. It was only with the onset of age and the coming to maturity of trustworthy young male relatives who could fill his place that Augustus abandoned his travels.

Hadrian's imitation of Augustus made it clear that he intended to rule in an orderly and law-abiding fashion, and his enthusiasm for great men of the past underscored his commitment to traditional *romanitas,* Romanness. It was on these foundations that he would build the achievements of his reign.

Like the first *princeps,* Hadrian looked back to paradigms of ancient virtue to guide modern governance. Augustus liked to see himself as a new Romulus, the second founder of a restored Rome; twelve vultures had flown overhead when he assumed his first consulship in his late teens, just as they had at the city's original establishment in 753 B.C.

Hadrian followed in his footsteps, associating himself with Romulus' peace-loving (and legendary) successor, Numa Pompilius. He had not forgotten those lines from Virgil about Numa that had foretold his imperial future. Known for his religious piety, the king was credited with the creation of Rome's religious institutions and, related to these, the annual calendar of sacred and profane days.

Florus, historian and friend of the emperor, wrote of Numa in his *Epitome*:

> In a word, he induced a fierce people to rule with piety and justice an empire which they had acquired by violence and injustice.

This could have been Hadrian's own political motto, with his strategies of nonaggression and competent administration.

According to Plutarch, writing in Hadrian's lifetime, Numa was a follower of the Greek mystic and mathematician Pythagoras. This was a historical impossibility, for the former lived more than a century before the latter was born. Nevertheless, the notion that the king was influenced by Greek philosophy, especially a creed with a spiritual dimension, would have appealed to the emperor. According to Aurelius Victor, "in the fashion of the Greeks or Numa Pompilius, he began to give attention to religious ceremonies, laws, schools, and teachers to such an extent that he even established a school of fine arts called the Athenaeum." The site of the Athenaeum has not been discovered, but the building was a theater or perhaps an amphitheater and was used for readings and training in declamation. It was seen as a token of the emperor's interest in supporting culture.

In December 119, Hadrian was dealt a heavy personal blow. His beloved mother-in-law and Trajan's niece, Matidia, died at the relatively early age of fifty-one. He arranged for her immediate deification and issued coinage to announce the fact: a denarius struck at Rome shows a bust of Matidia, wearing a triple diadem, and the legend *The deified Augusta Matidia*; on the reverse a veiled woman drops incense on an altar, the personification of *pietas Augusta,* or "the emperor's sense of duty and family affection."

The Augusta was given a splendid funeral and a formal *consecratio* as a goddess. After staging the "most immense delights," the emperor handed out spices to the people in her honor. The Arvals recorded their generous contribution in this regard by providing two pounds of per-

Competent but unsympathetic, Domitian was a domineering ruler. The Senate loathed him, and he repaid the compliment, terrorizing its members. MUSEI CAPITOLINI.

For much of his life, Nerva was the ultimate courtier, without convictions or shame, but as emperor his signal achievement was to reconcile the imperial system and its opponents in the Senate. PALAZZO ALLE TERME, ROME.

Trajan as triumphant commander. This was how the Romans liked to imagine their emperor, scoring victory after victory and presiding over an *imperium sine fine,* an empire without end. XANTEN, GERMANY.

Hadrian in energetic middle age, wearing a general's military cloak. He was the first Roman emperor to grow a beard in the Greek manner, setting a new fashion that many of his successors followed. British Museum.

A bust of Hadrian as a young man, but sculpted toward the end of his reign. This was how he may have imagined himself, reborn after the self-sacrifice of Antinous. FOUND IN THE VILLA AT TIVOLI.

But this was how the aging Hadrian really looked in a late study—disillusioned and ill. ARCHAEOLOGICAL MUSEUM OF CHANIA, CRETE.

Antoninus Pius succeeded Hadrian and maintained his policies. Unlike his predecessor he was neither a military man nor a traveler. He governed without incident and his reign was one of the most peaceful in the history of the Roman Empire. REAL ACADEMIA DE BELLAS ARTES DE SAN FERNANDO, MADRID.

TRAJAN'S COLUMN

Trajan's Column rises ninety-eight feet
from the ruins of his forum. It tells
the story, in the manner of a strip cartoon,
of Rome's victorious wars in Dacia.
It used to be topped by a heroically nude
statue of the emperor, but a statue of
Saint Peter has replaced him.

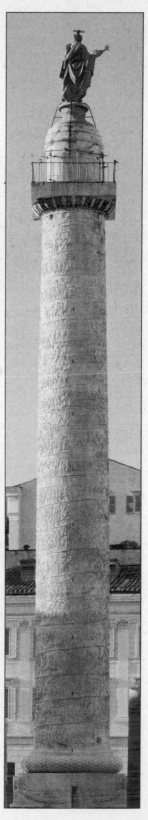

Two scenes from Trajan's Column illustrate the
outset of the Dacian wars. In the lower one, a
troop of Praetorian standard-bearers marches
across the Danube on a bridge of boats.
They are led by Trajan, as he sets foot on enemy
soil. He is preceded by trumpeters and dismounted
cavalrymen. Above, soldiers build a fortress
connected by a bridge to a marching camp.

THE WALL

The wall that Hadrian commissioned to run seventy-three miles across northern Britain, from South Shields on the east coast to Ravenglass on the west, was one of Rome's greatest engineering achievements. This view shows one of eighty milecastles near Steel Rigg in Northumberland.

VILLA ADRIANA

"MY HOUSE AT TIVOLI"

This model evokes the huge scale of Hadrian's villa near Tivoli. A road on the right of the picture skirts the long colonnaded terrace in the foreground and leads to the villa's formal entrance building. Beyond this lies a stretch of water called the Canopus, where summer banquets were held. Further still, at the top right, is a group of buildings, the so-called Academy, where the empress Sabina may have held her court. A temple of Antinous was discovered before the model was made; it should stand on the green land along the side of the entrance road where it approaches its destination. Villa Adriana.

In the heart of the villa complex stand the ruins of Hadrian's bolt-hole—a tiny circular building separated from the outside world by a moat. Here, in the midst of splendor and publicity, the emperor could be alone.

The Canopus at Hadrian's villa, so-called after a canal and popular tourist resort outside Alexandria in Egypt. This was the scene of large open-air dinner parties. The long pool was lined with statues, and sculptures of maritime beasts rose from the water. At the far end stands a vast, half-domed water feature, which towers above a semicircular stone dining couch. From this vantage point, the emperor could survey his guests.

THE YOUNG BITHYNIAN

Antinous as a chubby-faced teenager. This was how he looked when Hadrian first set eyes on him in Bithynia. He fell in love with the boy. BRITISH MUSEUM, LONDON.

Antinous lost his life in Egypt. Hadrian deified his dead lover and buried him in a temple built in his honor beside the entrance to the villa at Tivoli. It housed statues of Antinous, including this image of him as pharoah, the ruler who embodied the skygod Horus in life, and Osiris, god of the underworld, when dead. MUSEI VATICANI.

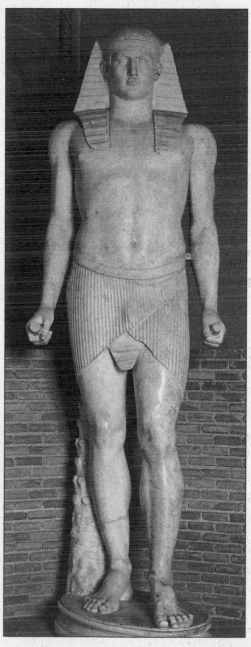

Antinous was the last sculptural type of male beauty to have been invented in the classical world—lush, melancholy, and demure. With his ivy and grape headband, he is shown here as an incarnation of the gods Dionysus and Osiris. Musei Vaticani.

HADRIAN'S OTHER BOYS

Hadrian adopted Lucius Ceionius Commodus and made
him his heir, renaming him Lucius Aelius Caesar. Critics
said unkindly that he was chosen for his looks rather than
his ability as a ruler. Unfortunately he was seriously ill,
probably suffering from tuberculosis. He soon died,
upsetting the emperor's plans for the succession.

Young Marcus Annius Verus. A solemn and dutiful
child, he was fascinated by philosophy. Hadrian was very
fond of him and affectionately teased him for his
virtuous behavior, nicknaming him "Verissimus" or
"truest." After the death of Aelius Caesar, Hadrian made
Antoninus Pius his heir and designated Marcus as his
next successor but one. He reigned as Marcus Aurelius.
MUSEI CAPITOLINI.

THE WOMEN IN HADRIAN'S LIFE

Trajan's wife, Pompeia Plotina, shown here on a sesterce. Devoted to Hadrian, she smoothed his way to power.

Salonina Matidia, shown here on a silver denarius, was Trajan's daughter and the mother of Hadrian's wife, Sabina. Hadrian adored her and was greatly saddened when she died.

Hadrian shared little with his wife, Vibia Sabina, except for mutual dislike; he greatly preferred her mother, Matidia. However, he treated his empress with respect and arranged for her to accompany him on many of his journeys. VILLA ADRIANA.

Lucius Julius Ursus Servianus. The image of a tough, ruthless Roman, Servianus served in the Dacian wars with distinction. He married Hadrian's sister, Paulina, but was critical of his brother-in-law.

MAUSOLEUM

An outsize cylinder standing on a cube, Hadrian's mausoleum was surmounted by
a roof garden and a colossal four-horse chariot. It was still under construction when
the emperor died. Similar in appearance to the mausoleum of Augustus but bigger, it
was not only designed for him but also as a resting place for his successors. In the Middle
Ages the tomb was transformed into a fortress, and later became a papal residence. It is
now known as the Castel Sant'Angelo. Hadrian also built the bridge, the *Pons Aelius,*
still in use but only for pedestrians.

Originally commissioned by Agrippa, Augustus's friend and partner in empire, the Pantheon was completely rebuilt by Hadrian. Best preserved of all the buildings of ancient Rome, it is still in use as a Christian church.

fumed ointment in their name and fifty pounds of frankincense as a gift of the association's servants.

The emperor delivered the eulogy. We have his own words, which have survived, mutilated but readable, on an inscription. He called Matidia his "most loving mother-in-law," whom he honored as if she were his own mother, and said that he was overcome with grief at her death.

> She came to her uncle [Trajan] after he had taken over the principate, and from then on she followed him until his last day, accompanying him and living with him, honoring as a daughter should, and she was never seen without him . . . [She was] most dear to her husband, and after his death, through a long widowhood, passed in the very flower and fullest beauty of her person, most dutiful to her mother, herself a most indulgent mother, a most loyal relative, helping all, not trouble- some to anyone, always in good humor.

Through the sorrow, can we perhaps detect an indirect dig at "my Sabina," his phrase for her in the speech, as a spoiled child? In any event, the emperor maintained good formal relations with his little-loved wife, and it may be now that he promoted her to Augusta in the wake of Matidia's death.

On the Palatine all was calm, order, and luxury, but when Hadrian walked down the hill into the busy, crowded heart of the world's first megalopolis what did he find? What was Rome like? Luckily, we have one man's personal view; his perspective was embittered and exagger- ated, but he offers us his eyes, senses, and feelings as he strives to survive, if not thrive. He was Juvenal, whose sixteen furious satirical poems describe, condemn, flay the skin off his fashionable or powerful fellow citizens.

Most of what we surmise of his life has been deduced from his poetry. Born probably in 55, he was the son of a rich freedman. Juvenal portrays himself in the satires as a needy client, who lived "in pretentious pov- erty" on the perilous edge of insolvency, a hanger-on of wealthy patrons.

His circumstances greatly improved after 117 and Hadrian's accession. This was no coincidence. For once he wrote kind things about an emperor.

All hopes for the arts, all inducement to write, rest on Caesar.
He alone has shown respect for the wretched Muses
in these hard times, when famous established poets would lease
an out-of-town bath concession or a city bakery . . .
But no one henceforth will be forced to perform unworthy labors . . .
So at it, young men: your Imperial Leader's indulgence
is urging you on, surveying your ranks for worthy talent.

Juvenal's unusual generosity of spirit seems to have been rewarded. He was granted (surely by the emperor) a pension and a small but adequate farmstead near Tibur, that home-away-from-home for the Aelii. Hadrian was, once again, modeling himself on Augustus, who was a generous patron of poets—as was his close friend and associate Maecenas, who bought the hard-up poet Horace a rural retreat at Tibur.

In his third satire Juvenal paints an unforgettable picture of daily life in ancient Rome, then a huddled conurbation of an estimated 1 million souls. Augustus claimed to have found a city of brick and left one of marble. This was an exaggeration, but successive emperors built or restored forums, basilicas, public baths, and theaters. After more than a century of nonstop construction, the result was a magnificent architectural assemblage in the old city center and on the Campus Martius. A network of streets, mostly unpaved and at best laid with pebbles, led to the city's main gates. Otherwise Rome was a huddle of narrow, dark alleys, punctuated by piazzettas and crossroads shrines. There were temples everywhere and, as Roman religion entailed numerous animal sacrifices, the groans and odors of the abattoir were added to the already complex soundscape and scent of city life.

Aqueducts brought water to numerous public fountains and the public baths and drains ran under main streets. But these amenities only mitigated a universal lack of hygiene and frequent visitations of infectious disease.

In the poem, a friend of Juvenal, a certain Umbricius, explains why he abandoned the city for "a charming coastal retreat." While the wealthy few lived in quiet, spacious homes with windowless walls on the street frontage and courtyards open to the sky, many ordinary people had single rooms in jerry-built multistory apartment blocks, which tended to come crashing down without warning. Nobody was afraid that his house in the country—"at Tibur perched on its hillside"— would collapse, says Umbricius.

> But here
> we inhabit a city largely shored up with gimcrack
> stays and props: that's how our landlords postpone slippage,
> and—after masking great cracks in the ancient fabric—assure
> the tenants that they sleep sound, when the house is tottering.
> Myself, I prefer life without fires, without nocturnal panics.

The night was noisy for other reasons. Since the days of Julius Caesar wheeled traffic was allowed on the streets only after sunset.

> Insomnia causes most deaths here . . . The wagons thundering past
> through those narrow twisting streets, the oaths of draymen caught in
> a traffic jam, would rouse a dozing seal . . .

There were no street lights, and in the hours of darkness the solitary walker was at risk of a severe beating up.

> . . . however flown with wine
> our young hothead may be, he carefully keeps his distance
> from the man in a scarlet cloak, the man surrounded
> by torches and big brass lamps and a numerous bodyguard.
> But for me, a lonely pedestrian, trudging home by moonlight
> or with hand cupped around the wick of one poor guttering candle
> he only has contempt . . .

The victim is slugged to a pulp and begs for his few remaining teeth— "as a special favor."

Immigrants were Umbricius' "pet aversion"—and, one suspects, Juvenal's too. They were mostly Greeks—meaning anyone from the eastern provinces. They poured into Rome with their outlandish habits, says Umbricius, including

> the whores pimped out around the Circus [Maximus]. That's where
> you go if you fancy a foreign pickup, in one of those saucy toques.

There were villains, con men, gangsters everywhere. Even at home the citizen was not safe.

> When every building
> is shuttered, when shops stand silent, when doors are chained,
> there are still cat-burglars in plenty waiting to rob you, or else
> you'll be knifed—a quick job—by some homeless tramp.

Like his imperial predecessors, Hadrian was determined to place his mark on the ugly, grubby, and higgledy-piggledy metropolis by commissioning masterworks of architecture. He was well aware that Trajan, Domitian, Nero, and Augustus had all spent vast sums of money beautifying Rome. An architectural enthusiast himself, one might even say an amateur architect, he was determined to outbuild them.

At the outset, he focused his attention on the Campus Martius. His aim was to create a visual connection between himself and the first *princeps,* between the structures that Augustus and Agrippa had left behind them and his own grand edifices, some brand-new and others radical remodelings of the old—beginning with the burned-out Pantheon.

Hadrian decided to reconstruct it using the existing floor plan—a conventional temple portico with columns and a pediment with a circular building behind it. If this circular building had had a roof it was probably made from wood—hence the successive fires. Hadrian had in mind something far more ambitious than Agrippa's temple, and gave his architect one of the most exciting and challenging commissions in history. With studied modesty he intended to retain the inscribed attribution to Agrippa, and nowhere would Hadrian's name be mentioned. The new Pantheon would be his homage to the admired founders of the imperial system—simultaneously eye-catching and discreet, a most Aelian touch.

The emperor restored two more of Agrippa's buildings, the basilica or stoa of Neptune, god of the sea, and his public baths. In addition to these exercises in radical refurbishment, there was one major item of new construction: next to the Pantheon he commissioned a large temple dedicated to that most recent of goddesses, the Augusta Matidia; it was to be flanked by deep, two-story porticoes on either side that came to be known as the basilicas of Matidia and her mother, Marciana. No *divae* had ever been so honored. In this magnificent new quarter, which stood within easy walking distance from Augustus' mausoleum and the Ara Pacis, and rivaled their visual impact, past and present were interlocked in marble.

His greatest project by far not only expressed Hadrian's delight in the art of architecture but also his determination to attach to the traditional governance of the empire something approaching the court of an absolute Hellenistic monarch. This was his celebrated villa on the plain beneath Tibur. As we have seen, the town and its environs were where a Spanish "colony" of expatriates from Baetica established itself and where the Aelian family may have had a country home. Perhaps this was the first-century B.C. house around which the emperor designed his new development; in that case, he was returning to the fields where he had played as a little boy.

For centuries wealthy Romans had built themselves rural retreats, whether on their estates or at seaside resorts like Baiae. Here they could relax from the noise and crowds of Rome. But Hadrian wanted much more than a place where he could get away from it all; he intended a center of government. His architects and he designed a campus of more than three hundred acres rather than a single edifice. Just as the palace of the Ptolemies in Alexandria was a city district, they had in mind a township, both pastoral and splendid, where public buildings, grand entry halls and audience chambers, temples, and baths would intermingle with gardens and terraces and canals.

Hadrian was careful not to be disrespectful of the institutions in the capital city, just visible on the horizon. Senators were bound to live within twenty miles of Rome so that they could easily attend meetings and take part in official duties, and Hadrian's "villa" was well within the limit.

As early as 117 work began, and it was to continue on and off for most of the rest of the reign. A development on this scale called for a team of architects, a clerk and office of works, and a wide range of experts (some doubtless seconded from the army), including mosaic artists, engineers, purchasing agents, garden designers, and sculptors, and hundreds if not thousands of manual workers.

Despite his engrossing construction projects, the emperor tired of Rome. Perhaps he was missing Athens, for he soon left the city for a tour of Campania, the nearest thing to Greece that Italy could provide. This was a long, fertile region in southern Italy, lying between the Tyrrhenian Sea and Italy's backbone, the Apennine mountain range. Strabo described it as "the most blest of plains, and round about it lie fruitful hills." The inhabitants had a reputation for luxury living.

Campania was settled from the eighth century B.C. by Greek colonists. The three great temples in the Doric manner at Paestum in the south still remind the visitor of the splendors of Greek culture. In the north Puteoli (today's Pozzuoli) began life as the city of Dicaearchia (from the Greek for "good rule") and was now a thriving harbor for the import of Alexandrian grain and a leading financial center.

Hadrian's departure may have reminded some of the celebrated occasion when his predecessor Tiberius left the city for Campania under the influence of astrologers—and never returned. When Tacitus described the incident in the *Annals,* he may have meant readers between the lines to think of their present emperor, also a devotee of the clairvoyant arts. Perhaps Hadrian was to abandon Rome for good. If that was what his contemporaries suspected, we must suppose that the opinionated emperor had already indicated his dislike of the capital.

On this occasion, Hadrian only had an excursion in mind, although he had no intention of spending the rest of his reign among the overblown splendors of the Palatine. His aim in Campania was to "aid all the towns of the region with benefactions and gifts, attaching all the leading men to him." Inscriptions have been discovered at various towns that record the completion of capital projects he commissioned and financed. Campania was a prosperous region, and the emperor was engaging in public relations rather than responding to some crisis or special need.

His itinerary is not recorded, but we must assume that, as the empire's commander in chief, he visited the naval base at Misenum and reviewed the fleet. Not far away was Neapolis itself ("new town"), or Naples. Thoroughly Hellenic in appearance and spirit, it was a center of learning and many upper-class young men went there to finish their education by cultivating rhetoric and the arts. Despite centuries of Roman rule, the inhabitants still spoke Greek. Strabo observed how their easy lifestyle attracted people from Rome who wanted

> a restful vacation—I mean the kind of people who have made their careers in education, or others who, because of old age or illness, are looking for somewhere to relax. Some Romans, enjoying this way of life and noticing the large number of men who share the same cultural attitudes as themselves staying there, gladly fall in love with the place and make it their permanent home.

Every five years Neapolis staged games in the traditional Greek manner where athletics alternated with musical and poetry competitions. According to the *Historia Augusta,* Hadrian was honored with the title of *demarch* (that is, "ruler of the people"), Neapolis' chief public official; although the date is not given it was probably now, in 119.

Nearby was the small town of Cumae. Here once lived its celebrated clairvoyant, the Sibyl. She let the god Apollo have sex with her if he granted her immortality; but like too many other attractive classical mortals, she forgot to ask for eternal youth as well. She shriveled up and dwindled over the centuries. According to Petronius, novelist and favorite of Nero, she lived in a cave where she sat in a jug moaning, "I want to die." The cave has been found, and some kind of oracular service seems to have been provided in historical times; if the Sibyl, or more precisely a living priestess, was open to inquiries we can be sure that Hadrian called by.

• • •

The journey around Campania gave the emperor a foretaste of how he would like to manage affairs. He conceived a plan to visit every province in his wide dominions. Like the first *princeps,* he liked to see things for himself, to go to where the problem was, to assess the evidence in person, to make a decision on the spot and not at a distance of tens or hundreds of miles. This, he was sure, was how the empire should be run.

After more than two years in Italy, Hadrian had convincingly asserted his authority. The new regime was no longer new, men loyal to him had been placed at all the power points, and the Senate and people now accepted, if grudgingly, the way things were. He could leave the capital without worrying what was going on behind his back.

The emperor was ready to set off on his travels.

XVI

THE TRAVELER

. . .

The emperor had not done quite enough to convince Rome that he loved it. People could still remember the young man who read out Trajan's letters to the Senate in a Spanish accent. A half foreigner, he had spent most of his adult career soldiering abroad on the empire's barbarian frontiers. If he was to take to the road for long years in the provinces, as he meant to do, *imperium* would accompany him—and the city would risk losing its proud sense of itself as capital of the world.

Hadrian took two steps that would prove beyond doubt his devotion, his *pietas,* that most traditional of virtues. First he designed a temple dedicated to the goddess Venus, mother of Aeneas, who renewed ruined Troy in the fields of Latium, and Roma, the city's divine spirit. This huge structure was to rest on a high man-made platform on the Velia, a low hill between the Forum and the Colosseum. It was to be large enough to rival the temple of Jupiter Optimus Maximus on the Capitol, at the Forum's other end, and no doubt that visual echo was what the emperor intended.

Second, the emperor felt that Rome deserved a birthday party. On April 21, 753 B.C., legend had it, Romulus founded his new city on the Palatine Hill, digging a trench along the route where its boundary, a strip of consecrated ground called the *pomerium,* would run. Hadrian announced an annual celebration on that day to mark the *Natalis Urbis Romae;* it was superimposed on an already existing festival, the Parilia, which honored a pastoral deity, Pales, and sought protection for shepherds and fecundity for their flocks. Interestingly, the birthday of the emperor's favorite king, Numa Pompilius, also fell on April 21.

This was all clever marketing, but Hadrian was not simply intent on seeking to please. In another ceremony evoking Rome's distant past, he reasserted his policy of containment rather than expansion. It was permissible to redraw the *pomerium* and take in a larger area, provided that the territory of the empire had also expanded. In Trajan's case it had obviously done so, but he had not gotten around to ordering an extension before his death. Rather than complete unfinished business from the previous reign, Hadrian confirmed the *pomerium* exactly as it was. He conducted a *lustratio,* a ritual of purification, along the route of the boundary, and in this way made his peaceful intentions absolutely clear.

In 121, not long after the reformed Parilia, the emperor left the city. According to Dio Cassius, he dispensed "with imperial trappings, for he never used these outside Rome." It was as if he were shaking himself free from the stifling grandeur and constricting rituals of the capital and embracing the freedom of the road.

Hadrian had little idea of the date of his return. He probably sailed to Massilia (Marseille), southern Gaul's main port, and made his way up the Rhône in the direction of Lugdunum (Lyon). Little information about his activities has come down to us. According to the *Historia Augusta,* he "went to the relief of all the communities with various acts of generosity." Evidently, he was still pursuing the popularity of the open hand. Years later imperial coins hailed him as *restitutor,* or "restorer," of the province; in one series, Gallia as a draped woman kneels before the *princeps,* who grasps her hand as if to raise her up.

Gaul was a sideshow, though, for Hadrian's real destination was the German frontier, where he was to unveil the military policy through which he meant to implement his strategy of nonexpansion.

For inspiration, Hadrian looked back to the generals of the Republic, not the flashy ones like Scipio Africanus who won brilliant victories, but those who had had to labor against disadvantage. Two men of the second rather than the first rank attracted his particular approval.

Publius Cornelius Scipio Aemilianus Africanus Numantinus was Africanus' adopted grandson. During the sack of Carthage, Rome's great rival, in 146 B.C., he turned to a friend and, with tears in his eyes, remarked: "A glorious moment, but I have a terrible fear that some day the same fate will be pronounced on my own country." He went on to quote from Homer the famous lines:

> There will come a day when sacred Troy shall perish
> and Priam, and the people of Priam of the strong ash spear.

This fusion of pessimism about the benefits of war and magnanimity will have appealed to Hadrian, but what really struck home was Aemilianus' generalship during a rebellion by Spanish tribes.

Fighting had been going on for a long time around the tribal settlement of Numantia, and the Roman troops were demoralized and ill disciplined. Aemilianus realized he would never win the war unless he brought his men under control. He arrived at the army camp with a small escort and immediately ordered the removal of everything that was not necessary to the war effort. The numerous civilians in the baggage train—tradesmen and prostitutes in the main—were sent away.

> [The soldiers'] food was limited to plain boiled and roasted meats.
> They were forbidden to have beds, and [Aemilianus] was the first one
> to sleep on straw. He forbade them to ride on mules when on the
> march; "for what can you expect in a war," said he, "from a man who
> is not able to walk?"

The harsh medicine worked; but Aemilianus knew that his legions were not yet ready for battle. So he instituted a severe and exhausting training regime. The troops were sent on route marches and were made to build, demolish, and rebuild camps. Tasks had to be completed within strict deadlines.

It was only when the legions were in good physical condition and morale had sharply improved that Aemilianus resumed his (ultimately successful) campaign against the Spaniards.

Hadrian's second military hero was Quintus Caecilius Metellus Numidicus, who flourished in the second century B.C. After holding the consulship, he was posted to North Africa to lead the campaign against the able and ambitious Numidian king, Jugurtha.

For him, too, training was the watchword. His predecessor in command had kept his forces in permanent camp, moving only when the bad smell or a lack of food supplies forced him. Men absented themselves from duty when the mood took them.

Just like Aemilianus, Metellus got rid of all the civilians, moved camp daily, undertook cross-country marches. At night he placed sentry posts at short intervals and did the rounds himself. When on the march, he moved up and down the column to check that no one left the ranks, that the men kept close to their standards and carried their own food and weapons. In this way, by inflicting exercise rather than punishment, Metellus soon restored discipline and morale.

The dowager empress's serious mind and quiet disposition owed much to her appreciation of the philosophy of Epicurus. His thinking derived from an atomic idea of nature (originally promoted by the fifth-century B.C. scientific theorist Democritus). The fundamental constituents of everything, he asserted, were indivisible little bits of matter, or atoms, and everything that happened was the consequence of these atoms colliding with one another. Unlike Hadrian's admired Epictetus, who saw the universe as the expression of a divine will, Epicurus held that it was no more than a sequence of random events.

On what foundation, then, was it possible to rest a system of ethics? The answer was that all good and bad originate in sensations of pleasure and pain. It was from these sensations that we construct a moral code. Epicurus also taught that death was the end of body and soul; it should not be feared, for there were no posthumous rewards and punishments. In later centuries Christian propagandists inaccurately labeled Epicurus as a hedonist (hence our terms *epicure* and *epicurean*). In fact, he sought no more than a tranquil life without pain, and cultivated simplicity.

Epicurus attracted a small band of devoted followers whom he taught in his house and garden just outside Athens. Above the garden gate a sign read: "Stranger, you will do well to linger here; here our highest good is pleasure."

On his deathbed he informed a friend, with a whiff of self-congratulatory sangfroid:

A painful inability to urinate has attacked me, and also dysentery, so violent that nothing can be added to the violence of my sufferings. But the cheerfulness of my mind, arising from the recollection of all my philosophical contemplations, counterbalances all these afflictions.

Epicurus left the house and garden to a nominated successor and they were handed on in turn from one philosopher to another, down to Hadrian's day. They were both a shrine and a continuing "school," known as the Succession of Epicurus. Its doctrines survived and thrived.

Plotina learned of a problem facing the Epicureans at Athens. The Successor at the time was a man called Popillius Theotimus. Popillius is a Latin name and indicates that he held Roman citizenship, and in this fact lay the difficulty. The provincial authorities insisted that the head of the Succession of Epicurus be a Roman citizen. Theotimus wanted the rule to be relaxed. Evidently he had someone in mind to take over from him who was ineligible.

He was fortunate to be well connected. He asked Plotina to intervene and she was happy to do so. She wrote a letter to her adopted son, which reached him during his European tour:

You know very well, sir, [the interest I] have in the sect of Epicurus. His school needs your help. [Since, as of now], a successor must be taken from those who are Roman citizens, the choice is narrowly limited. [I ask,] therefore, in the name of Popillius Theotimus, who is currently Successor at Athens, that it be permitted by you to him . . . to be entitled to appoint as successor to himself one of foreign nationality, if the distinction of the person should make it advisable.

Hadrian complied without demur and sent Theotimus the necessary permissions. The dowager empress was delighted and wrote to "all the Friends":

We have what we were so eager to obtain . . . We owe . . . a debt of gratitude to him who is in truth the benefactor and overseer of all culture and therefore a most reverence-worthy emperor, very dear to me in all respects as both an outstanding guardian and loyal son.

But she added a note of warning, knowing how personal feelings could warp judgment in tightly knit communities. It was important to choose as a successor "the best of all fellow-sectarians and to attribute more importance to his view of the overall interest than to his private congeniality with certain members."

Surely, Plotina had at the back of her mind another succession. She had had recent experience of an awkward handover of authority, in which she was widely supposed to have played a leading role. Hadrian had not been the most congenial personality at Trajan's court, but in her calm way the empress had acted firmly to ensure that the best man, in her opinion, followed her husband to the purple. The same principle, she was certain, should be applied in the garden of Epicurus.

When the emperor arrived at the German front he soon showed what he had learned about the art of command, both from his own experience and from a study of history. His strategy of defensive imperialism did not make him unwarlike or negate his many years in the army: quite the reverse, he was a soldier's soldier. Also, he needed to pacify his critics by demonstrating his prowess as a general.

Hadrian realized that the army had been growing slack thanks to the "inattention of previous supreme commanders," as the *Historia Augusta* has it: an interesting phrase, for, despite Hadrian's appreciation of Trajan's generalship, it implies that his adoptive father had been careless about the day-to-day routines of life in the camp and in the field.

Hadrian introduced the highest standards of discipline and kept the soldiers on continual exercises, as if war were imminent. In order to ensure consistency, he followed the examples of Augustus (once again) and Trajan by publishing a manual of military regulations. His approach to training was innovatory; he made his soldiers practice the fighting techniques of potential or actual opponents—Parthians, Armenians, Sarmatians, and Celts—and, according to Arrian, devised some of his own "with a view to beauty, speed, the inspiring of terror, and practical use."

He led by example, sharing the life of the rank and file and cheerfully eating "such camp fare as bacon, cheese, and vinegar." It may be while on campaign that he developed a liking for *tetrafarmakon,* a pie made from pheasant, sow's udder, and ham. The *Historia Augusta* writes: "He generally wore the commonest clothing—refusing gold ornamentation on his sword belt, fastening his cloak with an unjeweled clasp, and only reluctantly allowing himself an ivory hilt to his sword."

The emperor joined his men on the regular route marches he insisted on, walking with them for as many as twenty miles (the target was to cover this distance in five hours). He made a point of never setting foot in a chariot or sitting in a four-wheeled carriage, and always walked or rode on horseback. Whatever the weather, he went about with his head bare.

Hadrian was naturally inquisitive, and these qualities now came into their own. Dio Cassius writes: "He personally viewed and investigated absolutely everything." He inspected garrisons and forts, closing some down and relocating others. He examined all aspects of camp life—the weapons, the artillery, the trenches, ramparts, and palisades—making sure that every detail came up to his high standards.

The private lives of both rank-and-file soldiers and officers came under close scrutiny. The main aim was to eliminate luxury. Some officers behaved as if they were on vacation. The emperor put a stop to all that. According to the *Historia Augusta,* he "demolished dining rooms in the camps, and porticoes, covered galleries, and ornamental gardens."

The emperor also took steps to improve the professional caliber of officers. He was particularly anxious about military tribunes, who were, in effect, a legionary commander's general staff. He took care to appoint somewhat older men "with full beards or of an age to give to the authority of the tribuneship a full measure of prudence and maturity."

As for the ordinary legionary, Hadrian improved the quality of weapons and other equipment, and forbade the recruitment or maintenance in service of men who were either too young or too old to cope with the physical demands of military life. He found other ways of softening the severity of military regulations. He ruled that the death penalty should be used as sparingly as possible.

Soldiers were not allowed to marry during their term of enlistment, but often contracted informal partnerships with women and had children by them. On their discharge many married their mistresses and so legitimized any offspring. But if they died in service, their sons were bastards and not permitted to become principal heirs. In a letter discovered in the Egyptian desert, Hadrian discussed the matter with the prefect of Egypt. He had decided that it was time to allow illegitimate soldiers' sons the same limited property rights as relatives. The emperor was pleased to "put a more humane interpretation on the rather too strict rule established by emperors before me."

So far as we can tell, Hadrian's provincial survey was comprehensive. He visited the two Germanias, Lower and Upper, and the two small provinces along the upper Danube—Raetia (in today's geography, Bavaria and Swabia, with parts of Austria, Switzerland, and Lombardy) and Noricum (some of today's Austria and Slovenia).

Hadrian's army reforms should be seen alongside his defensive foreign policy. If war was to be discounted, his soldiers needed something else to ensure discipline and spur morale—namely, a leader who knew how to marry discipline with affection and concern for their welfare. Hadrian became very popular with them, and for the rest of his reign never found reason to doubt their loyalty. The impact of his reforms was deep and long-lasting. Through unremitting energy and skill, he forged a peacetime army into a powerful war machine. Hadrian's legions were one of the most valuable legacies he left to his successors.

The Roman had a different idea of a frontier than we do today. It was not a line demarcating the edge of a national or political territory, on the far side of which another power owned the freehold. Rather, he saw it as the edge of land that the state, the *Senatus Populusque Romanus,* directly administered.

Beyond lay a swath of territory also held to be in his possession, even if he chose not to govern it. Its inhabitants were to a certain degree imperial subjects. Some lived in client kingdoms, others were members of allied tribes who perhaps received subsidies from Rome or, alternatively, paid tribute. The result was that most frontiers were porous. Merchants and travelers, men looking for jobs, came and went. Goods were declared and dues paid. Embassies ferried complaints and compliments. At the same time, of course, the legions had to be on their guard against raiders, serious armed incursions, or even revolts. So a frontier was not like a city wall, the purpose of which was purely defensive. The job of guards was less to keep intruders out than to be traffic policemen.

When Hadrian arrived in Upper Germania he was especially interested in the *limes* that Domitian and, later, Trajan had erected. Originally a *limes* was a pathway between two fields, but here it meant a road lined with about one thousand watchtowers and two hundred or so forts and fortlets, running from the Rhine above Mainz southeast to the Danube above Regensburg. The *limes* bridged an awkward gap between the two great rivers that otherwise constituted Rome's natural borders between the North and Black seas.

When the emperor visited the *limes*, he made an important and innovative decision. On the "enemy" side of the road he ordered his soldiers to build an unbroken wooden palisade perhaps ten feet high, consisting of large oak posts, split in two with the flat sides facing out, and strengthened by crossbeams. This was a tremendous enterprise, for the *limes* was about 350 miles long. Wide swaths of German forest were harvested.

What problem was the emperor trying to solve? The existing fortifications seem to have been perfectly adequate, and the tribes in the hinterland posed no special threat of invasion. However, a wall would enable tax-hungry officialdom to discourage smuggling and increase customs dues, as well as control immigration. It would also be a time-consuming fatigue duty that would keep the legions busy for years.

But the sheer ambition of the project suggests another, overriding motive. The wall was a visible confirmation of Hadrian's policy of imperial stasis. It was a spectacular symbol both of the power of Rome and of its determination not to grow any further. This interpretation is supported by an observation in the *Historia Augusta* that Hadrian used artificial barriers to shut off or set apart barbarians "during this period [his first provincial tour] and on many other occasions." In other words, the German palisade was not a one-off project to meet a particular threat, but an example of an empire-wide policy that was bound to have a demonstrative as well as a practical effect.

The policy may well have been unpopular with his generals and with the Senate, but the emperor never wavered in his determination to implement it. With the passage of time, the benefits of defensive imperialism became widely accepted, at least in the provinces. Later in the century a commentator remarked approvingly: "An encamped army, like a rampart, encloses the civilized world in a ring."

Having introduced his new training regime and commissioned his palisade, the emperor was ready to move on. His next major destination was the island of Britannia, perched on the outer boundary of the known world.

XVII
EDGE OF EMPIRE

. . .

Halfway between the North Sea and the Solway Firth on the largely treeless and windswept moors of the northern Pennines, the fort of Vindolanda stood on a small plateau, well watered with springs. The beautiful, bleak landscape around it has changed little during the last two thousand years.

The fort's name brought together two Celtic words—*vindos,* "white" (winter derives from the same root), and *landa,* signifying enclosure or lawn. It was surely so-called because of a still-persisting trick of the weather. For about half an hour after sunrise in winter, the plateau remains in the shadow of a neighboring hill. While all around the frost on the ground melts away, the fort remains crisp and white—a magical shining enclosure.

Vindolanda was one of a series of strongpoints strung along a road (now known by its medieval name, Stanegate), rather like the *limes* of Domitian in Germania. High ramparts topped by a palisade formed a rectangle with rounded corners, and inside could be found the usual components of a Roman camp—tidy rows of barracks, storehouses, a hospital, and the commander's grand residence, the *praetorium.* The cultural amenities of urban life were available: a stone bathhouse stood outside the fort, and a temple.

Britannia's northern defenses were guarded by auxiliary troops, mainly Germans. Vindolanda was home variably to Tungrians, a Germanic tribe that had settled in northeastern Gaul, and the indispensable Batavians. It was not originally on the front line, but between 85 and 105 demands elsewhere in the empire led Domitian, and then Trajan, to pull back from forts in Scotland. The legions themselves were held in reserve in three towns whose Latin names were all drawn from native languages—Eboracum (York), Deva (Chester), and Isca Silurum (Caerleon).

The auxiliaries thought little of the locals' fighting quality—unfairly, for they had acquitted themselves well during their rebellion, probably led by a militant tribe, the Brigantes, who had controlled much of northern England and the Midlands before the coming of the Romans. Now it was policy to recruit from them, much to the disgust of the Batavians, who called them *Britunculi,* "miserable little Brits."

The early forts at Vindolanda were built of wood and were replaced every seven or eight years. Rather than clear a site before rebuilding, the Romans simply demolished it and overlaid the wreckage with a layer of clay or turf. The wet conditions ensured an environment without oxygen and preserved every object the legionaries discarded.

Since the early 1970s archaeologists have unearthed much priceless, well-preserved evidence of life as it was lived in an outpost of empire two thousand years ago. Shoes, belts, textiles, wooden tools, utensils of bronze and iron, have been discovered—and, most remarkable of all, correspondence, including personal letters, accounts, requests for leave, even drawings.

Most of the letters were penned in ink on slivers of oak or alder, usually the size and shape of a modern postcard or half a postcard (some were scratched onto wax-layered tablets). They reanimate the long-vanished dead—among them Flavius Cerealis, prefect of the ninth cohort of the Batavians, and his wife, Sulpicia Lepidina, who were in Vindolanda around the turn of the century.

A colleague apologizes to Cerealis for not having attended his wife's birthday party, and a woman friend dictates a note to Lepidina inviting her to *her* birthday celebrations. She has added, in her own slightly wobbly hand, "I shall expect you, sister. Farewell, sister, as I hope to prosper, and hail." The same woman gets her husband's permission for Lepidina to visit her at her home in another fort, for she had "certain personal matters" she wanted to discuss. Lonely in Vindolanda one winter and in need of society, Cerealis asks a highly placed correspondent, perhaps a senator, to "furnish me with very many friends that, thanks to you, I may enjoy a pleasant period of military service."

Cerealis and other cohort prefects appear to have been Germanic noblemen, and so well placed to win the loyalty of their men. However, the Vindolanda documents show that they and their families willingly Romanized themselves. Education of the young was a key tool: a couple of tablets reveal the efforts of a little boy, doubtless Cerealis and Lepidina's son, to learn lines from Virgil's *Aeneid*. He wrote down from memory a famous quotation: *interea pavidum volitans pinnata p' ubem,* or "meanwhile, the winged creature [Rumor] flying through the trembling city." He abbreviated *per* with *p'* and accidentally left out the *r* of *urbem*. A tantalizing glimpse of a young Batavian learning to grow up into a proper Roman.

It was not only the elite that corresponded. In their remote outpost ordinary people were needy for news. Solemnis wrote to his "brother" Paris (their names suggest they were slaves, not soldiers): "Many hellos. You should know that I am well, and I hope you are too. You are a most disloyal man, for you haven't sent me a single letter. I think I am behaving much more decently by writing to you."

The northern edge of Roman rule was the emperor's main destination, and there is evidence that the garrison at Vindolanda made expensive preparations to receive the great man in appropriate style. Archaeologists have discovered and explored a building that was erected at about the time of the emperor's visit to Britannia. It was more elaborate and substantial than anything seen before on the site; it had massive oak posts and the floors were laid with *opus signinum,* a pavement mix of material such as gravel, terra-cotta, or stone set in limestone or clay, a common feature of private houses. The internal walls were plastered and some were painted. These were spacious quarters specially commissioned for a personage of higher status than had ever stayed at the fort before. The obvious candidate was Hadrian, who had to have a domestic base appropriate for an emperor during his tour of the north. Vindolanda's central position made it a good choice, and doubtless provincial governors found it a convenient billet in the coming years long after the emperor had departed.

Hadrian probably crossed the sea to Britannia in June 122. He brought with him one of the Rhine legions, the VI Victrix (Victorious), which he added to the provincial garrison (perhaps replacing a legion lost in the late rebellion or transferred elsewhere). Also, three thousand men, borrowed from Spain and Germania, joined the expedition. The emperor was accompanied by the newly appointed governor, Aulus Platorius Nepos. Nepos was a friend and possibly a relative who originated in Hadrian's hometown of Italica. He had fought in the Parthian war and governed Thrace, before holding a suffect consulship in Hadrian's first year, 119. Platorius Nepos was to replace Falco, who had put down the stubborn British insurgents with efficiency but only after heavy losses.

Falco's last task was to organize the imperial visit, a feat comparable to staging the modern Olympic Games. Thousands of legionaries needed to be accommodated, as did a detachment of the Praetorian Guard and the Batavian cavalry. Then there was a phalanx of dignitaries—the members of the emperor's *consilium,* assorted *comites* and *amici.* Key members of the bureaucracy were present too, among them the *ab epistulis* Suetonius. A route had to be agreed and a series of hapless towns warned to prepare hospitality and plan to accommodate costly disruption with a smile.

The empress was of the party, there not from love but for decorum, and would have had her own court. The most politically significant of those accompanying the emperor was the praetorian prefect, Gaius Septicius Clarus (his colleague Turbo was still in charge in Rome). A distinguished *eques* and former governor of Egypt, this civilized man was a correspondent of Pliny and the dedicatee of Suetonius' masterpiece, *De Vita Caesarum,* "The Lives of the Caesars."

Information about Hadrian's movements in Britannia are scarce. He probably set sail from the main base for the Britannic fleet, the *classis Britannica,* at Gesoriacum (today's Boulogne), landing on the south coast and traveling up to the provincial capital, Londinium, where he doubtless parked the empress and most of the administrative staff. His subsequent itinerary is unknown, but a rational guess would have him visit the three legionary bases. Certificates were issued to soldiers from every army unit in the province whose service contracts had expired. These granted the usual privileges—in particular, "to their children and descendants, the citizenship and the right of legal marriage with the common-law wife they had at the time that citizenship was granted to them, or, if there are any bachelors, with the wife they subsequently marry"—the formula judiciously adds, "but only one at a time." This mass discharge was unusual and we may safely suppose was designed to justify a grand ceremony at which the emperor addressed his men, something he liked doing.

It appears that the VI Victrix sailed directly from the Continent to the river Tyne. On their arrival they dedicated two altars; one, to the sea god Neptune, was decorated with a dolphin curled around a trident, and the other, to Oceanus, with a ship's anchor. Oceanus was believed to be a vast river that encircled all land (of course, nobody knew then of the Americas, Australasia, and the Arctic). The event was powerfully evocative of a similar rite conducted by Alexander the Great on the eastern edge of the known world.

The emperor was surely present, and was perhaps making a political point about his predecessor. The glamorous ghost of Alexander ran through the Roman imagination like an obsession. Trajan had ruefully confessed that he was too old to emulate the conqueror of the Persian empire and reach Oceanus. And here was Hadrian offering the identical sacrifice at the other end of the world, where neither Alexander nor Trajan had ever been, at a time of peace rather than of war.

Britannia might have been a long way from the center of things, but the business of empire had to be maintained. One day a letter arrived from the governor of Asia asking for guidance on how to deal with Christians. By a happy chance the emperor's letters secretary, Suetonius, was able to offer well-informed advice: he had been Pliny's secretary in Bithynia a little more than ten years previously when Pliny had corresponded on the same subject with Trajan.

The governor wrote that he had received a petition to take action against local Christians and was unsure how to respond. The imperial government kept comprehensive archives, which enabled officials to keep an eye on precedents when requests, appeals, and petitions came in. While having no sympathy for the new sect, Trajan had had little wish to hunt down its adherents. They should be condemned only if the evidence against them was incontrovertible.

Hadrian took the same line. His reply survives (it found its way into Christian hands and is cited as an appendix in Justin's *First Apology,* Christian propaganda published some thirty or so years later). He makes clear that detractors should put up proofs, or shut up. "I will not allow them simply to beg and shout," the emperor insisted. If there was evidence, then the governor should hear it. If it was shown that the accused had committed offenses—in particular, that they were Christian and refused to make the appropriate sacrifices—then they should receive punishment proportional to their guilt. Provided that the text has not been tampered with, it looks as if Hadrian wanted to pursue Christians only for specific alleged crimes, not merely for membership in their church.

The emperor's anger is aroused less by the Christians than by their ill-natured critics. "And this, by Hercules, you shall pay special attention to, that if any man shall, through sheer ill will, bring an accusation against any of these persons, you shall sentence him to more severe penalties in proportion to his wickedness." The oath and the strangled syntax suggest that Hadrian was dictating the letter, and was in an irritated frame of mind.

The emperor may have adopted a tolerant policy because he saw through the hysterical prejudice against the sect and understood that it was not a group of fanatical criminals who practiced cannibalism, but was in fact pacific and posed no serious political threat. Alternatively, we know that he was fascinated by religion, especially the kind concerned with spiritual experience and individual commitment, and this may have motivated his approach.

One way or another, having won popularity with the Jews for his fairness toward them after their revolt in Egypt and Cyrene had been put down, the emperor became a favorite with Christian apologists. The *Historia Augusta* reports that Hadrian commissioned the building of temples throughout the empire without any divine images in them, and that it was thought they were dedicated to Christ. Apparently they came to be known as Hadrian's temples. It is difficult to be sure what to make of this: the story may simply be the product of authorial fantasy, but if there is anything in it, it is more likely to have been the emperor's general attempt to widen the scope of recognized or official worship than to single out any particular sect (rather as the Athenians did with their altar to the Unknown God). However, he could well have had Christianity in mind alongside other salvationist and monotheistic creeds of the day.

It was only a few years since rebellion in Britannia had marked the transition between Trajan and Hadrian. Curiously, though, the Vindolanda tablets do not convey an impression of military danger. Social life among senior officers was relaxed. A document of May 18 of an unknown year sets down the whereabouts of the members of the first cohort of the Tungrians, from which we learn that most of them, 456 soldiers out of a total complement of 752, were away from Vindolanda on every kind of errand and business. Of thirty-one soldiers who were sick, six were recovering from wounds—the only reference to fighting in all the Vindolanda texts. About half the cohort was at the neighboring fort of Coria (today's Corbridge), about twelve miles away to the east along the Stanegate for training or some military exercise. Nearly fifty were *singulares*—that is, soldiers deputed to the provincial governor's bodyguard. A number of small groups were in London or elsewhere; one detachment had gone to collect the cohort's pay, perhaps at York. Nine men and a centurion were in Gaul, probably on a mission to collect clothing.

All these traveling soldiers doubled as postmen, carrying messages and goods to and fro up and down the country. The Vindolanda tablets demonstrate how much of the army's time was devoted to economic activity and business trips. Nothing seems to have been exactly corrupt or incompetent, but the system would have been hard put to respond quickly and effectively to an emergency.

What did the emperor make of such commercial bustle? We are not told, but we may guess. There is plenty of evidence that discipline was a theme of his visit to Britannia. The *Historia Augusta* remarks that he "corrected many abuses." An altar found at Chesters, where a fort stood on the Tyne, was dedicated "To the discipline of the emperor Hadrian" by a regiment of horse "called Augustan because of its valor." Coins made the same point. A young military tribune with the VI Victrix at the time learned a lesson he never forgot. We hear of him forty years later as "a man of character and a disciplinarian of the old school"; arriving at a new posting, he saw that his soldiers were better clothed than armed. He

> ripped up their cuirasses with his fingertips; he found horses saddled with cushions, and by his orders the little pommels on them were slit open and the down plucked from their saddles as from geese.

We can reasonably infer that Hadrian tightened arrangements in the Britannic army that had worked themselves loose, and that the Batavians at Vindolanda awaited his arrival with justifiable anxiety.

Rather than fear of punishment, one man had high hopes of redress from the emperor. A draft letter of protest to him has been discovered at the fort, complaining of mistreatment. A civilian trader scribbled it on the back of some accounts he had prepared. He was not from Britannia, but a *transmarinus,* from overseas, and so believed he was exempt from corporal punishment. However, a centurion had given him a good flogging for delivery of substandard wine or oil. "I implore Your Clemency," he wrote, "not to suffer a *transmarinus* and an innocent one to have been made to bleed by a beating, as though I had committed some crime."

The single most telling feature of the letter is where it was unearthed—in the centurions' quarters. Someone must have found and confiscated the draft appeal, and we may doubt that a fair copy ever found its way to its addressee. Even if it did, the trader's accounts do not look altogether defensible. A best guess at an outcome is that the poor man merely earned himself another beating.

Something very strange took place during the *expeditio Britannica* that implies strongly that although the reign had already lasted four years the emperor's position was not entirely secure. Hadrian had a suspicious mind and he made full use of the secret police that had been developed from army supply officers. He had these agents pry into people's private lives, including those of his friends. They acted with the utmost secrecy so that their surveillance went unnoticed.

In one case, there was an amusing sequel. A woman wrote to her husband to complain that he spent too much time enjoying himself at the public baths and generally living a life of pleasure, and as a result neglected her. Hadrian found out about this from his *frumentarii,* and when the man applied for leave reproached him for his selfish conduct. He replied: "Oh, don't tell me she wrote to you as well to complain!"

More seriously, the *frumentarii* unearthed some delinquent behavior among senior members of the court. The details are obscure. With inexplicit brevity, the *Historia Augusta* says that Hadrian

> replaced Septicius Clarus, Praetorian prefect, and Suetonius Tranquillus, his letters secretary, and many others as well, because, without his consent, they had behaved at that time toward his wife, Sabina, in a more informal manner than respect for the imperial family required. He would have dismissed his wife, too, for being moody and difficult—if he had been a private citizen.

It is hard to work out from this what actually took place, but the impression given is of a venial offense. Sabina seems to have been innocent of any material wrongdoing, for she is criticized only for being a trying spouse. "More informally" (*familiarius*) could mean something as slight as a breach of court etiquette or something as damaging as a sexual flirtation. Hadrian made a point of not being a stickler for etiquette, but would have expected appropriately proper behavior in his wife's circle.

Whatever the offense was, we can only conclude that it was a pretext. The dismissal of two such senior figures was a political event of the first order, and so it must have been regarded at the time by informed opinion at court and in the Senate. Something grave had happened, but whatever it was is lost for good.

Sabina made her own, heavy riposte to Hadrian's treatment of her.

She used to say in public that because of his monstrous personality, she had taken pains not to become pregnant by him, for it would be "to the destruction of the human race." Contraception was an imperfect and inconvenient art in the ancient world, entailing such prescriptions as wiping the vagina with old olive oil or moist alum, or jumping up and down and sneezing. However, sympathy for the empress is unnecessary, for we cannot suppose that Hadrian often insisted on his conjugal rights.

Suetonius' dismissal has been bad news for classical historians, for he now no longer had access to the imperial archives. Only his biographies of Rome's first two emperors, Augustus and Tiberius, were complete. Thereafter, he was unable to quote from original papers.

The most famous Roman monument in the British Isles is Hadrian's Wall, the *Vallum Aelium*. Despite its celebrity today, there is only one literary reference to it in antiquity linking it to Hadrian. The *Historia Augusta* observes that he was "the first to construct a wall, eighty [Roman] miles long, which was to separate the barbarians from the Romans."

Much of the wall survives in good condition, especially the midsection, and is northern England's most popular tourist attraction. Its construction appears to have been planned before the emperor set off on his travels, if we can trust a much-restored inscription on two fragments of sandstone found at Jarrow and dating from 118 or 119, which asserted that the "necessity of keeping intact the empire [within its borders] had been imposed upon [Hadrian] by divine instruction" and announces the building of the wall.

The wall was a tremendous venture; all three of the British garrison legions, the Britannic fleet, and auxiliary troops were engaged in its construction. We may assume that the emperor took the closest interest in the design, and a sample length of wall could well have been built for his inspection.

At Newcastle a new bridge, made from timber on an estimated ten stone piers, was to cross the Tyne. This was the *Pons Aelius,* or "Hadrian's Bridge," which stood on the site of today's swing bridge. Here work on the great fortification began and proceeded westward for seventy-three miles to the Irish Sea. It was to be a stone wall, thirty feet broad and fifteen high, with added battlements (some parts survive today up to ten feet high). Along its northern side a huge ditch was dug, thirty feet wide and nine feet deep. The ditch was V-shaped, making it difficult for an attacker to climb out of, once he had fallen in.

Every Roman mile (slightly shorter than today's statute mile), measured from the *pons,* there was a guardpost or "mile castle," with barracks accommodating up to sixty or so men; and between each pair of guardposts, two signaling turrets every mile enabled the rapid communication of danger along the wall. The wall itself had a clay-and-rubble core with a stone facing, probably with a stone-floored walkway on top. It curved down the coast to guard against sea raiders.

The wall ran a few hundred yards north of the Stanegate, which enabled the rapid arrival of reinforcements when needed. An old Stanegate fortress such as Vindolanda ensured the ready presence of reserves.

The wall is believed to have taken about six years to complete. There was evidently some pressure applied to work as fast as possible, for some parts of it were reduced in width to six feet, and widened later. For the eastern third of its length from sea to sea, the wall was a turf rampart about sixteen feet wide, topped by a wooden palisade and walkway and punctuated by timber-framed turrets and mile castles. Perhaps this was because there were no ready supplies of stone and lime. Later the stretch up to the western coast was rebuilt in stone.

Originally the wall was to be garrisoned and patrolled by soldiers based at the mile castles, but this turned out to be unsatisfactory, so a number of large garrison forts were built, some for infantry and others for cavalry.

The single most striking feature of the wall was its visual appearance. It seems to have been finished with plaster, grooved to represent smooth courses of cut stone, and then whitewashed. A ribbon tracing the rise and fall of the rugged green moorland, it could be seen for miles as it shone in the sunlight, an almost magical metaphor for Roman *imperium.*

Soon after work on the wall had finished, another ambitious project was launched—the construction, south of the wall, of two turf banks, each about ten feet high, separated by a flat-bottomed, twenty-foot-wide ditch. Between each bank and the central ditch was a level space roughly thirty feet wide. This *vallum* was crossed by roadways running south from the wall forts toward the Stanegate.

What was Hadrian's Wall for? This is a harder question to answer than one might think. Little is known for sure about the population of northern Britannia (Scotland), but it is hard to believe that it posed much of a military threat. It is not obvious that building and managing a defended frontier along a fixed line was cheaper in manpower and treasure than annexing and governing the Scottish Lowlands (there was very little point, of course, in casting a covetous eye on the barren and sparsely populated Highlands). They could have been defended by a loose arrangement of forts that would cost no more, and maybe less, than manning a great wall from the Solway coast to the North Sea. It has been estimated that four thousand men, a little fewer than a legion, would have been a sufficient garrison.

As in Germania, the fact of a wall did not mean that Rome made no claim on land beyond it. Quite the opposite: it provided a secure baseline from which to project Roman power farther north as and when required. On a day-to-day basis we may safely assume that the fortification was permeable for migrants and merchants; indeed it bisected Brigantine territory, and tribesmen caught on the Pictish side were surely allowed access to their southern heartland. By enabling greater control of people's comings and goings the wall must have generated income through customs dues. But were the benefits accruing from the wall enough to justify the high cost of its construction?

The vast *vallum* presents its own particular mystery. It was not topped by a palisade, and so cannot have had a defensive function. If it was to mark a rearward boundary behind the wall, creating an exclusion zone, then surely something less elaborate—a fence of some sort—would have sufficed. Perhaps the *vallum* was a two-way communications route along either side of the central ditch, which troops and civilians could use, conveniently closer to the wall itself than the Stanegate. But little evidence of a road surface has been found, and the *vallum* sometimes traverses very steep terrain, unsuitable for travel. In any case, we know that a purpose-built supply road ran between the wall and the *vallum*.

One can only conclude that the emperor was restating his commitment to imperial containment. As with his building program in Rome, he used the visual language of architecture and engineering to make a political point. The white ribbon thrown across an empty landscape and the monumental *vallum* were politics as spectacular art.

XVIII
LAST GOOD-BYES

. . .

The great cavalcade that was the imperial court gathered itself together and moved on. The next stage in the emperor's travels was a return to Gaul, then Spain and North Africa.

Florus ribbed Hadrian for his inability to stay still and sent him a few satirical verses, detailing his movements so far in reverse order.

> I couldn't bear to be Caesar
> roaming up and down Britannia
> loitering around Germania
> freezing my balls off in Scythia.

"Scythia" was a poetic way of referring to the wild Danubian provinces. The emperor was amused and composed a good-humored but sharp reply.

> I couldn't bear to be Florus
> one of nature's pub crawlers
> who stuffs his face with burgers
> and lets bedbugs share his mattress.

As we have seen, Florus did not agree with what he saw as the emperor's do-nothing foreign policy, although he did remark that "it is harder to hold on to new provinces than to create them"—a dig at Trajan, one must suppose, which coincided with Hadrian's opinion. In a number of respects, the two men had prejudices in common. A couplet by Florus on the nature of women may well have won the concurrence of Sabina's husband.

Every woman's breast conceals a noxious slime,
sweet words pass her lips, but her heart contains venom.

However, consistency is not everything. Plotina's adopted son simultaneously cherished an affectionate opinion of the opposite sex. It depended on the woman in question. Some time about now, the news came from Italy of the much-cherished dowager empress's death. As Dio Cassius put it bluntly, she had been "the woman through whom he had secured the imperial office because of her love for him."

So far as we can tell, this love was platonic. The Augusta had run the oddest of happy households. At its center was a sexually uninterested emperor. Husband and wife liked and trusted each other, but they had no children, and probably no sex. Relations with the other senior ladies at court, Trajan's sister Marciana and her daughter Matidia, were harmonious. In fact, at the eye of the storm of power they lived lives of Epicurean calm, and present themselves as a high-minded, slightly monochrome sorority.

The empress was never accused of interfering in politics until the intestate Trajan's dying hours. On that occasion she did the state some service. She may have staged the less-than-convincing charade in Trajan's darkened bedroom, but the outcome had been worth the deceit.

Hadrian was very upset by her passing, for (says Dio) he "honored her exceedingly." He wore black for nine days and wrote some hymns in her honor (they are lost). In due course he arranged for her deification. He remarked of her: "Although she asked much of me I never refused her anything." By this he meant that he never *had* to refuse her anything, for her requests were always reasonable.

Plotina came from Nemausus (today's Nîmes, in southern France), capital of the Narbonesis province. The Pont du Gard, part of its aqueduct, and an extraordinarily well-preserved temple, now called the Maison Carrée, survive to the present day, but not the basilica "of marvelous workmanship" that Hadrian built in the empress's memory.

Hadrian retained his youthful passion for hunting. He had become so skillful that he famously brought down a huge boar with a single spear thrust. On one occasion, he broke his collarbone and on another suffered a leg injury that came close to crippling him.

When he visited Vindolanda during his tour of the Britannic frontier, he would have found to his delight that the sport was part of the garrison's culture. Presumably he made full use of the opportunities there to ride out with horses. And so he did in Gallia, too. We know of one particular hunt that came to a sad end. The Gallo-Roman town of Apta Julia (today's Apt, in Provence, some thirty miles or so from Aix) stood on the via Domitia, which led down to Spain, and so was on Hadrian's itinerary (Hannibal had traveled along it in the opposite direction on his march to Italy). There is mountainous hunting country nearby, and it is no accident that five dedications to the god of huntsmen, Silvanus, have been found in and near Apt.

The emperor's favorite horse, Borysthenes, died here, and the emperor prepared a tomb with an epitaph for him. The epitaph is a short poem of praise of little artistic worth, which must have been quickly scribbled by the bereaved, versifying owner.

> Borysthenes the barbarian
> Caesar's hunting horse
> was accustomed to flash by
> through sea and through bog
> and past Etruscan barrows.

It is a private tribute. Something amusing or untoward must have happened at a tumulus in Tuscany, but the author does not trouble to tell us what it was. He goes on to claim that no boar ever gored Borysthenes, so that cannot have been the cause of his death at Apta. Perhaps the horse fell and broke a leg, and had to be put down. In any event,

> Killed on his fated day
> here he lies beneath the soil.

Hadrian was very fond of animals, and Borysthenes was not the only creature to be buried with honors. According to the *Historia Augusta,* he loved his horses and dogs so much that he provided tombs for them all when they died.

The saddened emperor continued his journey south, spending the winter of 122 at the capital of the province of Hispania Tarraconensis. This was Rome's oldest foundation in Spain, Tarraco (today's Tarragona)—or to call it by its proper title, Colonia Julia Urbs Triumphalis Tarraco. A walled city built on terraces on high ground, it stood on the coast but lacked a safe harbor. It was well appointed with all the appurtenances of the civilized life.

According to the poet Martial, who, out of favor for his excessive flattery of Domitian, spent his last years in his native Hispania, Tarraco had much to recommend it, especially to a keen huntsman like his friend Licinianus.

> There you will slaughter deer snared in soft-meshed toils
> and native boars
> and run the cunning hare to death with your stout horse
> (stags you will leave to the bailiff).
> The nearby wood shall come down right to your own hearth
> and its girdle of grimy brats.
> The hunter will be invited; shout from close by,
> and a guest will come to share your dinner.

The simple life without luxuries in the countryside appealed to generations of world-weary urban Romans. This could be little more than a literary trope, and often meant lounging around in comfortable rural villas. But Hadrian had a genuine taste for roughing it in the company of ordinary, unpretentious folk. It was one of the delights that hunting guaranteed.

Hadrian would have known Tarraco. It had been the hometown of his dead patron and promoter, Licinius Sura, and was a regular stopping-off point for travelers from Baetica in the south as they made their way by the safe if slow land route to Italy.

Among the city's amenities were some gardens. They were probably those which, according to an inscription, a certain Publius Rufius Flavus left during his lifetime to four of his manumitted slaves. The legacy was to honor the "perpetual memory" of his dead wife, and the gardens could not be sold by the heirs or their successors, so we can deduce that they were to be a public park under the management of his freedmen and freedwomen.

It was here that the emperor took a stroll one day. According to the *Historia Augusta,*

> one of the slaves of the household rushed at him madly with a sword. But he merely laid hold of the man, and when the servants ran to the rescue handed him over to them. Afterward, when it was found that the man was mad, he turned him over to the physicians for treatment, and all this time showed not the slightest sign of alarm.

The attempt had no political implications—except that the emperor's calm and clement reaction won him widespread admiration.

Hadrian somewhat tarnished his popularity by announcing a recruiting drive for the legions. Roman citizens of Italian origin were not used to signing up in the army, and good-humoredly (but probably unsuccessfully) objected. It is a curious, and perhaps not unrelated, fact that on his journey south through Spain he failed to revisit his hometown of Italica, despite investing heavily in public buildings there over the years. His fellow citizens may have been preparing to submit a request to raise their town's municipal status, but they were disappointed. Any petition had to be put in writing, and the emperor merely promised to speak to the subject when next in the Senate.

Urgent matters were calling for the emperor's attention. While he was still in Britannia, reports had arrived of a renewed rebellion in Mauretania and riotous disturbances in Alexandria. It was only four years since the civil strife between rebellious Jews and the Greek community had been suppressed by Marcius Turbo (now the praetorian prefect in

Rome). But this time the trouble came from the native Egyptians in the form of a found bull.

According to their cosmogony the universe was dreamed of and then created by the god Ptah; in another epiphany he was Osiris, the murdered deity who rose from the dead and was the redeemer and merciful judge in the afterworld. Ptah's incarnation or messenger on earth was a sacred bull, Apis. The bull was recognized by special markings on his forehead, tongue, and flank, and was housed in Ptah's temple at Memphis. He was given a harem of cows and worshipped. On his death, he was interred alongside his predecessors in a huge sarcophagus in a necropolis known as the Serapeum.

A new Apis bull had recently been identified and coins minted in Alexandria welcomed the happy event. However, a dispute broke out; according to the *Historia Augusta,* different communities put in a claim to look after the Apis bull, and widespread disorder ensued. The nervous prefect of Egypt sought the emperor's presence.

The North African phase of Hadrian's travels is very poorly documented. We must assume that the Mauretanian problem was not as large as supposed; if there had been a major war and the emperor had had to intervene personally, we would have heard something about it. The provincial governor may have dealt with the matter before his arrival in the region, or the very fact of his arrival may have calmed angry breasts.

So far as Alexandria was concerned, good advice was at hand. Suetonius' successor as *ab epistulis* was very probably a Gallic intellectual, Lucius Julius Vestinus. A cultured man, he had been director of the imperial libraries and, germanely, had held the top academic post in the ancient world. He had been head of the Mouseion, a scientific research institution and literary academy in Alexandria with a celebrated library, which the ruling Ptolemies founded in the third century B.C. So Vestinus had direct knowledge of the Egyptian way of life, and was well placed to counsel his employer on the best course of action.

For the time being, Hadrian contented himself with a stern letter of reproof, which had the surprising effect of immediately stopping the rioting. Once again, the knowledge that he was slowly but inexorably journeying toward Egypt may have concentrated minds.

• • •

Hardly had these passing crises died away than a new and larger one loomed. Parthia was stirring. The emperor forwent a full inspection of the African provinces, probably setting sail for Antioch and arriving there in June 123. His aim was to meet the Parthian king, whichever member of the royal family happened to be on the throne for the moment, and dissuade him from aggression.

The city had not yet fully recovered from the devastating earthquake of eight years previously, and Hadrian scattered cultural largesse about him. He seems to have cherished an affection for the morally dubious gardens at Daphne and remained grateful to the clairvoyant Castalian springs there which had predicted his accession to the purple. He founded a "festival of the springs" to be held there every June 23, as well as commissioning a "theater of the springs" and a shrine of the nymphs. Although there is no record of the fact, presumably he removed the stones with which he had fearfully blocked the source in the first days of his reign.

Before setting off for the Parthian border Hadrian took care to honor Trajan's memory by ordering the construction of a "very elegant" temple dedicated to his predecessor. The honor of Rome, and the practicalities of negotiation with a resentful interlocutor, meant that Trajan's disastrous attempt to conquer the Parthian empire had to be presented as a victory.

Few details have survived about the quarrel, and it is even uncertain which of two rival rulers was occupying the throne at the time. It was probably Chosroes, whom Hadrian had acknowledged as rightful king in 117 when pulling the legions back from Parthia. As already noted, the new Roman emperor had deposed the puppet monarch whom Trajan had installed, Chosroes' renegade son Parthemaspates, awarding the young man the consolation prize of Osrhoene, the little kingdom in northwestern Mesopotamia.

Five years later, Chosroes may have objected to this continuing thorn in his side. He may also have pressed for the return of his daughter and his throne, both of them captured and held hostage during Trajan's campaign. One wonders, too, whether the king pressed for some kind of reparations for all the damage the legions had done during their blitzkrieg offensive. Rome was used to subsidizing neighboring states or tribes to keep them quiet.

The usual form for encounters between Roman and Parthian heads of state was for them to gather on either bank of the Euphrates, which marked the border between the two realms, and meet face-to-face on an island in the river; and that was presumably what happened on this occasion. As for the outcome, the *Historia Augusta* is brief and vague. "War with the Parthians had not at that time passed beyond the preparatory stage, and Hadrian checked it by a personal conference." From this we can safely deduce that the emperor gave ground. Because he was uninterested in recouping Trajan's brief gains, war would bring no practical advantage and would contradict his policy of self-containment. It would also consume vast quantities of treasure.

Coins tell the story of how the emperor presented the entente with Chosroes. For some time they made reference to an *expeditio Augusti,* or "the emperor on campaign," which covered the defense review of Britannia, putting down the Moorish rebellion, and addressing the Parthian threat. Then the image of Janus began to appear on the coinage.

Janus was the god of entrances and exits, of comings and goings, beginnings and endings. He was presented as two-faced "since he is the doorkeeper of heaven and hell," and presided over gates and doorways. A small temple in the Roman Forum was dedicated to him, the doors of which were opened in times of war and closed when the empire was at peace. The Romans understood peace to be the fruit of victory on the battlefield, so if, as seems very likely, the new coins mean that the emperor shut Janus' doors, he was claiming military success for what was at best an achievement of negotiation.

It can be no accident that the ruler he revered so much, Augustus, took the same line on Parthia as he did—namely, that talking is better than fighting. He, too, presented the deals he struck in 20 B.C. and A.D. 2 with Parthian monarchs as the result of compelling, rather than compromising with, a recalcitrant enemy. And it was the first *princeps* who made clever use of the doors of Janus; they had been shut only twice before in Rome's whole, warlike history, but Augustus closed them three times.

• • •

The past came vividly to life for the emperor when he visited the spot where a famous incident had taken place in the fifth century B.C. It was a rough pathway leading up to a mountain ridge that overlooked the Black Sea and the port of Trapezus in northern Cappadocia (today's Trebizond). It was here that one day in 401 B.C. a harassed band of Greek mercenaries found themselves after struggling through a high pass along a very narrow, steep, and winding route.

Greek infantry ("hoplites") were widely believed to be the best soldiers of their day, and about ten thousand of them had been hired by a pretender to the throne of the Persian empire. They joined his army and marched against the sitting king of kings. Near Babylon they helped the pretender win a decisive victory, but he fell in the fighting. The rebellion died with him, and the Greeks, now unemployed and unwelcome, had to fight their way through hundreds of miles of hostile territory to escape from the Persians. Their generals and senior officers were killed or captured, and the Athenian Xenophon, then an inexperienced but able young soldier, was elected as commander. He was a natural leader and, against the odds, brought his men to the safety of the Black Sea coast, with its Greek cities and ships to sail them home.

As the bedraggled regiment toiled its way up the slope, Xenophon and the rearguard heard a great shout from the brow of the hill and feared that it was some more enemies attacking from the front. Xenophon, who wrote a memoir of the long march home (modestly speaking of himself in the third person), described what happened next:

> However, when the shouting got louder and drew nearer, and those who were constantly going forward started running toward the men in front who kept on shouting, and the more there were the more shouting there was, it looked then as though this was something of considerable importance. So Xenophon mounted his horse and, taking . . . the cavalry with him, rode forward to give support and, quite soon, they heard the soldiers shouting out: "The sea! The sea!"

It was as famous a moment of return as Odysseus' homecoming in Ithaca from the Trojan war. Hadrian, who was inspecting the eastern frontier provinces after agreeing his entente with Chosroes, made sure he found the time to pay homage to one of his heroes. He regarded Xenophon highly not just for his courage and decency, but because he was an enthusiastic huntsman and, as we have seen, the author of a classic text on the subject.

Hadrian was touched by the place. To mark his visit, he added to memorial cairns built by the Greek soldiers by arranging for altars to be erected, plus a statue of himself. A few years later, Arrian, the emperor's friend and an even more fervent admirer of the Athenian, was appointed governor of Cappadocia and toured the area in that capacity. He was dismayed by what he found at the mountain ridge. He informed the emperor that the altars had indeed been built, but in rough stone with an inaccurately cut inscription, and he had decided to replace them. As for the statue of the emperor,

> although [it] has been erected in a pleasing pose—it points out to the sea—the work neither looks like you nor is beautiful in any way. So I have sent for a sculpture worthy to bear your name, in the same pose; for that spot is very well suited to an everlasting monument.

No doubt the replacements were a distinct improvement, but Arrian's reference to an "everlasting monument" was challenging fate. Nothing now remains of altars or statue—but the cairns are still there. Immortality, only where it is due.

The emperor's next stop was Bithynia-Pontus. The province was of strategic importance because it lay on the southern littoral of the Black Sea and was the main communication route between the Danube and Euphrates frontiers. According to ancient sources, the region was settled by Thracians from across the Propontis, but along the coastline a necklace of cities was founded by Greek colonists from the mainland and Asia Minor. Hellenic culture flourished there, as is borne out by the distinguished men whom the province produced—the famous rhetorician Dio Chrysostom of Prusa; Arrian, author and soldier; and, born later in the second century, the historian Dio Cassius.

There was plenty for an inquisitive visitor to inspect. The politics of Bithynia-Pontus was disputatious and corrupt and, for all Pliny's attempts at reform in the previous reign, it is unlikely that much had changed since. Also, his correspondence with Trajan discussed numerous building and engineering projects, exactly the kind of thing that fascinated the emperor. At the city of Amastris, for example, Pliny wrote of a "long street of great beauty" marred by an open sewer running down the middle of it; he won Trajan's permission to cover it and remove a "disgusting eyesore which gives off a noxious stench." Hadrian could not have resisted the temptation to inspect the street himself to make sure that the project had been completed satisfactorily and the problem solved.

An earthquake had struck the province, and Nicomedia, the provincial capital, and the town of Nicaea had sustained much damage. The emperor provided funds for the necessary restoration work and doubtless busied himself with the detail of public development projects.

He expected no especial surprises during his stay in the province and laid plans for his future destinations—Thrace and then northward to the frontier provinces on the Danube. Finally, to his huge pleasure and as a reward for his labors, he anticipated a lengthy stay in his spiritual homeland, Greece. However, before he went on his way a chance encounter took place.

He came across a country boy in his mid-teens, who was to transform his life.

XIX

THE BITHYNIAN BOY

. . .

He came from an upland town called Claudiopolis (today's Bolu). Named after the emperor Claudius, its citadel rose from a high plain in a mountain range that closed off the province's flat and fertile coastal fringe. The mountain slopes were covered with fir trees, oaks, and beeches, from which generations of fleets were constructed. There was little agricultural land but grass meadows fattened cattle and the area was well known for its milk and cheeses (and still is). In winters ice and snow could render the roads impassable.

Then as now, the lakes, forests, and mountains were rich in wildlife, including wild boar. This was excellent hunting country and it is very possible that Hadrian rode out here to take part in his favorite pastime.

Claudiopolis was a prosperous place and the local worthies were ambitious, sometimes overly so, for their city. Pliny reported indignantly to Trajan that they were "building, or rather excavating, an enormous public bath at the foot of a mountain." Not only was the site dangerously inappropriate, but its funding was dubious. He could not make up his mind whether to complete the original plans and hope that good money was not being thrown after bad, or to begin again at a new location and sacrifice the original outlay. Trajan replied shortly that the governor must decide for himself.

The main road from Cappadocia passed through Claudiopolis, and we can hardly doubt that Hadrian, copy of Pliny in his hand, stopped off to see how the dilemma had been resolved. It may be then and there that he met, or at least noticed, the boy.

• • •

Antinous was about fifteen or maybe a little younger in 123; if the year of his birth is uncertain, his birthday probably fell on November 27. History has not recorded his first encounter with the emperor. Before 130, when the pair went sightseeing in Egypt and North Africa, they are invisible. However, this was the only time when we find them in one place and they could have set eyes on each other.

It is possible to make a judgment by assessing the many statues of Antinous that have survived. Most of the images are posthumous—idealized and melancholy. But some survive from the beginning of Antinous' career that evoke a cheerful, chubby-faced teenager, almost a child (puberty seems to have arrived late in the ancient world, officially at fourteen for boys but in practice between fourteen and sixteen). In about 130 we see Antinous in a carved relief, as a whiskered young man with short hair, twenty or so years old.

So it is reasonable to infer that the paths of the forty-seven-year-old emperor and the young Bithynian crossed during the former's journey through the province. Rulers do not happen upon strangers in the street, and we must assume that Antinous was taking part in some public ceremony when he was noticed. This could well have occurred at Claudiopolis, but, if not, then at the capital, Nicomedia. Heraclea offers a third possibility, for games were founded and held there in the emperor's honor, and Antinous could have been a competitor.

Nothing whatever is known of the boy's parents, except that they claimed or assumed Greek descent. The people of Claudiopolis believed (whether rightly or wrongly is unclear) that migrants from Arcadia in the Peloponnese established their city. The capital of Arcadia was Mantinea, and it is relevantly curious that a woman called Antinoe was its secondary founder: inspired by an oracle and guided by a helpful snake, she moved the city to a new location. Antinous is the male form of her name, which was, we may suppose, popular in Claudiopolis.

A late reference to Antinous as Hadrian's "slave" can be discounted, for that would have been seen as a thoroughly disreputable provenance for an imperial favorite. We may guess, and it is no more than a guess, that Antinous belonged to a modestly prosperous family, prominent enough to enable their son to take part in some kind of public event, but not for a social position of any distinction. If they had belonged to the established, property-owning class that ran most local authorities, we might have expected some mention of this to survive in the record.

Whatever the details of the boy's origins and social status, the large, the overwhelming fact is that Hadrian fell in love with Antinous. The relationship was to color the rest of their lives.

But what did "falling in love," and for that matter in lust, mean for an elite citizen in the Roman empire? Something very different from our ideas today. Sex did not have the attributes of sin and guilt that Christianity brought to it. Most people in the ancient world found making love to be, in principle, an innocent, or at least an innocuous, pleasure.

There were limits, of course, to sexual freedom. The comic playwright Titus Maccius Plautus, writing as early as the third century B.C., set out a basic principle that remained current for centuries. A slave reassures his young master, who yearns for a prostitute rather than a freeborn girl:

> no one keeps you from coming here or forbids you from buying what is openly for sale—if you have the cash. No one keeps you from traveling on the public road; so long as you do not make your way through a fenced-off farm, so long as you keep away from a married woman, an unmarried woman, a maiden, young men, and free boys, love whatever you like.

The point was that sex with Roman citizens outside marriage was beyond the pale, for not even the shadow of a doubt should be allowed to fall across a citizen's paternity. Slaves and foreigners of either gender, though, were fair game.

It follows from this that Hadrian would have broken the rules when sleeping with Antinous if he was a Roman citizen. However, this was probably not the case, for citizenship was an honor usually granted only to members of local elites in the provinces.

The second rule for the Roman male was that he should be sexually "active" rather than "passive." It did not greatly matter into whom he inserted his penis, but he must never allow anyone to insert theirs into him. To be sodomized was to fall under someone else's power, and to be classed as a pseudo-woman.

The Romans had no particular theory of same-sex behavior and saw it simply as one among a number of sexual variations. Through a law passed in the second century B.C., the *lex Scantinia,* they tried to control homosexual acts of which they disapproved (male prostitution, for example), but by the time of the empire legal sanctions had more or less become a dead letter.

By contrast, the Greeks developed an idealized and specialized version of homosexual behavior. It involved relations between young men and postpubertal teenagers. The older partner was expected to educate his boy lover in virtue in the public square and courage on the battlefield. Some form of sexual activity was an expected, but (so far as we can tell) not absolutely essential, component in these relationships. The boy was not meant to desire his mentor, however charming or good-looking, but allowed himself to be the object of desire; provided discretion was exercised, he might even agree to being sodomized, whether intercrurally or rectally. The wider function of the pairings is uncertain, but people at the time believed that they encouraged martial valor. Also, just as marriage was a useful means of uniting families, so these love affairs facilitated the creation of informal networks of political alliances.

Homosexual practices varied from state to state, and were often restricted to aristocrats or elite groups. In Sparta and Thebes close affection between young men was part of the military ethos. The Cretans engaged in a procedure that resembles tribal initiation ceremonies in different parts of the world. A young man asked a boy's friends to abduct him and hand him over. He then gave the boy expensive presents, after which they went out into the countryside with all the boy's friends and spent two months hunting and feasting. The *philetor,* or befriender, and the *parastates,* or stander-beside-in-battle, as they were called, were now a recognized couple.

The Athenian system is well described in Plato's *Symposium,* or "The

Drinking Party" (dialogues were a popular form of "faction" in Greco-Roman culture, combining real-life debaters and fictional debates). Pausanias, one of the speakers, makes it clear that a love affair between an *erastes,* or lover, and an *eromenos,* or beloved one, was highly respectable.

> Lovers of their own sex . . . do not fall in love with mere boys, but wait until the age at which they begin to show some intelligence, that is to say, until they are near growing a beard. By choosing that moment in the life of their favorite they show, if I am not mistaken, that their intention is to form a lasting attachment and a partnership for life.

In other words, the heat of passion, *eros,* would give way over time to a deep but nonphysical friendship between adults, *philia.* A sexual relationship, intense or otherwise, was in the nature of things ephemeral. It came to an end when a beard replaced a smooth cheek.

The theory and practice of "Greek love" survived the fall of the free city-states and their absorption into the Roman empire, and remained current in Hadrian's day. In one of his numerous dialogues, Plutarch, the emperor's older and much admired contemporary, the leading Hellenic intellectual of his day, gave the floor to a spokesman for same-sex relationships, a certain Protogenes.

> The true genuine love is that of boys, not afire with lust . . . nor besmeared with perfumed ointments, nor alluring with smiles and rolling glances; but you shall find this love plain and simple and undebauched, delighting in the schools of the philosophers, or in the wrestling lists and gymnasia . . . and exhorting to virtue all that he finds to be fit objects of his attention.

How seriously should we take assurances of this kind? Cynics such as Cicero suspected the motives of the *erastes* who claimed to be interested only in the soul of his *eromenos.* Why is it, he mused, that no one falls in love with an *ugly* youngster?

Men did not categorize themselves as homosexual, for, until the inventions of modern psychology, there was no concept, and so no term, for man-to-man sexual preference as a viable and exclusive alternative to heterosexuality and as a describer of personality. But too much can be made of this apparent lack of definition. There were impolite terms for the "out," feminized homosexual (*cinaedus,* for example); and, more pertinently, Romans were quite capable of telling straights from gays even without our words for them. Many slept impartially with members of both sexes. (We have little clear idea of homosexual behavior among women, except that sophisticated circles knew of it. Martial certainly did when he played on the two meanings of girlfriend, sexual and amicable.

> Lesbia of the Lesbians, Philaenis, how right you are
> to call the woman you fuck "my girlfriend."

It is a pity that more is not known of attitudes in Trajan's womanly household, in which heterosexual males were conspicuous by their absence.)

One of the remarkable features of this period is that for nearly fifty years the imperial government was headed by two men who engaged predominantly, if not exclusively, in homosexual behavior. There are no references at all to Trajan sleeping with women. As for Hadrian, Sabina's remark about taking precautions to avoid pregnancy implies at least occasional coitus, if we are to credit an angry witness. The *Historia Augusta* cites reports of his "passion for males and adulteries with married women," but there is not a sliver of supporting evidence for the latter in any of the sources. Whatever the exact nature of the emperors' sexuality, it was not felt to be of political significance since they never allowed their private lives to influence their public decisions, and no one complained.

However, it is hard to believe that this homosexual preference did not have some impact on cultural and social attitudes, although such evidence as remains fails to show causal links. A literature of pederasty flourished. A poet called Straton, who came from Sardis in the fertile Hermus Valley in Asia Minor and was a contemporary of Hadrian, happily acknowledged that he was a *philopais,* or boy lover. He published an anthology of gay epigrams, *Mousa Paidike,* or "The Boyish Muse," many of which he wrote himself. Playful lip service to love concealed a more cynical motive—how to find a pretty lad and have his way with him; abuse masked as flirtatiousness.

Juvenal takes a bleaker view of Rome's ubiquitous and corrupt gay scene. He sympathizes with a male prostitute "who used to fancy himself as a soft, pretty boy, a latter-day Ganymede" and has grown up to be no more than a well-hung "two-legged donkey" buggering old men up their depilated, distended rear passages. This, we may gloomily infer, was the fate awaiting Straton's little favorites.

Where do we place the *philopais* emperor and his Antinous in this variegated landscape of the senses? Hadrian's reported behavior at Trajan's court suggests a strong libido and a promiscuous nature. He could well have regarded his Bithynian boy as a plaything—the kind of golden lad that graces Straton's pages. With Hadrian's reputation as a procurer of every luxury and licentiousness, Antinous was simply another in a long line of conquests.

There is a more attractive alternative—that this most Hellenic of emperors cast himself as an *erastes* with Antinous as his *eromenos*. If he followed the rules, he would have treated the boy with respect, wooed him, and given him the choice whether or not to accept his advances. Any "favors" Hadrian was granted would have been matched by a serious commitment to Antinous' moral development as he grew into an adult.

The strongest argument in favor of this hypothesis is that the relationship did indeed endure. Antinous was no brief fling. However, social equality was implicit in Greek love, and the disparity of power between the man and the boy was far too wide to allow genuine freedom of choice, however much an idealistic lover may have wished to confer it on his beloved. Who says no to an autocrat? Also, it was inconceivable that someone of Antinous' class could be trained for a political and military career when an adult, for Rome's political elite would have been shocked to its core by such a promotion.

The most likely conclusion is that Hadrian's emotions were complicated. Antinous may have started off as the kind of boy whom Straton hymns, but for some reason, unknowable and unguessable now, he attracted the emperor's deepest feelings. So what looked to outsiders like a routine liaison, Hadrian decorated with the anachronistic appurtenances of Greek love.

The relationship between an *erastes* and an *eromenos* was meant to ripen into *philia,* a lifelong friendship. But what would happen five or so years later, when summer inevitably gave way to fall, and stubble grew on Antinous' cheeks? Would Hadrian stay true?

Hadrian traveled in style, serviced by an *agmen comitantium,* a "moving multitude of companions." There were the bureaucrats, who looked after his correspondence with provincial governors and the Senate in Rome, helped him reply to petitions that poured in from every corner of the empire, and controlled the finances. There were the Praetorians, and the fiercely loyal Batavians. There were specially recruited "cohorts on the model of military legions" of workmen, stonemasons, architects, and "every kind of specialist in the construction and interior decoration of great buildings."

If it was what the emperor wanted, it was easy enough to add a boy to the retinue. However, Antinous needed an induction into the mysterious and complicated ways of life at court, and it seems rather more likely that he was packed off to the imperial Paedogogium in Rome, the ruins of which have been excavated by archaeologists. This was a boarding school for boys between twelve and eighteen years, where they trained to be pages at court; the gravestone of one of its directors about this time reveals that his name was, aptly enough, Titus Flavius Ganymedes. Inscriptions suggest that they were well looked after, for we hear of a "master medical rubber of distinguished children"—an anointer—and a hairdresser. Youth and good looks were insufficient for a complete career, and students also acquired the wider skills they would need for the rest of their lives as servants or slaves. These were to be the chamberlains, bookkeepers, secretaries, valets, and butlers of the future.

As well as writing, arithmetic, and so forth, the students would learn how to serve drinks and present food. One disapproving observer spoke of such establishments as "colleges for the most contemptible vices—

the seasoning of food to promote gluttony and the more extravagant serving of courses." And Juvenal grumpily complained of a carver of meat who danced and gestured at the same time as wielding his "flying knife."

Something of the mood of the place can be discerned in some two hundred graffiti low down on the walls of small rooms in the Paedogogium. Most of them are happy messages of delight from students after graduation. "Corinthus is leaving the Paedogogium!" "Narbonensis is leaving the Paedogogium!" Two friends or brothers write their names together, and another scrawl refers to "lovers." The most striking image is of a boy kneeling in front of a cross on which hangs a male figure with a donkey's head. Underneath, a scornful legend reads: "Alexamenos worships his god!" Presumably he was a young Christian, teased for his beliefs.

Hadrian traversed the narrow stretch of water dividing Asia from Europe and reviewed the multitribal, now Hellenized province of Thrace. He then recrossed the Propontis and toured Mysia. Once more the emperor indulged his fascination with the past. He visited the site of the battle of Granicus, where in 334 B.C. Alexander the Great had daringly charged across a stream with a steep slope to confront and defeat the massed forces of the Persian commander. The emperor moved on to Troy, then a tiny coastal settlement devoted entirely to tourists, where he was the latest in a long line of distinguished leaders to pay his respects, among them Alexander himself. Hadrian noticed that the so-called tomb of the Greek warrior Ajax was in a state of disrepair. Apparently the sea had washed open the entrance to the grave mound and revealed bones of gigantic size; the kneecaps alone were as large as a boy's discus. The emperor had them reinterred. It is hard to say what had been unearthed, perhaps some misinterpreted fossils.

Hadrian took time off for some highly successful hunting. He was so pleased with killing a she-bear in Mysia's wooded mountainous hinterland that he founded a town on the spot called Hadrianutherae, or Hadrian's Hunt. It may have been at this point that there was another apparent assassination attempt on the emperor, during which nothing seems to have happened (like the one with which his reign began).

A friend of his, a member of his entourage at the time, told the story. He was Marcus Antonius Polemon, a leading Hellenic intellectual and orator, who was about ten years younger than the emperor; descended from kings of Pontus, he lived in the grand manner, at some cost to the imperial budget, but in compensation he could not have been a more enthusiastic proponent of Greek culture. He ran a school of rhetoric in Smyrna, where he taught "select and genuinely Hellenic" students.

Polemon, via an unsure translation of his Greek text into Arabic, wrote: "Once I accompanied the greatest king, and while we were traveling with him from Thrace to Asia with his troops and vehicles, that man mingled with them." The identity of "that man" is not revealed, but Polemon thought very little of him; he was insolent, shameless, an inciter of trouble against authority, and, worst of all, an alcoholic who took his drink badly.

Before the hunt got under way Polemon was shocked to see the man with his companions, and all of them armed. They surrounded Hadrian, but this "was in no way to show honor to the emperor or because he was well disposed toward him. No, he was looking to do him harm and carrying out his evil designs, which allowed him no rest."

Meanwhile the supposed victim was getting ready to set off, aware of nothing untoward. This prevented Polemon and his friends from entering into conversation with him. So, instead, they chatted among themselves about Hadrian—"what an uneasy position he was in, how far removed from the pleasant life people used to say he enjoyed." They also mentioned the unnamed delinquent, who had crept up on the group and was eavesdropping. "You must have been talking about me," he said. Polemon admitted the charge, and counterattacked.

"We did mention you," I said, "and expressed amazement at your manner. Out with it, then! Tell us how you have imposed this burden on yourself and how you can bear such tensions in your soul." This resulted in an instant outburst. He had a demon in him, the man admitted, that was responsible for the evil desire in his soul. He began to weep—"Woe is me, I am destroyed!"

This is a most curious episode, and we never learn the outcome. Polemon may have simply meant to smear someone who was a disagreeable and undependable host or fellow guest. But, as we have already seen, a hunt was a good place to kill an emperor, it being the only occasion when people were officially allowed to carry weapons in his presence. Perhaps the truth is that a grumbling opposition to Hadrian lingered on for some time into his reign and occasionally threatened to coalesce into a plot—but never quite succeeded in doing so.

Polemon certainly had a point when he wrote of the emperor's life not being the *vie de luxe* that many imagined. Even an idle *princeps* had his hands full with the business of government, but the hyperactive Hadrian kept himself extremely busy addressing a multitude of detailed issues, as his tour of Asia Minor goes to show.

It is surprising to see the degree of micromanagement to which the Roman state committed itself. The collection of taxes was, naturally and always, a high priority, but most emperors cast themselves as well-meaning arbiters of civic disputes and assessors of local needs; Hadrian was unusual only for the ubiquity of his engagement—and for his propensity to turn up in person to look into matters himself. One consequence was the large number of cities and towns that renamed themselves after their benefactor; a Hadrianopolis here and a Hadriane there mark the emperor's interventionist progress throughout the eastern provinces.

The prosperous city of Stratonicea (today an Anatolian village called Eskihisar) is a case in point. It hosted the emperor in 123, and renamed itself Hadrianopolis as thanks for some now forgotten favors. The relationship persisted in the following years. Three letters from the emperor show him taking action on the city's behalf. He grants it the right to collect taxes in the rural hinterland that previously went to the Roman *fiscus,* and decides that a wealthy absentee landlord should "either repair [a property in Stratonicea] or sell it to one of the local inhabitants so that it does not collapse from age and neglect." He also indicates that he has briefed serving provincial governors to look kindly on the city.

Two anecdotes suggest that the pressure of the emperor's administrative duties sometimes led to a brief, regretted explosion. While on one of his journeys (the date is unknown, but it could have been now) a woman stepped forward as the emperor passed by, and made a request. "I haven't got the time," Hadrian said. With considerable presence of mind, perhaps powered by desperation, she replied, "Well, stop being emperor, then!" This struck home. The emperor relented and gave her a hearing.

While in Asia Minor, he visited Pergamum, an opulent city of more than one hundred thousand inhabitants. Here, according to Aelius Galenus (or Galen, the famous medical researcher and theorist), in his book on mental illness,

> the emperor Hadrian struck one of his attendants in the eye with a pen. When he realized that [the slave] had become blind in one eye as a result of this stroke, he called him to him and offered to let him ask him for any gift to make up for what he had suffered. When the victim remained silent, Hadrian again asked him to make a request of whatever he wanted. He declined to accept anything else, but asked for his eye back—for what gift could provide compensation for the loss of an eye?

The story has a good provenance, for its source was probably Galen's father, a Pergamese architect at the time of Hadrian's visit. At least, the anecdote is evidence that Hadrian wrote letters himself, pen to parchment, as well as dictating to secretaries. The clear implication is that on this occasion the *princeps* lost his temper over something, even if (as is probable) the injury itself was unintended.

Wherever Hadrian went he invested in urban infrastructure; he commissioned aqueducts and canals, new roads or the refurbishment of old ones, and he paid lavishly for the construction of temples and other public buildings.

He was constitutionally unable to turn down an architectural challenge. At Cyzicus, a busy port on the Propontis, work on a vast temple of Zeus had been started three centuries before, but never finished. Hadrian agreed with Pliny that it was a Roman emperor's duty to "accomplish what kings could only attempt" and arranged for the temple's completion. Its columns were about seventy feet high and were carved out of single blocks of marble. "In general," observed Dio Cassius, "the details of the edifice were more to be wondered at than to be praised." In this case, Hadrian's good intentions came to nothing, for in the following reign an earthquake brought the temple down.

The emperor faced an even more tempting test of his construction team's abilities. Approaching the end of his long tour, he renewed his acquaintance with Ephesus, where "young men of the city sang a hymn in the theater for the emperor, who listened to it in a gracious and friendly manner," as we can well imagine. From there he made for Rhodes. Sailing into the island's port, he passed the recumbent remains of the Colossus of Rhodes, one of the Seven Wonders of the ancient world. This was a huge statue of the god Helios, the Sun himself. Built in the early third century B.C., it stood at the harbor mouth (or on a breakwater nearby) and was more than one hundred feet high (about three-quarters the height of the Statue of Liberty). It was made from brick towers encased by bronze plates and was mounted on a white marble pedestal fifty feet high. The Colossus had stood for only fifty-six years when it was felled by one of the region's frequent earthquakes.

The statue, still apparently in one piece, lay on the ground for centuries and was so impressive that many traveled to see it. Hadrian was one of these tourists and, according to a late and not altogether dependable source, a Byzantine chronicler called John Malalas, had it reerected, providing cranes, ropes, and craftsmen. The difficulty with this account is that there is no corroboration. However, Malalas claims to have seen an inscription commemorating the event. What is more, it was exactly the kind of project to which Hadrian would have been attracted. Perhaps the task proved in the event too difficult and eventually had to be abandoned. Alternatively, the restoration took place, only for the Colossus soon to collapse again. One way or another, by then the emperor was long gone, and the locals could safely leave the god to rest in peace.

• • •

On his travels Hadrian was concerned not only with building programs and economic development; he also took a close interest in the administration of justice. He is the first emperor whose legislation and rulings have been preserved to any extent. This is in large part due to his decision to commission a legal expert, Lucius Salvius Julianus, to compile and systematize in a single document, sometimes called the Perpetual Edict, the diffuse laws and judgments that had grown up over the centuries. As well as laws on the statute book, officeholders such as praetors and provincial governors, who had judicial functions, issued edicts at the beginning of their terms of office that set out their legal priorities. Under the empire the findings of recognized jurists also had legal force, as did the judgments of emperors themselves. This mass of material contained many inconsistencies and disagreements that needed to be resolved.

The tendency of Julianus' work was to reinforce the authority of the emperor. The preamble to Justinian's *Digest,* published in the sixth century A.D., observed:

> Julianus himself, that most acute framer of laws and of the Perpetual Edict, laid it down in his own writings that whatever was found to be defective should be supplied by imperial decree, and not he alone but the deified Hadrian as well in the consolidation of the Edict and in the decree of the Senate which followed it most clearly prescribed that where anything is not found set out in the Edict shall be provided for in accordance with the rules of the Edict, and by inferences from and analogies to the rules, by more recent authority.

At last the emperor could say farewell to his eastern provinces. He had a much-anticipated, long-delayed pleasure in store. This was a return to Athens, after a decade's absence. In the last couple of years he had been in touch with the city fathers and, at their request, helped them recast their constitution. Now he had a more radical ambition to fulfill. This was nothing less than making Greece an equal partner with Rome, and rebalancing the empire. The imperial flotilla left Rhodes and set a course across the Aegean Sea.

XX

THE ISLES OF GREECE

. . .

The piglet squealed and wriggled as it tried to escape from Hadrian's arms. They were on the seashore near Athens and it was his awkward task to wash the pair of them in the water. Once he had accomplished this, the emperor took the young animal and offered it up for sacrifice to Demeter, goddess of the earth's fertility and provider of grain. Its death was intended to stand in place of his own.

Then followed a ritual of purification. Wearing a blindfold, the emperor sat down on a stool covered with a ram's fleece. A winnowing fan was waved over him and then a flaming torch brought close to him. In this way he was cleansed by air and fire.

Hadrian was now a *mustes,* a novice whose initiation would be complete only when he took part in the Mysteries, at the small harbor town of Eleusis in Attica. This religious ceremony took place every year in the autumn month of Boedromion, the first in Athens' calendar year. The emperor had arrived in Greece from Rhodes in the late summer, to ensure he was in time for his spiritual induction.

In the prehistory of the world, Zeus and his fellow deities lived and schemed against one another on the snowy peaks of Mount Olympus in northern Greece. One day the goddess Demeter's beautiful daughter, Persephone, disappeared. She had been kidnapped by Zeus' brother, Hades, lord of the underworld, but her mother had no idea where she was. So Demeter roamed the earth looking for Persephone. Eventually she learned of the abduction and was shocked to discover that the king of the gods had approved the crime in advance. She abandoned her divine status and disguised herself as an old Cretan woman. Eventually she arrived at Eleusis, where she got a job as nanny to a local chieftain's son.

At night when everyone else was asleep Demeter anointed her infant charge with ambrosia, a cream which with repeated use conferred immortality, and put him into the hearth-fire, where he lay unharmed. Unfortunately the boy's mother spied on her once and screamed when the flames touched his body.

An incensed Demeter resumed her full divine form and demanded that a temple be built in her honor. There she would teach people her special rituals—and, just as usefully, the art of agriculture. With that promise she vanished. Meanwhile the earth began to undergo a great famine, for Demeter refused to let the seeds grow. A compromise solution was agreed among the gods: Persephone would spend one third of the year in the underworld and nature would temporarily stop work, but for the rest of her time she would return to her mother and the copious earth.

So the fundamental myth of Eleusis was the death and rebirth of growing and flowering things. But the huge popularity for more than one thousand years of the Eleusinian ceremonies was less that they guaranteed the safely turning seasons than that they offered initiates the promise of a happy afterlife. Becoming an adept of Demeter was an attractive insurance policy to ensure a prosperous posthumous future. Men and women, slaves and freedmen, all were entitled to become initiates (provided only that they could speak Greek). Murderers burdened with blood guilt were excluded. Upper-class Romans, weary of the arid superstitions of their state religion, often participated in the Mysteries at Eleusis. Cicero believed that the Mysteries helped to civilize his rough-and-ready compatriots. "We have learned from them the beginnings of life, and gained the power not only to live happily, but also to die with a better hope."

Initiates were sworn to perpetual secrecy, on pain of death, about what they saw, heard, and experienced. Luckily, some disrespectful Christian apologists revealed what they knew, or thought they knew. The broad shape of the ceremony in which Hadrian took part is understood, although significant details can only be guessed.

* * *

On the fourteenth day of Boedromion, 124, a band of young men collected the *hiera,* or "sacred things" (ritual utensils of some kind), from Eleusis, and deposited them at a small shrine at the foot of the Acropolis. Usually they carried knives during religious ceremonies, but Hadrian had learned his lesson by now about the danger of allowing armed men into his presence, and this year weapons were banned.

On the nineteenth of the same month a multitude of people formed a procession and proceeded along the Sacred Way, the road that ran for twenty-one miles from Athens to Eleusis. Priestesses carried the sacred things in closed hampers. As well as Hadrian and the other *mustai,* there were the more numerous *epoptai,* those who had already been initiated and witnessed Demeter's secrets at Eleusis at least once before. A rhythmic shout, *Iakh' o Iakhe,* was repeated again and again, perhaps referring to a boy god, Iakchos, in Demeter's service. The crowd danced itself into a state of euphoria and waved bundles of branches in the air.

At a certain point on the road masked figures mocked the passing *mustai,* shouting and making obscene gestures. This commemorated an old woman who met Demeter when she was mourning her daughter and offered her a refreshing drink. On being rebuffed, she had pulled aside her skirt and "uncovered her shame, and exhibited her nudity." The goddess had "laughed and laughed"—and swallowed the drink after all.

The procession crossed a new bridge over the river Kephisos, about a mile from Eleusis. A couple of years previously a flood had swept away its predecessor and Hadrian had commissioned a replacement. He would have been pleased with the result: 165 feet long and 16 wide, it was built of well-cut limestone blocks and has survived in good condition to the present day, although the river itself silted up in modern times.

At last twilight fell and the stars appeared. Once they had arrived at Eleusis, the *mustai* were allowed to break their fast. Hadrian and the rest drank down (just as the goddess had once done) a beverage called *kukeon,* which consisted of barley meal and water mixed with fresh pennyroyal mint leaves. Some modern scholars believe that the barley was contaminated naturally with ergot, which causes hallucinations (among other more distressing symptoms), or that some other intoxicating ingredient was added to the potion.

The initiates passed through two columned gateways into a large walled enclosure. After uttering an enigmatic password, they walked on and found themselves in front of a square, windowless building with a columned porch, like a blind temple. This was the Telesterion, or hall of mysteries. Inside its dark interior were rows of columns and stepped benches along the walls, from which thousands of participants watched the proceedings. Hadrian, like the other new initiates, was accompanied by a guide and was not allowed to see all the sights (he probably wore a veil).

What took place now is known only approximately. In the center of the Telesterion was an oblong stone construction with a doorway opening onto a piece of natural, unhewn rock, the Anactoron. Dreadful, ineffable things took place by flickering torchlight, possibly reenacting the story of Persephone's abduction and all that followed.

On top of the Anactoron, which functioned like an altar, a fire blazed. Perhaps there was some sort of apotheosis by fire, recalling the unharmed boy in the flames. Perhaps animals were killed and burned. The officiating priest, or Hierophant, announced: "The holy Brimo ['the raging one,' a name for Demeter] has been delivered of a holy son, the Brimos."

When the drama came to an end, the priest withdrew through the Anactoron doorway, and then reemerged with the sacred things, a great light shining out when the door opened. This was the culminating revelation, and we have no idea today of what it consisted. A Christian source claimed that it was "an ear of corn in silence reaped. [This was] considered among the Athenians to constitute the perfect enormous illumination."

The religious authorities were well aware of the presence of their illustrious guest. The female partner of the Hierophant, who helped induct Hadrian into the rites, wrote a poem honoring the

> ruler of the wide, unharvested earth,
> the commander of countless mortals,

> Hadrian, who poured out boundless wealth
> on all cities, and especially famous Athens.

The emperor did not reveal what the experience of initiation meant to him. At one level he was merely treading in the footsteps of many Roman predecessors, among them Augustus. But the fact that the *Historia Augusta* mentions the initiation at all suggests that for Hadrian it was more than a routine experience. He was committed to religion as a transcendent experience, and had been fascinated since childhood by magic and astrology. For someone of this cast of mind Eleusis conveyed a powerful spiritual meaning. On a point of detail, the example of the piglet whose life had been sacrificed to secure his own survival may have lodged in his mind, to be exploited when future occasion demanded.

However, Eleusis was also important for reasons of state. Oddly, the *Historia Augusta* claims that the emperor was following the example of Alexander the Great's father, Philip of Macedon, a reference that must derive from a statement in Hadrian's memoirs. Presumably (although there is no direct evidence for it) the king had taken part in the Mysteries, and for some reason Hadrian had wanted to draw attention to the association. But why?

Philip had brutally extinguished Greek liberty at the famous battle of Chaeronea in 338 B.C., and was the last man the emperor would have been expected to cite as a distinguished forerunner. But the message Hadrian wished to convey was that the Macedonian monarch united all the disputatious Greeks under his leadership, and that he had done so by force was less telling than that he was a Panhellene. He had seen Greece as a single entity—an ideal very close to the emperor's heart.

For Hadrian, the Mysteries at Eleusis, which bound together all initiates of whatever nationality and class, were the religious dimension of this single entity. It is no accident that an inscription found at Eleusis, carved after his death, refers to "Hadrian, god and Panhellene."

When he was at Eleusis, Hadrian characteristically kept his eyes open. He noticed, or was informed, that locally caught fish were being sold at an inflated price during the busy period of the Mysteries, and that supply failed to meet demand. He soon discovered that professional retail merchants bought the catch from the fishermen, or from first purchasers, and then sold it to the public with a steep markup. He published a letter to the authorities forbidding this practice and exempting anyone selling fish from the regular purchase tax. He ruled: "I want the vendors to have been stopped from their profiteering or else a charge to be brought against them."

Hadrian now set off on a tour of the Peloponnese, taking Sabina with him. Wherever the imperial court went, ancient cities received the emperor's largesse. Sometimes this was practical, at others extravagantly useless. Not far from the uninhabited ruins of Mycenae stood a great shrine to Hera, queen of the gods, at which Hadrian dedicated "a peacock in gold and glittering stones, because peacocks are considered to be Hera's sacred birds."

In return, names were changed to honor the donor, statues were erected, and temples dedicated. The small town of Megara, for example, received the full force of the emperor's benevolence; a brick temple was rebuilt in stone and a road widened to allow chariots to drive past each other in opposite directions. Grateful inscriptions hailed Hadrian as their "founder, lawgiver, benefactor, and patron," and the empress was enrolled as a "New Demeter." However, Megara remained an impoverished backwater. According to Pausanias, second-century author of a guidebook to Greece, "not even the emperor could make the Megarians thrive: they were his only failure in Greece." This implies there was more to the emperor's munificence than self-aggrandizement. It had a practical purpose—economic development.

Hadrian visited the obvious tourist destinations—among them, austere Sparta, where boys were still whipped until the blood flowed to prove their bravery (and to entertain visitors), and Corinth, systematically devastated by the Romans in 146 B.C. and resettled by Julius Caesar.

But at Mantinea, Hadrian's personal feelings were engaged. On a plain four miles or so south of the town a great battle was fought in 362 B.C. between Thebes, then the leading power in Greece, and an allied army of other city-states. The brilliant and charismatic general Epaminondas led the Thebans and won the day. However, he and his *eromenos*, or beloved, were mortally wounded. They were buried at the roadside. A pillar with a shield on it engraved with a serpent, denoting his clan, marked the spot. Hadrian was touched by the fate of these tragic lovers and wrote a poem about them, which he inscribed on a memorial stone by the tomb (it has not survived).

The walled city of Mantinea also had a special significance, being the reputed origin of the Greek settlers at Claudiopolis, Antinous' birthplace. We do not know of the boy's whereabouts at this time. However, more than a year had passed since they had (probably) first set eyes on each other. If Antinous did go to Rome for training at the Paedogogium, he would surely have graduated by now and been ready for service at court. If we speculate that the couple were together, *princeps* and *pais* will have enjoyed researching the latter's family tree.

Although there is not a jot of evidence, it is hard to believe that Hadrian failed to visit Xenophon's farm near Olympia, thirty miles or so from Mantinea. When the Greek adventurer and huntsman Xenophon bought the estate he built a small temple to Artemis (the Greek Diana), for having helped to save him from the Persians, and he held an annual celebration in her honor. The goddess will have been delighted, for the hunting on his land was excellent. Nothing much had changed over the centuries. Hadrian encouraged Antinous to hunt, and here was ideal country, rich in game, for the young man to learn the art of the chase.

The emperor made sure that he was back in Athens in time for the great theater festival of the Dionysia in March 125 (which he had first attended in 112). He presided as its *agonothetes,* or president, and made a good impression on the locals. Dio Cassius reports: "He wore local dress and carried it off brilliantly."

His hosts during his stay were the international Romanized superrich. One of these had been Philopappus, whom Hadrian met during his first visit to the city, but he had died in 116. His sister, Balbilla, built a grandiose monument for him near the Acropolis, decorated with statues of Philopappus and his ancestors, kings of Commagene. Courtesy of Balbilla, Hadrian may well have billeted himself at the family town house or a villa in the countryside.

Another successful Greek was Gaius Julius Eurycles Herculanus Lucius Vibullius Pius, to give him his complete nomenclature. He was of Spartan stock and descended from a Eurycles who had fought on Augustus' side at Actium and had enthusiastically albeit fruitlessly chased after Antony and Cleopatra as they sped away by sail to Egypt and their doom. A Roman senator and former praetor, he was a senior member of the imperial elite. Plutarch knew him well and dedicated an essay to him (tongue in cheek?) entitled, "How to Praise Oneself Without Incurring Disapproval."

Hadrian was fond of the twenty-four-year-old Lucius Vibullius Hipparchus Tiberius Claudius Atticus Herodes Marathonios (Herodes Atticus, for short). He was an Athenian aristocrat, and fabulously wealthy. His grandfather was reputed to be the richest man in the Greek world. Both he and his son were generous patrons of the arts and architecture, and more than happy to cooperate with the emperor on the beautification of Athens.

Self-interest mingled with the cordiality. Both sides, Romans and Greeks, were aware that there was latent hostility among provincials to the empire. Pliny, writing earlier in the century, warned a prospective governor of Achaea (the province of Greece) that tact was essential when dealing with the locals.

> Do not detract from anyone's dignity, independence, or even pride . . . To rob [Athenians and Spartans] of the name and shadow of freedom, which is all that now remains to them, would be an act of cruelty, ignorance, and barbarism.

But however discreetly the Roman rulers conducted themselves, the reality of Greek subordination was clear enough to the intelligent observer. Plutarch, who admired and liked Romans, argued that anyone entering public office should recognize this, but avoid unnecessary subservience. "Those who introduce the emperor's opinion into every decree, committee debate, act of patronage, and administrative act, force emperors to have more power than they want."

Well, perhaps not in Hadrian's case; it was in his nature to interfere and he loved to consume detail. But was he sensitive to the underlying Hellenic reservation? He was too intelligent not to recognize it, but he did

not value it. As deeply as he respected Greek culture, he was not a senti-
mental naïf like Nero, who believed that he could free all the famous
city-states and return to them their ancient liberties. That experiment
had failed, and Hadrian had a different idea, which was not to liberate
Greece from the empire but to make it equal to Rome *inside* the empire.

There was nothing new in appointing men such as Philopappus and
Eurycles to the Senate and other high positions in the government, but
it was a growing trend that the emperor happily fostered. However, he
wanted to do more than promote meritocrats. His extended stay in
Athens witnessed an astonishing expenditure on new buildings. The result, which gradually became apparent during the years of construction,
was the transformation of an ancient, slightly dusty "university town"
into a new metropolis. Where Rome remained the center of government, Athens was to be the empire's spiritual capital.

Hadrian's coup was to complete the enormous temple of Olympian
Zeus, which stood about one third of a mile southeast of the Acropolis.
The foundations had been laid as long ago as about 520 B.C., the original
plan being to outdo the Temple of Artemis in Ephesus, one of the Seven
Wonders of the world. The project was soon abandoned and, although
work on it briefly recommenced in the second century B.C., since then
nothing had been done. Hadrian now brought matters to a successful, if
extremely expensive, conclusion. In the temple, he installed a colossal
sculpture of Olympian Zeus. The temple was enclosed by a marble-
paved precinct filled with statues of Hadrian, each dedicated by a Greek
city.

Other developments included an aqueduct, a pantheon, a gymnasium, and, in Pausanias' eyes best of all, a cultural center and library,
which had a "hundred columns, walls and colonnades all made of Phry-
gian marble; and pavilions with gilded roofwork and alabaster."

A statue has survived, an official portrait of the emperor in ceremonial armor, which expresses in visual form Hadrian's view of the relation
between Athens and Rome. The breastplate shows in relief the goddess
Athena, patron of Athens, being crowned by divine personifications of
victory. She is standing on a she-wolf suckling the baby boys Romulus
and Remus—the traditional symbol of Rome. It is almost as if Rome
were not the conqueror, but had itself been conquered.

Hadrian cast himself as the unifier; after all, it was on *his* breastplate that images of the empire's two cultures were brought together. As a boy he had incorporated in his own personality a passion for all things Hellenic and at the same time a deep admiration for the old-fashioned moral fiber of the Roman Republic. That balance he now applied, this time in political terms, to the empire of which he was the head.

Four years had passed since Hadrian had last seen Rome, and it was time to go home. He needed to meet the Senate again and check that discontent was not simmering unseen. More excitingly, the villa complex at Tibur was, if not complete, ready for habitation. In the spring of 125 the emperor left Athens and set off northward to the Adriatic port of Dyrrachium (today's Durrës, in Albania).

En route he took the opportunity to explore central and western Greece. Once more he was the indefatigable tourist, calling in at Delphi, home of the classical world's most celebrated oracle. The aged Plutarch served as high priest of the shrine and had dedicated a statue of the emperor; if he was still alive, Hadrian would have held discussions with him. In any case, he adjudicated a complicated dispute concerning the membership of the Amphictyonic League, an association of neighboring city-states, the aim of which was to protect and administer the temple of Apollo at Delphi, where the oracle was based.

As usual, wherever he went, Hadrian busied himself with resolving long-standing local disagreements and deciding on development projects. The town of Coronea disputed grazing rights with its neighbor Thisbe and local tax dues with Orchomenus. The emperor made his judgments, but the vendettas outlived him, and were eventually to trouble his successor on the imperial throne.

Whenever Hadrian's emotions were captured, he wrote a poem to mark the event. His visit to Thespiae was such an occasion. This town in Boeotia was dedicated to sexual love, as personified by the boy god Eros, Aphrodite's attractive, mischievous son. Every four years the Erotidia, a "very magnificent and splendid" festival of love, was held.

The love most admired here was that between the *erastes* and his *eromenos,* but heterosexual romance was celebrated too. In his dialogue *On Love,* Plutarch tells the story, ostensibly a true one, of a merry widow at Thespiae who arranged the kidnap of a handsome *ephebos* and then married him—much to the annoyance of his male admirers. And Heracles was remembered at a sanctuary in his honor for sleeping with forty-nine women, all daughters of the same father, during a single night. A fiftieth daughter declined the honor, and the angry demigod sentenced her to be his virgin priestess for life. Her latest successor still managed the sanctuary.

During his stay, the emperor went hunting on nearby Helicon, the most fertile mountain of Greece, writes Pausanias, where wild strawberry bushes offered delicious fruit for goats. This was the home of the Muses, and "the people who live there say that not a single herb or plant can harm human life; even the venom of snakes is weakened."

Animals were less fortunate: the emperor downed a bear and dedicated it to Eros, accompanied by a short poem in Greek. He asked the god:

> . . . be gracious, kindly receive
> the best parts of this bear from Hadrian,
> the one he killed with a blow from horseback.
> You, of your own accord, in recompense let grace
> be breathed soberly on him by Aphrodite Urania.

How are we to interpret this prayer? Antinous is not mentioned by name, and, if he was absent, this may simply be a lonely emperor's plea for love. But an alternative and more plausible hypothesis may be hazarded. "Urania" means heavenly or spiritual, so Hadrian was seeking the blessing of nonphysical love. On the assumption that Antinous was with him in Greece at this time, the emperor, as a responsible *erastes,* was seeking relief from sexual passion and its transcendence by something more honorable—a love that, as Plutarch puts it, leads "the soul from the world below to truth and the fields of truth, where full, pure, deceitless beauty dwells."

XXI

HOME AND ABROAD

· · ·

As the darkness lightened and the stars went out, rosy-fingered dawn materialized, looking her most delightful. Although he was covered in black volcanic dust and exhausted, Hadrian's spirits lifted as he gazed across from the summit of Mount Etna at the brightening horizon.

He had decided on a long, risky night climb so that he could see the sunrise, which, according to the *Historia Augusta* (quoting doubtless from the emperor's autobiography), was "many-colored, it is said, like a rainbow." He had done exactly the same at Mount Casius in Syria, just before his accession, and his nocturnal ascent had culminated in a storm. He had nearly been struck by lightning. This time the danger was even greater, for he was ascending a live volcano.

Etna stands about nine thousand feet above sea level, and the emperor and his party grew light-headed as they climbed and the oxygen thinned. They found their way up to the crater by torches. The mountain was restive; not long before, in 122, its entire crest had been blown off in a violent explosion. Ash, cinders, and volcanic blocks had fallen from the air for miles around and many roofs in the nearby town of Catania had collapsed.

The countryside had not yet recovered, and the beautiful sunrise revealed desolation all around. It must have been much the same scene as after the eruption of Vesuvius, about which Hadrian had learned, horrified and fascinated, as a little child, with its evocation of the end of the world.

Having sailed south from Dyrrachium, the emperor's flotilla probably put in at the great harbor of Syracuse, which was not far from Etna.

After his volcanic ascent and a brief inspection of western Sicily, he resumed his journey to Rome.

The emperor's arrival in the capital had been heralded by public prayers for his safety. Coins were struck celebrating his impending *reditus*. The bloodstained events of 117 still rankled, but it was now clear that he was no Domitian. While ruling decisively, he consistently acted as a *princeps,* a first among equals, not as a *dominus.* There had been no more executions of senior senators. The settlement between the supporters of the imperial regime and the Stoic opposition that Nerva had struck was holding firm.

There was much building work for Hadrian to inspect. Best of all, the Pantheon was ready. An architectural masterpiece, it is one of the very few Roman buildings that has survived complete to the present day (in the guise of a Christian church). Approached from the front, the building has the appearance of a conventional temple, with three rows of columns supporting a pediment with a pitched roof. Visitors pass through bronze doors (the originals, although repaired in the sixteenth century) and find themselves in a round space surmounted by a great coffered dome, with a circular opening through which the sky can be seen. The exterior of the dome was covered in gold leaf.

The Pantheon retained its dedication by the man who commissioned the original structure, Augustus' friend and partner in rule, Agrippa. Hadrian had a rule of not having his name inscribed on buildings he commissioned; but he made one exception, the newly completed majestic temple of Trajan and Plotina, which he dedicated *parentibus suis,* to his adoptive father and mother.

An even more tempting architectural treat awaited the emperor outside the city—the villa complex at Tibur. He intended to stay there for some time, and it cannot reasonably be doubted that Antinous was now living with him.

A senator or ambassador summoned to Tibur to enjoy the emperor's hospitality was driven in a carriage up a long hill from the plain below. To his left he looked across gardens to a stone theater and a circular temple of Venus. The road skirted a high, colonnaded terrace about 250 yards long; supporting it was a long multistory block of tiny rooms, quarters for the service staff—the cooks, cleaners, gardeners, engineers, builders—who made the villa function. It has been estimated that as many as two thousand people—slaves, servants, officials, and guests—could occupy the villa at any one time.

The distinguished visitor stepped down from his conveyance and walked up some steps into a large vestibule where there was a shrine to Hadrian's beloved Matidia. He was guided to his quarters, or directly to a presence chamber, through a labyrinth of halls, banqueting suites, columned porticoes, baths, peristyles and atria, covered walkways and formal gardens.

First impressions were overwhelming. The place was garishly multi-colored. Public rooms were decorated with frescoes and marble of every hue, and bright mosaics covered their floors. A phrase on an inscription, which may have been Hadrian's own words, speaks of "the Aelian villa with the colorful walls." In niches or on plinths, indoors and out, every-where there were groves of statues, all of them, as was the convention, painted in brilliant colors.

Another, equally ubiquitous feature of the villa was water. It spurted, fell, or flowed in monumental fountains, ran along sluices, or stood still and glassy in rectangular pools. Martial spoke approvingly of *rus in urbe,* or the countryside in the town. The Romans had a pronounced taste for intermingling nature with urban artifice. In Hadrian's villa, greenery was civilized by statuary and architecture set off by a touch of nature, of the wild. As much space was given over to gardens and fields as to build-ings.

The *Historia Augusta* reports that the emperor

built his villa at Tibur in wonderful fashion, and actually gave to parts of it names of provinces and places there, and called them, for exam-ple, the Lyceum, the Academy, Prytaneum, Canopus, Poecile, and Tempe. So that he might omit nothing, he even made a Hades.

In this memorial nomenclature, Hadrian was not original. For genera-tions wealthy Romans had built country villas on much the same lavish principles as he applied to what he liked to call, modestly, his "house at

Tibur." They took pleasure in naming features after admired originals, usually Greek; so Cicero had his "Academy" a century and a half before Hadrian established his. The difference was one of scale and scope. Even Nero's famous Domus Aurea, or Golden House, a luxuriant mix of town and country in the heart of Rome, occupied only between 100 and 200 acres to Hadrian's 250 or more.

It is not known for certain which parts of the villa corresponded to which Roman province or place. Hadrian made room at Tibur for the great Greek philosophers: the Lyceum was a gymnasium outside the walls of Athens where Aristotle gave lectures and Plato's Academy a walled olive grove. The Poecile was the Painted Stoa (*Poikile Stoa*) at the northern end of the Athenian marketplace, where Zeno, the founder of Stoicism, met his students. Their equivalents in the villa were not copies, but at most stylized evocations or perhaps on occasion simply the names given to a building or a piece of land. For visitors they were presumably identifiable by appropriate statues and decorations.

Presumably the Canopus canal in Egypt and the Vale of Tempe in Thessaly had personal associations for Hadrian that cannot now be recovered with any assurance; with the former (to be named some years later), an allusion to Antinous may be hazarded (see pages 283–84), and Tempe's reputation for sorcery points to one of the emperor's abiding interests. The Prytaneum, the town hall of Athens, seems out of place, but perhaps it was in some way connected with Hadrian's service as archon.

Whether or not the trapezium of underground tunnels beneath open land to the south of the estate was intended as a metaphor for Hades is unsure, but possible. Such an ambitious engineering project must have had some important function. So far as can be told, the tunnels had no practicable exits except for a subterranean link to an open-air stone theater. Some scholars suggest that this may have been a cult theater, used for religious events, and that in the tunnels initiates experienced chthonic rituals, not unlike the terrifying ceremonies at Eleusis, where darkness and sudden bright light induced ecstatic visions of truth. An underworld, indeed.

The villa was both a palace and a vacation resort, accommodating on one site the public and the private. For the rituals of state the architects—among whom we assume the talented amateur, Hadrian himself—designed spaces of more than sufficient grandeur. At the same time, the emperor enjoyed the good things in life: he was "devoted to music and flute players, and was a great eater at great banquets." At Tibur there were open-air dining rooms, leafy terraces for pleasant promenades, quiet gardens populated with rural deities in marble— Dionysus, Pan, Silenus—and, very probably, rough country for hunting. Where Domitian built a despot's palace on the Palatine, Tibur was the home of a sociable citizen-emperor.

Hadrian wished to maintain a personal life away from the public gaze and his official duties. His most astonishing architectural innovation was a round structure at the heart of the complex. Almost exactly of the same diameter as the Pantheon in Rome, it is still substantially in place, but unroofed and ruined. Inside the external wall are a colonnade and a moat surrounding a circular island on which a building stood—an intertwining confection of stone curves and straight lines. As well as living and sleeping areas, it contained two lavatories and a small bathhouse (with access to the moat for swimming). A minivilla within the villa, it could be reached only by wooden bridges that were easily removed to give a sense of complete inaccessibility. Here was the emperor's hideaway. Here he could relax alone, or be alone with Antinous.

A building can scarcely be cited as reliable evidence of the psychology of its maker. However, beautiful as the marble cottage is, the suspicion arises that it was the invention of a man with negative affect, with a weak fellow-feeling for others. Here we see Hadrian, solitary in his deluxe hermitage, hidden in the crowd, as a misanthropic Timon of Athens, although much too rich to be ruined by his unbefriending generosity.

The villa was an elaborate reminder of imperial power. It was no accident that its splendors matched those of the court of a Hellenistic monarch. Even though Hadrian was a *civilis princeps,* who walked with kings nor lost the common touch, he governed in an even more executive manner than his predecessors. In the capital, the fiction of the emperor as the first citizen of a republic was still observed and Hadrian politely followed the constitutional conventions. However, when he was in Italy, the center of government was to be found at Tibur not

Rome. Also, Hadrian spent more than half his reign traveling. Consulting the Senate, attending its meetings, and seeking its advice was not possible.

Of course, an emperor seldom acted alone and when announcing a decision often indicated the many experts whom he had consulted. He increasingly depended on his *amici* (literally, "friends"), chosen advisers and senior officials who accompanied him wherever he happened to be. A favored *amicus* might be appointed a *comes* (or "companion," hence the later title of *count*) and given a particular area of responsibility. The emperor also made use of a *consilium,* a council of state that could consider, even develop, policy and endorse major decisions. This was not a permanent committee but a shifting group of men of high rank. They were drawn from a pool of senators, including some with a legal background, and *equites* (among them, heads of government departments), and were selected for their expertise on any given topic on which the emperor needed advice.

The imperial bureaucracy was growing, but, more important, its administrative departments, previously managed by freedmen, were increasingly headed by *equites,* for whom the public service offered a well-paid career path. This change meant that not only senators had an opportunity to participate in government.

There was nothing new about these centralizing trends, which (as already observed) can be detected in previous reigns; the novelty was the pace with which they were moving forward under an autocrat whose benevolence was matched by his decisiveness.

Most of the women in his family were dead by now, but Hadrian had a number of male kinsfolk, some of whom he liked better than others. Servianus had married Hadrian's eldest sister, Paulina, by thirty years her husband's junior. He had criticized his young brother-in-law during Trajan's reign, but he was now seventy and enjoying the twilight of a successful career.

He retained a certain political importance, for his daughter had married a man called Gnaeus Pedanius Fuscus Salinator and given birth to a son, Pedanius Fuscus. He had been born in or about 113 and was now a boy of twelve or so. His importance lay in the fact that he was Hadrian's great-nephew and the only other male Aelian. Everyone could see that the emperor, approaching his fiftieth birthday, was most unlikely to sire offspring at this late stage, and showed no inclination to secure the succession with an adoption. Little Pedanius Fuscus could expect to be the emperor's heir when he grew up.

A more congenial personality than Servianus was Marcus Annius Verus, a wealthy senator and a member of the Spanish set at Rome. The family came from Baetica and may have been related to the Aelii: like them, its fortune probably originated in the export of olive oil. Verus had four children, two boys and two girls, all of whom made highly advantageous matches. He was high in favor with Hadrian, who appointed him to a third consulship, for the year 126; this was an unprecedented distinction on the part of an emperor who had served as consul only three times himself.

Servianus was a friend of Verus and sent him an odd little congratulatory poem. In it a man called Ursus claims to be a leading player in the "glass-ball game," but admits that "I myself was beaten by the thrice consul Verus, my patron, not once but often." Sometime many years previously Servianus had adopted the name of Ursus; as he had only held the consulship twice, he was ruefully admitting defeat in the great game of politics, for which playing with a fragile glass ball was an apt metaphor.

One of Verus' sons, also Marcus Annius Verus, married an heiress who owned a vast brickworks outside Rome (and no doubt profited from Hadrian's many building schemes). In 121 a son arrived, yet another Marcus (confusingly, every male Verus, not simply the firstborn, shared the same given name). By the time of the emperor's return to Italy he was a toddler of four.

The father died in the year of his praetorship, probably in 124, and the child was adopted by his grandfather. Many years later Marcus remembered the old man for "his kindly disposition and avoidance of bad temper." Despite her exceptional wealth, his mother instilled austere habits in her son: he reported that she was god-fearing and virtuous, and lived "the simple life, far removed from the habits of the rich."

His grandfather was not the only man to busy himself about this little boy. Lucius Catilius Severus, his maternal great-grandfather, played so active a part in his upbringing that Marcus added the names Catilius Severus to his original Marcus Annius Verus. Catilius, a Bithynian of Italian descent, was a close friend of the emperor, having given him crucial support during the first nervous days of his accession to the purple.

On his return to Italy, Hadrian met the orphan, now about four, and took a liking to him. According to the *Historia Augusta,* he was a "solemn child from the very beginning," a quality that pleased the emperor. As time passed, his interest and affection grew; Marcus was brought up under the emperor's close supervision—literally "in Hadrian's lap," *in Hadriani gremio*. Evidently, the child seldom lied, and Hadrian nicknamed him Annius Verissimus, or "most truthful"—a pun on his *cognomen* Verus, which means "true" in Latin.

At the unusually young age of six, before he started his education proper, Marcus was enrolled as an *eques*, by Hadrian's specific arrangement. A year later the emperor enrolled him among the Salii, a priestly college founded by the legendary king Numa Pompilius, Hadrian's antique model of the just and wise ruler. These were the "leaping priests" of Mars—twelve young patricians who wore outlandish outfits originally worn by warriors in the remote past. Every March they purified the sacred trumpets that the Romans carried to war and sang the "Carmen Saliare," a chant the function of which was to keep Rome safe in battle. Hadrian's intervention was unusual, for the college usually elected new members itself, and was a sign of special favor.

Hadrian's relationship with Marcus was political as well as personal. It recalls Augustus' grooming of the two sons of Marcus Agrippa, Gaius and Lucius Caesar. The first emperor removed them to his own house and personally attended to their upbringing, as if he were a very grand *paedogogus*. He was thinking in the long term; he hoped that he would live long enough for the boys to become adults and enter politics. Fate dashed his plans, for they died young. The echo with Hadrian was not fortuitous. If he were allowed enough time, it made sense to train up a successor from childhood. After all, Augustus had survived to the age of seventy-seven: that would give Hadrian more than a quarter of a century; plenty of time.

The emperor was unenthusiastic about young Pedanius Fuscus. It was not simply a question of his kinship with the little-trusted Servianus, but he seems to have been a bad lot, being "erotic and fond of gladiators." It was sensible to have more than one option at his disposal.

Even the lovely villa at Tibur could not keep Hadrian in one place for long. On March 2, 127, after no more than a year and a half since returning from his grand tour, the emperor left Rome for a tour of northern Italy.

On his return he decided to reorganize the governance of the peninsula. Augustus had divided it into eleven districts, but this appears to have been for statistical convenience when managing periodic censuses. Local authorities were largely left to themselves under the general supervision of the Senate. Hadrian disagreed with this laissez-faire approach. He arranged Italy into four administrative regions headed by ex-consuls called *iuridici*. The extent of their powers is unclear, but it looks as if the emperor wanted to place the homeland of the empire on a level with other provinces. This demotion paralleled the promotion of all things Greek. The reform was unpopular, and was repealed after his death.

Hadrian was back in Rome to celebrate an important moment in his life. August 11 marked the tenth anniversary of his accession. Ten days of games were held to mark the occasion and thirty Pyrrhic dances (a war dance performed by men in full armor) staged in the Circus Maximus.

The emperor then fell ill, or so the evidence strongly suggests. According to the *Fasti Ostienses,* the annual record of official events, the games were to promote "the emperor's health." A number of coins also refer to the *salus Augusti;* on their reverse they show the personification of health as an attractive woman, feeding a snake in a basket. Snakes were often used in healing rituals and were associated with Asclepius (Aesculapius in the Latin form), the god of healing and medicine. Patients slept in healing temples and nonvenomous snakes were encouraged to slither therapeutically around the dormitories. Another coin type of the same period shows Hope, *Spes,* holding up a flower.

The supposition of bad health is supported by a report in the *Epitome de Caesaribus* that for a long time he endured a painful "subcutaneous disease" that left him "burning and impatient with pain." It is possible, of course, that the emperor had been incapacitated by an accident. The *Historia Augusta* mentions a fractured collarbone and rib sustained while hunting; no date is given, and the summer of 127 is as good a time as any for an accident to have taken place. However, the balance of the evidence suggests a bout of illness lengthy enough and grave enough to have warranted numismatic propaganda.

As to what the emperor was suffering from, retrospective diagnoses in the absence of the patient are risky. However, his symptoms are consistent with erysipelas, a streptococcus bacterial infection. This infects the underskin, or dermis, and the fatty tissue beneath, and often inflames the face or bodily extremities. A red, swollen, warm, hardened, and painful rash occurs. The patient can go on to suffer fever, tiredness, headaches, and vomiting. In the days before antibiotics erysipelas could be fatal, or, if not, quite likely to recur.

In the following year, with his tenth anniversary behind him and his health presumably having improved, the emperor judged the time right to accept the title of *Pater Patriae,* father of his people. Like Augustus, and probably in imitation of him, he had declined the Senate's offer for a long time; despite the fact that it conferred no additional power and was not an official post, the honor was not to be treated lightly. The wise emperor regarded it as a reward for substantial attainment. Hadrian could feel sure that he had at last put the deaths of the four ex-consuls behind him: they had been forgotten, or at least forgiven.

Hadrian laid plans for further expeditions. His first stop was to be the provinces of northern Africa, rich, urbanized, and fertile (although then suffering from a severe drought). No *princeps* had ever been there before, and in 123 he himself had had to cut short a tour to deal with a sudden Parthian crisis. The visit got off to an excellent start. According to the *Historia Augusta,* "it rained on his arrival for the first time in the space of five years, and for this he was extremely popular with the Africans."

The provinces received the by-now-familiar treatment. Hadrianopolises bloomed along the itinerary: even Carthage was so renamed. Great building works were announced, an aqueduct, temples, and so forth. Emperors such as Nero had confiscated many African estates to refill the treasury, so large areas were crown land, sublet to tenants-in-chief. Hadrian checked carefully that they were not oppressing the peasants who tilled the land. He introduced new regulations, giving tax breaks to those who cultivated marginal or previously unused land. An inscription recording some of the details refers to "Caesar's untiring concern by which he assiduously keeps watch for the advantage of humankind."

Three key features of Hadrian's reign, its recurring melodies, were given another hearing—building the *limes* that marked out the edge of empire; recruiting the victims of empire to help the victors run it; and, ultimately the most essential of all, maintaining the morale and (much the same thing) the efficiency of the legions. Hadrian extended what were called Latin Rights, according to which political leaders and their families who headed town councils automatically received Roman citizenship. Although the details are not altogether clear, he now opened citizenship to ordinary town councillors.

Visitors to the predesert of Algeria and Tunisia today can see substantial stretches of wall and ditch. They are the remains of the *fossatum Africae,* already under construction by the time of Hadrian's arrival. This series of border defenses had many features in common with the Britannic wall, although local materials were used—in this case mud bricks. The longest unbroken stretch ran for about forty miles, with a gateway every Roman mile and an additional watchtower equidistant from two gates. Rome had widened its zone of control under the Flavian emperors and Trajan, and the *fossatum* made it clear that this process of expansion had now concluded.

However, if the wall asserted a border, it was not there to exclude. Rather, its main purpose was to enable the legions to manage relations between a settled agricultural population to the north and southern nomads who needed to move their herds and flocks to and from summer and winter pastures. This entailed controlling water sources, especially in times of low rainfall.

By the end of June, Hadrian had reached the former kingdom, now province, of Numidia, where the III Augusta legion was waiting for his inspection. Its legate, Quintus Fabius Catullinus, was an intelligent officer who had obviously been warned what to expect of his demanding commander in chief. He trained his troops to the highest possible level of efficiency, and in an elegant piece of indirect flattery to Hadrian the rainmaker erected two altars, one dedicated to "Jupiter Best and Greatest, lord of the heavenly rainstorms" and the other to "Winds that have the power to bring generous rainstorms."

The legion had just moved to a new base at Lambaesis and was busy constructing a fortress. Large parts of an inscription, on the base of a column erected to commemorate the imperial visit, have been found, which transcribe speeches the emperor made to the troops. A shorthand writer must have been in attendance, for his remarks have been taken down verbatim. It is one of the few times we have Hadrian's own words as he spoke them, and can almost hear his voice.

Addressing legionary cavalry after they had performed in front of him, he said, "Military exercises, in a manner of speaking, have their own rules, and if anything is added to or subtracted from them, the exercise becomes too insignificant or too difficult. The more difficulties that are added, the less pleasing is the result. Of all difficult exercises the most difficult was the one you performed, throwing the javelin in full battledress . . . I approve of your eagerness."

On July 1 the emperor praised a Spanish cohort for building a stone wall for the new fortress in record time. "A wall requiring much work, and one that is usually made for permanent winter quarters, you constructed in not much longer a time than it takes to build one of turf."

The officers came in for a fair share of praise, but there was criticism of a cavalry commander whose name is lost. "I commend Catullinus, my legate, . . . because he directed you to this exercise, which took on the appearance of a real battle and which has trained you in such a way that I can also praise you. Your prefect Cornelianus also has performed his duties very well. However, the cavalry skirmish did not please me. [————] is the person responsible. A cavalryman should ride across from cover and pursue with caution, for if he cannot see where he's going or if he cannot restrain his horse when he wishes, it is perfectly possible that he will be exposed to hidden traps."

A week later the emperor congratulated some Pannonian auxiliaries for their maneuvers. "If anything had been missing, I would have noticed it, and if anything had stood out as bad, I would have pointed it out. In the entire exercise you have pleased me uniformly."

It is easy to see why the emperor was popular. We can imagine him in the African sun in front of hundreds of sweating men. His words crackled with energy. He knew exactly what he was talking about, and had precise ideas of how things should be done. His praise was worth having, and his listeners were fearfully aware that he would not hide his disapproval.

This was how to keep an army fighting fit when there was no fighting to be done.

XXII

WHERE HAVE YOU GONE TO, MY LOVELY?

. . .

Hadrian was in a hurry. The summer of 128 was drawing to a close and he had an appointment he wanted to keep in September. The date of the Eleusinian Mysteries was approaching and he meant to attend for a second time. So he and his traveling court sailed back to Rome, where he spent a few quick weeks dealing with essential business before setting off for Greece.

He was an *epoptes,* a full and complete initiate, and, we may guess, so was Antinous, now about eighteen and on the verge of beards and adulthood. No account has come down to us, but one wonders if, in this Greek setting, they felt able to present themselves publicly as an honorable and traditional couple, a mature *erastes* with his maturing *eromenos*.

Having witnessed the most secret rituals, Hadrian broadcast the significance of his participation through an Asiatic coin, a tetradrachm worth six sesterces, which showed him holding a bunch of corn ears; the legend reads *Hadrianus P[ater] [Patriae] Ren[atus],* "Hadrian, Father of the Fatherland Reborn." The corn ears indicate his status as an initiate of Eleusis, and *renatus* his spiritual rebirth. On the obverse is a head of Augustus, the first emperor to attend the Mysteries.

In the heyday of Athens in the fifth century B.C., its undisputed leader was Pericles. For many years, he was its democratically elected first citizen (its *princeps,* as a Roman might put it). His contemporaries nicknamed him, flatteringly, "the Olympian," a title usually reserved for Zeus, king of the gods.

Greece was still recovering from the destruction wreaked during the Persian invasion. The Persians had been driven back, and Athens headed a league of city-states and island communities whose aim was to continue the struggle against the "barbarians." Pericles transformed the league into a maritime empire and spent much of the wealth Athens acquired thereby by rebuilding the city as splendidly as possible; the masterpiece was the Parthenon, Athena's temple on the Acropolis.

Plutarch writes that Pericles "introduced a bill to the effect that all Hellenes wheresoever resident in Europe or in Asia, small and large cities alike, should be invited to send deputies to a council at Athens." The aim was to discuss matters of common interest—restoration of the temples the Persians had burned down, payment of vows to the gods for the great deliverance, and clearing the seas of pirates. The Greek colonies of Sicily and Italy were not invited, for they had not been directly involved in the war. Nothing came of the project owing to opposition from the Spartans, then the great military rival of Athens. Pericles let the idea drop.

More than half a millennium later Hadrian picked it up where it had fallen. During his previous visit, his attention had been caught by the *synedrion,* or council, at Delphi for the Amphictyonic League, but it did not include enough Greek cities. He decided to launch a new Panhellenion along Periclean lines. As before, a grandly refurbished Athens was to be the headquarters and Greek cities would be invited to send delegates to an inaugural assembly. Member communities had to prove their Greekness, both culturally and in genetic descent, although in practice some bogus pedigrees were accepted.

The enterprise had a somewhat antiquarian character. So far as we can tell from the fragmentary surviving evidence, Hadrian aimed at roughly the same catchment area as Pericles had done—in essence, the basin of the Ionian Sea. Italy and Sicily were excluded once again, and there was no representation of Greek settlements in Egypt, Syria, or Anatolia. The emperor made a point of visiting Sparta, presumably to ensure that it did not stay away as it had done in the fifth century.

A renaissance of old glories was reflected in the development of archaized language; so, for example, Spartan young men (*epheboi*) suddenly took on an antiquated Doric dialect in their dedications to Artemis Orthia, a patron goddess of the city. It seems clear that one of the purposes of Hadrian's policy was to recruit the past to influence and to help define and improve the decadent present.

Hadrian began to call himself the "Olympian," echoing the example of Pericles as well as reflecting the completion of the Olympieion, the vast temple to Olympian Zeus. He was soon widely known throughout the Hellenic eastern provinces as "Hadrianos Sebastos Olumpios," *Sebastos* being the Greek word for Augustus, or indeed "Hadrianos Sebastos Zeus Olumpios."

What did the Panhellenion actually do? It administered its own affairs, managed its shrine not far from the Roman Agora and offices, and promoted a quadrennial festival. It also assessed qualifications for membership. But Hadrian was careful to give it no freestanding political powers. All important decisions were referred to him for approval. Rather, the focus was cultural and religious, and a connection was forged with the Eleusinian Mysteries. In essence, the task was to build spiritual and intellectual links among the cities of the Greek world, and to foster a sense of community. The Panhellenion also furthered the careers of delegates, who were usually leading members of Greek elites (but not necessarily Roman citizens), and created an international "old-boy network" of friends who advanced one another's interests.

A good deal of notice was required for the summoning of the new assembly, and the buildings the emperor had commissioned in 125 were probably not yet finished. But the future look of Athens was already evident. The city was being transformed and the area around the Olympieion was defined as a new district, named (not difficult to guess) Hadrianopolis. At its boundary an arch was erected, which can still be seen today. On the west side, facing the Acropolis, an inscription on its architrave reads, "This is Athens, the onetime city of Theseus," Theseus being the city's legendary founder. On the east side, facing the Olympieion, another reads, "This is the city of Hadrian, not of Theseus."

It was cheek of a very high order. However warmly they welcomed the emperor's pro-Hellenic policies, this expropriation of their city must have irritated many Athenians. But they had no alternative to biting their lips.

• • •

About March 129, with the sea lanes open again, Hadrian set sail for Ephesus. He roamed around the eastern provinces, scattering buildings, instructions, and benefactions in his wake. As usual, he refused to tolerate poor performance by public officials, punishing delinquent procurators and governors, the *Historia Augusta* reports, "with such severity that it was believed that he incited those who brought the accusations."

The emperor's main political object for this tour was a gathering of client kings along the frontier with the Parthian empire. This "durbar" was the mirror image of the Panhellenion, originally summoned as it had been to manage a continuing Persian threat. The Parthians had now assumed the role of the sinister Other. Hadrian, of course, had not the slightest intention of provoking a war. Instead, he mounted a spectacular but peaceful demonstration that the Roman empire was safe from invasion.

We do not know if the Parthian king, Chosroes, still embattled by ambitious relatives, was invited to another riverine summit meeting, but he was at least offered sweeteners for good behavior. His daughter, held as hostage in Rome for twelve years, was at last sent back to Parthia and the emperor promised to return the royal throne, which Trajan had captured during his ruinous invasion of Mesopotamia. However, before anything could be decided, Chosroes was deposed and his successor had more important matters on his mind than playing a walk-on role in Hadrian's political theatricals.

So far as the client kings were concerned, they were a mixed bunch with uncertain loyalties. Conventional opinion disapproved of Rome's purchasing peace with subsidies, but the emperor was proud of his achievements. According to the *Epitome de Caesaribus,* "after procuring peace from many kings by means of secret subventions, [Hadrian] liked to boast openly that he had won more by doing nothing than from waging war."

Dealing with distant rulers who knew that it was impractical for the Romans to punish lack of cooperation by military action sometimes led to embarrassment. Pharasmenes was king of the Iberi, a tribe that lived between the Black and Caspian seas (today's Georgia), and was a case in point. He haughtily declined Hadrian's invitation to his grand assembly, despite being the recipient of generous gifts—among them an elephant and a detachment of fifty soldiers. When Pharasmenes reciprocated with some gold-embroidered cloaks, the irritated Hadrian apparently ridiculed the king's presents by sending three hundred condemned men to be killed in the arena dressed in cloth of gold.

The emperor's next destination was Egypt, for which he planned an extensive tour, but en route he passed through Judaea. Here he made a fateful decision.

Since the devastation that followed Titus' capture of Jerusalem in 70, the ruined and depopulated province had hardly recovered. Jewish society became localized into villages. The high-priestly families that had dominated Judaea disappeared from history, the Sanhedrin, ancient Israel's supreme court, ceased operations, and the old upper class vanished. As for Jerusalem, the city's fortifications were left in ruins and the Temple remained rubble. This was typical Roman behavior: in previous ages Carthage had been razed and years passed before reoccupancy of the site was allowed. A similar fate had befallen Corinth.

The bitter uprising among Jews of the diaspora at the end of Trajan's reign seems not to have affected Judaea, presumably because the Moorish general Lusius Quietus had been appointed its governor with a brief to stamp out any discontent. Once the uprising had been quashed, Hadrian, newly in power, had won a reputation for being sympathetic to the Jewish cause when he acted as a disinterested arbiter in disputes between Alexandrian Jews and Greeks.

The emperor's sympathy seems to have been tactical and did not represent his real opinion. He now determined that enough time had passed to reconstitute Judaea as an ordinary province, by which he meant that it should be Hellenized. Quite a number of affluent Jews, he observed, were willing to become collaborators. It may even be that some of them actively encouraged the emperor to pursue his Hellenizing agenda.

Circumcision had been outlawed by Domitian and Nerva. Interestingly, Christians, too, disapproved of the procedure: Paul of Tarsus called it mutilation and argued that those who inflicted it should be "cut off," or castrated. Hadrian renewed the prohibition and made the offense punishable by death.

At Jerusalem the emperor refounded the city and commissioned a temple of Jupiter Capitolinus, to be built on the ruins of Herod's temple. He brought in settlers and seems to have established a *colonia* of Roman citizens, which in the course of time would produce recruits for the garrison legion that had been based nearby for sixty years, the X Fretensis.

To underline the point that Jerusalem was now a Roman city with Greek-speaking inhabitants and no longer had the slightest association with Jewry, Hadrian named it Aelia Capitolina, in honor of his own family, the Aelii, and the king of the Olympian gods whose great shrine stood on Rome's citadel. Jehovah was banished. If we can trust the new city's celebratory coinage, the emperor personally helped to plow a furrow around its boundary. Cities in the neighborhood also signaled his presence. Shrines in his honor were founded at Caesarea and Tiberias, and Gaza launched a Hadrianic festival.

So far as Hadrian was concerned, the Jewish question was settled.

The emperor had been greatly looking forward to touring Egypt, with its strange animal-headed gods, its lauded skill in magic, and its extraordinary temples and palaces. Here was a mysterious, age-old civilization that had largely preserved its unique character. The Macedonian dynasty of the Ptolemies, ruling from Alexandria on the Mediterranean coast, had only partly Hellenized it. A Roman province since the defeat and deaths of Antony and Cleopatra, Egypt was the emperors' private domain, and nothing was allowed to imperil its huge strategic value as a grain producer for the capital. Senators were forbidden to visit, and few emperors bothered to go there either, despite their having the title of pharaoh. The kingdom's governance was entrusted to a prefect, who was always a nonpolitical *eques*. Unless there was trouble, Egypt was largely left to its own devices.

Hadrian, ever the missionary, was determined to deepen Egypt's conversion into a worthy member of the Greco-Roman world. What he had in mind was to found yet another Hadrianopolis, somewhere many miles south in the country's traditional heartland.

He may have had another, more personal reason for his visit. A fourth-century church father, Epiphanius, claims that he suffered from leprosy, which none of his doctors could heal, and that he went to Egypt to find a cure. At first sight, the story is unconvincing. It is highly unlikely that he contracted leprosy, a disease which is hard to catch and often associated with poverty and a bad diet. However, the assertion may be a faulty echo of the emperor's previously reported subcutaneous affliction. Egypt had a high reputation for medicine; the healing and magical arts were closely allied, something that would have appealed to Hadrian. A recurrence of erysipelas could well have made him abandon conventional treatment for the arcane nostrums of the Egyptian priesthood.

No later than the end of August 130, Hadrian traveled down the coast road from Gaza to Pelusium, the fortress town that guarded the entry into Egypt. It lay between the marshes of the Nile and the Mediterranean shore. It was on the beach here that in 48 B.C., at the start of Rome's long civil war, Pompey the Great (Gnaeus Pompeius Magnus) was lured ashore from his ship and stabbed to death by a renegade legionary in Egyptian pay. He had been fleeing from Julius Caesar after his army's decisive defeat in Pharsalus in Greece and was hoping to find sanctuary with the pharaoh. "Dead men don't bite," said one of the king's advisers. Pompey's head was cut off and presented to Caesar.

The body was buried on the shore and a small monument erected above it. With the passage of time sand blew over it and covered it from view. Never one to pass up the chance to mourn a dead celebrity, the emperor located the grave and had the sand brushed away. And, of course, he wrote a poem, which was inscribed on the monument. Referring to the fact that many shrines had been erected in Pompey's name throughout the empire, one line reads:

How pitiful a tomb for one so rich in temples.

The high point of Hadrian's visit was to be a journey up the Nile. The expedition had to wait until late September or October, when the river's annual flood would abate. In the meantime the emperor spent some time in Alexandria, where there was plenty to see and do. The Greek community had long believed that the Romans always favored the Jews at their expense. Now there were hardly any Jews left in the city, following the suppression of their uprising, and Hadrian the Hellenizer made himself popular by investing in restoration projects to make good the damage that had been done.

The old palace of the Ptolemies was not a single edifice but a royal campus filled with buildings of every kind. Among them was the Mouseion, which housed the ancient world's most distinguished scholars, intellectuals, and authors. Membership was a high privilege, and brought with it the honor of free meals. "By Mouseion," wrote Philostratus, a third-century expert on Greek intellectuals, "I mean a dining table in Egypt to which the most distinguished men from all over the world receive invitations."

Hadrian took a close interest in the Mouseion's work. He is known to have appointed two members, and, as already noted, his *ab epistulis,* successor to the dismissed Suetonius, was a former head of the Mouseion, the Gallic scholar Julius Vestinus. The emperor was not going to miss dinner at the high table for anything. However, it is not certain that his visit was well received. Behaving as usual with uneasy uppitiness to the gathered scholars, the emperor "put forward many questions for consideration," claims the *Historia Augusta,* "only to provide the answers himself."

The emperor's relations with intellectuals were often fraught.

Although he wrote verse and composed speeches with great facility he treated academics as though he were their intellectual superior and liked to ridicule, scorn, and humiliate them. He competed with these professors and philosophers, with both sides in turn publishing books and poems.

He was said to have been jealous of celebrated philosophers and rhetoricians, and promoted others to attack them and try to destroy their reputations. In response, a victim, Dionysius of Miletus, said acidly to one of Hadrian's officials, who had tried to rival him in public speaking, "The emperor can give you money, but he can't make you an orator."

Apparently Hadrian did not publish under his own name, but under those of his freedmen with literary reputations. One of his offerings was *Catachannae* (presumably some sort of miscellany, for the word refers to a tree onto which several different types of fruit have been grafted). This was an "extremely obscure work" of which nothing is known except that it was a homage to Antimachus, himself an extremely obscure poet from about 400 B.C. who sought consolation for the death of his mistress by retelling stories of legendary disasters.

One of the most original academics of the age was the Sophist Favorinus of Arelate (Arles); he was described as a hermaphrodite and was beardless with a high-pitched voice. When Hadrian criticized a word he had used, he accepted the point. His friends later reproached him for giving way, to which he replied: "You are giving me bad advice. You must allow me to regard as the greatest of scholars the man who commands thirty legions."

However much he tormented them with his cross-examinations, Hadrian lavished honors and money on anyone who professed the arts. At the beginning of his reign he conferred a series of immunities on practitioners of the liberal professions—philosophers, rhetoricians, grammarians, and doctors—that remained in force until the latter part of the second century. Although he was himself responsible for hurting people's feelings, he took it to heart, he used to say, whenever he saw anyone upset as a result of his disputatiousness.

Hadrian allowed himself some free time with Antinous. He relaxed at the Canopic canal, which ran from Alexandria to the port of Canopus. Although it was well known for a temple of Serapis where the sick could sleep overnight and hope for healing, the place was mostly notable for its disreputable pleasures. Strabo, the Greek travel writer and geographer, observed:

> Some writers go on to record the cures, and others the virtues of the oracles there. But to balance all this is the crowd of revelers who go down from Alexandria by the canal to the public festivals; for every day and every night it is crowded with people on boats who play the

flute and dance without restraint and with extreme licentiousness, both men and women.

By an odd coincidence there was a village called Eleusis on the canal. But there were no mysteries there, rather rooms for hire and "commanding views for those who wish to engage in revelry." Shameless things were done that marked the "Canopic lifestyle."

There is no record of an imperial visit, but the fact that Hadrian gave the name Canopus to a stretch of water and a large *nymphaeum,* or artificial grotto, at his villa at Tibur suggests that the Egyptian resort held some special meaning for him. We can infer that he and Antinous went there—and memorably enjoyed themselves.

Hadrian would not have been Hadrian without finding time for a hunt. He and Antinous made a foray into the countryside in Cyrenaica, the province adjoining western Egypt, and went in search of lions. On a fragment of papyrus a poem, composed in the high, heroic epic manner by a certain Pancrates, describes what happened. This is, in fact, the only occasion where there is an explicit written record of the couple being together in one place.

There is also evidence in stone confirming that the pair hunted together. Eight large *tondi,* or circular reliefs, now displayed on the Arch of Constantine in Rome but once adorning a memorial of the emperor's exploits, show Hadrian and his party hunting various kinds of animals including a lion, and making sacrifices. In at least one of the carvings a huntsman can be seen who strongly resembles the young Bithynian— but with a difference. What we see is no longer a boy but a short-haired young man of about twenty with sideburns and down on his cheeks, no longer gracefully feminine but strong and active.

The desert adventure nearly had an unhappy ending. Hadrian and Antinous came across a fierce lion. According to the poet,

> First Hadrian with his brass-fitted spear wounded the beast,
> But did not kill him, for he purposely missed the mark,
> Wishing to test to the full the sureness of aim
> Of his lovely Antinous, son of the Argus slayer.

The infuriated lion charged at Antinous and gored his horse. It was then struck in the neck, evidently by Hadrian (the papyrus breaks up at this point), and fell beneath the hooves of the emperor's horse. It was a close shave, but the lover had triumphantly rescued the beloved from the threat of serious injury, or even death.

At last Hadrian was able to set off on his journey up the Nile. We may suppose that a grand barge was prepared for him and a flotilla of boats assembled, including warships from the Alexandrian fleet, to carry the court and the guard. As usual, places warned to expect an imperial visitation had been making preparations for many months and stockpiling generous supplies of food and other necessaries. One of these was the town of Oxyrhyncus, which laid in 700 pecks of barley, 3,000 bales of hay, 372 suckling pigs, nearly 200 pecks of dates, and 2,000 sheep, together with olives and olive oil. The imperial cavalcade, locustlike, consumed everything in its path.

Pachrates (whose Hellenized name was Pancrates) was a magician and priest, as well as a poet. He looked the part of a holy ascetic— "with shaved head, clothed in white linen, speaking Greek with an accent, tall, flat-nosed, with thick lips and thin legs."

He was based at the ghost town of Heliopolis (a Greek name meaning Sun City; the Egyptians called it Iunu, or "place of pillars"). Since time immemorial it had been a revered center of learning, but competition from Alexandria, founded in 334 B.C., removed its raison d'être. By the first century A.D. the place was deserted except for a handful of hierophants, who, according to Strabo, "performed the sacrifices and explained to strangers what pertained to the sacred rites."

With his lifelong interest in the dark arts, Hadrian stopped off at the city for an explanation of the rites. He consulted Pachrates and, according to an ancient papyrus, received instruction in the art of a spell to "attract those who are uncontrollable . . . It inflicts sickness excellently and destroys powerfully, sends dreams beautifully." The priest prepared a magic recipe, which included, among assorted ingredients, a field mouse and two moon beetles, all drowned in the Nile, the fat of a virgin goat, and the dung of a dog-faced baboon, pounded together in a mortar. A little of this unpleasant paste was burned on a charcoal fire as an offering, and a charm recited. The papyrus warned that the procedure should not be used rashly and only in the case of "dire necessity."

Pachrates knew how to lay on a good performance. He cast the spell, which was credited with never failing: one victim fell sick in two hours and, apparently, another died in seven. Hadrian received dreams "as he thoroughly tested the whole truth of the magic." Deeply impressed, he doubled the magician's fee.

What was the emperor's purpose in making this consultation? Curiosity is a likely enough motive, for Egyptian magic was an exotic mix of spells and remedies drawn from Greek and Jewish as well as indigenous religious traditions. But, one wonders, did he also have anyone in mind whom he wished to fall ill, or even die? Did he anticipate a "dire necessity"? The questions are relevant, for some days later an astonishing death did occur.

A few miles south of Heliopolis, Hadrian, Antinous, and their entourage toured Memphis, founded more than three thousand years previously and the original capital of the old kingdom of Egypt. They inspected the pyramids and the Sphinx. Then the imperial party sailed on upriver and moored at Hermopolis (Egyptian Khemennu). Situated on the border between Upper (or southern) and Lower Egypt, this was a populous and opulent city, with a famous sanctuary of Thoth, god of magic, heart and tongue of Ra, arbiter of good and evil and judge of the dead.

On October 22 the festival of the Nile was celebrated—usually a happy celebration of the renewed fertility that the river's annual inundation brought about, but on this occasion a glum affair, one suspects, for it was the second year when there had been a disastrously poor flood. Then two days later came the anniversary of the death of Osiris and worshippers chanted for his yearly rebirth, analogous with the rise and fall of the river.

Opposite Hermopolis the riverbank curved and the current strengthened. A small, impoverished settlement of mud huts lay along the shore and close by stood a modest temple of Ramses the Great, Egypt's most famous pharaoh (1298–1235 B.C.). One day during the last week of the month, here or hereabouts, the lifeless body of Antinous was recovered from the river. He had drowned.

Hadrian broke down. The *Historia Augusta* noted, disapprovingly, that he "wept for the youth like a woman." He declared that he had seen a new star in the sky, which he took to be that of Antinous. Courtiers assured him that the star was new and had indeed come from Antinous' spirit as it left his body and rose up into the heavens. The emperor decided that Antinous was to be deified. Dead, he was to be reborn as a god.

From the point of view of Roman convention, such a thing was unheard of. Emperors, and wives or close relatives, received divine honors by approval of the Senate—but not boyfriends of no political or social significance. Hadrian did not even trouble the Senate with the matter, for "the Greeks deified him at Hadrian's request." What precisely this means is unclear, but there was a long-standing tradition in the eastern Mediterranean of potentates declaring themselves gods, and in the popular mind the boundary between the human and the divine was porous.

As it happened, there was a local precedent for the conferral of divine honors. A drowning in the Nile had magical properties. When Pachrates' spell called for a mouse and beetles to be drowned in the Nile, the actual word he used was "deified." This was because many believed that the Nile conferred immortality on anyone it took to itself by drowning. (Importantly, suicides were excepted.) Only the priests could touch the corpses and these were buried at the public expense. Two brothers, Petesi and Paher, who drowned in Roman times even had a temple devoted to them. In the second-century tomb of a girl, Isidora, who drowned in the river, a funerary poem has her father say: "O my daughter, no longer will I bring you offerings with lamentation, now that I know that you have become a god."

So Antinous joined the immortals—but how did he come to die in the first place? This is difficult to ascertain, for nothing is known about the exact circumstances. In his memoirs Hadrian asserted that the death was an accident, but the ancient sources were not so sure. Three texts give accounts of what happened—Dio Cassius, the *Historia Augusta,* and Aurelius Victor. They were written long after the event, are not altogether reliable, and (some say) betray signs of malice. According to Dio, the best of the bunch,

> Antinous . . . had been a favorite of the emperor and had died in Egypt, either by falling into the Nile, as Hadrian writes, or, as the truth is, by being offered in sacrifice. For Hadrian, as I have stated, was always very curious and employed divinations and incantations of all kinds.

Aurelius Victor agrees, reporting that

> when Hadrian wanted to prolong his life and magicians had demanded a volunteer in his place, they report that although everyone else refused, Antinous offered himself and for this reason the honors mentioned above were accorded him. We shall leave the matter unresolved, although with someone of a self-indulgent nature we are suspicious of a relationship between men far apart in age.

The *Historia Augusta* takes a similar line, but with less certainty.

> Concerning this incident there are varying rumors; for some claim that he had devoted himself to death for Hadrian, and others—what both his beauty and Hadrian's excessive sensuality indicate.

What is intended by this insinuation is unclear; presumably the reader is to infer that Antinous killed himself in order to escape the emperor's sexual advances.

The first and most ordinary of explanations is that the emperor's favorite was drowned by accident, just as Hadrian claimed. A youth, high spirits, unpredictable currents or underwater plants trapping an unwary diver or swimmer—this is a familiar and plausible concatenation of circumstances. But a personage of Antinous' importance would seldom be alone, and if he went for a swim help would surely have been close at hand.

A second possibility is that he committed suicide, evading notice and slipping silently into the river, perhaps under cover of darkness. It is not too hard to guess at motives. He was now about twenty, and no longer the pretty lad who had first caught the emperor's eye. If Hadrian fancied only smooth-cheeked teenagers, then indeed Antinous faced an uncertain future. What use would his patron and lover have for him once he had graduated from *puer,* boy, to *iuvenis,* young man?

There is evidence, though, that Hadrian had catholic tastes. Aurelius Victor claims that "malicious rumors spread that he debauched adult males (*puberibus*)." While no necessary blame attached to a youthful *eromenos* for having sex with his *erastes* and even privately allowing himself to be buggered, it was, as we have seen, shameful for an adult to accept the receptive role. Antinous, having reached manhood, may have been unwilling to go on sleeping with the emperor. In his eyes, if he allowed things to continue as before, he would be little better than a male prostitute. All too credibly, he could imagine himself aging into the superannuated gigolo of Juvenal's satire.

Even if there was something to these fears, that one member of the pair was losing interest or that the other was feeling shame, the evidence of Hadrian's behavior after the drowning points to the passionate sincerity of his love, and so surely mitigates them. That is to say, Antinous could count on the emperor's continuing affection even if for one reason or another the love affair itself were to end. He had no grounds for anticipating that he would either be discarded or abused.

We are left with the opinion of the literary sources, although from a modern perspective they propose by far the most implausible of the options. However, the idea of compensatory self-sacrifice was familiar to the ancient world. Euripides' famous tragedy *Alcestis* told the story of a wife volunteering to hand herself over to death in place of her husband, Admetus, whose time was due. Admetus would be permitted to survive

> if he could find another
> to take his place and join the dead below.
> He asked in turn of all his family,
> his father, and his mother; but found no one
> willing to quit the world and die for him—
> except his wife.

This account neatly parallels Hadrian's alleged search for a volunteer, according to Aurelius Victor.

At some point after 130 or 131, Hadrian's friend the historian and public official Arrian wrote a guide to part of the Black Sea coastline in the form of a long letter to the emperor. It includes a description of an island called Leuke, deserted except for a few goats. Here, legend had it, the Greek hero Achilles once lived as a boy. Visitors left votive offerings to him and his older *erastes,* Patroclus, for whose death Achilles had wreaked a terrible vengeance during the siege of Troy before himself being killed. Arrian concluded:

> I myself believe that Achilles was a hero second to none, for his nobility, beauty, and strength of soul; for his early departure from mankind . . . and for the love and friendship because of which he wanted to die for his beloved.

Although Hadrian and Antinous are hardly a perfect match for the Greek couple, Arrian was surely linking two doomed *eromenoi* who, in different ways, put their lives on the line for their lovers. It was a delicate allusion, well judged to touch and comfort his desolate correspondent.

In sum, then, Hadrian was suffering from a serious illness of some kind; he and Antinous believed that the emperor would recover his health if he, Antinous, gave up his life in his stead. So the verdict of suicide stands, but for religious or magical reasons rather than from private unhappiness.

Another unappetizing option is that, with or without Antinous' consent, Hadrian arranged for his sacrificial execution, as he had sacrificed the piglet during his Eleusinian initiation. This would have been very odd behavior. The Romans had outlawed human sacrifice long ago during the Republic, and the Egyptians are not known to have practiced it in remembered times. But magic may be a different matter: the Pachrates papyrus at least purports to deal in spells that cause death. The lethal power of witches was widely believed: Horace summed up the fearful fantasies of popular opinion in his little horror poem about a boy who was buried alive up to his neck and starved to death so that his marrow and liver could be used in a love potion. Whether such crimes were commonplace may be doubted, but it is conceivable that Pachrates or some other magico-religious authority was consulted about a ritual sacrifice to restore the emperor's health, and that Antinous was, willy-nilly, cast into the river. At least that would justify Hadrian's denial of suicide.

Any conclusion on these matters has to be guesswork. Such evidence as there is points to the offering of one life for another. Two marble busts, one of them from Tibur, and dating from about this time or later seem to offer confirmation. They show the emperor as a young man again. A new coin type shows an equally youthful Hadrian. Thanks to wishful thinking, it was supposed that the death in the Nile had worked its magic. The emperor had been aging and ill, but now, look, here was the proof—he had been rejuvenated, this time literally, not symbolically, *renatus*.

Within a week of the drowning the emperor decided to found a new city opposite Hermopolis where Antinous had been taken from the water. He had already had in mind the creation of a Hadrianopolis to be located at some as yet undetermined place in the center of Egypt, but now this general project was transformed into a massive memorial to the dead boy.

Plans were quickly drawn up for a splendid new city, to be called Antinoopolis after its founding divinity. Settlers, a mix of people of Greek descent and army veterans, were attracted by generous tax concessions from other Hellenized Egyptian cities. Although almost nothing remains today (thanks to the depredations of local people), three centuries ago many buildings were intact. An eighteenth-century visitor remarked: "This town was a perpetual peristyle." Antinoopolis was arranged in a grid and two main streets with double colonnades crossed in the city center, where a large shrine was erected, dedicated (we may reasonably suppose) to the new divinity.

This layout echoes that of Alexandria where the Sema, a building that housed the body of Alexander the Great, stood at the intersection of two grand avenues; here the mummified conqueror lay in a crystal coffin. It is possible that Hadrian's first thought was to inter Antinous at the new foundation, within hailing distance of where he died. If so, he soon changed his mind and commissioned a shrine to house his remains at his villa at Tibur. Construction began almost at once in a very prominent location just by the villa's grand entrance and proceeded with great speed.

The Antinoeion was a walled enclosure with two small temples inside it. Facing the entrance was a semicircular colonnade, or *exedra,* at the back of which a porch led into a sanctum, the tomb itself. In the center of the enclosure a specially commissioned obelisk was installed (now called the Barberini obelisk, it stands on the Pincian Hill in Rome). It bears four inscriptions; the first expresses good wishes to the emperor and empress, and the other three concern Antinous and his cult as the new god Antinous-Osiris. One passage reads: "Antinous rests in this tomb situated inside the garden [that is, Hadrian's villa and its park], property of the emperor of Rome."

Antinous had a marvelous life after death. His cult spread with great speed and his popularity grew with the years. As a god who dies and is resurrected, he even became a rival to Christianity for a while; it was claimed that "the honor paid to him falls little short of that which we render to Jesus."

One of the characteristics of religion in the Mediterranean was that an equivalence was assumed among the gods of different religions. Antinous was associated immediately on deification with Osiris, something he may dimly have guessed at while still alive. It is likely that he died on October 24, the day of the festival of Osiris; if so, this was a date he or Hadrian very possibly chose for its spiritual resonance. Osiris was the merciful judge of the dead and, by the same token, the underworld power that gave life. He inspired the annual flooding of the Nile and the vegetable renewals of spring.

Antinous did not only overlap with Osiris, he was also linked to Hermes (the Egyptian Thoth and the Roman Mercury), patron of boundaries and the travelers who cross them. This is why Pancrates called him "son of the Argus slayer" in his poem about the hunt, which was written in the weeks following the drowning. Argus was a many-eyed monster whom Hermes killed. As well as being the messenger of the gods, he was a psychopomp, a conductor of souls to the underworld. In Athens Antinous merged with Dionysus, and the priest of his cult was allocated a best seat for the theatrical performances of the Dionysia, which the new god had originally attended, we may assume, as an ordinary member of the audience.

A coin has been found that shows Antinous as Iakchos, the minor deity who played a part in the Eleusinian Mysteries. Having first encountered the visions and secrets of Demeter as a humble initiate, he returned as a divine being.

Apart from founding Antinoopolis and establishing a cult at Mantinea, Hadrian did not insist on the worship of his lost lover. But local elites seeking his favor quickly realized that commissioning temples and statues was one sure way to obtain it. When the contemporaneous travel writer Pausanias visited Mantinea, he noticed a new temple dedicated to Antinous. "I never saw him in the flesh," he commented, "but I have seen statues and images of him."

This was no exaggeration. Soon Antinous was everywhere. Dio writes that Hadrian "set up statues, or rather sacred images of him, practically all over the world." The emperor must have commissioned an artist of great ability to produce a sculptural paradigm, which was then widely copied. It is an unforgettable type of masculine beauty—melancholy, heavy-locked, large-chested, eyes modestly downcast.

Around the Mediterranean, temples, altars, priesthoods, oracles, inscriptions, and games were established in his name, all of which required images. It has been estimated that as many as 2,000 were carved, of which more than 115 still exist, and more are emerging from the ground as the years go by. A colossal seated statue recently excavated in the Peloponnese shows Antinous tying a fillet around his head as if he were a victorious athlete. The villa at Tibur was filled with Antinous; at least ten statues have been found there. At Delphi his effigy was ritually oiled for so many generations that it acquired, and even now possesses, the translucency of alabaster. Remarkably, the distant Iberi, realm of the difficult-to-please King Pharasmenes, yielded to the spell. In the grave of one of his noblemen, a very fine silver dish embossed with Antinous' head has been unearthed. It was probably an official gift, much prized by the recipient.

The worship of Antinous long outlasted the reign of his imperial lover. Free of Hadrian he drew his own mass following, and his image can be found not only in high-status artworks but in the artifacts of daily life—lamps, plates, and bowls. Whatever the original intention behind his deification, the ageless Bithynian became a talisman by which the Greek inhabitants of the empire could simultaneously celebrate their own identity and their loyalty to Rome. He personified the reconciliation between the two dominant cultures of the Mediterranean world. He was the ideal of the Panhellenion made flesh.

Even today his is the most instantly recognizable and memorable face from the classical world. Antinous is one of the very few ancient Greeks and Romans to have his own active websites.

XXIII

"MAY HIS BONES ROT!"

. . .

The death of Antinous did not halt the imperial tour. The journey up the Nile and the sightseeing continued. The party visited the so-called singing statue of Memnon at Thebes; this was one of two seated figures of a pharaoh. It lost its top half in an earthquake; thereafter at dawn, when the sun's rays warmed the stone, a singing sound could be heard— "very like the twanging of a broken lyre string or harp string." This curious phenomenon was irregular, and on the first visit it failed to sing. The next day Sabina and her friend Balbilla returned and the statue performed, as it did soon afterward for Hadrian. Balbilla carved some poems on the stone, in one of which she wrote

> The emperor Hadrian then himself bid welcome to
> Memnon and left on stone for generations to come
> this inscription recounting all that he saw and all that he heard.
> It was clear to all that the gods love him.

Hadrian spent some months in Alexandria, coming to terms with his loss and planning the construction of Antinoopolis. Pancrates produced his poem on the lion hunt, in which he suggested that the rosy lotus should be renamed antinoeus on the fictive grounds that it sprang from the blood of the lion Hadrian killed. Pleased with the conceit, the emperor enrolled the poet as a member of the Mouseion.

He left Egypt in the spring of 131 and toured the provinces of Syria and Asia. Then, for his third visit as emperor, he returned to Athens, where he spent the winter. No doubt he attended the Eleusinian Mysteries again, this time alone. His benefactions continued; in an inscription he asserts: "Know that I take every opportunity to benefit both the city publicly and individual Athenians."

In the spring the delegates of the Panhellenion met for the first time, probably on the occasion of the dedication of the Olympieion. The first games, the Panhellenia, did not take place until 137, but with new Panathenaic games, new Olympic games, and the Hadriania, in honor of the emperor (perhaps instituted only after his death), every year in a quadrennial cycle was to see Athens host a great international celebration, with large influxes of visitors from all over the eastern Mediterranean. Athens was to become a festival city and the acknowledged center of the Greek-speaking world.

A catastrophe now befell Hadrian for which he had only himself to blame. The Jews were infuriated by the ban on circumcision and deeply offended by the rebuilding of Jerusalem as Aelia Capitolina, a Jewless and Hellenic city. It looked to them very much as if the Romans intended to ethnically cleanse Judaea. Also, the diversion by Titus of the half-shekel tax levied on all Jews for the upkeep of the Temple on the Mount to the upkeep of the temple of Jupiter Best and Greatest on the Capitol in Rome still rankled half a century on.

They were reminded of Antiochus IV Epiphanes, king of the Seleucid empire in the Near East, who flourished in the second century B.C. In a number of respects he was an anticipatory echo of Hadrian. He had tried (but failed) to complete the Olympieion in Athens and promoted the cult of Zeus Olympios. At his capital, Antioch, he behaved informally with ordinary people and was very much the *civilis* ruler that Hadrian sought to be. He sacked Jerusalem and introduced his own cult into the Temple, erecting a statue of himself there. His aim, like Hadrian's, was to Hellenize Jewry.

The Jewish leadership felt it had no choice but to collaborate. According to Josephus, a renegade Jew who defected to Titus in the great Jewish war of two generations previously, they told the king

they wanted to leave the laws of their country, and the Jewish way of living as they understood it, and to follow the king's laws, and the

Greek way of living . . . Accordingly, they left off all the customs that belonged to their own country, and imitated the practices of other nations.

A rebellion broke out, known as the Maccabean uprising, after one of its leaders, Judah Maccabee. Antiochus' forces were incapable of coping with the guerrilla tactics of the insurgents. The Seleucid monarch was distracted by the Parthians and then unexpectedly died. The Jews had won their independence.

Almost exactly three hundred years later, history appeared to be repeating itself. Tacitus wrote in his *Histories,* a book that Hadrian is very likely to have read, that Antiochus "endeavored to abolish Jewish superstition and to introduce Greek civilization; the war with the Parthians, however, prevented him from improving this basest of peoples." That was precisely Hadrian's program, but he was sure that, in the event of any resistance, he would not have to worry about Parthian interference, now that he had renewed his entente with Rome's most dangerous neighbor. In fact, so far as he knew, the emperor had no grounds for fearing any real trouble.

However, Jewish activists were preparing carefully for war, in the greatest secrecy. Hadrian was still in Egypt and they did not want to alarm him. They armed themselves without attracting notice, by means of an ingenious trick. Legitimate, state-regulated armorers in Judaea produced faulty weapons ordered by Roman garrisons in the region; when these were returned as substandard they were reworked and held in readiness for later use.

Those planning the rebellion well understood that it would be fruitless to challenge the Romans in the field. Just as the Maccabees had done, they adopted guerrilla tactics. Dio Cassius writes that, not unlike the tunneling Vietcong of our own day,

they occupied the advantageous positions in the country and strengthened them with mines and walls, in order that they might have places of refuge whenever they should be hard pressed, and might meet together unobserved under ground; and they pierced these subterranean passages from above at intervals to let in air and light.

Archaeologists have identified more than three hundred tunnel complexes, building on an infrastructure of cisterns, wine and oil presses, storehouses and burial caves. With ventilation shafts, water tanks, and storerooms for supplies, they were designed for long stays underground.

During the great rebellion put down by Titus the Jews paid a heavy price for being disunited. This time they had the considerable advantage of strong, self-confident, and intelligent leadership. Their commander was Shim'on ben Kosiba, who signed his letters as prince of Israel and usually traded under the name of Bar Kokhba, "Son of the Star." The phrase alluded to a prediction made by the prophet Balaam:

> I look into the future,
> And I see the nation of Israel.
> A king, like a bright star, will arise in that nation.
> Like a comet he will come from Israel.

In other words, Bar Kokhba was casting himself as the Messiah, or "anointed one"—a leader who would rebuild Israel, cast out the wicked, and ultimately judge the whole world. Some rabbinic opinion supported the claim. A celebrated rabbi, Aqiba ben Joseph, chief teacher in the rabbinical school of Jaffa, was reported to have said when he met Bar Kokhba: "This is the Messiah." It may have been he who proposed the stellar sobriquet. Another rabbi begged to differ, telling Aqiba: "Grass will grow on your cheeks and still he [namely, the Messiah] will not come."

The revolt broke out in 132. An immediate cause, the last straw, may have been the collapse of the tomb of King Solomon in Jerusalem, probably caused by workers engaged in building Aelia Capitolina. A narrative account of the course of the fighting has not come down to us, but the general sequence of events is clear enough. The first phase was near-terminal defeat for the Romans.

The governor of Judaea, Quintus Tineius Rufus, had at his disposal two legions and a dozen auxiliary cavalry units. He underestimated the threat. What appeared at first sight to be a local crisis soon acquired a regional dimension. The Jewish diaspora was involved (although not in Egypt, Cyrenaica, and Cyprus, where Jewish communities had more or less vanished after the suppression of the uprising there in 116–17 at the beginning of Hadrian's reign). There was probably fighting, or at least disorder, in the neighboring provinces of Syria and Arabia. Dio paints the scene.

> At first the Romans took no account of [the rebels]. Soon, however, all Judaea had been stirred up, and the Jews everywhere were showing signs of disturbance, were gathering together, and giving evidence of great hostility to the Romans, partly by secret and partly by overt acts; many outside nations, too, were joining them through eagerness for gain, and the whole earth, one might almost say, was being stirred up over the matter.

Tineius Rufus was rapidly overwhelmed. The governor of Syria sent reinforcements down from the north. The legion XXII Deiotariana was rushed to Judaea from Egypt, but appears to have been annihilated. Roman casualties were exceptionally severe.

Usually when generals sent dispatches to the Senate they began with the phrase "If you and your children are in health, it is well; I and the legions are in health." It is telling that when Hadrian reported on the military situation in Judaea, he omitted this introduction. The army was in dire straits.

The emperor learned of the revolt when still in Athens or perhaps having started on the journey back to Rome. He made a number of necessary decisions. Sailors or marines were hurriedly transferred to the legion X Fretensis, presumably to make up for losses, and for the first time in many years new troops were raised in Italy, an unpopular move.

According to Dio, Hadrian "sent against [the Jews] his best generals." First among them was his highly competent governor of Britain, Sextus Julius Severus, a reliable troubleshooter, whom he ordered to make his way to Judaea, picking up reinforcements en route. It is a sign of the scale of the emergency that Severus was moved from the most remote of provinces and had to cross the complete length of the empire to reach the theater of operations. He must have spent some months on the road. But in Hadrian's eyes merit outweighed distance and delay.

Dio's account implies that Severus was not in overall command but that all the generals were placed on a level footing. This sounds like a very bad idea, for armies with a collective of commanders seldom thrive. It can only be assumed that the emperor himself took personal charge of the campaign, at least for a time. This is confirmed by a reference in inscriptions listing the service careers of officers and men to the *expeditio Judaica,* the Jewish expedition. Use of the word *expeditio* signifies the presence of the emperor.

It would indeed have been surprising if such a hands-on ruler stayed away from what was both the greatest military crisis of his reign and a perfect opportunity to check that his military training methods, to which he had devoted so much time and energy, were fit for the purpose.

In the flush of victory Bar Kokhba established a disciplined state, and Judaea was totally free of foreign influence or control. A good deal is known about how he governed, thanks in part to coins but most of all to astonishing discoveries in caves in the desert wadis west of the Dead Sea—legible papers and artifacts in perfect condition thanks to the arid weather conditions.

A new calendar was decreed and appeared on coins and in letters. The year 132 became "the First Year of the Redemption of Israel." Religious ceremonies were restored and a new high priest appointed. A highly placed officer wrote to colleagues requesting ritual necessaries for a festival; subordinates of Bar Kokhba, they were commanders (apparently) at En-gedi, an oasis on the shore of the Dead Sea.

> Soumaios to Ionathes, son of Baianos, and to Masabala, greetings. Since I have sent Agrippa to you, hurry up and send me stems of palms and citrons and they will be set up for the Festival of the Tabernacle of the Jews. Don't do anything else. This was written in Greek because [a name is lost] could not be found to write it in Hebrew. Let

him [i.e., Agrippa] return quickly because of the festival. Don't do anything else. Soumaios. Farewell.

The letter, with its needless repetition of the phrase "Don't do anything else," speaks eloquently of the excitement, the urgency, and, implicitly, the optimism of a revolutionary moment.

A note from the prince of Israel himself reveals a ruthless touch. Its subject is a certain landowner, wealthy but uncooperative. The produce from his orchards and his livestock would be of material benefit to the rebel cause.

Shim'on Bar Kosiba to Yehonatan son of Ba' ay an, and to Masabala, son of Shim' on, that you will send to me Eleazar son of Hitta immediately, before the Sabbath.

If Eleazar was found and delivered, he would have had a distinctly uncomfortable interview. One rather hopes that he smelled trouble and made himself scarce.

Another letter suggests Yehonatan and Masabala were not altogether dependable officers. Bar Kokhba ordered them to send him reinforcements. "And if you shall not send them, let it be known to you, that you will be punished."

Bar Kokhba's approach to religion was rigorously exclusive and he had no time for Christians. The church fathers returned the compliment. Justin, writing contemporaneously, claimed: "In the present war it is only the Christians whom Barchochebas [i.e., Bar Kokhba], the leader of the rebellion of the Jews, commanded to be punished severely if they did not deny Jesus as the Messiah and blaspheme him."

Jerome goes further: "Barcocheba, leader of a party of the Jews, because the Christians are not willing to help him against the Roman army, murders them with every sort of torture." Christians regarded Bar Kokhba as a butcher, a bandit, and a con man. In order to meet a prophecy that the Messiah breathed fire, Jerome accused him of "fanning a lighted blade of straw in his mouth with puffs of breath so as to give the impression that he was spewing forth flames."

If we can generalize from names in the discovered papyri and the location of coin finds, the new Jewish state was of limited extent. It controlled at least a territory running south of Jerusalem and along the Dead Sea and extending to within eighteen miles of the Mediterranean. There may have been pockets of insurgent activity farther north and on the eastern shore of the Dead Sea. However, Bar Kokhba failed to capture the abomination of desolation that was Aelia Capitolina. Rebel coins have been found in many other places in Judaea but none there.

Eventually the regrouped and reinforced Romans returned to the fight. Tineius Rufus wreaked vengeance for his early defeat, if we can trust hysterical Talmudic sources. Eusebius records:

> When military aid had been sent him by the emperor, [Tineius Rufus] moved out against the Jews, treating their madness without mercy. He destroyed in heaps thousands of men, women, and children, and under the law of war, enslaved their land.

The hapless rabbi Aqiba fell into Roman hands. Apparently he was flayed alive. He is said to have endured the punishment with composure, but his messiah was unable to save him.

Hadrian hired the services of the architect and engineer Apollodorus of Damascus, builder of the stone bridge across the Danube and designer of many of Trajan's buildings in Rome, despite their being reputed to be on bad terms. Apollodorus was an expert on siegecraft, and in an epistolary preface to his classic text on the subject, *Poliorcetica,* he addressed an emperor who needed his advice: "I am honored that you think me worthy of sharing your concern in this matter." He writes that although he is not familiar with the terrain in question he has been invited to supply designs for siege works to be used against elevated fortified positions—heights rather than cities.

Apollodorus lists devices suitable for employing against a hill fort; these included defenses against heavy objects, such as wagons and barrels that could be rolled down a hill onto attackers; screens to protect an assault force against missiles as it made for the top; and techniques for undermining a wall, ramming a gate, or using assault ladders.

The emperor in question is most likely to have been Hadrian, for the task Apollodorus describes exactly fits the challenge facing the Romans in Judaea. When Julius Severus eventually arrived, he adopted the only rational tactic to subdue a lawless countryside speckled with guerrilla groups. As Vespasian had done before him, he proceeded slowly and methodically, taking and securing every hill and strongpoint and destroying everything he encountered before he advanced farther.

The Romans had assembled overwhelming force. It is impossible to gauge how many troops took part in the campaign, but a best estimate indicates that the number of legions, either with a complete complement or represented by sizable *vexillationes*, or detachments, was twelve or thirteen (albeit not necessarily present at the same time). This was a disproportionately huge deployment for tiny Judaea, but nothing was to be left to chance.

Bar Kokhba responded vigorously, if we can trust Talmudic tales. It was said that "he would catch missiles from the enemy's catapults on one of his knees and hurl them back, killing many of the foe." This can be interpreted as meaning that the rebels acquired some Roman artillery and put it to good use.

However, letters have been found which suggest that loyalty to the prince of Israel was beginning to wear thin. In one of them, the unsatisfactory duo Yehonatan and Masabala continued to disappoint. "In comfort you sit, eat, and drink from the property of the House of Israel," he wrote angrily, "and care nothing for your brothers."

The endgame approached. The civilian Jewish population, not only in Judaea but also in Arabia, grew desperate. Whether sympathetic to the rebel cause or not, everyone was caught up in the approaching catastrophe. Well-to-do families, together with their gold and silver, hid in the insurgents' network of tunnels and in caves. That some failed to survive their ordeal is confirmed by the discovery of cooking utensils, correspondence, and human remains in caves at Wadi Murabba' and Nahal Hever.

Bar Kokhba's final redoubt was the fortress of Betar, six miles south-west of Jerusalem. We do not have the details, but Apollodorus' advice on siegecraft was good. A fragmentary letter evokes the despair of total defeat: ". . . till the end . . . they have no hope . . . my brothers in the south . . . of these were lost by the sword."

In November or December 135 Betar fell. According to Eusebius, the siege lasted a long time, but eventually "the rebels were driven to final destruction by famine and thirst and the instigator of their madness paid the penalty he deserved." Bar Kokhba's head was taken to Hadrian (or perhaps to Severus). Dio reports that 50 of the most important strongholds of the Jews had been captured, 985 villages razed, and 580,000 Jews killed. A hyperbolic rabbinical tradition had it that gentiles fertilized their vineyards for seven years with the blood of Israel without using manure.

The Jewish state lasted three years, before the dream of liberty was extinguished. The man whose nom de guerre was Shim'on bar Kokhba, Son of the Star, was renamed by embittered survivors as they contemplated the ruins of Judaea; he was now Shim'on bar Kozeba, Son of the Lie.

The emperor determined to root out Judaism. So many prisoners were put up for auction at Hebron and Gaza that each fetched no more than the value of a horse. Judaea was, in effect, depopulated of Jews either by death or enslavement, and any few who remained were forbidden to enter the district around Jerusalem. This was to prevent them from even seeing, let alone visiting, their ancestral capital. The teaching of Mosaic law was banned, as was the ownership of scrolls (the essential medium on which the scriptures and rabbinical commentaries were written).

The building of Aelia Capitolina proceeded apace and an equestrian statue of Hadrian, still in place more than a century later, was erected on the site of the Holy of Holy. Pagan shrines were built over Jewish places of worship. By the city gate for the Bethlehem road, a marble sow was erected, insultingly offensive to Jews and denoting their subjection to Roman power. Judaea was abolished as a territorial entity. It was added to Galilee and the enlarged and purified province was known as Syria

Palaestina, the first time the term *Palestine* was ever employed. It was to be as if the chosen people had never existed.

Hadrian was acclaimed *imperator* for the first time in his reign, a title adopted by an emperor only after a signal victory, and his three chief generals, Severus and the governors of Syria and Arabia, were granted triumphal honors, *ornamenta triumphalia,* the highest military honor to which they could aspire. The emperor was unusually parsimonious with such titles, and his generosity on this occasion signals the shock that had rocked the empire. It had taken a huge effort to put down the revolt.

For Hadrian, his victory was in part a defeat. His policy was to attract the fullest possible consent to Roman rule, to entice provincial elites to join him in government, to recast the empire as a commonwealth of equals. There is no reason to doubt the sincerity of this approach, but, for all that, the revolt had exposed its falsity. The final guarantee of the *pax Romana* was the brute force of the legions. This, in turn, was a reminder of the implicit fragility of the imperial system. If the army were ever to fail, what would then preserve Rome's dominion?

When the rabbinical authors mention the name of Hadrian they often add the phrase "May his bones rot!" No wonder, for it was now clear that, after recurrent revolts at the end of Nero's reign and then at the end of Trajan's, the Jews would never again give Rome any trouble.

XXIV

NO MORE JOKES

. . .

In the spring of 134 Hadrian returned to Rome from the east, probably revisiting the Dacian provinces en route. The war in Judaea was by no means over, but he had made all the necessary arrangements and he had confidence in his generals. That dependably undependable client king Pharasmenes stirred up trouble for the Parthians by encouraging a neighboring people, the fierce Alani, to invade their empire as well as the Roman province of Cappadocia; the Parthian king complained to Hadrian, but luckily the governor, Arrian, was on hand. He deployed a Roman force with masterly skill to deter the incursion; being a writer as well as a man of action, he wrote a book on the subject, which is the fullest record of the Roman army in the field to have survived.

· Despite these alarms, coins celebrating the emperor's *adventus* breathed optimism. In one series, a galley rides on the waves with the goddess Minerva in the prow brandishing a javelin and holding a spear: underneath, a legend reads *Felicitas Aug,* "the emperor's happiness." Other coins from this time boast of Mars the Avenger and Rome holding a statuette of Victory.

The emperor's brother-in-law, Servianus, was still vigorous in his ninth decade. After a long, resented wait, he had been appointed to serve as consul *ordinarius* this year for the third time (in April he handed over, as was usual, to a *suffectus*). This was a high honor, which, despite a history of chilly relations with the emperor, he owed to being a leading member by marriage of the imperial family. Paulina, his wife and Hadrian's sister, had died a few years previously. Nothing is heard of his daughter and son-in-law. Servianus' grandson Pedanius Fuscus was now in his late teens and, via his grandmother, was the only adult male linked by blood to Hadrian. For so long as the emperor did not adopt someone else, he was entitled to regard himself as the heir presumptive. He was probably in the imperial entourage, where an eye could be kept on him.

As previously noted, the only other senator to have held a third consulship was Annius Verus, and we can take it that Hadrian was looking forward warmly to seeing his loyal old friend's grandson again. Little Marcus, his *verissimus,* was now thirteen years old. It was six years that the emperor had been away, a very long period in the life of a child. It would be a pleasant task to find out how he had developed.

Always serious-minded, the boy proved to be a hardworking pupil when his elementary education began at the age of seven. His maternal great-grandfather Catilius Severus was city prefect and an important man at court. However, he found time to guide the boy's schooling; Marcus recalled gratefully in later life that he was "allowed to dispense with attendance at schools and to enjoy good teachers at home." Two family slaves or freedmen taught him the rudiments of Greek and Latin. Specialists gave him a grounding in the arts—literature, music (mainly singing), and geometry.

A tutor looked after Marcus' moral formation, and seems to have instilled worthy but slightly dull values in the growing teenager. He was taught "not to side with the Greens or the Blues at the chariot races, or to back Thracian [swordsmen] or Samnite [heavy-armed] gladiators; to tolerate pain and limit my needs; to work with my own hands and mind my own business and not to listen to malicious gossip."

A year or so before Hadrian's return to Italy, Marcus entered his secondary education under various *grammatici.* But his most influential teacher was his art master, Diognetus, from whom he learned not only painting but the rudiments of philosophy. He wrote dialogues in the manner first established by Plato and "set my heart on the pallet bed and coverlet of animal skins, and everything else that tallied with the Greek [philosophical] system." In fact, according to the *Historia Augusta,* Marcus would have preferred to sleep on the ground, were it not for his mother's veto.

Diognetus also imparted a subversive principle that presumably would have annoyed Hadrian had he learned about it. This was "not to give credence to the claims of miracle-mongers and magicians and such matters."

Marcus sounds as if he was becoming rather priggish, but the emperor liked what he saw of him. This may have had something to do with the fact that he was a nice-looking boy, as a bust of him in his teens shows. More to the point, Hadrian believed he could foresee an intelligent and responsible adult in the making.

During the emperor's absence, building work in Rome had proceeded busily. The spectacular temple of Venus and Rome was dedicated in 135. Hadrian was very proud of the result. According to Dio Cassius, he invited Apollodorus to offer his comments. Hadrian bore him a grudge, because years before he had interrupted with some smart remark a conversation between Apollodorus and Trajan about a building project. The architect had snapped back at Hadrian, who was practicing his draftsmanship at the time: "Go away, and get back to your drawing exercises. You don't understand any of this."

The emperor hoped that this time Apollodorus would compliment him, but he was disappointed. The architect remarked that the temple

> ought to have been built on high ground and that the earth should have been excavated beneath it, so that it might have stood out more conspicuously on the Sacred Way from its higher position . . . Second, in regard to the statues [of Venus and Rome], he said that they had been made too tall for the height of the *cella* [the temple's inner chamber]. "For now," he said, "if the goddesses wish to get up and go out, they will be unable to do so."

Dio has it that the emperor was so angry that he banished the architect and later put him to death. This is a tall story. The joke about the goddesses had already been made centuries previously against Phidias' famous statue of Zeus at Olympia, and there is evidence that Hadrian continued to make use of Apollodorus' services. However, the exchange is consistent with what we know of the emperor's bossy nature. It may well be that the amateur and the professional got on badly. If they quarreled, though, the worst that can have happened was that the architect died soon after and malicious tongues made the most of the coincidence.

Rome was still a construction site. On the right bank of the river the emperor's huge mausoleum, long planned, was rising from the ground. A bridge connecting it to the Campus Martius had already been constructed. The tomb itself was similar to that of Augustus, which was full. Nerva had been squeezed in there and Trajan's remains lay at the foot of his column; the dynasty needed a long-term replacement. The design was a large drum rising from a square base and faced with marble. It probably supported a superstructure decorated with statues and surmounted by a colonnaded tower, on top of which stood a colossal four-horsed chariot.

The emperor was wise to plan his final resting place, for he was feeling unwell. He suffered from recurrent and increasingly copious nosebleeds. He remained in or near Rome, presumably spending most of his time at the villa complex at Tibur, where there was the construction of the temple of Antinous to superintend. The text on the obelisk there included a prayer from Osirantinous to Ra-Harachte, a union of the sun god Ra and Horus, king of the heavens, that the emperor "live eternally, like Ra, / With a prospering and newly risen age!"

Hadrian had believed that the death of Antinous would cure him of his chronic ailment. Perhaps he had benefited for a time from this most selfish of placebos, but, of course, the truth was otherwise. By the time he celebrated his sixtieth birthday, on January 24, 136, and doubtless long before, it was obvious that the magic had failed. Mumbo jumbo was mumbo jumbo and Hadrian was sicker than ever. A portrait study from sometime in the 130s from Diktynna in Crete shows a weary, disillusioned face. The loss of his beloved had been for nothing.

The emperor's state of mind grew irritable. Some thought that the stress released an innate cruelty. He began to throw over old friends and allies for reasons that are now obscure, but do not appear to be altogether rational. He dropped Aulus Platorius Nepos, who had probably accompanied him on his visit to Britannia and who, as governor, had organized the building of the wall. He now held him "in the greatest abhorrence," writes the *Historia Augusta*. "Once, when he [Platorius Nepos] went to see him when he was ill he refused him admittance."

Saddest of all, Quintus Marcius Turbo, who had been a centurion with the legion II Adiutrix when Hadrian was a military tribune in his first army posting, fell from favor about now. Turbo had had a glittering career, quashing the Jewish uprising in 117 and serving with distinction in Dacia. One of the emperor's closest advisers and confidants, he had been Praetorian prefect since 125. Dio Cassius reports that

> he spent the entire day near the palace and often he would even go there before midnight, when other people were just going to bed.

Turbo was never to be found at home during the daytime, even when he was unwell. Hadrian once asked him to calm down and live a quiet life; he replied, adapting Vespasian's famous last words: "The prefect ought to die on his feet."

Turbo was removed from office and replaced. A strong link to the past was broken.

Hadrian only just survived a major hemorrhage in the villa at Tibur, perhaps another unstoppable nosebleed. He realized that he was approaching the end of his life, and that it was time to think of the succession. Among his relatives, Servianus was much too old. A quarter of a century previously Trajan had once considered him worthy of the purple, but his time had passed. Anyway, Hadrian disliked him. What, then, about Pedanius Fuscus? The young man harbored great expectations, and so presumably thought himself to be in favor with the emperor.

However, for some reason, now impossible to ascertain, Hadrian disregarded his claim. Instead, he chose as heir someone who could hardly have been less suitable for the imperial throne. The political world was amazed when during the second half of 136 the emperor unexpectedly announced that he was adopting as his son Lucius Ceionius Commodus. He was renamed Lucius Aelius Caesar (from now on the word *caesar* ceased being an ordinary *cognomen*, but became the title of the nominated successor to the throne).

The *Historia Augusta* asserts that "his sole recommendation was his beauty." His pleasures were "not discreditable but somewhat unfocused": he enjoyed sex (with women, for a change) and kept by his bedside copies of Ovid's book of naughty poems, "My Love Affairs" (*Amores*). Frivolity went hand in hand with poor taste; apparently Martial was his Virgil. On the face of it, there was little to choose between him and Pedanius Fuscus. That said, Ceionius Commodus was now a man in his late thirties and was running a successful political career. This year he was consul and, although the appointment was in the emperor's gift and could have had a personal rather than a political significance, he seems to have commanded a certain competence.

It is possible that Lucius had been Antinous' predecessor as *eromenos*, albeit with a significant difference. If he was an attractive boy, he was also a freeborn Roman citizen of high status. A love affair on the traditional Greek model was feasible, but any sexual expression of affection would have necessarily been conducted with restraint. By the same token, the imperial *erastes* would have been expected to train his noble boyfriend for public life. Once Lucius had grown up, the relationship should have matured into *philia*, a deep and loyal friendship. Perhaps this was the background to his surprising promotion.

It is relevant to note that two or three years later, young Marcus Annius Verus and his tutor Marcus Cornelius Fronto exchanged letters about their love for each other. Fronto, holding back, says, "So far as I am concerned you shall be called καλὸς ['beautiful,' usually applied to victorious athletes] and not ἐρώμενος [*eromenos,* or 'beloved']." Marcus objects: "You shall never drive me, your lover, away." There is something artificial about the correspondence, but even if Marcus and Fronto were only playing at having an affair it does strongly suggest that Greek love was a respectable and accepted convention at court.

It is also worth observing that Ceionius Commodus had been the stepson of Avidius Nigrinus, one of Hadrian's four consular victims in the opening weeks of his reign—the crime for which the Senate had never quite forgotten. Could it be, wondered contemporaries, that a dying emperor was seeking to make amends by this remarkable adoption?

The real problem had nothing to do with favoritism or lack of outstanding ability, but with health. The new caesar was very ill, more so indeed than his adoptive father. He was known to cough up blood and, so far as we can tell, was suffering from tuberculosis. He was too ill even to appear in the Senate to offer his thanks to the emperor for the adoption.

Nevertheless, great celebrations were held. His health improved enough to allow Aelius Caesar to preside over games in the Circus Maximus, and he handed out lavish donatives to the People (that is, citizens living in or near Rome) and to the legions. He was designated consul again for 137 and was given the tribunician power that was an essential ingredient of imperial authority. Deciding that his heir needed a military grounding, Hadrian sent him to the Danube as governor of the two Pannonian provinces.

Pedanius Fuscus nursed a grievance. His hopes of succeeding Hadrian had been dashed, and he staged a coup. A second-century horoscope of the emperor claims that he nearly died when he was sixty-one years and ten months old, namely November 137. To be technical, "the degrees of the Horoscopos and the moon in Aquarius come into quartile to Saturn, which, however, is not destructive because Venus is in aspect to it (Saturn) also the second time." This was presumably a reference to Pedanius' plot. It failed, and it was the great-nephew who lost his life, not the emperor.

A horoscope of Pedanius reports him as coming "of an illustrious family of the highest level—I speak of his father and mother, both of high repute." The document continues (minus planetary data): "Having been born with great expectations and thinking he was coming into the imperial power, he was given bad advice and fell from favor about his twenty-fifth year. He was denounced to the emperor and was destroyed along with a certain old man of his own family, who was himself slandered because of him. In addition, all members of his family because of him were done away with in a lowly manner."

The "certain old man" was Servianus. Whether or not he was implicated in the conspiracy, it was unsafe to let him live once Pedanius had been removed. He was either executed or (so the *Historia Augusta* says) instructed to commit suicide. The alleged offense was ambition for the throne, presumably on his grandson's behalf rather than his own. The evidence, such that we have, smells of prosecutors making the most of little: the charge sheet noted that "he gave a feast for slaves in the royal household, sat in a royal chair placed close to his bed, and, though an old man of ninety, used to go out and meet the soldiers on guard duty [at the palace]."

Before he died, Servianus asked for fire with which to burn some incense. As he made the offering he exclaimed: "That I have done nothing wrong, you gods know very well. As for Hadrian, this is my only prayer, that he may long for death, yet be unable to die."

Two literary sources claim that "many others" or "many from the Senate" were also put to the sword, either openly or by subterfuge. However, they name no names, and the accusation may be false—a malicious lie, an exaggeration of a purge of officials, or a simple mistake. If there is truth in it, though, the deaths were doubtless related to the Pedanius affair. To many they echoed the scandalous executions of 117, and the Senate's old resentment against the emperor returned.

At about this time (or perhaps in the following year) another illustrious death occurred—that of the empress. A late source reports that "his wife, Sabina, while she was nearly being incapacitated by servile affronts, was driven to a voluntary death." A forced suicide is possible, but improbable. Although the husband and wife cordially loathed each other, the emperor took great pains to ensure that Sabina was treated with respect. She accompanied him on many of his travels and received all the honors due to an empress. Hadrian immediately had his late wife deified, enabling her to join her mother, Marciana, and Plotina on Olympus. Her apotheosis was recorded on an aureus, on the reverse of which she is shown seated on a flying eagle.

However, her disappearance just when the regime was undergoing a painful succession crisis is odd. The empress was still only in her late forties or early fifties and, in the normal course of events, should have expected another ten or twenty, even thirty, years of life. If there really was a Hadrianic bloodbath, it is conceivable that Sabina would have joined the other victims, should the emperor have suspected that she would scheme against his settlement when he was gone. The *Historia Augusta* mentions a rumor that he poisoned her, but there is no other evidence for this. Apart from the mysterious scandal during the visit to Britannia when Suetonius lost his job as imperial secretary for lèse-majesté, Sabina had no more recorded involvement in politics than Plotina had as Trajan's consort. The timing of her departure is most likely to have been merely a coincidence of fatalities.

Marcus Annius Verus was fifteen in April 136, by which time he had come of age and exchanged the red-striped *toga praetexta* of the child for the adult's plain *toga virilis*. As had been the case with the teenage Hadrian, the consuls appointed him to the honorary, and highly honorific, post of prefect of the city, *praefectus urbi* (not to be confused with the official of the same name who was in charge of the city's administration). The prefect, a boy from an aristocratic or imperial family, was left nominally in charge of the city of Rome when all the officeholders from the consuls down processed to the Alban Mount a few miles outside Rome and celebrated there the Feriae Latinae.

Marcus was still the apple of Hadrian's eye. He won golden praises for his ceremonial performance as prefect, and at banquets given by the emperor. He loved boxing and wrestling, running and fowling: he was a huntsman and an excellent ball player. However, he remained a studious youth. According to the *Historia Augusta*,

> His enthusiasm for philosophy led him away from all these pursuits and made him an earnest and serious-minded person. Yet it never completely took away a certain personal warmth . . . he was austere but not unreasonably so, reserved but not shy, serious but not depressive.

It was at the emperor's express wish that Marcus had been betrothed to Ceionia Fabia, one of Ceionius Commodus' daughters. This may provide a clue of Hadrian's real intention when deciding on the adoption. Aware of the man's poor health, he only wanted him to keep the seat warm for Marcus until *he* was old enough to assume the purple (as a matter of fact, Ceionius had a son of his own, but he was no more than seven years old and perhaps only five, young enough to be disregarded). Augustus' efforts to plan for the long-term succession of a grandson provided a precedent, although not a happy one as things turned out. He had expected Tiberius, a capable general and administrator, to govern the empire until young Gaius Caesar was ready to hold the reins of power. Tiberius refused to play the part allotted to him, and both Gaius and his younger brother Lucius died prematurely.

Once again, the fates put an end to an emperor's hopes. Hadrian had not originally realized just how ill Aelius Caesar was, but he came to see that the prognosis was poor. He repeatedly used to say, "We have leaned against a tottering wall and have wasted the four hundred million sesterces which we gave to the people and the soldiers on the adoption of Commodus."

Aelius Caesar spent less than a year on the Danube, where he had by no means been a failure as a commander. Before the end of 137 he was back in Rome. He was due to deliver an important speech before the Senate on January 1, but on the preceding night he collapsed. He took an overdose of some medicine, and his condition deteriorated further. He hemorrhaged badly and lost consciousness, dying on New Year's Day. The emperor forbade mourning, so as not to prevent the annual vow-taking ceremony for the safety of the state. The adoption had been greeted with "universal opposition," and there was no question of deification.

It was a near-disastrous setback. Hadrian himself was failing; he was looking emaciated and suffered from dropsy. A new succession plan was urgently needed. On January 24, his sixty-second birthday, he summoned leading senators to his sickbed, from which he addressed them.

My friends, I have not been permitted by nature to have a son, but you have made it possible by legal enactment . . . Since Heaven has bereft us of Lucius [Aelius Caesar], I have found as emperor for you in his place the man whom I now give you, one who is noble, mild, tractable, prudent, neither young enough to do anything reckless nor old enough to neglect anything.

This time Hadrian's choice had fallen on someone entirely unexceptionable. He confessed later: "I made my decision even when Commodus was alive." His successor was to be Titus Aurelius Fulvius Boionius Arrius Antoninus. He was a middle-aged senator of great wealth and with impeccable antecedents. He was orphaned as a child and his grandfather Titus Arrius Antoninus had brought him up. An amiable friend of Pliny, an intimate of Nerva, and a skilled versifier in Latin and Greek, Arrius was a senator of the old school who held the consulship "with the dignity of a bygone age."

The adoption of Arrius Antoninus' grandson as the new Caesar was an astute move on Hadrian's part, for it symbolized the entente between the two parts of the ruling class—those who were willing to collaborate with the emperors and traditionalists, including survivors of the Stoic opposition, still in mourning for the Republic. This entente had been Nerva's great achievement, and Antoninus was an assurance of its continuance into the future.

Good-natured and distinguished in appearance, Antoninus was an excellent public speaker. From Hadrian's point of view he had the overriding advantage of being a man of peace. He had no military experience of any kind and so there was little chance of a return to military aggression and imperial expansion.

The emperor had privately contacted Antoninus immediately after Aelius Caesar's death, but the senator asked for time to consider the invitation before accepting it. Perhaps he had something of Arrius in him and feared that the attractions of power were overrated. Also, Hadrian's offer came with conditions. Antoninus was to adopt Marcus, his *verissimus,* now seventeen years old, along with the dead Commodus' little son—probably confirmation that the boy had been the emperor's preferred choice all along. His solution was not without risk: Antoninus might disregard the adoptions after his death, or die before Marcus was old enough to take over. But if all went well, the empire would be in the hands of two competent and well-intentioned rulers for another couple of generations. It was a bet worth taking.

After due thought, Antoninus accepted the emperor's offer. He insisted on retaining his *cognomen* and was known as Titus Aelius Hadrianus Antoninus. Marcus became Marcus Aurelius Antoninus Augustus; today we call them Antoninus Pius (*pius* means "loyal" or "dutiful") and Marcus Aurelius.

The end was near. The emperor suffered from bad dreams; in one of them he asked his father, fifty years dead, for a sleeping draft. On another occasion he was overcome by a lion, a distorted memory perhaps of his last hunt with Antinous in the sands of Libya. He was no longer really in a fit condition to attend to affairs of state, but he insisted on trying to do so. In practice, Antoninus, officially endowed with proconsular *imperium* and *tribunicia potestas,* very soon found himself in charge of the government machine.

The emperor still placed confidence in "charms and magic rituals" and he received temporary relief from his dropsy, but his limbs soon filled up with fluid again. It would seem that Hadrian had contracted congestive (that is, fluid-retaining) heart disease, a condition that could have lasted for a couple of years or so. As has been seen, he may also have been suffering from chronic erysipelas.

It is impossible to assign a definite cause at this distance in time, but one clear possibility is reduced blood flow to the heart through the coronary blood vessels. If reports of Hadrian's heavy drinking with Trajan are correct and reflect a long-standing habit, this may have led to alcoholic cardiomyopathy, a weakening of the heart muscle or a change in its structure. Cardiac failure means that the heart's function as a pump to deliver oxygen-rich blood is inadequate to meet the body's needs. This in turn reduces the kidneys' normal ability to excrete salt and water. As a result the body retains more fluid which descends to the legs when the sufferer is standing or sitting. Hence the symptoms of dropsy.

Hadrian would have found temporary relief by lying down, but that risked fluid gathering in the lungs and shortness of breath. Sometimes he would have awoken at night, gasping for air. He may have had to learn how to sleep seated upright. Excess fluid also prompts increased urination, especially at night, and when it accumulates in the liver and intestines causes nausea, stomach pain, and a loss of appetite.

The emperor felt as if he were dying every day, and came to long for an immediate end. He asked for poison or a sword, but nobody would give them to him even if he promised money and immunity from prosecution. The curse of Servianus had come to pass.

Finally, Hadrian sent for Mastor, the captive tribesman from the Iazyges, who had acted for years as his hunting assistant. According to Dio Cassius,

> partly by threatening him and partly by making promises, he forced the man to promise to kill him. He drew a colored line about a spot beneath the nipple that had been shown him by Hermogenes, his physician, in order that he might be struck a fatal blow there and die without pain.

Antoninus was informed of what was happening and went to see Hadrian, taking the guards and city prefects with him. He begged the emperor to endure the course of his illness with equanimity. Now that Antoninus was his adopted son, he would be guilty of patricide if he allowed him to be killed. Hadrian lost his temper and ordered the whistle-blower to be put to death (Antoninus ensured that the sentence was not carried out).

He now drew up a will. Somehow he acquired a dagger, but the weapon was taken from him. He instructed his doctor to give him poison, and the doctor committed suicide to avoid having to administer it.

Two eccentric visitors called, both of them claiming to be blind. First, a woman said she had been told in a dream to coax Hadrian from suicide, for he was destined to make a full recovery. After meeting the emperor, she recovered her sight, or so he was assured. Then an old man turned up when Hadrian was suffering from a fever. He touched the patient, whereupon he saw again and the fever vanished. The emperor's biographer, Marius Maximus, believed that these were benevolent hoaxes. The court knew its Hadrian, and his penchant for magic.

Hadrian enjoyed periods of remission, or at least quiescence, for he managed to muster the energy to write an autobiography during these last months, almost certainly in the form of a letter to Antoninus. A fragment of a copy on papyrus of its opening lines has been found at Fayum in Egypt. It reads like an indirect apology for attempting to do away with himself (at some point about now he asked those close to him to keep a suicide watch). He wrote:

> I want you to know that I am being released from my life neither before my time, nor unreasonably, nor piteously, nor unexpectedly, nor with faculties impaired, even though I shall almost seem, as I have found, to do injury to you who are by my side whenever I am in need of attendance, consoling and encouraging me to rest.

His mind turned to his birth father, who, he calculated, "fell ill and passed away as a private citizen at the age of forty, so that I have lived half as long again as my father, and have reached nearly the same age as my mother."

He also wrote a poem, a short address to his soul as it quits its body and sets out for the unknown. It is a fine piece of work, allusive, adroitly opaque—and owing more to Hadrian's favorite, Ennius, than to fluent, smooth Virgil.

> *animula vagula blandula*
> *hospes comesque corporis*
> *quae nunc abibis? In loca*
> *pallidula rigida nudula*
> *nec ut soles dabis iocos*

> Little soul, you charming little wanderer,
> my body's guest and partner,
> where are you off to now? Somewhere
> without color, savage and bare;
> you'll crack no more of your jokes once you're there.

The failing emperor retreated from Rome to an imperial villa at the seaside resort of Baiae. He abandoned his medical regimen and ate and drank whatever he liked. This precipitated a final crisis and he lost consciousness after shouting out loud: "Many doctors killed a king."

On July 10, 138, the man who entered life as Publius Aelius Hadrianus left it as Imperator Caesar Divi Traiani filius Traianus Hadrianus Augustus. His next name was due to be Divus Hadrianus, Hadrian the God. But he very nearly failed to make the grade.

XXV

PEACE AND WAR

. . .

Although by any objective standard he had been a successful ruler, Hadrian never won over the Senate and the ruling class. He was widely believed to have been innately cruel, and to have hidden his true nature beneath an affable veneer. An opposing view came from someone who had no reason to be kind, being a cousin of one of the former consuls Hadrian had killed at the beginning of his reign. He wrote that the emperor "mixed justice with kindheartedness in accordance with the care he took when making decisions."

Dio Cassius gives a levelheaded summary:

> Hadrian was hated by the people, in spite of his generally excellent reign, on account of the murders committed by him at the beginning and end of his reign, since they had been unjustly and impiously brought about. Yet he was so far from being of a bloodthirsty disposition that even in the case of some who clashed with him he thought it sufficient to write to their native places the bare statement that they did not please him.

A generous epitaph was written near the end of the reign by the emperor's friend, the historian, administrator, and general Arrian. Quoting Terpander on the virtues of the Spartans, he writes:

> The following words, it seems to me, are better applied to the present government of which Hadrian has been the *princeps* for twenty years than to old Sparta:

> ἔνθ' ᾿αιχμά τε νέων θάλλει καί μῶσα λίγεια
> καί δίκα ᾿ευρυάγια καλῶν ᾿επιτάρροθος ᾿έργων.

*When the young men's spear prospers, so do the sweet-toned Muse
and holy Justice, the defender of fine deeds.*

The army (the "spear"), the arts (the "Muse"), and holy justice can indeed be seen as the three foci of Hadrian's life's work.

Antoninus conveyed Hadrian's remains to Rome and arranged his burial "in the gardens of Domitia." This park was the location of the late emperor's mausoleum. The building had not yet been completed, for it was dedicated the following year; perhaps a temporary interment took place nearby. We know that eventually Hadrian lay in the grandiose tomb he had built for himself and his successors, for Antoninus' memorial stone has been found there.

The Senate, remembering its embittered relationship with Hadrian, did not wish him to deify him, but Antoninus insisted (hence perhaps the *cognomen* Pius). The consecration ceremony was modeled on the obsequies of Augustus. An artificial body, made from wax and wearing the costume of a *triumphator,* a general at a triumph, represented Hadrian and lay in state in the Forum Romanum. Here it repeated symbolically the dying of the already deceased emperor; for some days doctors examined the "patient" and issued bulletins. Then, when death had eventually been acknowledged, Antoninus delivered a eulogy after which a long procession of dignitaries headed by the Senate made its way to the Campus Martius. Here the effigy was placed on a tall, richly decorated multistory pyre. The consuls set light to it and an eagle, caged on the top tier, was released, which signified Hadrian's spirit flying up through the flames to join the immortal gods.

What are we to make of Hadrian? The judgment of his contemporaries was much too harsh. Whatever the truth about the killings at the beginning and end of his reign, he governed humanely and equitably. He was immensely industrious and exercised good judgment. He loved the arts and was an enthusiastic and not ungraceful poet.

However, his personality puzzled people; he was gregarious and friendly in manner, but he dropped intimates easily and without apparent regret. In specialist fields such as architecture, he was that annoying person, the self-taught (if talented) amateur who insists on competing with the professional. A Christian poet, Tertullian, called him *omnium curiositatum explorator,* "a seeker-out of every kind of curiosity." A hostile witness notes and overstates his faults, but cannot help sounding a note of admiration: Hadrian was

> diverse, manifold, and multiform . . . He adroitly concealed a mind envious, melancholy, hedonistic, and excessive with respect to his own ostentation; he simulated restraint, affability, clemency, and conversely disguised the ardor for fame with which he burned. With respect to questioning and likewise to answering in earnest, in jest, or in invective, he was very skillful; he returned verse to verse, speech to speech, so you might actually believe that he had given advance thought to everything.

In his reflections many years later, in which he reviewed those to whom he owed gratitude, Marcus Aurelius surprisingly makes no affectionate mention of his adoptive grandfather. "Do not be upset," he wrote, addressing himself as a good Stoic. "In a little while you will be no one and nowhere, as is true now even of Hadrian and Augustus." His friend and mentor, Fronto, found it hard to warm to Hadrian, whom he compared unfavorably to his successor.

> I wished to appease and propitiate [him], as I might Mars or Jupiter, rather than loved him. Why? Because love requires some confidence and intimacy. Since, in my case, confidence was lacking, I dared not love someone whom I so greatly revered. Antoninus, by contrast, I love, I cherish . . . and feel that I am loved by him.

Hadrian cuts a lonely figure. His moated refuge in the heart of the villa-city at Tibur suggests an emotional self-sufficiency into which few if any were allowed to intrude, except perhaps Antinous. But if it is true that the emperor agreed to the boy's sacrificial death in the Nile, we can only conclude that here, too, self-sufficiency—and its subset, self-interest—trumped love.

It is a curious feature of Hadrian's protracted death that no close family members or friends are recorded as having been at the patient's bedside. They had died, or been killed or dropped. His secretary, Caninius Celer, "saw Hadrian to his grave, then went to his own grave." Two otherwise unknown men, Chabrias and Diotimus, kept vigil by his coffin; their Greek names suggest that they were members of the emperor's household, on a par with Trajan's Phaedimus. *Raison d'état* brings cruel consequences for even the most lovable ruler, but it seems entirely appropriate that Hadrian spent his last days in the care of slaves and freedmen, and of an heir who, until recently, had only been a political colleague.

If we examine Hadrian's political and military record, he scores very high. His emphasis on the training and disciplining of the army complemented his unpopular but wise policy of nonaggression to neighbors. He introduced no important structural reforms, but improved the efficiency and morale of the legions in an age when serious fighting was seldom required. Dio Cassius, himself an experienced public servant, observed: "Even today the methods he then introduced are the soldiers' law of campaigning."

In another passage earlier in his *Roman History,* Dio sets out his view of the ideal emperor. In a fictional debate, he has a speaker advise Augustus: "Because of your intelligence and because you have no desire to acquire more than you already possess, you should be strongly disposed toward peace, but in your preparations you should be thoroughly organized for war." As we have seen, until the very end of his reign, Augustus was an uncompromising and bellicose imperialist. Dio's prescription fits Hadrian much more closely, and he must surely have had his example in mind when penning these words.

It is difficult to judge the impact of Hadrian's pan-Hellenic strategy, but he wisely maintained and developed the Roman tradition of encouraging provincial elites to take part in the governance of the empire as partners. In his day more men than previously from "old" or mainland Greece joined the Roman Senate and even governed provinces in the Latin West. In succeeding centuries there was a great flourishing of Greek culture. That the Hellenic easterners increasingly bought into the empire and regarded it as theirs is reflected in their description of themselves during late antiquity as Ρωμαιοι (*Romaioi*), or Romans. Hadrian can claim some of the credit.

However, his attempt to forcibly Hellenize the Jews precipitated the worst crisis of his reign. The Bar Kokhba rebellion cost thousands of Roman lives, and the number of Jewish victims was many times greater. The elimination of Judaea as a national homeland meant that Jewry no longer posed a political threat—in fact it no longer had a political existence. It was a blunt reminder that, in the last resort, the Roman empire was sustained by violent force.

Roman law functioned as a kind of international law, in the sense that plaintiffs could appeal to it from local jurisdictions, and it helped bind people to the imperial system. Hadrian was very interested in the administration of law, and his judicial decisions reveal a disinterested and detailed concern for fair treatment. The codification and publication of the praetor's annual edict into "perpetual" or definitive form was an important step in the development of European law.

Like emperors before him, Hadrian was a great builder, and architecture fascinated him. The Pantheon in Rome and the villa complex at Tibur provided a treasure-house of ideas that inspired the architects of the Renaissance and later ages.

Despite his defects of character, Hadrian meant well. He had the great good fortune to preside over an empire at its zenith and of following two well-meaning predecessors. He faced no serious external military threats or economic challenges. His genius lay in the fact that he was a consolidator. Determined not to squander the advantages he inherited, he made the empire safe, purging it of military adventurism, binding its inhabitants to the imperial idea, and embedding the rule of law.

Later in the second century Aelius Aristides, a celebrated Greek orator, addressed a personified Rome in a speech that he delivered in the presence of the emperor Antoninus. It attributes to the spirit of Rome achievements to which Hadrian made a significant contribution.

> The sea is not a hindrance to becoming a citizen, nor is the mass of intervening land, nor is any distinction made here between Asia and Europe. Everything lies within reach of everyone. Nobody is a stranger

who is worthy of magistracy or trust, but a free commonwealth, in which the whole world shares, has been established under one excellent ruler and director, and everyone meets as if in a common assembly, each to receive his just reward.

In the original Greek, the word the speaker used for "commonwealth" was *democracy,* which in this period meant a government in which the civil rights of citizens were protected.

It is telling that it was a Greek who paid these lavish compliments; the average, conservative Roman did not feel quite so warm toward an idea of empire as an equal community of peoples. This was one of the reasons Hadrian never really won their hearts, but it was through tirelessly promoting this idea that he helped to ensure the prosperous and pacific continuance of Roman rule.

Antoninus generally maintained Hadrian's policies and preserved, in the elder Pliny's phrase, "the immeasurable majesty of the Roman peace." We hear of no dramas, and the reign exemplifies the truth of the maxim: Happy the country that has no history. There was occasional frontier trouble; in Britain an insurgency led to a new rampart north of Hadrian's Wall, only for it to be abandoned twenty years later. Thereafter the Romans manned Hadrian's Wall until the end of their occupation of Britannia.

Such disturbances attracted little attention. Aelius Aristides remarked: "Wars, if they once occurred, no longer seem real." The empire ran smoothly, he asserted, thanks to the emperor's watchfulness, but not to his presence. "He can stay quietly where he is and govern the whole world by letters."

Hadrian's succession plan worked. When Antoninus died after reigning for more than twenty years, Marcus Aurelius, the *verissimus,* and Lucius Commodus (later Verus, who soon succumbed to a stroke) assumed office without opposition. Foreign policy became more aggressive, again. After a successful war with Parthia the legions brought back a plague that ravaged the empire and caused a famine. Troops had been withdrawn from the Danube provinces for the campaign, allowing a mass breakthrough of tribes from the far side of the river.

The fighting continued on and off for most of the reign, and Marcus died in camp at Vindobona (today's Vienna), still struggling to protect the empire's northern frontier. Breaking the precedent set by his predecessors, he left the empire to his son by birth, the eighteen-year-old Commodus. He was a handsome blond whose hair shone in the sunlight as if dusted with gold powder. A lazy good-for-nothing, he devoted his time to having a good time. In 192 he was assassinated in a well-managed palace plot. In this way, a run of five good emperors came to a miserable end. Some very old men were able to recall the day when Hadrian announced his sequence of adoptions, and to regret the return of inheritance by bloodline.

Migrating tribes pressed harder and harder against the borders. From now on Rome was on the defensive. Its long endgame had begun.

ACKNOWLEDGMENTS

I am most grateful to Will Murphy, my editor, and Courtney Turco of Random House for their unstinting support, combining patience with optimism. As always, my agent, Christopher Sinclair Stevenson, has been a constant and wise adviser and guide.

Professor Robert Cape of Austin College, Texas, very kindly read a draft and offered valuable comments and corrections. Dr. Peter Chapman and the heart surgeon Philip Hayward offered most helpful medical analysis, despite the absence of a patient to inspect, but are not responsible for my speculative diagnoses of Hadrian's illnesses. I am enormously indebted to Alessandro La Porta, Responsabile d'Area per Pierreci Soc. Coop. a.r.l., who kindly showed me around Hadrian's villa at Tivoli and brought me up-to-date on the latest archaeological discoveries.

As ever, the London Library was an invaluable aid to a writer who lives in the country and required a constant supply of books.

I am grateful to Penguin Books for permitting me to quote from *Juvenal: The Sixteen Satires*, translated by Peter Green.

NOTES

ABBREVIATIONS

Acts	Acts of the Apostles
Ael Arist Rom	Aelius Aristides, *Ad Romam (To Rome)*
Alexander	P. J. Alexander, "Letters and Speeches of the Emperor Hadrian"
Amm Marc	Ammianus Marcellinus, *Res Gestae (History of Rome)*
Anth Pal	*Palatine Anthology*
App Civ War	Appian, *Civil Wars*
App Iberica	Appian, *Wars in Spain*
App Pun	Appian, *Wars with Carthage*
Apul Apol	Apuleius, *Apologia*
Apul Met	Apuleius, *Metamorphoses*
Arafat	K. W. Arafat, *Pausanias's Greece*
Arr Alan	Arrian, *Order of Battle with Array*
Arrian Alex	Arrian, *Campaigns of Alexander*
Arrian Parth	Arrian, *Parthica*
Arrian Peri	Arrian, *Periplus Ponti Euxini*
Arrian Tact	Arrian, *Ars Tactica*
Aul Gell	Aulus Gellius, *Noctes Atticae*
Aur Vic	Aurelius Victor, *De Caesaribus*
Bennett	Julian Bennett, *Trajan: Optimus Princeps*
Birley	Anthony Birley, *Hadrian, the Restless Emperor*
Birley Vind	Anthony Birley, *Garrison Life at Vindolanda*
BMC III	H. Mattingly, *Coins of the Roman Empire in the British Museum*, vol. 3
Bowman	Alan K. Bowman, *Life and Letters on the Roman Frontier*
Brunt	P. A. Brunt, *Roman Imperial Themes*
Burkert	Walter Burkert, *Greek Religion*

CAH	*Cambridge Ancient History,* vol. XI
Camp	J. M. Camp, *The Archaeology of Athens*
CCAG	*Catalogus Codicum Astrologorum Graecorum*
Char	Charisius, *Ars Grammatica*
Cic Att	Cicero, *Epistulae ad Atticum* (*Letters to Atticus*)
Cic Fam	Cicero, *Epistulae ad familiares* (*Letters to His Friends*)
Cic Leg	Cicero, *Leges* (*Laws*)
Cic Tusc	Cicero, *Tusculanae Quaestiones* (*Tusculan Disputations*)
CIL	*Corpus Inscriptionum Latinarum*
Clem	Clement of Alexandria, *Proteptious*
Col	Keith Hopkins and Mary Beard, *The Colosseum* (*Wonders of the World*)
Colum	Columella, *De re rustica* (*On Farming*)
Digest	*Digesta* (Justinian I)
Dio	Dio Cassius, *Roman History*
Dio Chrys	Dio Chrysostom, *Oratio* (*Discourse*) 21
Diod	*Diodorus Siculus Bibliotheke* (*Library*)
Dio Laer Epicurus	Diogenes Laertius, *Lives and Opinions of Eminent Philosophers: Epicurus*
Eck	Werner Eck, "The Bar Kokhba Revolt: The Roman Point of View"
Ennius	Ennius, *Annales* (*Annals*)
Ep de Caes	*Epitome de Caesaribus* (*Summary of the Caesars*)
Epict	Epictetus, *Discourses*
Epiph	Epiphanius, *Weights and Measures*
Eur Alc	Euripides, *Alcestis*
Euseb Ch Hist	Eusebius, *Church History*
Eutropius	Eutropius, *Historiae romanae breviarium*
FIRA	*Fontes Iuris Romani Antejustiniani*
Florus Ep	Florus, *Epitome*
Fronto Ad L Ver	Fronto, *Ad Lucium Verum* (*to Lucius Verus*)
Fronto Ad M Caes	Fronto, *Ad Marcum Caesarem* (*To Marcus Caesar*)
Fronto de bell Parth	Fronto, *De bello Parthico* (*On War with Parthia*)
Fronto de fer Als	Fronto, *De feriis Alsiensibus*
Fronto Princ Hist	Fronto, *Principia Historiae*
Galimberti	Alessandro Galimberti, *Adriano e l'ideologia del principato*
Gibbon	Edward Gibbon, *History of the Decline and Fall of the Roman Empire*
Goldsworthy	Adrian Goldsworthy, *In the Name of Rome*

Gray	William D. Gray, "New Light from Egypt on the Early Reign of Hadrian"
Greek Horo	*Hephaestio of Thebes*
Green	Peter Green, *Juvenal: The Sixteen Satires*
Gyn	Soranus, *Gynaecologia*
HA Ant	*Historia Augusta, Antoninus Pius*
HA Ael	*Historia Augustus, Aelius Caesar*
HA Hadr	*Historia Augusta, Hadrian*
HA Marc	*Historia Augusta, Marcus Aurelius*
HA Ver	*Historia Augusta, Aelius Verus*
Herodian	Herodian, *History of the Empire After Marcus*
Homer Il	Homer, *Iliad*
Hor Ep	Horace, *Epistulae* (*Letters*)
Hor Epo	Horace, *Epodes*
Hor Ser	Horace, *Sermones* (*Satires*)
IG	*Inscriptiones Graecae*
ILS	*Inscriptiones Latinae Selectae*
Jer Chron	Jerome, *Chronicle*
Jer Contra Ruf	Jerome, *Contra Rufinum* (*Against Rufinus*)
Jer de vir ill	Jerome, *De viris illustribus* (*Of Famous Men*)
Jer In Esaiam	Jerome, *In Esaiam* (*Commentary on Isaiah*)
Johnson	Paul Johnson, *A History of the Jews*
Jones	Brian W. Jones, *The Emperor Domitian*
Jos AJ	Josephus, *Jewish Antiquities*
Jos BJ	Josephus, *Jewish War*
JRS	*Journal of Roman Studies*
Julian Caes	Julian, *The Caesars*
Justin Apol App	Justin, *Apologia Appendix*
Justin First Apol	Justin, *First Apologia*
Juv	Juvenal, *Saturae* (*Satires*)
Lambert	Royston Lambert, *Beloved and God*
Levine	Lee I. Levine, *Jerusalem: Portrait of the City in the Second Temple Period*
Livy	Livy, *Ab Urbe Condita* (*History of Rome*)
Lucian Philospeud	Lucian, *Lover of Lies*
Lucr de Rerum Nat	Lucretius, *De rerum natura* (*On the Nature of Things*)
MacDonald	William L. MacDonald and John A. Pinto, *Hadrian's Villa and Its Legacy*
Macr	Macrobius, *Saturnalia*

Malalas	John Malalas, *Chronographia*
Marc Aur	Marcus Aurelius, *To Himself (Meditations)*
Mart	Martial, *Epigrammata (Epigrams)*
Mart Lib de Spect	Martial, *Liber de Spectaculis (Show Book)*
MLP	*Minor Latin Poets,* Loeb Classical Library
Mommsen	Theodor Mommsen, *A History of Rome Under the Emperors*
Naor	Mordecai Naor, *City of Hope*
Oliver	J. H. Oliver, *Greek Constitutions of Early Roman Emperors from Inscriptions and Papyri*
Opper	Thorsten Opper, *Hadrian—Empire and Conflict*
Paus	Pausanias, *Description of Greece*
Petr	Petronius, *Satyricon*
Phil	Saint Paul, *Letter to the Philippians*
Philo Apoll	Philostratus, *Life of Apollonius of Tyana*
Philo Her	Philostratus, *Heroicus*
Philo v. Soph	Philostratus, *Lives of the Sophists*
Pindar Dith	Pindar, *Dithyrambs*
Plato Symp	Plato, *Symposium*
Plaut Curc	Plautus, *Curculio*
Pliny Ep	Pliny the Younger, *Epistulae (Correspondence)*
Pliny NH	Pliny the Elder, *Naturalis Historia (Natural History)*
Pliny Pan	Pliny the Younger, *Panegyricus*
Plut Crass	Plutarch, *Life of Crassus*
Plut Mor	Plutarch, *Moralia (Essays)*
Plut Per	Plutarch, *Life of Pericles*
Plut Pomp	Plutarch, *Life of Pompey the Great*
Pol Physio	Polemon, *De Physiognomia*
POxy	*Oxyrhyncus Papyri*
Quint	Quintilian, *Institutio Oratoria*
RIC	H. Mattingly and E. A. Sydenham, *The Roman Imperial Coinage*
Rossi	Lino Rossi, *Trajan's Column and the Dacian Wars*
Script Phys Vet	*Scriptores Physiognomoniae Veteres*
Sen Contr	Seneca, *Controversiae*
Sen Ep	Seneca, *Epistulae (Correspondence)*
Shakespeare, A & C	Shakespeare, *Antony and Cleopatra*
Sherk	Robert K. Sherk, ed., *The Roman Empire: Augustus to Hadrian*

PREFACE

ix **"the fair prospect of universal peace"** Gibbon, p. 36.

x **"persisted in the design"** Ibid., p. 37.

xii **"repellent" and "venemous"** Mommsen, p. 340.

INTRODUCTION

Full information on Hadrian's villa at Tivoli can be found in the site guidebook and MacDonald.

xxviii **"And in order not to omit anything"** HA Hadr 26 5.

I. INVADERS FROM THE WEST

Main literary source—*Historia Augusta*

3 **born on the ninth day** HA Hadr 1 3.

4 **"exceedingly miserable place to live"** Strabo 3 1 2.

4 **"Turdetania . . . is marvelously blessed"** Ibid., 3 2 4.

7 **The Aelii were friendly with the Ulpii** For this paragraph and the next, see Syme Tac, p. 603.

7 **four hundred active senatorial families** CAH, p. 222.

8 **"should be not younger than twenty"** Gyn 2 19.

8 **Paulina appointed a woman called Germana** See CIL 14 3721 for an inscription about her.

9 **"Should I express wonder at gilded beams"** Stat Silv 1 3 35–37.

9 **"they grow up lying around in litters" and "broad daylight of a respectable school"** Quint 1 2 7–9.

11 **Now thirty-two** Eutropius 8 5 2 reports that Trajan died in his sixty-third year. It follows that he was born in A.D. 53. Other literary sources suggest different years of death, but most modern scholars follow Eutropius.

11 **Tall and well made** For Trajan's appearance, see statues and Pliny Pan 4 7.

11 **"setting foot on rocky crags"** Pliny Pan 81 1.

11 **liked having sex with young men** Although biographers such as Bennett write of Trajan's bisexuality, the emperor may have been exclusively homosexual, although most Romans appear not to have specialized.

II. A DANGEROUS WORLD

Main literary sources—*Historia Augusta;* Xenophon and Arrian on hunting

12 **the celebrated Quintus Terentius Scaurus** HA Ver 2 5 identifies Scaurus as "Hadrian's *grammaticus.*" It has been argued that this simply means a "*grammaticus* of the age of Hadrian," but the context implies that a personal teacher is meant.

12 *obiter* Char 13 271.

13 **"he preserved my chastity"** Hor Ser 1 6 82–84. Although Horace wrote in the first century B.C., there is no reason at all to believe that children's safety improved under the empire.

13 **"require that he take"** Juv 7 237–41.

14 *manum subducere ferulae* Op. cit. 1 15.

14 **"that genius"** Sen Contr 1 Praef 11.

15 **"An orator, son Marcus"** Sen Contr 1 Praef 9.

15 **"happiest days of my life"** Pliny Ep 2 18 1. This citation from Pliny and the one that follows date from the early second century, but there need be little doubt that they are equally relevant to educational attitudes in Hadrian's youth.

15 **the slightest hint** In HA Hadr after the sentence recording Hadrian's father's death, we read *"imbutusque impensius Graecis studiis"*—"and he steeped himself rather enthusiastically in . . . " The *que,* or "and," could imply a connection.

15 **his guardian's new wife, Plotina, encouraged him** A persuasive speculation in Galimberti, pp. 21–22.

16 **"When Greece was taken"** Hor Ep 2 1 156–57.

17 **"Like Indians under the British Raj"** Green, p. 316.

18 **"from this day, from this moment"** Sherk 168, p. 217.

19 **casting an emperor's horoscope was high treason** Ulpian, *De Officio Proconsulis* 7.

19 **"*moribus antiquis*"** Ennius 467.

20 **singling out for bravery** Pliny NH 8 11.

20 **celebrated his fifteenth birthday** Hadrian's coming of age is an assumption that convincingly explains his visit later in the year to the family estates in Spain, a natural step for their new owner to take.

21 **Hadrian had visited Baetica once before** It is argued in Birley 19 that "returned," *rediit,* HA Hadr 2 1, is probably a way of saying "went back to the old plantation" without meaning that Hadrian had been there before. Possibly so; but there is no reason not to take the word literally.

22 **a *collegium* in the province of Africa** See inscription in *L'année epigraphique,* Paris 1888ff., 1958.

22 **We can safely assume** The following section on hunting makes use of Xenophon's and Arrian's monographs, *Hunting with Dogs*.

23 **"Surely everyone is liable to make mistakes"** Pliny Ep 9 12 1.

23 **"these Graeculi"** Ibid., 10 40 2.

III. YOUNG HOPEFUL GENTLEMAN

Main literary source—Quintilian, *Institutio Oratoria*

25 **"The man who can really play his part"** Quint 1 p. 10.

26 **one likely candidate is Lucius Licinius Sura** A helpful speculation in Birley, p. 27.

26 **"The (person) who has the stars"** Greek Horo pp. 79 80.

27 **"your antiquated vocabulary"** Martial 7 47 2.

28 **"gave orders respectfully"** Sherk 173 A.

28 **Tombstones from the early empire** Sherk 173 B to Z.

29 **"has a lovely family"** Sen Ep 41 7.

32 **"all the flower of the colonies"** FIRA I 43 Col II lines 2–4.

32 **perhaps 17 percent of its six hundred members** Lambert, p. 26.

34 **"Robbers of the world"** Tac Agric 30 4–5.

IV. CRISIS OF EMPIRE

Chief literary sources—Suetonius on Nero, Vespasian, Titus, and Domitian; Josephus and the Talmud

35 **"There were people"** Suet Nero 57 1.

35 **"Even now everyone wishes [Nero] to be alive"** Dio Chrys 21 *On Beauty* 10.

36 **"The Greeks alone are worthy"** Ibid., 22 3.

36 **"Other leaders," he said** Sherk 71.

36 **the decree earned Nero reincarnation** Plut Mor *Delays of God's Vengeance* 567F.

36 **of an empire of about 60 million souls** For population estimates see CAH, pp. 813–14.

37 **Tacitus exemplifies the general opinion** The account that follows draws on Tac His 5 2–8.

38 **"hid the circumcision"** Jos AJ 12 5 1.

38 **"Cursed be the man"** Mishnah Sota 49B.

38 **"The great Jewish revolts"** Johnson, pp. 112, 133.

39 **a population perhaps of 100,000** Levine, p. 342.

39 **a snowcapped mountain peak** Jos BJ 5 6 223. The description of the city and Temple draws on Jos BJ 5 136–8 247.

40 **"In this stood nothing at all"** Jos BJ 6 282.

41 **A military incident** Jos BJ 3 31 289–306.

42 **"What an artist"** Suet Nero 49 1.

43 **between thirty thousand and forty thousand men** Goldsworthy, p. 337.

43 **a silver shekel** Naor, p. 55.

45 **"Following the directions and plans"** Sherk 83 (ILS 264).

45 **"Why was the First Temple destroyed?"** Yoma 9b.

V. A NEW DYNASTY

Chief literary sources—Suetonius, Dio Cassius, and Pliny the Younger

46 *pecunia non olet* See Dio 65 14 5.

48 **"This is what it means"** Epict 1 1 31–32.

48 **verbatim notes** These are *The Discourses of Epictetus,* written by Arrian.

49 **in the expected high Roman fashion** See Shakespeare, A & C 4 15 92.

49 *Paete, non dolet* Pliny Ep 3 166.

49 **"It is in your power"** Epict 1 2 19–21.

50 **"Dear me, I seem to be becoming a god!"** Suet Vesp 23 4.

50 **"An emperor ought to die on his feet."** For the two versions of the story, see Suet Vesp 24 and Dio 66 17 1–3.

50 **Vespasian had in fact been poisoned** Dio 66 17 1.

51 **"people did not know"** Dio 66 23 5.

51 **"the whole world was dying with me"** Pliny Ep 6 20 17.

51 **"At the beginning of his reign"** Suet Dom 3 1.

52 **"shaking the thunderbolt of purity"** Stat Silv 5 2 102.

53 **the senior Vestal, Cornelia** For Cornelia's trial and execution see Pliny Ep 4 11 *passim.*

53 **unfazed by the contrast** There is no good reason to resist the unanimity of the sources on this topic.

53 **"he was not only physically lazy"** Dio 67 6 3.

53 **"bed-wrestling"** Ep de Caes 11 7.

54 **"shrewd in his understanding of warfare"** Dio 67 6 1.

55 **"dreaming of battle"** Juv 4 111–12.

55 **subsidy of about 8 million sesterces** See Jones, p. 74.

55 **the emperor agreed to provide military engineers** Dio 67 4.

55 **exhibits displayed as campaign spoils** Dio 67 7 2.

57 **"Rulers find themselves"** Suet Dom 21.

57 **Trajan received the culminating reward** In the ensuing brief discussion about Trajan's career, I follow Bennett, pp. 43–45.

VI. ON THE TOWN

Chief literary sources—Suetonius, Dio Cassius, Pliny, and Epictetus

60 **"young patrician who had had his tunic torn off"** Pliny Ep 4 16.

60 **behest of one of the consuls for 94** A plausible speculation in Birley, p. 30, regarding the consul C. Antius A. Julius Quadratus.

61 **"We want bears!"** Hor Ep 2 1 182–213.

62 **The emperor Caligula** Suet Cal 36, 55, 57.

62 **Nero acted as one himself** Suet Nero 16, 26.

62 **an eccentric old noblewoman** Pliny Ep 7 24.

62 **Apuleius, in his picaresque novel** Apul Met 10 29–35, for the following paragraphs.

63 **a similar spectacle actually occurred** Mart Lib de Spect 6 (5).

63 **Appuleius Diocles** For Diocles' detailed and boastful funerary inscription, see Sherk 167 (CIL 6 1000 48; ILS 5287).

64 **Eutyches** Sherk 168 (CIL II 4314; ILS 5299).

64 **"standing down there below them"** Dio 62 17 4.

65 **Cicero found the whole business vulgar** Cic Fam 7 1 3.

66 **An ingenious recent calculation** Col pp. 91–94.

66 **one dud arm** Juv 6 106–10.

67 **one beast, beaten for failing to learn a trick** Pliny NH 8 6.

67 **death of a pregnant wild sow** Mart Lib de Spect 14.

67 **"Time was when their plebiscite"** Juv 10 78–81.

68 **the complete gallery of horrors** According to the HA Hadr 19 8, Hadrian was a frequent spectator at gladiatorial shows when emperor. He presumably acquired the taste when young.

69 **Massa . . . served as governor of Baetica** For Massa's trial and its consequences, Pliny Ep 7 33.

70 **"A soldier marched in"** Plut Mor *Curiosity* 522d.

71 **"I stood among the flames"** Pliny Ep 3 11 3.

71 **"In Rome reckless persons"** Epict 4 13 5.

VII. FALL OF THE FLAVIANS

Chief literary sources—*Historia Augusta,* Dio Cassius, and Pliny

73 **Pannonia was famous for a plant** Pliny NH 21 20 and 83: probably *Valeriana celtica*.

74 **"A distant look at a camp"** Pliny Pan 15 2.

75 **an estimated salary of 18,000 sesterces** For army pay, see Speidel *passim* and Table 7.

77 **"an ostentatious lover of the common people"** HA Hadr 17 8.

77 **an uncanny memory for names** Pliny Pan 15 5.

77 **identified as Quintus Marcius Turbo** Birley, p. 32, but see Syme, "The Wrong Marcius Turbo," p. 91, for an opposing view.

79 **"the charge brought against them"** Dio 67 14 1–2.

79 **"man of the most contemptible laziness"** Suet Dom 15 1.

79 **"on the slightest of suspicions"** Ibid., 15 1.

80 **He was a handsome man** For Nerva's appearance see Julian Caes 311A, his coins. His vomiting is recorded in Dio 68 1 3, and drinking in Aur Vic 13 10.

81 **"Whoever is familiar with the poet Nero's verses"** Mart 8 70 7–8.

81 **reported to have seduced Domitian** Suet Dom 1 1.

81 **"Your great enemy, Clemens"** Phil Apoll 8 25 1. The usually unreliable Philostratus seems to be reporting a credible account.

VIII. THE EMPEROR'S SON

Chief literary sources—Dio Cassius, Pliny, and *Historia Augusta*

83 **personification of Liberty** BMC III p. 3 16.

84 **provision of grain for the capital city** Ibid., p. 21 115.

84 **"Harmony of the armies"** Ibid., p. 4, 25ff.

84 **"Assuredly we have been given a signal proof"** Tac Agric 2 3, 3 1.

85 **Despite the embargo** For this episode and quotations, Pliny Ep 9 13.

85 **"bloodstained servility"** Pliny Ep 9 13 16.

85 **"whose loss of sight"** Ibid., 4 22 5.

85 **"I wonder what would have happened"** Ibid., 4 22 4–5.

85 **"I have done nothing"** Dio 68 3 1.

86 **The Guard took over the palace** For this episode, see Dio 68 3 3–4, Ep de Caes 12 7–8.

86 **A laureled dispatch** If I am wrong, and Trajan was governing one of the Germanys, then the victory must have been someone else's. However, this would render Pliny's reference Pan 7–8 2 rather odd; he says that the Pannonian victory marked "the rise of a ruler [i.e., Trajan] who would never be defeated." That makes little sense if it was not for Trajan's success on the battlefield.

86 **"May good fortune attend"** Dio 68 3 4.

87 **"May the Danaans"** Homer Il 1 42.

87 **he moved Trajan from his posting in Pannonia** For Trajan's postings and movements I follow Bennett, pp. 44–50.

87 **"All disturbances died at once"** Pliny Pan 8 5.

87 **"You had to be pressed"** Ibid., 5 6.

88 **"foretold" the principate of Trajan** Tac Agric 44 5.

88 **"wanton tyranny of power"** Pliny Pan 7 6.

89 **he had famously congratulated** Ep de Caes 12 3.

90 **an unprecedented third posting** Only one case is attested: see Birley, p. 37.

90 **and was impressed** An inference drawn from Hadrian's later development of the *limes* principle.

91 **revealed "what he was spending"** HA Hadr 2 6.

91 **The news angered Trajan, as was intended** The Latin has "*odium in eum movit*" ("he stirred anger against him"). The "*movit*" implies intention.

91 **Aquae Mattiacae** Pliny NH 31 17.

91 **Hadrian seized the hour** HA Hadr 2 6, for the race to Colonia Agrippinensis.

IX. "OPTIMUS PRINCEPS"

Chief literary sources—Pliny and Dio Cassius

93 **"Who is that in the distance"** Virg Aen 6 808–12.

94 **Plotina was probably in her mid-thirties** I follow Bennett, p. 24, in supposing that Trajan married Plotina about A.D. 78, and that, like most Roman girls, she was between thirteen and fifteen at the time of the union.

95 **"he thought that an old man"** Dio 68 5 1.

95 **"he would not kill or disenfranchise"** Dio 68 5 2.

95 **"If the public interest demands it"** Pliny Pan 67 8.

96 **"ridicule that had greeted"** Tac Agric 39 1.

96 **"One could see swords everywhere"** Dio Chrys 12 16–20.

97 **"I enter here such a woman"** Dio 68 5 5.

97 **"Nothing was so popular"** Pliny Pan 34 3–4.

98 **"Well, let them go!"** Ibid., 34 5.

99 **"The weather was . . . particularly bad"** Pliny Ep 3 18 4.

99 **"critical sense of my audience"** Ibid., 18 8.

99 **"Times are different"** Pliny Pan 2 3–4.

100 **"provoked a laugh"** HA Hadr 3 1.

100 **he picked up un-Italian speech patterns** Birley, p. 46.

101 **Some said she was in love with him** Dio 69 1 2.

101 **more interested sexually in men than women** This is an assumption, but everything in the records of Hadrian's life points to this conclusion. I discuss his sexuality on pp. 239–44.

102 **According to Aulus Gellius** Aul Gell 10 10.

103 **she was a wealthy woman** Opper, p. 204.

103 **"it was a bit crowded"** BBC *Panorama* interview with Diana, Princess of Wales, November 21, 1995.

X. BEYOND THE DANUBE

Chief literary sources—Dio Cassius, Pliny, and *Historia Augusta*. Trajan's Column is an important "document."

106 **"O Jupiter, Greatest and Best"** Smallwood II 1 24–37.

107 **"Imperator Caesar, son of the deified Nerva"** *L'Année Épigraphique* 1973, 473.

107 **"because of the danger of cataracts"** JRS 63 (1973) pp. 80–81.

108 **a notorious rogue** Dio 68 32 4–5.

110 **"how high a hill and place have been excavated"** Smallwood 378.

110 **The column picks up the tale** The interpretation of the reliefs on Trajan's Column in the following paragraphs is indebted to Rossi, pp. 130–212.

112 **"I have had no letter from you"** Pliny Ep 3 17 1–3. It is highly probable, though not certain, that this letter was sent to Servianus during the first Dacian war.

112 **Servianus and Sura returned to Rome** In the ordinary course of things, they should have served or at least opened their consulships in Rome. They may have stayed with Trajan, but I follow Bennett, p. 93.

112 **An inscription . . . sets out his early career** Smallwood 109. The reference to *donis militaribus* is associated with Hadrian's quaestorship and appointment as *comes* during the Dacian expedition.

112 **military decorations** See Rossi, pp. 79–80.

112 **"into a position of fairly close intimacy"** HA Hadr 3 2–3; and the next quotation.

112 **"opulent rewards"** Ibid., 3 3.

112 **appointment as *tribunus plebis*** The *Historia Augusta* confuses the dates, placing the tribuneship in A.D. 105, later than the praetorship, which it must have preceded. See discussion in Birley, p. 47.

113 **"he was given an omen"** HA Hadr 3 5.

113 **There is some misunderstanding** Birley, p. 48.

114 **"seized some fortified mountains"** Dio 68 9 3.

115 **The celebratory coins he issued** BMC III 191, 236, and 242.

115 **"agreed to surrender his weapons"** Dio 68 9 5–6.

115 **"excessively keen on poetry"** HA Hadr 14 8.

115 **would write verse as a relaxation** Pliny Ep 7 9 9.

116 **"rage powers my poetry"** Juv 1 79.

116 **"the poverty of our native tongue"** Lucr de Rerum Nat 1 139.

116 **"When you speak, the honey"** Pliny Ep 4 3 3. See also Homer *Iliad* 1 249.

116 *lascivus versu* Apul Apol 11.

117 **"glory of the empire"** Pliny Ep 10 14.

118 **seems to have been made urban praetor** The sources are not explicit, but this must be the assumption, for only the urban praetor held games. Confusion in the *Historia Augusta* has left the date of the praetorship uncertain. I agree with Birley, p. 47.

120 **arrested "on suspicion"** Dio 68 11 3.

120 **about this time that a telling exchange took place** I follow the plausible speculation in Birley, p. 50ff.

120 **"To the strongest"** Arrian Alex 7 26.

120 **it distinctly appealed to Trajan** In the event (as the reader will discover), Trajan did seek to follow Alexander's precedent, except perhaps in his very last hours.

121 **"I commend the provinces"** HA Hadr 4 8. By its location in the text, this story (if true) took place near the end of Trajan's life. The Dacian wars seem a more likely date, seeing that Trajan would be naming a nearby general; Priscus could take over in the event of his being killed or incapacitated.

122 **offered to negotiate without preconditions** For Longinus' story see Dio 68 12 1–5.

122 **the freedman's safety** Ibid., 68 12 5.

123 **"with the help of some captives"** Ibid., 68 14 4–5.

123 **about 500,000 pounds of gold** Sherk 118 (Joannes Lydus De Mag 2 28). Lydus' numbers are fantastic because of a transmission fault in the text, but this can be easily corrected to produce a rational result.

123 **gray marble inscription** Sherk 117. For a photograph see Rossi, p. 228.

124 **"his many remarkable deeds"** HA Hadr 3 6.

XI. THE WAITING GAME

Chief literary sources—*Historia Augusta,* Dio Cassius, and Pliny. Also the *alimenta* tablets.

125 **"held back the Sarmatians"** HA Hadr 3 9.

126 **"restrained the procurators"** Ibid., 3 9.

126 **"One was said to ask a wealthy man"** Ep de Caes 42 21.

127 **"maintained military discipline"** HA Hadr 3 9.

127 **in recognition of his successful record** HA Hadr 3 10.

128 **"So great was the friendship"** Dio 68 15 4–6.

128 **One of these concerned a spring** Pliny Ep 4 30.

129 **"He was no longer despised"** HA Hadr 3 10.

129 **"zeal that he had secured *imperium*"** Epit de Caes 13 6.

130 **with its thirty legions** This was the legionary strength after Trajan raised two additional legions, probably during the Dacian wars.

131 **He treated them as personal friends** Eutropius 8 4.

131 **"He joined others in animal hunts"** Dio 68 7 3; and the next quotation, "took more pleasure . . ."

132 **"what the emperor decides"** Digest 1 4 1Pr.

132 **"*Appello Caesarem*"** Acts 25 11.

132 **defendants condemned in absentia** Digest 48 19 5.

132 **a remote bridge in Numidia** Smallwood 98.

132 **he was nicknamed "the Wallflower"** Amm Marc 27 3 7.

133 **Even the decisions of a "bad" emperor** For example, see Pliny Ep 10 66.

133 **the celebrated *tabula alimentaria*** Now in the National Archaeological Museum of Parma.

133 **The tablets give detailed information** CIL 1455 and 11.1147.

133 **identify needy children** CAH, vol. XI, p. 115, argues against poverty as a criterion. While Roman citizenship in the provinces was selective and indicative of membership in an affluent local elite, in Italy it was universal; so many citizens there must have been poor. What would the point have been of an *alimenta* system that did not target their offspring? *Epitome de Caesaribus* 12 4 claims the chosen children were those in greatest need.

134 **cost the state annually 311 million sesterces** Bennett, p. 83.

134 **"As a result, most of [them] have lost interest"** Pliny Ep 9 37.

134 **one with the proud slogan *Italia restituta*** RIC II 278 no. 470.

134 **writing the emperor's speeches** HA Hadr 3 11.

135 **"My own view is that we should compromise"** Pliny Ep 10 115.

135 **"I think then that the safest course"** Ibid., 10 113.

136 **So he wrote to Rome for guidance** Ibid., 10 96.

136 **It was impossible, he wrote** Ibid., 10 97.

XII. CALL OF THE EAST

Chief literary sources—Dio Cassius, *Historia Augusta*, and Epictetus. Also Camp for background on Roman Athens.

138 **"to the pure and genuine Greece"** Pliny Ep 8 24 2.

139 **"O glittering, violet-crowned"** Pindar Dith 76 (46).

139 **In 112 Hadrian made his way to Athens** The dating is supported by Hadrian's year as archon, known to be 112. Because the Athenian official year ran from summer to summer, this could mean either 111–112 or 112–113. That Panathenaic Games were held in 112 makes it very likely that Hadrian chose 112–113 for his stay in Athens.

139 **became a friend and admirer** HA Hadr 16 10.

140 **a number of remarks in his lectures** I am indebted to Birley, pp. 60–61, for this happy speculation.

140 **"If the emperor adopts you"** Epict 1 3 2.

140 **"Shall kinship with the emperor"** Ibid., 1 9 7.

140 **"Some men . . . have excessively sharp tongues"** Ibid., 1 25 15–16.

141 **"Maximus: I sit as a judge over Greeks"** Ibid., 3 7 30–33.

143 **They then awarded him their highest honor** The *Constitution of Athens* 55 makes clear that archons entered office immediately after election. I assume that the antiquarian Athens of the first century A.D. maintained the old tradition.

145 **"He devoured the pursuits and customs"** Ep de Caes 14 2.

145 **"Euphranor"** The Latin has "Euphranoras," but Euphranor must be meant.

145 **He was tall and . . . elegant in appearance** For Hadrian's appearance see HA Hadr 26 1–2. I have also used the evidence of statues.

145 **"a pleasant man to meet"** Dio 69 2 6².

145 **"languishing, bright, piercing"** Script Phys Vet 2 51f (Adamantius).

145 **Augustus prided himself** Suet Aug 79 2.

146 **"bristly farmer with a kiss like a billy-goat's"** Martial 12 59 4–5.

146 **Cicero called them** *barbatuli* Cic Att 1 16 11.

146 **cover some natural blemishes** HA Hadr 26 1.

146 **"Can anything be more useless than hairs"** Epict 1 16 9.

146 **"So we ought to preserve the signs"** Ibid., 1 16 14.

146 **very plausible that he did so now** See Birley, p. 61, for this notion.

147 **"Friend of the Greeks"** Smallwood 44a.

147 **Plutarch recalls how Roman soldiers** Plut Crass 24 2.

147 **Trajan, while mindful of the dignity** See Arrian Parth frag. 33.

148 **"was a desire to win glory"** Dio 68 17 1.

148 **Coins were issued** BMC III p. 108 531; p. 106 525; p. 101 500; p. 112 569ff.

148 *legatus* **to the emperor** HA Hadr 4 1.

148 **"assigned to Syria for the Parthian war"** Dio 69 1.

149 **"large force of soldiers and senators"** Malalas 11 3–4.

150 **"satisfactory neither to the Romans"** Dio 68 17 2–3.

150 **"Friendship is decided by actions"** Ibid.

150 **Hadrian waited in Antioch** Hadrian's movements and whereabouts during this period are uncertain. Malalas (11 3–4) says that he accompanied the emperor on his journey east, presumably after Athens. But Dio (69 1) and HA (Hadr 4 1) seem to indicate a preparatory role; it follows that he preceded Trajan to Syria.

150 **the legions he had assembled** Little detail has come down to us of Hadrian's responsibilities, but it can be inferred that preparing an army for the Parthian campaign was one of them.

150 **the superstitious Hadrian** Amm Marc 22 12 8. The reference is undated, and could have taken place during Hadrian's brief governorship of Syria in 117.

151 **The imperial pair presented** Arrian Parth frag. 36.

151 **"To Zeus Kasios has Trajan"** Anth Pal 6 332.

XIII. MISSION ACCOMPLISHED

Chief literary sources—Dio Cassius, *Historia Augusta,* and Arrian's *Parthica*

152 **"At this same time [Hadrian] enjoyed"** HA Hadr 4 2.

153 **cocommander of the Guard** Attianus' partner was Servius Sulpicius Similis. He stayed in Rome while Attianus accompanied Trajan on his *profectio.*

153 **owner of twin boys** Martial 9 103.

153 **"He displayed neither effeminacy"** Dio 69 18 1.

153 **"always his enemies"** HA Hadr 4 3.

153 **distinction of public statues** Dio 68 16 2.

154 **arrived toward the end of May** Bennett, p. 192.

154 **Abgarus, king of Osrhoene** Dio 68 21 1.

154 **"Afraid of Trajan and the Parthians alike"** Ibid., 68 18 1.

155 **Parthamasiris turned up late** Arrian Parth frags. 38–40.

155 **laid his diadem** Dio 68 19 2–20 3.

155 **coin issues that depict the *rex Parthus*** BMC III 103, 106.

156 **Armenia was soon reduced** The timing and order of events in the Armenian and Parthian campaigns are hard to determine from our sketchy

sources. Dio seems to conflate the fighting in 114 and 115, and I follow Bennett in placing the Mesopotamian campaign in 115; the earthquake at Antioch in late 115 or early 116; and the capture of Ctesiphon in 116. Certainty cannot be had.

156 **"became Trajan's friend"** Dio 68 21 3.

156 **"Sometimes he even made his scouts"** Ibid., 68 23 1–2.

157 **"laureled letter"** See *fasti Ostienses*, Smallwood 23.

157 **Early one morning in January** Malalas 11 275 3–8. Malalas can be unreliable. Birley, p. 71, believes that because the *ordinarius* consul Pedo had given way to a suffect long before December, the earthquake must have taken place in January 115. But there is no need to disturb Malalas' precision; he very probably called Pedo consul because as *ordinarius* he gave his name to the year.

157 **"able neither to live any longer"** Dio 68 24 6.

157 **the emperor "hurried" back** Ibid., 68 26 1.

158 **civil strife had removed Parthia's capacity** Ibid., 68 26 4².

158 **a military trophy . . . with two captives** For example, BMC III 606.

158 **raising the ferry charges** Fronto Princ Hist 16.

158 **a third new province, Assyria** The location of the Roman *provincia* Assyria is disputed. It may be that historic Assyria was mislabeled Mesopotamia, the year before the capture of Ctesiphon in the south, and that Mesopotamia was called Assyria later, when the name Mesopotamia had already been used for the northern reaches of the Euphrates and Tigris. Strabo seems to have thought that Assyria was located in the lands we take to be Mesopotamia. Other scholars now argue that the new province lay along the eastern bank of the Tigris.

158 **down the Tigris** Arrian Parth frag. 67.

158 **"four of them carried the royal flags"** Ibid.

158 **"I would certainly have crossed over"** Dio 68 29 1.

159 **"Because of the large number of peoples"** Ibid., 68 29 2.

159 **"would eat the flesh"** Ibid., 68 32 1–2.

160 **"The one hope"** Sherk 129 E.

160 **"Not only because of my long absence"** Ibid., F.

160 **"clean them out"** Euseb Ch Hist 4 2 5.

161 **"in grandiloquent language"** Dio 68 30 3.

161 **emperor crowning Parthemaspates** BMC III p. 223 no. 1045.

162 **"So great and so boundless"** Malalas 11 274 11–13.

XIV. THE AFFAIR OF THE FOUR EX-CONSULS

Chief literary sources—Dio Cassius and *Historia Augusta*

163 **"sharing his daily life"** Dio 69 1 1. Although the phrase is undated, it is placed in a passage referring to this time.

163 **related to one of those onetime royal families** Sherk 128.

164 **Well known for his promiscuity** Aur Vic 14 9, 10.

164 **"Widespread rumor asserted"** HA Hadr 4 5.

164 **"The blood, which descends"** Dio 68 33 2.

164 **In modern terms** I owe this analysis to Bennett, p. 201.

164 **sure . . . he had been poisoned.** Dio 68 33 2.

165 **Apparently Trajan at dinner** Ibid., 69 17 3. One epitome mistakenly attributes the incident to Hadrian.

165 **"My father, Apronianus"** Ibid., 69 1 3.

166 **A gold piece showed Trajan** BMC III, p. 124. Galimberti, p. 19, sees this coin as evidence that the story of a deathbed and/or fake adoption is false, and that in fact Trajan adopted Hadrian earlier in the year 117, before he was approaching death. But while the literary sources may have been hostile to Hadrian they would hardly have made up a story that many eyewitnesses would have known to be false. Also, Dio's citation of his father's account has the ring of truth. However, the coin is awkward and calls for a convincing explanation, which I seek to provide.

166 **the *cognomina* "Augustus" and "Caesar"** Aur Vic 13 21.

166 **He climbed Mount Casius** Dio 69 2 1; and HA Hadr 14 3. Dio refers to a dream, but HA more convincingly writes of an actual event. This is one incident in different versions, not two.

166 **"To [the memory of] Marcus Ulpius Phaedimus"** Smallwood 176.

168 **Hadrian drafted a polite, carefully worded letter** HA Hadr 6 1–2.

168 **Trajan handing a globe to Hadrian** BMC III, p. 236 1.

168 **image of the phoenix** Ibid., p. 245, 48 and 49.

168 **the "Golden Age"** Ibid., p. 278 312.

168 **The dowager empress** Ibid., p. 246.

169 **a coin with two obverses** Ibid., p. 124.

169 **"advised him by letter"** HA Hadr 5 5.

170 **"he swore that he would do nothing"** Dio 69 2 4.

170 **boarded ship** An assumption on my part. A cortege could have made its way to Antioch by land, but it would have been a journey through uncomfortable terrain and taken a week or more.

171 **"Noting from your letter"** Oliver, pp. 154–56.

171 **blocked up with a huge mass of stone** Amm Marc 22 12 8.

171 **"The nations that Trajan had conquered"** HA Hadr 5 2.

172 **"The Romans have aimed to preserve their empire"** App Civ War pref. 7.

173 **"all catalogued by Augustus"** Tac Ann 1 11.

173 **he must have known of the policy** HA Hadr 5 1.

173 **"Because it is impossible to keep them under our care"** Ibid., 5 3. This translation paraphrases the compressed Latin.

174 **Rome was to abjure military expansion** Some contemporary scholars wonder whether Hadrian really did abandon the principle of *imperium sine fine*. Hadrian's actions and those of his successor, together with what we know or can infer about the practicalities of administering a large empire, persuade me that Hadrian did indeed introduce a strategic change. For less firm opinions, see Opper, chapter 2, and the brilliant chapter 8 in CAH.

174 **"From the time of Caesar Augustus"** Florus Ep 1 8.

175 **in his post on or before August 25** POxy 3781.

175 **Hadrian himself probably paid a quick visit** I follow Gray, pp. 25–28.

175 **the *tributum soli*** For more information see Brunt, p. 335.

175 **known for his shrewdness and sharpness of wit** Marc Aur 8 25.

175 **Hadrian presided over the trial** This account derives from fragmentary papyri, the so-called Acts of Paulus and Antoninus; these nationalistic texts are semifictional, but it is possible to interpret the bedrock of actuality on which they rest. The events described seem most likely to have taken place now and in Egypt, although it is possible that they occurred later and elsewhere. Delay in dealing with the aftermath of the Jewish revolt was not in Rome's interest.

176 **"he had fallen under suspicion"** HA Hadr 5 8.

176 **"And after him shall rule"** Or Syb 5 65–69. The quotation comes from the Sibylline Oracles, a collection of Greek hexameters, much amended and added to over the centuries, probably composed between the second century B.C. and the sixth century A.D. The original Sibylline Oracles were in the possession of the Roman Republic and were destroyed by fire in 83 B.C. These surviving texts reflect Jewish and Christian hostility to the Roman empire.

177 **appoint the reliable Gaius Avidius Nigrinus** This is plausible speculation; we know that Nigrinus was governor of Dacia from an inscription found in Sarmizegetusa (Smallwood 192), but not exactly when. See Birley, p. 86, for a discussion.

178 **the emperor's favorite horse, Borysthenes** A speculation by Birley, p. 86. There are, of course, other possible donors among Rome's client kingdoms that lined the Black Sea.

178 **"energetic enough in mobilizing his friends"** Fronto Princ Hist 10. Also the following quotation "with amusing games."

178 **the supposed talents of a later emperor** Lucius Verus, co-emperor with Marcus Aurelius. See Galimberti, p. 99.

179 **"a well-phrased statement"** Pliny Ep 5 13 6.

180 **"in reality because they had great influence"** Dio 69 2 5.

180 **while he was conducting a sacrifice** HA Hadr 7 1.

180 **the occasion was a hunt** Dio 69 2 5.

181 **Trajan had accessed the public courier or postal service** Aur Vic 13 5–6.

182 **a German-born centurion, Marcus Calventius Viator** Speidel pp. 47–48. ("German-born" because the Dacian altar was dedicated to Celtic deities; bodyguards usually consisted of Germanic recruits.)

182 **His name appears on two altars** Smallwood 192 and 332.

182 **"This slavish passivity"** Tac Ann 16 16.

XV. THE ROAD TO ROME

Chief literary sources—Dio Cassius, *Historia Augusta,* and Juvenal on Rome

184 **"They are made exclusively for war"** Tac Germ 29 2.

184 **"I was once the most famous of men"** Smallwood 336 1–5 (my translation).

184 **"No Roman or barbarian"** Ibid., 7, 11.

185 **a certain Mastor** Dio 69 22 2.

187 **declared on oath** Ibid., 69 2 6.

187 **he would never put a senator to death** HA Hadr 7 4.

187 **it showed Clemency** BMC III p. 271 no. 252.

187 **Hadrian wanted to do away with his former guardian** HA Hadr 9 3.

188 **"burned the records of old debts"** Suet Aug 32 2.

188 **"who remitted 900 million sesterces"** Smallwood 64a.

188 **A carved relief shows the scene** Chatsworth House, Derbyshire, inv. no. A 59.

189 **a *lictor* setting fire to a pile of bonds** Smallwood 64b.

189 **maintaining the government courier service** HA Hadr 7 5.

189 **"crown gold"** Ibid., 6 5.

189 **supplementary distribution** BMC III p. 402 nos. 1125, 1126, and 1127.

190 **"bread and circuses"** Juv 10 78–81.

190 **"the waxed tablets"** Smallwood II 6, February 26 p. 20.

190 **permission to hang an ornamental shield** The date of this request is unknown. I refer to it here for convenience.

191 **a high-value silver coin, a tetradrachm** BMC III p. 395 no. 1094.

191 **"That he was surnamed Thurinus"** Suet Aug 7 1.

191 **"On the day of a meeting of the Senate"** Ibid., 53 3.

192 **"he frequently attended the official functions"** HA Hadr 9 7–8.

192 **a dangerous faux pas** Dio 69 6 1–2.

193 **He had not forgotten those lines from Virgil** See page 93 above.

194 **"In a word, he induced a fierce people"** Florus Ep 1 2.

194 **"in the fashion of the Greeks or Numa"** Aur Vic 14 2–3; "fine arts" is my paraphrase of *ingenuarum artium*.

194 **the emperor's interest in supporting culture** Green, p. 164.

194 **denarius struck at Rome shows a bust of Matidia** BMC III p. 281 no. 332.

194 **"most immense delights"** HA Hadr 19 5.

194 **The Arvals recorded their generous** Smallwood II 7 4–9 (p. 23).

195 **We have his own words** Ibid., 114 4 (p. 56).

196 **"All hopes for the arts"** Juv 7 1–4, 17, 20–21.

197 **"a charming coastal retreat"** Juv 3 4.

197 **"at Tibur perched on its hillside"** Ibid., 3 191.

197 **"But here we inhabit a city"** Ibid., 192–97.

197 **"Insomnia causes most deaths here"** Ibid., 232, 236–38.

197 **"however flown with wine"** Ibid., 282–88.

197 **"as a special favor"** Ibid., 301.

198 **"the whores pimped out"** Ibid., 64–65.

198 **"When every building"** Ibid., 302–5.

198 **commissioning masterworks of architecture** This section is indebted to Opper, pp. 110–25.

200 **"the most blest of plains"** Strabo 5 4 3.

200 **the celebrated occasion when his predecessor** Tac Ann 4 57 and 58.

200 **His aim . . . was to "aid all the towns"** HA Hadr 9 6.

201 **Inscriptions have been discovered at various towns** CIL X 4574, 6652, and ILS 843.

201 **"a restful vacation"** Strabo 5 4 7.

201 *demarch* HA Hadr 19 1.

201 **According to Petronius . . . she lived in a cave** Petr 48.

XVI. THE TRAVELER

Chief literary sources—Dio Cassius and *Historia Augusta*

204 **dispensed "with imperial trappings"** Dio 69 10 1.

204 **"went to the relief of all the communities"** HA Hadr 10 1.

204 *restitutor,* **or "restorer," of the province** BMC III p. 350f, 521f.

204 **the generals of the Republic** HA Hadr 10 2 refers to Hadrian's debt to Scipio Aemilianus and Metellus. The information must have come from Hadrian's lost autobiography via Marius Maximus. Hadrian would have first heard about these generals in his youth.

204 **"A glorious moment"** App Pun 132.

205 **"There will come a day"** Homer *Iliad* 6 448–449.

205 **"[The soldiers'] food"** App Iberica 85.

206 **"Stranger, you will do well to linger here"** Sen Ep 21 10.

207 **"A painful inability to urinate"** Dio Laer Epicurus 10 22.

207 **"You know very well, sir, [the interest I] have"** Oliver, pp. 174ff.; Smallwood 442.

207 **"We have what we were so eager to obtain"** Smallwood 442.

208 **"the best of all fellow-sectarians"** Ibid.

208 **"inattention of previous supreme commanders"** HA Hadr 10 3.

208 **a manual of military regulations** Veg 1 8.

208 **"with a view to beauty, speed, the inspiring of terror"** Arr Tact 32 3.

209 **"such camp fare as bacon, cheese, and vinegar"** HA Hadr 10 2.

209 **"He generally wore the commonest clothing"** Ibid., 10 5.

209 **"He personally viewed and investigated"** Dio 69 9 2.

209 **"demolished dining rooms in the camps"** HA Hadr 10 4.

209 **older men "with full beards"** Ibid., 10 6.

209 **the death penalty should be used** See Digest 49 16 6–7, and 48 3 12.

210 **"put a more humane interpretation"** Smallwood 333.

211 **"during this period [his first provincial tour]"** HA Hadr 12 6.

212 **"An encamped army"** Ael Arist Rom 82.

XVII. EDGE OF EMPIRE

Chief literary sources—Dio Cassius and *Historia Augusta*. Also Birley and Bowman on Vindolanda.

213 **a still-persisting trick of the weather** Birley Vind p. 50.

214 *Britunculi* See Bowman p. 103, TVII 164.

214 **"I shall expect you, sister"** Bowman, p. 135.

214 **"furnish me with very many friends"** Ibid., p. 129.

215 **a couple of tablets reveal the efforts** See Birley Vind p. 76.

215 **"Many hellos"** Bowman, pp. 141–42.

215 **Archaeologists have discovered and explored** See Birley Vind p. 76.

217 **Certificates were issued** Smallwood 347.

218 **His reply survives** Justin Apol App.

218 **"I will not allow them simply to beg"** Ibid.

218 **"And this, by Hercules"** Ibid.

219 **A document of May 18** TVII 154 (see Bowman, pp. 101–2).

219 **"corrected many abuses"** HA Hadr 11 2.

220 **"To the discipline of the emperor"** Birley Vind p. 97.

220 **"ripped up their cuirasses"** Fronto Ad L Ver 19.

220 **"I implore Your Clemency"** TVII 344 (see Bowman, pp. 146–47, but NB variant translation). It is just possible that the letter was for the provincial governor, but the use of the term "Majesty" (not quoted here) suggests that Hadrian was the addressee.

221 **there was an amusing sequel** For this anecdote, HA Hadr 11 6–7.

221 **"replaced Septicius Clarus, Praetorian prefect"** HA Hadr 11 3. "Without his consent" translates *iniussu eius,* but some prefer a modern emendation *in usu eius,* or "in their association with her." I prefer the former, the latter being somewhat repetitive of *apud,* "in the presence (or company) of."

222 **because of his monstrous personality** Epit de Caes 14 8.

222 **"the first to construct a wall"** HA Hadr 11 2.

222 **"necessity of keeping intact"** Sherk 141. Hadrian was consul in 118 and 119.

XVIII. LAST GOOD-BYES

Chief literary sources—*Historia Augusta* and Dio Cassius. Also Xenophon on reaching the sea.

226 **"I couldn't bear to be Caesar"** HA Hadr 16 3–4. This and the following quatrain is a free rendering of *ego nolo Caesar esse / ambulare per Britannos / [latitare per Germanos] / Scythicas pati pruinas* and *ego nolo Florus esse / ambulare per tabernas / latitare per popinas, / culices pati rotundos.* A line has dropped out of the first squib, but it can be reconstructed by reference to the emperor's reply and his itinerary since accession.

227 **"Every woman's breast"** MLP Florus 3. The Latin runs: *Mulier intra pectus omnis celat virus pestilens; / dulce de labris loquuntur, corde vivunt noxio.*

227 **"the woman through whom he had secured"** Dio 69 10 3.

227 **"honored her exceedingly"** Ibid.

227 **"Although she asked much of me"** Ibid., 3².

227 **he famously brought down a huge boar** Ibid.

228 **he broke his collarbone** Ibid., 69 10 2.

228 **"Borysthenes the barbarian"** MLP Hadr 4. *Borysthenes Alanus, / Caesareus veredus, / per aequor et paludes / et tumulos Etruscos / volare qui solebat / . . . die sua peremptus / hic situs est in agro.* The Alani were Iranian nomads who reared Borysthenes. Also the next quotation.

229 **he loved his horses and dogs** HA Hadr 20 13.

229 **"There you will slaughter"** Mart 1 49 23–30.

230 **a certain Publius Rufius Flavus** Sherk 180, CIL II 4332.

230 **"one of the slaves of the household"** HA Hadr 12 5.

230 **he failed to revisit his hometown of Italica** Dio 69 10 1.

231 **Suetonius' successor as *ab epistulis*** We know that Vestinus became Hadrian's *ab epistulis,* but it is not certain that he followed immediately on Suetonius.

232 **Hadrian scattered cultural largesse** Birley, p. 153. Malalas 278f.

232 **"very elegant" temple** See Birley p. 153, Suda sv Jovianus.

233 **"War with the Parthians"** HA Hadr 12 8.

233 *expeditio Augusti* BMC III p. 425 no. 1259ff., pp. 434–35 no. 1312ff.

233 **Janus began to appear on the coinage** Ibid., p. 254 no. 100, p. 437 no. 1335.

233 **"doorkeeper of heaven and hell"** Macr 1 9 13.

234 **"However, when the shouting got louder"** Xen Anab 4 7.

235 **memorial cairns built by the Greek soldiers** Diod 14 29 4.

235 **"although [it] has been erected"** Arrian Peri 1 3–4.

236 **"long street of great beauty"** Pliny Ep 10 98 1.

236 **"disgusting eyesore"** Ibid.

236 **An earthquake had struck the province** Syncellus Chron p. 659 7–8.

XIX. THE BITHYNIAN BOY

Chief literary sources—Plato, Plutarch, and others on love. Polemon on a possible assassination attempt.

237 **"building, or rather excavating"** Pliny Ep 39 5–6.

238 **his birthday . . . November 27** Smallwood 165, line 5.

238 **a cheerful, chubby-faced teenager** Bust, Munich Glyptothek, Inv. No. GL286; head, British Museum, Inv. No. 1900. Juvenile portraits

may or may not have been posthumously carved or copies of earlier ones, but, even if posthumous, are an indication of contemporaries' understanding of Antinous' age when first noticed.

238 **In about 130 we see Antinous in a carved relief** Tondo, Arch of Constantine, Rome.

238 **a woman called Antinoe** Paus 8 8 4–5. Also, after Antinous' death, a divine cult in his honor was established at Mantinea; so the connection was credited, even if mistakenly.

238 **A late reference to Antinous as Hadrian's "slave"** Jer de vir ill 22.

239 **"no one keeps you from coming here"** Plaut Curc 33–38.

240 **The Cretans engaged in a procedure** Strabo 10 4 21.

241 **"Lovers of their own sex"** Plato Symp 181 D.

241 **"the true genuine love"** Plut Mor 751a.

241 **no one falls in love with an *ugly* youngster?** Cic Tusc 4 33 70.

242 **"Lesbia of the Lesbians"** Mart 7 70.

242 *Mousa Paidike* This is Book 12, Anth Pal.

243 **"who used to fancy himself"** Juv 9 46–47.

243 **a procurer of every luxury** Aur Vic 14 7.

244 *agmen comitantium* Ep de Caes 14 4 5.

244 **"cohorts . . . every kind of specialist"** Ibid.

244 **the imperial Paedogogium in Rome** I accept here the traditional location on the Palatine Hill, although another address places the Paedogogium on the Caelian Hill. Perhaps there were two similar or related establishments. In this section, I am indebted to Clarence A. Forbes, "Supplementary Paper: The Education and Training of Slaves in Antiquity," *American Philological Association* 86 (1955), 321–60; also to Lambert, pp. 61–63.

244 **the gravestone of one of its directors** ILS 1831. The widow of the "paedogogus of the slave boys of our Caesar" was called Ulpia Helpis, which suggests that she won her freedom from Trajan. So Ganymedes would have died not before Trajan's reign and very possibly in Hadrian's.

244 **"colleges for the most contemptible vices"** Colum 1 praef. 5.

245 **Juvenal grumpily complained** Juv 5 121–22.

245 **some two hundred graffiti** The Paedogogium had a long life, and the dating of these graffiti ranges from the first to the third century.

245 **tomb of the Greek warrior Ajax** Philo Her 1 2; the reference at Paus 1 35 3 must refer to Hadrian's visit, unless it is to be supposed that the tomb needed restoration twice in the same period.

245 **Hadrianutherae, or Hadrian's Hunt** HA Hadr 20 13.

246 **"select and genuinely Hellenic"** Philo v. Soph 1 25 3.

246 **his Greek text** A book called Polemon's *Physiognomica*.

246 **"Once I accompanied the greatest king"** Pol Physio (ed. G. Hoffmann, in R. Forster, *Scriptores Physiognomici* I, pp. 138ff.); also the succeeding quotations. See Birley, pp. 164–66.

247 **The prosperous city of Stratonicea** Oliver, pp. 201–4.

248 **a woman stepped forward** Dio 69 6 3.

248 **"the emperor Hadrian"** Galen, *The Diseases of the Mind,* 4.

249 **"accomplish what kings could only attempt"** Pliny Ep 10 41 5.

249 **"In general," observed Dio** Dio 70 4 2.

249 **"young men of the city"** Smallwood 72b.

249 **a late and not altogether dependable source** Malalas, p. 279.

250 **"Julianus himself"** Digest, Constitution "Tanta . . ." 18.

250 **recast their constitution** Jer Chron 280–81.

XX. THE ISLES OF GREECE

Chief literary source—Pausanias on Greece. Also Burkert on Eleusis.

251 **The piglet squealed** For my account of the Mysteries I am mainly indebted to Burkert, especially pp. 285–90. There are many theories of what took place during the rites, but I try to take a conservative line. The first section concerns what were called the Lesser Mysteries, where initiates were purified; these usually took place in March, but could be held at other times. Special arrangements were surely put in place for an emperor. It appears that Hadrian was not initiated during his previous visit to Athens.

252 **for more than one thousand years** Legend has it that the Mysteries started in 1500 B.C. Their popularity was long sustained. Peter Levi writes: "As late as 1801 Demeter was still worshipped at Eleusis; when her last cult image, a two-ton kistophorus from the inner porch, was stolen by Professor E. D. Clarke of Cambridge, the visitors were terrified. An ox ran up, butted the statue repeatedly and fled bellowing. The people prophesied the shipwreck of Clarke's ship: it occurred off Beachy Head, but the statue is now in Cambridge." Paus vol. 1, book 1, note 231.

252 **"We have learned from them the beginnings of life"** Cic Leg 2 14 36.

253 **weapons were banned** HA Hadr 13 2.

253 **"uncovered her shame"** Clem 2 176–77.

253 **a new bridge over the river Kephisos** Jer Chron 280–81.

254 **"ruler of the wide, unharvested earth"** Smallwood 71a.

255 **"Hadrian, god and Panhellene"** IG 2² ²⁹⁵⁸.

255 **When he was at Eleusis** It is a reasonable assumption that the *princeps* noticed the distorted market in fish during his visit to Eleusis, but it *is* only an assumption.

256 **"I want the vendors to have been stopped"** Oliver, pp. 193–95.

256 **a tour of the Peloponnese** See Birley, pp. 177–182.

256 **"a peacock in gold"** Paus 2 17 6.

256 **"founder, lawgiver, benefactor"** IG VII 70–72, 3491.

256 **"not even the emperor"** Paus 1 36 3.

256 **buried at the roadside** Ibid., 8 11 7–8.

257 **an annual celebration** Xen Anab 5 3 9–10.

257 **"He wore local dress"** Dio 69 16 1.

258 **"Do not detract from anyone's dignity"** Pliny Ep 8 24.

258 **"Those who introduce the emperor's opinion"** Plut Mor 814–15.

259 **"hundred columns, walls and colonnades"** Paus 1 18 9.

260 **a complicated dispute** CIG 1713.

260 **"very magnificent and splendid"** Plut Mor 748–49.

261 **"be gracious, kindly receive"** IG 7 1828.

261 **"the soul from the world"** Plut Mor 764–65.

XXI. HOME AND ABROAD

Chief literary source—*Historia Augusta*. Also the guidebook, and MacDonald and Pinto, on Hadrian's villa; and the speech at Lambaesis.

262 **"many-colored, it is said, like a rainbow"** HA Hadr 13 3.

262 **entire crest had been blown off** M. Coltelli, P. Del Carlo, and L. Vezzoli, "Discovery of a Plinian basaltic eruption of Roman age at Etna Volcano, Italy," *Geology* 26 (1998), 1095–98.

264 **"the Aelian villa with the colorful walls"** CIL 14 3911.

264 *rus in urbe* Mart 12 57 21.

264 **"built his villa at Tibur"** HA Hadr 26 5.

264 **his "house at Tibur"** Oliver, p. 74 bis.

265 **Some scholars suggest . . . a cult theater** MacDonald, pp. 162ff.

266 **"devoted to music and flute players"** Fronto de fer Als 4.

266 **His most astonishing architectural innovation** It is possible that Hadrian was influenced by the palace of Dionysius the Elder of Syracuse, which was isolated by a canal, and the Herodion, Herod the Great's circular palace-fortress.

267 **He had been born in or about 113** Dio has Pedanius Fuscus about six

years younger. An ancient horoscope places his birth in 113, and because of its broad contemporaneity (it would have been published not long after his death when he was still "news") is more likely to be accurate.

268 **an odd little congratulatory poem** ILS 5173. It survives in an inscription. See the inspired interpretation by Edward Champlin in *Zeitschrift für Papyrologie und Epigraphik* 60 (1985) 159ff.

268 **"his kindly disposition"** Marc Aur 1 1.

268 **"the simple life"** Ibid., 13.

269 **"solemn child from the very beginning"** HA Marc 2 1.

269 **"in Hadrian's lap"** Ibid., 4 1.

270 **"erotic and fond of gladiators"** CCAG 8, 2 p. 85, 18 to p. 86, 12.

270 **"the emperor's health"** Smallwood 24 16.

270 **the personification of health . . . feeding a snake** BMC III 476 etc.

270 **Hope, *Spes,* holding up a flower** Ibid., 486.

271 **"subcutaneous disease" . . . "burning"** Ep de Caes 14 9.

271 **"it rained on his arrival"** HA Hadr 22 14.

272 **"Caesar's untiring concern"** Smallwood 464, col. II 4–5.

272 ***fossatum Africae*** See Birley, pp. 209–10.

273 **"Jupiter Best" . . . "Winds that have the power"** CIL 8 2609–10.

273 **"Military exercises"** Sherk 148 (and the further quotations).

XXII. WHERE HAVE YOU GONE TO, MY LOVELY?

Chief literary sources—Dio Cassius and *Historia Augusta*. Also *Epitome de Caesaribus* and Aurelius Victor on Antinous. Lambert on Antinous. Betz on magic.

275 **tetradrachm worth six sesterces** BMC III p. 395.

275 **first citizen** Thuc 1 139.

276 **"introduced a bill to the effect"** Plut Per 17.

276 **He decided to launch a new Panhellenion** On Hadrian's Panhellenion, see A. J. Spawforth and Susan Walker, "The World of the Panhellenion: I. Athens and Eleusis," *The Journal of Roman Studies* 75 (1985).

276 **to recruit the past** Arafat, p. 30.

277 **its shrine not far from the Roman Agora** There has been debate about its location. I follow Camp, p. 203.

277 **"This is Athens, the onetime city"** IG II^2 5185.

278 **"with such severity that it was believed"** HA Hadr 13 10.

278 **"after procuring peace from many kings"** Epit de Caes 14 10.

278 **Pharasmenes was king of the Iberi** HA Hadr 13 9, 17 11–12 and 21 13.

279 **Paul of Tarsus called it mutilation** Phil 3 2–3.

280 **the new city's celebratory coinage** Birley, p. 233.

281 **A fourth-century church father, Epiphanius** Epiph 14.

281 **No later than the end of August** Alexandrian coinage celebrating Hadrian's *adventus* is dated in the fourteenth year of the reign, which ended on August 28, 130. See Birley, p. 237.

281 **"Dead men don't bite"** Plut Pomp 77 4.

281 **"How pitiful a tomb"** App Civil War 2 86.

282 **investing in restoration projects** Jer Chron 197.

282 **"By Mouseion," wrote Philostratus** Phil v. Soph 1 22 3.

282 **"put forward many questions"** HA Hadr 20 2.

282 **"Although he wrote verse and composed speeches"** HA Hadr 15 10–11.

282 **"The emperor can give you money"** Dio 69 3 5.

283 **"extremely obscure work"** HA Hadr 16 2.

283 **"You are giving me bad advice"** Ibid., 15 13.

283 **"Some writers go on to record the cures"** Strabo 17 1 17.

284 **a village called Eleusis** Ibid., 17 16.

284 **"First Hadrian with his brass-fitted spear"** MS Gr Class d 113 (P), Bodleian Library, Oxford.

285 **the town of Oxyrhyncus** Birley, p. 246.

285 **"with shaved head"** Lucian Philopseud 34f.

285 **"performed the sacrifices"** Strabo 17 1 29.

285 **instruction in the art of a spell** Betz, pp. 82ff.

286 **Opposite Hermopolis the riverbank curved** See Lambert, p. 127, for this description.

287 **"wept for the youth like a woman"** HA Hadr 14 5.

287 **"the Greeks deified him"** Ibid.

287 **"O my daughter"** Laszlo Kakosy, "The Nile, Euthenia, and the Nymphs," *Journal of Egyptian Archaeology* 68 (1982), 295.

288 **"Antinous . . . had been a favorite"** Dio 69 11 2.

288 **"when Hadrian wanted to prolong his life"** Aur Vic 14 9–10.

288 **"Concerning this incident there are varying rumors"** HA Hadr 14 6.

289 **"malicious rumors spread"** Aur Vic 14 8.

289 **the superannuated gigolo** See page 243 above.

289 **"if he could find another"** Eur Alc 13–18.

290 **"I myself believe that Achilles"** Arrian Peri 23 4.

290 **his little horror poem** Hor Epo 5.

291 **A new coin type shows an equally youthful Hadrian** BMC III p.

318, no. 603. The reverse shows heads of Trajan and Plotina, and another interpretation concerns the legitimacy of his adoption.

291 **"This town was a perpetual peristyle"** Lambert, p. 198.

292 **a shrine to house his remains . . . at Tibur** The account I give of the Antinoeum at Tibur is drawn from Mari and Sgalambro passim. Brick date-stamps show that building started soon after 130. The site was excavated from 1998.

292 **"Antinous rests in this tomb"** Ibid., p. 99.

292 **"the honor paid to him falls little short"** Origen 3 36.

293 **Antinous as Iakchos** Opper p. 190.

293 **"I never saw him in the flesh"** Paus 8 9 7.

293 **Hadrian "set up statues"** Dio 69 11 4.

294 **his own active websites** Current at the time of writing: sites include http://antinous.wai-lung.com/, http://www.antinopolis.org/, and the homoerotic http://www.sacredantinous.com/.

XXIII. "MAY HIS BONES ROT!"

Chief literary sources—Dio Cassius and Bar Kokhba papyri on Judaea. Also Christian writers and Talmudic references.

295 **"very like the twanging"** Paus 1 42 3.

295 **"The emperor Hadrian"** Bernand, *Les inscriptions grecques et latines du Colosse de Memnon.*

296 **"Know that I take every opportunity"** Smallwood 445.

296 **"they wanted to leave"** Jos AJ 12 5 1.

297 **"endeavored to abolish Jewish superstition"** Tac His 5 8.

297 **Hadrian was still in Egypt** Dio 69 12 2.

297 **They armed themselves** Ibid.

297 **"they occupied the advantageous positions"** Ibid., 69 12 3.

298 **"I look into the future"** Numbers 24 17.

298 **"This is the Messiah"** Midrash Rabbah *Lamentations* 2 2–4.

299 **"At first the Romans took no account"** Dio 69 13 1–2.

299 **Roman casualties** Fronto de bell Parth 2.

299 **"If you and your children are in health"** Dio 69 14 3.

299 **"sent against [the Jews] his best generals"** Ibid., 13 2.

300 **Severus was not in overall command** Regarding the Roman response I follow Eck.

300 **"the First Year of the Redemption of Israel"** For example, Sherk 151 E.

300 **"Soumaios to Ionathes, son of Baianos"** Ibid., 151 C.

301 **"Shim'on Bar Kosiba"** Yadin Bar-K, p. 128.

301 **"And if you shall not send them"** Ibid., p. 126.

301 **"In the present war it is only the Christians"** Justin First Apol 31 5–6.

301 **"Barcocheba, leader of a party of the Jews"** Jer Chron p. 283.

301 **prophecy that the Messiah breathed fire** 4 Ezra 13 9–11.

301 **"fanning a lighted blade of straw"** Jer Contra Ruf.

302 **"When military aid had been sent him"** Euseb Ch Hist 4 6 1.

302 **"I am honored"** See Birley, p. 273.

303 **"he would catch missiles"** Midrash Rabbah *Lamentations* 2 4.

303 **"In comfort you sit, eat, and drink"** Yadin Bar-K, p. 133.

303 **Well-to-do families** Jer In Esaiam 2 12 17.

304 **A fragmentary letter evokes the despair** Yadin Bar-K, p. 139.

304 **"the rebels were driven to final destruction"** Euseb Ch Hist 4 6 3.

304 **Bar Kokhba's head was taken to Hadrian** According to Midrash Rabbah *Lamentations* 2 2–4.

304 **forbidden to enter the district around Jerusalem** Euseb Ch Hist 4 6 4.

304 **still in place more than a century later** Jer In Esaiam 1 2 9.

304 **a marble sow was erected** Jer Chron p. 283.

305 **"May his bones rot!"** For example, Midrash Rabbah *Genesis* 78 1.

XXIV. NO MORE JOKES

Chief literary sources—*Historia Augusta* and Dio Cassius

306 **the fullest record of the Roman army in the field** Arr Alan.

306 **Other coins from this time** BMC III p. 325f, p. 329.

307 **"allowed to dispense with attendance at schools"** Marc Aur 1 4.

307 **"not to side with the Greens or the Blues"** Ibid., 1 5.

307 **"set my heart on the pallet bed"** Ibid., 1 6.

307 **"not to give credence to the claims of miracle-mongers"** Ibid.

308 **a bust of him in his teens** MC279 Musei Capitolini, Rome.

308 **"get back to your drawing exercises"** Dio 69 4 2. Literally, "get back to drawing your gourds." These were plants like pumpkins or squash and resembled domes being built at the time.

308 **"ought to have been built on high ground"** Ibid., 4 4–5.

309 **the emperor's huge mausoleum** For a fuller description see Opper, pp. 208f.

309 **The text on the obelisk** See H. Meyer, *Der Obelisk des Antinoos: Eine kommentierte Edition,* Munich, 1994.

309 **A portrait study from . . . Diktynna in Crete** The bust is in the Archaeological Museum of Chania, Crete. See illustration in photo section.

309 **an innate cruelty** Dio 69 18 3.

309 **He now held him "in the greatest abhorrence"** HA Hadr 23 4.

310 **"he spent the entire day"** Dio 18 1–2.

310 **Turbo was removed** It is conceivable that he was somehow caught up in the Pedanius Fuscus plot—see below.

311 **The *Historia Augusta* asserts** The *Life of Aelius* is largely fiction, but the details quoted in this paragraph are plausible: see HA Ael 5 3 and 9.

311 **"his sole recommendation was his beauty"** HA Hadr 23 10.

311 **"not discreditable but somewhat unfocused"** HA Ael 5 3.

311 **their love for each other** Fronto, *On Love,* 5; Marc Aur to Fronto 1, Epist Graecae 7.

312 **he staged a coup** It is possible that Pedanius acted before the public announcement of the adoption: that is the order of events in the *Historia Augusta.*

312 **"the degrees of the Horoscopos"** CCAG No. L 76, 90–91.

312 **"of an illustrious family"** Sherk 159.

313 **instructed to commit suicide** HA Hadr 23 8.

313 **"he gave a feast for slaves"** Ibid., 8–9.

313 **"That I have done nothing wrong"** Dio 69 17 2.

313 **"many others"** HA Hadr 23.

313 **"many from the Senate"** Epit de Caes 14 9.

313 **A late source reports that "his wife, Sabina"** Ibid., 14 8.

313 **Her apotheosis** Smallwood 145 b.

314 **a rumor that he poisoned her** HA Hadr 23 9.

314 **"His enthusiasm for philosophy"** HA Marc 4 9–10.

315 **he had by no means been a failure** HA Ael 3 6.

315 **"universal opposition"** HA Hadr 23 11.

315 **"My friends, I have not been permitted"** Dio 69 20 2.

316 **"with the dignity of a bygone age"** Pliny Ep 4 3 1.

317 **bad dreams** HA Hadr 26 10.

317 **affairs of state** Ibid., 24 11.

317 **"charms and magic rituals"** Dio 69 22 1.

317 **congestive . . . heart disease** The suggestion that diagonal creases in earlobes, as seen in some portrait busts of Hadrian, are an indicator of heart disease (e.g., see Opper pp. 57–59) is now discounted by cardiac specialists, according to Philip Hayward (see Acknowledgments).

318 **"partly by threatening him"** Dio 69 22 2.

318 **He now drew up a will** HA Hadr 24 12–13.

319 **a suicide watch** Ep de Caes 14 12.

319 **"I want you to know"** Smallwood 123.

319 **owing more to Hadrian's favorite, Ennius** Lines 3–4 in Hadrian's poem recalls Ennius' evocation of the underworld as *"pallida leto, nubila tenebris loca."*

319 *animula vagula blandula* HA Hadr 25 9.

320 **"Many doctors killed a king"** Dio 69 22 4.

XXV. PEACE AND WAR

321 **"mixed justice with kindheartedness"** Smallwood 454b 7–8.

321 **"Hadrian was hated by the people"** Dio 69 23 2.

321 **"The following words, it seems to me"** Arr Tact 44 3.

321 **ἐνθ' 'αιχμά τε νέων θάλλει** T. Bergk Terpander, *Poetae Lyrici Graeci,* 4th ed., Leipzig, iii 12 frag 6.

322 **The army . . . the arts . . . and holy justice** I owe this elegant observation to Alexander, p. 175.

322 **"in the gardens of Domitia"** HA Ant 5 1. HA is confusing, for elsewhere it claims that Antoninus "built a temple for [Hadrian] at Puteoli instead of a tomb" (HA Hadr 27 3). Why would he have commissioned a new building, with the mausoleum at Rome nearing completion? Perhaps the allusion is to a temple in Hadrian's honor.

322 **The consecration ceremony** See Opper, pp. 209–10; Suet Aug 100 for Augustus' apotheosis; Dio 75 4–5 and Herodian 4 2 for two later emperors, Pertinax and Septimius Severus.

323 *omnium curiositatum explorator* Tert Apol 5.

323 **"diverse, manifold, and multiform"** Ep de Caes 14 6.

323 **"Do not be upset"** Marc Aur 8 5.

323 **"I wished to appease and propitiate"** Fronto ad M Caes 2 1.

324 **"saw Hadrian to his grave"** Marc Aur 8 25.

324 **Chabrias and Diotimus** Ibid., 8 37.

324 **"Even today the methods"** Dio 69 9 4.

325 **"The sea is not a hindrance"** Ael Arist Rom 59–60.

326 **"immeasurable majesty of the Roman peace"** Pliny NH 27 3.

326 **"Wars, if they once occurred"** Ael Arist Rom 70.

326 **"He can stay quietly where he is"** Ibid., 33.

SOURCES

ANCIENT HISTORY

The prime challenge facing the biographer of Hadrian is the inadequacy of the leading literary sources.

The first of these is the *Historia Augusta,* an abbreviation of its traditional title, "The Lives of Various Emperors and Tyrants from the Deified Hadrian to Numerianus, Composed by Various Hands." The names of six authors are listed, and a number of references suggest that the book was written in the early fourth century after the abdication of Diocletian and before the death of Constantius. However, other allusions and anachronisms do not fit with this dating.

The mystery was solved by a German scholar in the nineteenth century who convincingly argued that in fact the book was the product of one writer only, and had been written nearly a century later than previously thought, toward the end of the fourth century.

The strangeness of the *Historia Augusta* does not cease with its authorship. The text itself is mendacious, mixing historical fact with fantasy and citing bogus sources. Fortunately, the life of Hadrian, the first in the series, is more or less free of base matter, although the same cannot be said of the brief account of his adopted son, Aelius Caesar—and indeed of many of the later lives.

We will never know who wrote the *Historia Augusta,* and what he was thinking of when he did. Maybe he was a hoaxer, sharing some kind of private joke with a coterie of friends.

Although the life of Hadrian does not include much fantasy, it is poor-quality history. Written in the manner of Suetonius' *Lives of the Caesars,* it is clumsily put together and dully written. It is sometimes difficult to disentangle the order or dating of events, and incidents are described with obscure brevity.

All of that allowed, the *Historia Augusta* contains much useful information, often confirming and usually being consistent with evidence from other sources.

By contrast, the *Roman History* of Dio Cassius is a serious, if uninspired, work. A leading imperial politician who flourished around the turn of the third century, a onetime consul and provincial governor, Dio wrote a history of Rome in eighty volumes, beginning with the Trojan prince Aeneas' landfall in Latium after the fall of Troy and ending with the year A.D. 229. The difficulty in his case is that much of the narrative, including everything concerning the events of Hadrian's lifetime, survives only in fragments and an inadequate summary by an eleventh-century monk, John Xiphilinus.

Two fourth-century texts, one attributed to Aurelius Victor and the other by an unknown hand, offer minibiographies of emperors, each the length of a substantial paragraph—helpful if handled with care. Bits and pieces can be gleaned from Christian writers such as Jerome and Eusebius, especially on Christian and Jewish matters.

Invisible in the shadows stand two lost books that underpin much of what has survived. These are Hadrian's own autobiography, written in the last months of his life, and *The Caesars* (*Caesares*), a continuation of Suetonius by Marius Maximus; like Dio a leading senator of the Severan dynasty, he wrote in the early years of the third century. His quality as a historian is debated, but he was a substantial author and, it is supposed, influenced both Dio and the *Historia Augusta*.

Of Hadrian's contemporaries, few writers have anything to say explicitly about him; however, they fill in much of the background to his life and times. He lived out his childhood and teen years under the Flavian dynasty, covered by Suetonius' lives of Vespasian, Titus, and Domitian. The invaluable correspondence of Pliny the Younger, a senator of moderate views connected to the Stoic opposition, shows how Nerva and Trajan arrived at a concordat with Rome's estranged ruling class—a concordat that Hadrian as emperor endorsed, but placed under severe strain.

The *Histories,* by the great historian Tacitus, deals with the period from the fall of Nero and the Year of the Four Emperors up to the death of Domitian. Only the first four books and part of the fifth survive; this is fortunate, for they describe Rome's most serious crisis since the civil wars of the first century B.C.; it haunted imperial politics for many years afterward, and avoiding a repetition was a preoccupation of the ruling class. Tacitus' *Agricola* is useful for observations on Domitian; taken with the *Germania,* it also reveals much of Roman attitudes to the tribal peoples of northern Europe. The *Annals,* which covers the Julio-Claudian era after the death of Augustus, sometimes comments allusively on later events.

Specialist authors of various kinds cast light on aspects of the age. They in-

clude the great biographer and essayist Plutarch; Hadrian's friend, the soldier
and administrator Arrian, who wrote on hunting, military matters, and the
philosophy of Epictetus, all of them topics dear to the emperor's heart; the
poets Martial and Statius, evocative flatterers of Domitian; Juvenal, excoriator
of Roman decadence; the engineer and architect Apollodorus, who wrote a
textbook on siegecraft; Aulus Gellius, who recorded instructive or curious information he came across in his reading or in conversation; Philostratus' *Lives of
the Sophists;* the homoerotic versifier Straton; three orators—Dio Chrysostom,
the valetudinarian Aelius Aristides, and the egregious Polemon; Pausanias, author of the first guidebook to Greece; and the magical-realist storyteller
Apuleius. Pliny the Younger's letters illuminate the values of Rome's upper
class, from which Hadrian and his colleagues in government sprang. Marcus
Aurelius' *Meditations* reveals much about the boy whom Hadrian singled out to
be his ultimate successor to the throne; and Marcus' mentor Fronto offers an
insight into contemporary judgments of Hadrian. Strabo's *Geography,* although
written in the days of Augustus, is a mine of topographical data.

If the main sources are gravely deficient, then, there is much useful material
to offer a rounded view of the Roman world during the late first and early second centuries. And, thanks to the labors of scholars and archaeologists, the
physical remains of the past have yielded an almost inexhaustible mine of inscriptions, papyri, and coins. These speak directly to the present-day reader,
and mitigate a pervading anti-Hadrianic bias in many of the literary sources.
Important letters, decisions, and speeches of emperors were transcribed onto
stone reliefs for the public benefit, often recording their verbatim remarks. A
vital medium for propaganda, coins reveal an emperor communicating with his
subjects (and, of course, placing the best possible spin on events).

Perhaps the most exciting discoveries are documents found in Judaean caves,
written by Jewish fighters in the Bar Kokhba revolt against the Romans; and a
papyrus describing a magical spell conducted by an Egyptian priest, whom
Hadrian consulted shortly before the drowning of Antinous.

Although important items are to be found elsewhere, three invaluable col-
lections assemble much of this material—Harold Mattingly's magisterial *Coins
of the Roman Empire in the British Museum,* volume 3; J. H. Oliver's *Greek Constitutions of Early Roman Emperors from Inscriptions and Papyri;* and (in Latin or Greek
only) E. Mary Smallwood's essential *Documents Illustrating the Principates of
Nerva, Trajan and Hadrian.*

Most of the mainstream ancient authors appear, in both Greek or Latin and
English translation, on the Loeb Classical Library's list (Harvard University

Press, Cambridge, Massachusetts). Hadrian's poetry in Latin is included in Loeb's *Minor Latin Poets,* volume 2; so far as I know, his attributed verses in Greek are not collected.

Penguin Classics publishes Ammianus Marcellinus, *The Later Roman Empire AD 354–378,* trans. Walter Hamilton; Marcus Aurelius, *Meditations,* trans. Martin Hammond; Cicero, *Selected Letters,* trans. D. R. Shackleton Bailey, and *On Government,* trans. Michael Grant; the first half of the *Historia Augusta* as *Lives of the Later Caesars,* trans. Anthony Birley; Horace, *Satires of Horace and Persius,* trans. Niall Rudd, and *Complete Odes and Epodes,* trans. W. G. Shepherd and Betty Radice; Josephus, *The Jewish War,* trans. G. A. Williamson, rev. E. Mary Smallwood; Juvenal, *Sixteen Satires,* trans. Peter Green; Martial, *The Epigrams* (a selection), trans. James Michie; Pausanias, *Guide to Greece: Southern Greece* and *Central Greece* (two volumes), trans. Peter Levi; *Odes of Pindar,* trans. Maurice Bowra; Plato, *The Symposium,* trans. Christopher Gill; Pliny the Elder, *Natural History,* trans. John F. Healey; Pliny the Younger's *Letters,* trans. Betty Radice; Plutarch, *Essays* (a selection), trans. Robin H. Waterfield, also selected biographies under various titles from *Parallel Lives;* Suetonius, *The Twelve Caesars,* trans. Robert Graves, rev. James Rives; Tacitus, *Annals of Imperial Rome,* trans. Michael Grant, *Agricola and Germania,* trans. H. Mattingly, rev. S. A. Handford, *The Histories,* trans. Kenneth Wellesley; Xenophon, *The Persian Expedition,* trans. Rex Warner.

With rare titles, I have directed readers to Web sites, accurate and active at the time of writing.

For works not published by Loeb, the reader may consult the following (where possible in translation).

Aelius Aristides, P. *Complete Works,* trans. Charles A. Behr (Leiden: Brill, 1981–86)

Apollodorus. *Poliorcetica,* see *Siegecraft,* trans. Dennis F. Sullivan (Cambridge, Mass.: Harvard University Press, 2000)

Apuleius. *The Apologia and Florida of Apuleius of Madaura,* trans. H. E. Butler (Dodo Press, 2008)

Arrian. *Circumnavigation of the Black Sea,* trans. Aidan Liddle (Bristol Classical Press, 2003)

———. *Arrian's Anabasis of Alexander and Indica,* ed. E. J. Chinnock (London: George Bell and Son, 1893)

———. *The Greek Historians. The Complete and Unabridged Historical Works of Herodotus, Thucydides, Xenophon and Arrian* (New York: Random House, 1942)

————. *Indica*. See http://www.und.ac.za/und/classics/india /arrian.htm

————. *Ars Tactica,* trans. Ann Hyland, in *Training the Roman Cavalry from Arrian's Ars Tactica* (Alan Sutton: Dover, N.H., 1993)

————. *Order of Battle with Array.* See http://members.tripod.com /~S_van _Dorst/Ancient_Warfare/Rome/Sources/ektaxis.html

————. *Parthica* in *Arrianus, Flavius: Scripta: Vol. II. Scripta minora et fragmenta,* A. G. Roos and Gerhard Wirth (eds.), *Biblioteca scriptorum graecorum et romanorum teubneriana* (Leipzig: Teubner, 2002)

Arrian and Xenophon. *Xenophon and Arrian on Hunting,* trans. A. A. Phillips and M. M. Willcock (Warminster, UK: Aris and Phillips, 1999)

Aurelius Victor. *De Caesaribus,* trans. H. W. Bird (Liverpool: Liverpool University Press, 1994)

Charisius, *Ars Grammatica,* ed. K. Barwick. See http://kaali.linguist.jussieu.fr/ CGL/text.jsp

Epiphanius. *Weights and Measures.* See http://www.tertullian.org/fathers/ epiphanius_weights_03_text.htm

Epitome de Caesaribus, trans. Thomas M. Banchich. See http://www.roman-emperors.org/epitome.htm

Eusebius. *Church History.* See http://www.ccel.org/ccel/schaff/npnf201.iii.vi .html

Eutropius. *Historiae romanae breviarium.* See http://www.thelatinlibrary.com/ eutropius.html; Adamantius, *Physiognomica,* ed. J. G. Franzius (Altenburg: Scriptores Physiognomiae Veteres, 1780)

Galen. *The Diseases of the Mind,* 4; translation from T. Wiedemann, *Greek and Roman Slavery* (London: Croom Helm, 1981)

Hephaestio of Thebes. *Hephaestionis Thebani Apotelesmaticorum libri tres,* ed. D. Pingree (Leipzig: Teubner, 1973)

Jerome. *Chronicle.* See http://www.tertullian.org/fathers/jerome_chronicle_ 00_eintro.htm

————. *Contra Rufinum.* See http://www.ccel.org/ccel/schaff/npnf203.vi.xii .html

————. *De viris illustribus.* See http://www.fourthcentury.com/index.php/ jerome-famous-men

Justin. See http://www.earlychristianwritings.com/justin.html

Justinian. *Corpus Iuris Civilis* (including the *Digest*). See http://web.upmf-grenoble.fr/Haiti/Cours/Ak/

Macrobius. *Saturnalia,* trans. Peter Vaughan Davies (New York: Columbia University Press, 1969)

The Chronicle of John Malalas: A Translation, by Elizabeth Jeffreys, Michael Jeffreys, Roger Scott, et al. *Byzantina Australiensia* 4 (Melbourne: Australian Association for Byzantine Studies, 1986)

Philostratus. *Heroicus.* See http://zeus.chsdc.org/chs/heroes_test#phil_her _front_b3

Polemon. *De Physiognomia,* trans. (from Arabic into Latin) G. Hoffmann (Leipzig: 1893)

Sententiae Hadriani. See N. Lewis, *Greek, Roman and Byzantine Studies* 32 (1991), 267–80

Sibylline Oracles/Books. See http://thedcl.org/heretics/misc/terrymil /thesibora/ thesibora.html

Soranus' Gynaecology, trans. Owsei Temkin, et al. (Baltimore: Johns Hopkins University Press, 1956)

Strato. *Puerilities: Erotic Epigrams of the Greek Anthology* (Princeton: Yale University Press, 2001)

Syncellus, Georgius. *Chronographia.* Corpus Scriptorum Historiae Byzantinae, ed. B. G. Niebuhr et al., vol. 1 (Bonn, 1829)

Talmud. See text links at http://en.wikipedia.org/wiki/Talmud

Vegetius. *Epitoma rei militaris* (*Military Institutions of the Romans*), trans. John Clark (Whitefish, Mont.: Kessinger Publishing, 2007)

MODERN COMMENTARY

Of modern studies the one on which I most depended was Anthony Birley's *Hadrian, the Restless Emperor.* A quarry of scholarly information, it assembles all that is known or can be guessed about its subject; in particular, through scrutiny of the tiniest clues and clever speculation, it establishes a clear outline of Hadrian's journeys.

For those with a general interest in the classical world I recommend from below Balsdon's *Life and Leisure in Ancient Rome,* Bowman's *Life and Letters on the Roman Frontier—Vindolanda and Its People,* Connolly's wonderful visual reconstructions in *The Ancient City: Life in Classical Athens and Rome,* Goldsworthy's *In the Name of Rome: The Men Who Won the Roman Empire,* Hopkins and Beard's revisionist *The Colosseum,* Paul Johnson's *A History of the Jews,* Royston Lambert's (somewhat overcolored) *Beloved and God,* Thorsten Opper's catalogue, *Hadrian—Empire and Conflict,* and, of course, Marguerite Yourcenar's study in melancholy, *Memoirs of Hadrian.*

For a full bibliography, readers can consult the *Cambridge Ancient History,* volume 11, *The High Empire*. What follows is a selection of books and articles that I found useful.

Adembri, Benedetta. *Hadrian's Villa* (Rome: Ministero per I Beni e le Attività Culturali, Soprintendenza Archeologica per il Lazio, Electa 2000)

Alexander, P. J. "Letters and Speeches of the Emperor Hadrian," *Harvard Studies in Classical Philology* 49, 1938

Alon, G. *The Jews in Their Land in the Talmudic Age II* (Harvard University Press, 1984)

Antinous: The Face of the Antique, exhibition catalogue (Leeds, UK: Henry Moore Institute, 2006)

Arafat, K. W. *Pausanias's Greece, Ancient Artists and Roman Rulers* (Cambridge, UK: Cambridge University Press, 1996)

Balsdon, J.P.V.D. *Life and Leisure in Ancient Rome* (London: The Bodley Head, 1969)

Beard, Mary, John North, and Simon Price. *Religions of Rome,* vol. 1: *A History* (Cambridge, UK: Cambridge University Press, 1998)

Benario, H. W. *A Commentary on the Vita Hadriani in the* Historia Augusta (The Scholars Press, 1980)

Bennett, Julian. *Trajan: Optimus Princeps,* 2nd ed. (London: Routledge, 2001)

Bernand, A., and E. Bernand. *Les Inscriptions grecques et latines du Colosse de Memnon* (Archeolog Caire, 1960)

Betz, H. D. *The Greek Magical Papyri in Translation,* 2nd ed. (University of Chicago Press, 1992)

Birley, Anthony. *Garrison Life at Vindolanda—A Band of Brothers* (Stroud, UK: Tempus, 2002)

———. *Hadrian, the Restless Emperor* (London and New York: Routledge, 1997)

———. *Marcus Aurelius: A Biography* (London: Batsford, 1987)

Boatwright, Mary T. *Hadrian and the Cities of the Roman Empire* (Princeton, N.J.: Princeton University Press, 2000)

———. *Hadrian and the City of Rome* (Princeton, N.J.: Princeton University Press, 1987)

Bowerstock, G. W. *Greek Sophists in the Roman Empire* (Oxford: Oxford University Press, 1969)

Bowman, Alan K. *Life and Letters on the Roman Frontier—Vindolanda and Its People,* 3rd ed. (London: British Museum Press, 2003)

Brunt, P. A. *Roman Imperial Themes* (Oxford: Clarendon Press, 1990)

Burkert, Walter. *Greek Religion* (Cambridge, Mass.: Harvard University Press, 1985)

Cambridge Ancient History, vol. 11: *The High Empire* (Cambridge, UK: Cambridge University Press, 2005)

Camp, J. M. *The Archaeology of Athens* (New Haven: Yale University Press, 2004)

Cantarelli, L. *Gli scritti latini di Adriano imperatore, Studi e documenti di storia e diritto* 19 (1898), 113–70

Castle, E. B. *Ancient Education and Today* (Harmondsworth, UK: Penguin Books, 1961)

Catalogus Codicum Astrologorum Graecorum, 12 vols. (Bruxelles: Lamertin, 1898–1953)

Claridge, A. "Hadrian's Column of Trajan," *Journal of Roman Archaeology* 6, 1993

Clarke, John R. *Looking at Lovemaking: Constructions of Sexuality in Roman Art 100 BC–AD 250* (University of California Press, 2001)

Coarelli, Filippo. *Rome and Environs* (Berkeley, Los Angeles, and London: University of California Press, 2008)

Collingwood, R. G., and R. P. Wright. *Roman Inscriptions of Britain I: Inscriptions on Stone* (Oxford: Clarendon Press, 1965)

Connolly, Peter, and Hazel Dodge. *The Ancient City: Life in Classical Athens and Rome* (Oxford: Oxford University Press, 1998)

Connor, W. R. *The Acts of the Pagan Martyrs/Acta Alexandrinorum (Greek Texts and Commentaries)* (Ayer Co. Publications, New Hampshire)

Corpus Inscriptionum Latinarum (Berlin: Berlin-Brandenburg Academy of Sciences and Humanities, 1893–2003)

Corpus Papyrorum Judaicorum I–III. V. A. Techerikover and A. Fuks, eds. (London and Cambridge, Mass.: 1957–64)

Duncan-Jones, R. P. *Structure and Scale in the Roman Economy* (Cambridge, UK: Cambridge University Press: 1990)

Dupont, Florence. *Daily Life in Ancient Rome* (Oxford: Blackwell, 1992)

Eck, Werner. "The Bar Kokhba Revolt: The Roman Point of View." *Journal of Roman Studies* 89 (1999)

Encyclopedia Judaica. Cecil Roth, ed. (New York: Macmillan, 1972)

Epigrammata Graeca. Georg Kaibel, ed. (Berlin: 1888)

Fontes iuris romani antejustiniani in usum scholarum [FIRA]. S. Riccobono et al., eds. (Florence: S.A.G. Barbèra, 1941–64)

Fuks, Alexander. "Aspects of the Jewish Revolt in A.D. 115–117." *The Journal of Roman Studies* 51, parts 1 and 2 (1961), 98–104

Gibbon, Edward. *History of the Decline and Fall of the Roman Empire* (London: Folio Society, 1983)

Goldsworthy, Adrian. *In the Name of Rome: The Men Who Won the Roman Empire* (London: Orion, 2003)

Gray, William D. "New Light from Egypt on the Early Reign of Hadrian." *The American Journal of Semitic Languages and Literatures* 40:1 (Oct. 1923)

Green, Peter. *From Alexander to Actium* (London: Thames and Hudson, 1990)

Hoff, Michael C., and Susan I. Rotroff. *The Romanization of Athens: Proceedings of an International Conference held at Lincoln, Nebraska (April 1996).* Oxbow Monograph 94 (Oxford: Oxbow Books, 1997)

Hopkins, Keith, and Mary Beard. *The Colosseum* (London: Profile Books, 2005)

Inscriptiones Graecae (Berlin-Brandenburgische Akademie der Wissenschaften, 1893ff)

Inscriptiones Graecae ad res Romanas pertinentes (Paris, 1906–27)

Inscriptiones Latinae Selectae. H. Dessau, ed. (Berlin, 1892–1916)

Johnson, Paul. *A History of the Jews* (London: Weidenfeld and Nicolson, 1987)

Jones, Brian W. *The Emperor Domitian* (London: Routledge, 1993)

Jones, C. P. *Plutarch and Rome* (Oxford: Oxford University Press, 1972)

————. *The Roman World of Dio Chrysostom* (Cambridge, Mass.: Harvard University Press, 1978)

Jones, David. *The Bankers of Puteoli: Finance, Trade and Industry in the Roman World* (Stroud, UK: Tempus, 2006)

Keppie, Lawrence. *The Making of the Roman Army from Republic to Empire* (London: Routledge, 1984)

Lambert, Royston. *Beloved and God: The Story of Hadrian and Antinous* (New York: Viking Books, 1984)

Lamberton, Robert. *Plutarch* (New Haven: Yale University Press, 2001)

Lepper, F. A. *Trajan's Parthian War and Arrian's Parthica* (Chicago: Ares, 1985)

Levine, Lee I. *Jerusalem: Portrait of the City in the Second Temple Period* (Philadelphia: Jewish Publication Society of America, 2002)

Lewis, N. *The Documents from the Bar Kokhba Period in the Cave Letters, Greek Papyri* (Jerusalem: 1989)

MacDonald, William L., and John A. Pinto. *Hadrian's Villa and Its Legacy* (New Haven: Yale University Press, 1995)

Mantel, H. "The Causes of the Bar Kochba Revolt." *Jewish Quarterly Review* 58 (1967)

Mari, Zaccaria, and Sergio Sgalambro. "The Antinoeion of Hadrian's Villa: Interpretation and Architectural Reconstruction." *American Journal of Archaeology* 3:1 (Jan. 2007)

Mattingly, H. *Coins of the Roman Empire in the British Museum III: Nerva to Hadrian* (London: British Museum, 1936)

Mattingly, H., and E. A. Sydenham. *The Roman Imperial Coinage I–III London [1923–30]* (London: Spink and Son, 1968)

Mommsen, Theodor. *A History of Rome Under the Emperors,* German ed. trans. Demandt, Barbara and Alexxander, ed., Krojze, Clare (London: Routledge, 1976)

Naor, Mordecai. *City of Hope* (Chemed Books, 1996)

Oliver, J. H. *Greek Constitutions of Early Roman Emperors from Inscriptions and Papyri* (Philadelphia: American Philosophical Society, 1989)

Opper, Thorsten. *Hadrian—Empire and Conflict,* exhibition catalogue (London: British Museum, 2008)

Panegyrici Latini. R.A.B. Mynors, ed. (Oxford: Oxford University Press, 1964)

Petrakis, N. L. "Diagonal Earlobe Creases, Type A Behavior and the Death of Emperor Hadrian." *Western Journal of Medicine* 132.1 (January 1980), 87–91

Platner, Samuel Ball (as completed and revised by Thomas Ashby). *A Topographical Dictionary of Ancient Rome* (Oxford: Oxford University Press, 1929)

Rawson, Beryl. *Children and Childhood in Roman Italy* (Oxford: Oxford University Press, 2003)

Richardson, L., Jr. *A New Topographical Dictionary of Ancient Rome* (Baltimore: Johns Hopkins University Press, 1992)

Rossi, Lino. *Trajan's Column and the Dacian Wars* (Ithaca, N.Y.: Cornell University Press, 1971)

Schäfer, P. "Hadrian's Policy in Judaea and the Bar Kokhba Revolt: A Reassessment," in P. R. Davies and R. T. White (eds.), *A Tribute to G. Vermes, Journal for the Study of the Old Testament* Supp. Ser. 100 (1990), 281–303

Schürer, E. *History of the Jewish People in the Age of Jesus Christ (175BC–AD135),* vol. I, rev. ed., G. Vermes and F. Millar (Edinburgh: T and T Clark, 1973)

Sherk, Robert K., ed. *The Roman Empire: Augustus to Hadrian* (Cambridge, UK: Cambridge University Press, 1988)

Smallwood, E. Mary. *Documents Illustrating the Principates of Nerva, Trajan and Hadrian* (Cambridge: Cambridge University Press, 1966)

———. *Jews Under Roman Rule* (Leiden: Brill, 1976)

Spawforth, A. J., and Susan Walker. "The World of the Panhellenion: II. Three Dorian Cities." *The Journal of Roman Studies* 76 (1986), 88–105

Speidel, M. P. "Swimming the Danube Under Hadrian's eyes. A Feat of the Emperor's Batavi Horse Guard." *Ancient Society* 22 (1991), 277–82

———. *Riding for Caesar: The Roman Emperors' Horse Guard* (London: Routledge, 1994)

———. "Roman Army Pay Scales." *The Journal of Roman Studies* 82 (1992)

Stambaugh, John E. *The Ancient Roman City* (Baltimore and London: Johns Hopkins University Press, 1988)

Strack, P. L. *Untersuchungen zur römische Reichsprägung des zweiten Jahrhunderts II. Die Reichsprägung zur Zeit des Hadrian* (Stuttgart: 1933)

Swain, S. *Hellenism and Empire. Language, Classicism and Power in the Greek World AD* (Oxford: Clarendon Press, 1996)

Syme, Ronald. "The Career of Arrian." *Harvard Studies in Classical Philology* 86 (1982), 181–211

———. "Fictional History Old and New: Hadrian." *Roman Papers* VI (1991)

———. *Tacitus* (Oxford: Oxford University Press, 1958)

———. "The Wrong Marcius Turbo." *Journal of Roman Studies* 52, parts 1 and 2 (1962)

Toynbee, J. M. C. *The Hadrianic School: A Chapter in the History of Greek Art* (Cambridge: Cambridge University Press, 1934)

Williams, Craig A. *Roman Homosexuality: Ideologies of Masculinity in Classical Antiquity* (Oxford: Oxford University Press, 1999)

Winter, J. G. "In the Service of Rome: Letters from the Michigan Collection of Papyri." *Classical Philology* 22:3 (July 1927)

Yadin, Yigael. *Bar-Kokhba: The Re-discovery of the Legendary Hero of the Last Jewish Revolt Against Imperial Rome* (London: Weidenfeld and Nicolson, 1971)

Yourcenar, Marguerite. *Memoirs of Hadrian,* trans. Grace Frick (London: Secker and Warburg, 1955)

INDEX

Individuals are listed in alphabetical order of *nomen,* the clan or family name, except for emperors and Romans who are usually referred to by Anglicized names (for further information on Roman names see pages xiv–xv).

PHOTO: © BARRY BURKE

ANTHONY EVERITT, visiting professor in the visual and
performing arts at Nottingham Trent University, has written
extensively on European culture and is the author of *Cicero*
and *Augustus*. He has served as secretary general of the Arts
Council for Great Britain. Everitt lives near Colchester,
England's first recorded town, founded by the Romans.